THIRD EDITION

SOGGY SNEAKERS

A GUIDE TO OREGON RIVERS

Kayaking a class 6 drop (photo by Jason Bates)

THIRD EDITION

SOGGY SNEAKERS

A GUIDE TO OREGON RIVERS

WILLAMETTE KAYAK AND CANOE CLUB, INC.

**THE
MOUNTAINEERS**

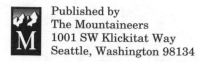

Published by
The Mountaineers
1001 SW Klickitat Way
Seattle, Washington 98134

Published simultaneously in Canada by Douglas & McIntyre, Ltd.,
1615 Venables Street, Vancouver, B.C. V5L 2H1

Published simultaneously in Great Britain by Cordee, 3a DeMontfort
Street, Leicester, England, LE1 7HD

0 9 8 7 6
5 4 3 2

Manufactured in the United States of America

Edited by Kris Fulsaas
Maps by Brian Metz/Green Rhino Graphics
Cover design by Watson Graphics
Layout by Nick Gregoric
Book design and typesetting by The Mountaineers Books

Cover photograph: Owyhee River (photo by Paul Kauffman)

Library of Congress Cataloging in Publication Data

Soggy sneakers : a guide to Oregon rivers / Willamette Kayak and Canoe
    Club. -- 3rd ed.
                p.   cm.
    Includes bibliographical references (p.) and index.
    ISBN 0-89886-330-9
    1. Canoes and canoeing--Oregon--Guidebooks. 2. Rivers--Oregon--
Recreational use--Guidebooks. 3. Oregon--Guidebooks.
    I. Willamette Kayak and Canoe Club.
GV776.O6S63   1993
797.1'09795--dc20   93-45840
                                               CIP

CONTENTS

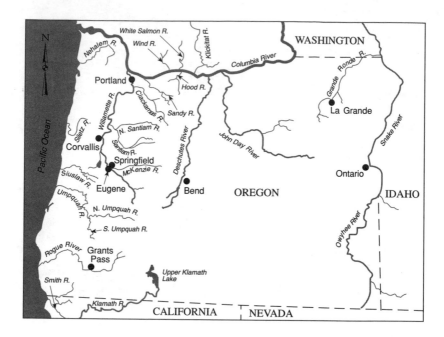

REGION 5. MID-WILLAMETTE VALLEY

REGION 6. LOWER WILLAMETTE VALLEY AND CLACKAMAS RIVER

REGION 7. COLUMBIA GORGE

Legend

Symbol	Description	Symbol	Description
5	Interstate Highway		Put-in or Take-out
20	Highway	85	Run Number referred to in text
34	Road	●	Town or City
	River, Creek	▲	Mountain or Butte
	Run referred to in text	⊼	Park or Picnic Area
	Border	▲	Campground

MAPS

PREFACES

PREFACE TO THE FIRST EDITION

The *Soggy Sneakers Guide to Oregon Rivers* has as many beginnings as the state has rivers. Willamette Kayak and Canoe Club, Inc. (WKCC) members had been keeping notes and collecting trip reports for many years. Some had the idea of publishing; some merely wanted to aid their friends in running rivers. Periodically, individual trip reports had been written by club members for publication in the club newsletter. Bill Ostrand, president of WKCC in 1979, brought these beginnings together. George and Gene Ice, Ron Mattson, and Rob Blickensderfer turned over all of their material to the club project, and a guidebook for Oregon rivers was begun.

Lance Stein, president of WKCC in 1980, soon had club members volunteering for various committees and duties. The call went out to paddling partners throughout the state. Trip reports on rivers near and far began to arrive. A technical review committee checked reports for accuracy and sometimes sent them back to authors for clarification. An editorial committee unified the text. Gradually, trip reports merged into chapters and the *Soggy Sneakers Guide to Oregon Rivers* became a reality.

PREFACE TO THE SECOND EDITION

The second edition of the *Soggy Sneakers Guide to Oregon Rivers* began in the summer of 1984. Gary Adams, then president of WKCC, and Lance Stein began discussing with club members ideas for a new edition. Soon there were so many "great ideas" that an editorial committee was formed, and the call for new write-ups went out. More than 100 new write-ups were received, including an entire chapter on surf kayaking on the Oregon Coast. *Soggy Sneakers* more than doubled in size.

PREFACE TO THE THIRD EDITION

In recent years, more and more sections of rivers and creeks have been run that were not described in previous editions of *Soggy Sneakers*. The boating community of Oregon has generously submitted reports and descriptions of many of the new runs as well as corrections on many of the previous runs. The third edition contains more than sixty new runs and is reorganized for easier use.

The editorial policy for the third edition was similar to that of the

A quiet moment at Big Windy, Rogue River (photo by Phil DeRiemer)

previous editions. An attempt was made to edit the articles for clarity and consistency, while allowing the myriad of styles of the many different authors to shine through. The result is a book that's not only the most complete guide to Oregon rivers, but also very interesting reading, even if you aren't going boating!

ACKNOWLEDGMENTS

As the length of the book grows, so does the list of people to whom we are indebted for getting it into print.

First we acknowledge the authors, without whose contribution the book would not be possible. The compilers of the third edition can fully appreciate the enormous efforts made by the creators of the first edition, who got *Soggy Sneakers* off the ground and into print before the days of word processors. Bill Ostrand provided the first push; Ron Mattson, Gene Ice, George Ice, and Rob Blickensderfer gave up personal publishing goals; Kim Hummer, Dan Valens, T. R. Torgersen, Ellen Oliver, Richard Hand, and Lance Stein carried the manuscripts through the process of typing, editing, typesetting, and printing for the first edition.

Gary Adams provided the inspiration for the second edition, and kept it rolling through the initial stages. Rob Blickensderfer, Laurie Pavey, and John Westall edited the initial set of new write-ups. Gary Adams and Laurie Pavey managed the editorial correspondence with the authors. Rich Brainerd produced all of the maps. Naomi Weidner and Tee Taylor proofread the manuscript. Steve Holland obtained the data on gauges and river flow; Bryan Tooley worked on river classification, and Richard Hand on typesetting. Dan Valens proofread the entire book. Three people are recognized for service above and beyond the call of duty. Laurie Pavey did more than her share of typing, editing, and other jobs. Lance Stein, a veteran of the first edition, contributed his talents as printing consultant, business manager, and typesetter for the maps. John Westall is acknowledged for his endurance as an editor, and the one who tied all the loose ends together for the second edition.

Rich Lague provided the incentive for the third edition. Lance Stein's experience in publishing again proved invaluable, particularly since he acted as the club representative in negotiating the publishing contract with The Mountaineers. The following people contributed to the preparation of the manuscript for the third edition: Lance Stein also served as primary photo coordinator for the third edition. Rob Blickensderfer acted as primary text rewriter and compiler. Naomi Weidner typed the new river descriptions. Jim Reed and Steve Cramer helped organize data and maps, and with Dan Vallens, did many other tasks. Gina de Grassi carefully read the entire manuscript. Terry Wyatt helped gather write-ups for southern Oregon.

INTRODUCTION

What kayaker, canoer, rafter, drift boater, or pilot of those newest whitewater craft, riverboards, catarafts, and inflatable kayaks, doesn't have a trusty pair of soggy sneakers in his or her past? They epitomize our eagerness, our willingness, indeed our need to embrace the rushing waters of stream, river, and sea. They lead a journey in time and space over these waters of sheer delight and pleasure, of challenge and daring, of sport and skill, and of companionship and sharing. In doing so, they give us an opportunity to come to grips with truths in our own lives and to see vividly the powerful and subtle connections that guide all that lives, all that exists, from the past into the future.

We hope *Soggy Sneakers* proves to be an effective guide for you in boating Oregon's whitewater rivers and streams and coastal surf. It is the voice of Oregon boaters past and present. They have invested in our future and in the future of Oregon's water resources. We owe them much for their unique "boaters'" view and for the skill and thoroughness they bring to the individual descriptions of runs in this guide.

One of the pleasures of compiling these many voices is recording the new runs pioneered. Improvement in boater skills, a growing willingness to explore more distant rivers and streams, and better accessibility to stream flow data create these opportunities. More than sixty new runs have been added to *Soggy Sneakers* since the second edition was published. Of course, boaters will continue to push into new watersheds to find additional runs.

Most of the known runs in Oregon are described, and all of the popular runs are included. Most of the runs can be done in a day; some runs may be combined to provide multiday trips with river camping or car camping. A number of multiday runs in remote areas are described. The difficulty of the whitewater runs ranges from class 1 (least difficult) to class 6 (most difficult).

Class 1 and 2 runs are boated by the greatest number of paddlers, whereas class 5 and 6 water is boated by only a few experts, in a team, after close study and with all precautions taken. Some of the popular class 1 runs are fully described. Other class 1 runs are briefly described in Supplement 1, Other Class 1 Rivers. A number of more difficult, remote, or unpopular runs are included in Supplement 2, Yes, It Has Been Run.

Region 10 describes surf kayaking on the Oregon Coast. It is a unique feature of this guide. Surf kayaking represents the crossover in skills and equipment now taking place in the paddling community for those who "surf" the standing wave trains of rivers and those who "surf" the moving wave trains of the ocean. However, there are special problems and dangers involved in paddling the ocean surf that are not encountered on rivers. Regardless of skill, boaters engaged in surf kayaking must respect the power and unpredictability of ocean currents.

Oregon whitewater will take you from the high desert to the ocean surf, from steep creeks to gentle streams and rivers, from runs within 1 hour of urban areas to remote rivers where hiking out is a serious event. Oregon whitewater is a year-round activity. We have fall and winter rains, spring snowmelt, and summer dam releases. *Soggy Sneakers* brings you more than 2,300 miles of whitewater runs for the state. Enjoy!

We will see you on the rivers.

The authors

HOW TO USE THIS BOOK

Most of the known river runs in Oregon are described. They have been grouped into nine chapters organized around the seventeen drainage basins of the state. Multiple runs on one river are listed beginning from upstream and heading downstream. All river runs reported in this book were run by the authors.

First-descent dates and persons involved are included when known, although first-descent information is not well documented within the boating community. The earliest known date for the run is given.

General river descriptions are given for major rivers and river systems. Each river run begins with an information block that lists **class** designation, **flow** in cubic feet per second (cfs), **gradient** in feet per mile (fpm), **length** in miles, **character** of the surroundings (the most significant topographic, geographic, and/or scenic features), and **season** in which the river can be run. Because the class designation of a river varies depending upon the flow, multiple information-block entries, separated by semicolons, are given for some runs. Detailed information on some of these information-block categories and how they are used in this book is given later in this section.

Following the information block is a description of the run. The character of the river is described, as well as the rapids and landmarks that are found on the run. Unless otherwise indicated, "right" and "left" are used with respect to an observer looking downstream (river right and river left). Each run concludes with short sections on **hazards, access**, and **gauge** information (no gauge information is given for the surf sections in chapter 10).

The maps in this book show the principal rivers and roads, the sections for which runs are described, the locations of access points, and major landmarks such as campgrounds and towns. Although the main shuttle roads are shown, it is intended that a state road map be used with this book. (For more information on maps, see the end of this section).

The appendices include important additional information. Appendix A lists the river-regulating agencies that provide information on stream flow or gauge readings. Appendix B is a listing of the whitewater boating organizations in Oregon. These organizations provide an invaluable voice in the ongoing battles over how our rivers and streams will be used. Through clinics, workshops, and trips, they are a source of information and training on safety and paddling skills. Best of all, they put you in touch with a great bunch of paddlers and open the door to a rich agenda of river activities.

Below are definitions of some of the categories used in this book.

Class. The class designations indicate the class of the majority of the run, according to the American Whitewater Affiliation International Scale of River Difficulty, as reprinted below. If the water temperature is below 50 degrees Fahrenheit, the American Whitewater Affiliation states that the river should be considered one class more difficult than normal. If only one or two spots are more difficult than the majority of the run, the class of these spots is given in parentheses, for example, South Santiam as 4(6) or Lower McKenzie as 1(2). The letter "T" is given after the number designation for a run that is predominantly technical in nature, and the letter "P" is used to indicate that at least one portage is mandatory.

Class 1. Moving water with a few riffles and small waves. Few or no obstructions.

(Still water and class 1 are sometimes subdivided by water speed: Class A, standing or slow-flowing water, not more than 2.5 mph; Class B, current between 2.5 and 4.5 mph, but back-paddling can effectively neutralize the speed; Class C, current more than 4.5 mph, thus back-paddling cannot neutralize the speed of the current, and simple obstacles may occur that require a certain amount of boat control.)

Class 2. Easy rapids with waves up to 3 feet, and wide clear channels that are obvious without scouting. Some maneuvering is required.

Class 3. Rapids with high, irregular waves often capable of swamping an open canoe. Narrow passages that often require complex maneuvering. May require scouting from shore.

Class 4. Long difficult rapids with constricted passages that often require precise maneuvering in very turbulent waters. Scouting from shore is often necessary, and conditions make rescue difficult. Generally not possible for open canoes, except experts. Boaters in covered canoes or kayaks should be able to Eskimo roll.

Class 5. Extremely difficult, long, and very violent rapids with highly congested routes that nearly always must be scouted from shore. Rescue conditions are difficult and there is significant hazard to life in event of a mishap. Ability to Eskimo roll is essential for kayaks and canoes.

Class 6. Difficulties of class 5 carried to the extreme of navigability. Nearly impossible and very dangerous. For teams of experts only, after close study and with all precautions taken.

Flow. The rate of flow, which is normally measured at the gauge location, is reported in cubic feet per second (cfs). The flow may differ significantly upstream or downstream of the gauge, depending upon flow in any tributaries. Flows are estimated by the authors where necessary.

Gradient. The average gradient of the run is the elevation change over the length of the run, in units of feet per mile (fpm). The letters "PD" are used to indicate that a run is primarily "pool-drop" in nature; that is, relatively flat stretches are connected by relatively steep sections in which most of the elevation changes occur. The letter "C" is used to indicate that a run is primarily "continuous" in nature; that is, the elevation change is relatively uniform over its length.

Season. The time of year that a river can normally be run is related to the weather and the type of source for the river. The classifications used in this book are:

Year-round. There is adequate water for boating all year. The sources of these rivers are generally impounded or spring-fed.

Dam-controlled. The flow of these rivers is controlled by dams or irrigation diversions, but there is no requirement for minimum flow. Water may be shut off or reduced to less than runnable flows by the controlling agency.

Rainy. Runnable levels are reached after several days of rain. Many of the rivers of western Oregon are in this group, with a season from about October to April.

Snowmelt. Most of the water comes from melting snow in the spring and early summer. Such rivers are at high elevations or in eastern Oregon.

Rainy/snowmelt. The water is received from both rain and snow. The rivers are runnable after a few days of good rain and into early summer because of melting snowpack.

Hazards. The most difficult rapids are described, and some suggestions are made about how they can be approached or portaged. Other hazards, such as sweepers, weirs, and dams, are also mentioned.

Access. Directions to the river, primary and optional put-ins and take-outs, and directions on running the shuttle are described.

Gauge. The location of the river gauge and the agency for obtaining the flow is given, where applicable. The authors' opinion of "high runnable," "low runnable," and "optimum" flows are provided when possible. Further information is available from the agencies listed in Appendix A. Some gauge information is telemetered, that is, transmitted automatically from a gauging station to a central recording station.

Maps in this book are intended to be used with a state road map. The *Oregon Atlas and Gazetteer* is probably the single most useful collection of maps for boaters in Oregon. It is extremely useful for locating all of the runs and shuttle routes, and is available at most bookstores. Most counties in Oregon publish a county road map, although the quality varies considerably. Some have all roads, some have only main roads, and others have only a portion of the county. Check at each county's courthouse for maps and prices. Privately published maps of small, county-size areas abound. The quality and usefulness of these maps vary considerably; *caveat emptor!* These maps include the Thomas Brothers Maps, Pittmon Maps, Metzger's Maps, Big Sky Series of maps, and Phillip Arnold's Maps. Most of these are available from bookstores and sporting goods stores.

The Oregon Water Resources Department publishes an excellent set of drainage basin maps for the state.

For smaller streams and forest service roads, the U.S. Forest Service maps are useful. All of the roads in the national forests in Oregon and Washington were renumbered in 1982, and the maps have been republished. National forest maps are available from the Pacific Northwest Region Field Office (319 SW Pine Street, Portland, OR 97208), or from any of the national forest headquarters offices throughout the state.

U.S. Geological Survey (USGS) topographical maps are indispensable for exploratory boating. However, their coverage of Oregon's whitewater country is not extensive, and many of the maps are at least twenty to thirty years old. Most maps are in 15-minute quadrangles with 80-foot contour intervals. This scale limits their accuracy in figuring stream gradient, but they're better than nothing. The 7.5-minute maps are the ones to obtain if they are available. Many sports stores, bookstores, and libraries carry some of the topographical maps.

RIVER SAFETY

The river-run descriptions in this book reflect the general character of a river, but the character can change dramatically in the course of a day, a season, or a year. Thus, while this book is a guide to the rivers and what to expect, it must in no way be regarded as the exact description of what you will find on a particular day. Each boater must accept personal responsibility for finding out what lies around the next corner, and for possessing sufficient skills to cope.

Persons running rivers are responsible for their own safety. This book is offered only as a guide. The authors are not responsible or liable for any loss of life or property that may befall others running the rivers.

People run rivers for different reasons; some seek a relaxing aesthetic experience, others seek adventure or challenge. Many seek a combination of the two. For whatever reasons you choose to boat, your river-running experience will be more fun and more rewarding if done safely. On any river, even innocently small ones, the price of ignorance or carelessness can be anything from lost or damaged equipment to personal injury or the loss of life.

Working the Hole at Bob's, Clackamas River (photo by Eric Larson)

A large part of safe boating lies in identifying potential dangers. Prevention is the key, not just reacting to a hazardous situation already in motion. Recognizing potential hazards requires experience. Boating clubs offer the novice a way to acquire that experience and learn boating safety other than by trial and error. Clubs normally have people who teach boating and are willing to share their experience and instill safe boating practices. Many clubs provide instruction in boat handling (for a listing of boating organizations, see Appendix B). Another way of learning boating skills and safety is through classes offered by city parks and recreation departments, community colleges, the Red Cross, or the YMCA. Many of the books in the Bibliography at the back of this book discuss safety, rescue techniques, and safety equipment.

The Safety Code of the American Whitewater Affiliation, slightly condensed, is reprinted here with permission. It should be read carefully.

T. R. Torgersen

I. PERSONAL PREPAREDNESS AND RESPONSIBILITY

1. Be a competent swimmer with ability to handle yourself underwater.

2. Wear a life jacket.

3. Wear a solid, correctly fitted helmet.

4. Keep your craft under control. Control must be sufficient to stop or reach shore before reaching danger. Do not enter a rapids unless you are reasonably sure that you can run it safely or swim it without injury.

5. Be aware of river hazards and avoid them. The following are the most frequent killers.

    A. High water. The river's power and danger, and the difficulty of rescue, increase tremendously as the flow rate increases. It is often misleading to judge river level at the put-in. Look at a narrow, critical passage. Be aware that sun on a snowpack, hard rain, or a dam release may greatly increase the flow.

    B. Cold. Cold quickly drains strength and robs the ability to make sound decisions. Dress to protect from cold water and weather extremes. When the water temperature is less than 50 degrees Fahrenheit, a wetsuit or drysuit is essential. Next best is wool or pile clothing under a waterproof shell. In this case, also carry matches and a complete change of clothes in a waterproof bag. If, after prolonged exposure, one experiences uncontrollable shaking or loss of coordination, or has difficulty speaking, one is hypothermic and needs assistance.

    C. Strainers. These are brush, fallen trees, bridge pilings, or anything else that allows river current to sweep through but pins boats and boaters against the obstacle. The water pressure on anything trapped this way can be overwhelming. Rescue is often extremely difficult. Pinning may occur in fast current with little or no whitewater to signal the danger.

    D. Dams, weirs, ledges, reversals, and holes. When water drops over an obstacle, it curls back on itself, forming a strong upstream current that can hold boats or swimmers. Some holes make for sport; others are proven killers. Hydraulics around man-made dams are especially dangerous. Despite their benign appearance, they can trap a swimmer. Once trapped, a swimmer's only hope is to dive below the surface, where downstream current is flowing beneath the reversal.

    E. Broaching. When a boat is pushed sideways against a rock or log by strong current, it may collapse and wrap. Kayakers and decked canoe paddlers especially may become trapped and drowned. To avoid pinning, throw your weight downstream and lean downstream toward the obstacle. This allows the current to slide harmlessly underneath the hull.

6. Boating alone is not recommended. The preferred minimum is three craft.

7. Have a frank knowledge of your boating ability. Don't attempt waters beyond that ability.

    A. Develop paddling skills and teamwork to match the river you plan to boat. Attempts to advance too quickly compromise safety and enjoyment.

    B. Be in good physical and mental condition. Make adjustments for loss of skills due to age, health, or fitness. Explain any health limitations to your fellow paddlers.

8. Be practiced in self-rescue, including escape from an over-

turned craft. The ability to Eskimo roll is strongly recommended.

9. Be trained in rescue skills, CPR, and first aid, with special emphasis on recognizing and treating hypothermia.

10. Be suitably equipped. Wear shoes that will protect your feet during a bad swim or a walk for help. Carry a knife, a whistle, and waterproof matches. If you wear eyeglasses, tie them on and carry a spare pair. Do not wear ponchos, heavy boots, or anything that will reduce your ability to survive a swim.

11. Individual paddlers are ultimately responsible for their own safety, and must assume sole responsibility for the following:

   A. The decision to participate on any trip.
   B. The selection of appropriate equipment.
   C. The decision to scout any rapids, and to run or portage according to their best judgment.
   D. Constantly evaluate their own and their group's safety, voicing concerns when appropriate. Speak with anyone whose actions on the water are dangerous.

II. BOAT AND EQUIPMENT PREPAREDNESS

1. Test new and unfamiliar equipment before relying on it on the river.

2. Be sure craft is in good repair before starting a trip. Eliminate sharp projections that could cause injury during a swim.

3. Install flotation bags in noninflatable craft, securely fixed and designed to displace as much water as possible. Inflatable craft should have multiple air chambers and should be test-inflated before launching.

4. Paddles or oars should be strong and adequately sized for controlling the craft. Carry sufficient spares for the length and type of trip.

5. Outfit your craft safely. Be certain there is absolutely nothing to cause entanglement when coming free from an upset craft, such as a spray skirt that won't release or will tangle around legs, life jacket buckles or clothing that might snag, canoe seats that lock on shoe heels, foot braces that fail or allow feet to jam under them, flexible decks that collapse on the boater's legs when trapped by water pressure, baggage that dangles in an upset, loose ropes in the craft, or badly secured bow and stern lines (painters).

6. Provide ropes to allow you to hold onto your craft in case of upset, and so that it may be rescued. Following are the recommended methods:

   A. Kayaks and covered canoes should have grab loops attached to bow and stern. A stern painter 7 or 8 feet long may be used if properly secured to prevent entanglement.

B. Open canoes should have bow and stern lines (painters) consisting of 8 to 10 feet of ¼- or ⅜-inch rope. These lines must be secured in such a way that they are readily accessible but cannot come loose accidentally. Attached balls, floats, and knots are *not* recommended.

C. Rafts and dories should have taut perimeter grab lines threaded through the loops usually provided. Rafts should have flip lines for righting in case of upset.

7. Respect rules for craft capacity and know how these capacities should be reduced for whitewater use. In open canoes, do not carry more than two paddlers when running rapids.

8. Carry appropriate repair materials: cloth repair tape for short trips, complete repair kit and tools for wilderness trips.

9. Car-top racks must be strong and positively attached to the vehicle, and each boat must be tied to each rack. In addition, each end of each boat should be tied to the car bumper. The entire arrangement should be able to withstand all but the most violent vehicle accident.

III. GROUP PREPAREDNESS AND RESPONSIBILITY

1. Organization. A river trip should be regarded as a common adventure by all participants, except instructional or commercially guided trips. Participants share the responsibility for the conduct of the trip, and each is responsible for judging his or her own capabilities.

2. River conditions. The group should have a reasonable knowledge of the difficulty of the run. Be aware of possible rapid changes in river level and how these changes can affect the difficulty of the run. Secure flow information. If the trip involves important tidal currents, secure tide information.

3. Participants. Determine if the prospective boaters are qualified for the trip. All decisions should be based on group safety and comfort. Difficult decisions regarding the participation of marginal boaters must be based on total group strength.

4. Equipment. Plan so that all necessary group equipment is present on the trip: 50- to 100-foot throw rope, first aid kit with fresh and adequate supplies, extra paddles, repair materials, and survival equipment if appropriate. Check equipment as necessary at the put-in, especially life jackets, boat flotation, and any items that could prevent complete escape from the boat in case of an upset.

5. Organization. Keep the group compact, but maintain sufficient

spacing to avoid collisions. If the group is large, divide into smaller groups, each with appropriate boating strength, and a designated leader and sweep.

A. The lead paddler. Set the pace and do not get in over your head. Never run blind drops. When in doubt, stop and scout.

B. Keep track. Each boat keeps the one behind it in sight, stopping if necessary. Know how many people are in your group and take head counts regularly. Less-skilled paddlers should stay near the center of the group.

C. Courtesy. Do not cut in front of a boater running a drop. Always look upstream before leaving eddies to run or play. Never enter a crowded drop or eddy when there is no room.

6. Float plan. If the trip is into a wilderness area, or for an extended period, plans should be filed with appropriate authorities or with someone who will contact them after a certain time. It may be wise to establish checkpoints along the way where civilization could be contacted if necessary. Knowing the location of possible help and preplanning could speed rescue.

7. Drugs. The use of alcohol or mind-altering drugs before or during river trips is not recommended.

IV. GUIDELINES FOR RIVER RESCUE

1. In case of an upset, recover with an Eskimo roll if possible. Evacuate your boat immediately if there is imminent danger of being trapped against logs, brush, or any other form of strainer.

2. If you swim, hold onto your craft. It has much flotation and is easy for rescuers to spot. Get to the upstream end so the craft cannot crush you against obstacles.

3. Release your craft if this improves your safety. If rescue is not imminent and water is numbingly cold, or if worse rapids follow, then strike out for the nearest shore.

4. When swimming in shallow or rocky rapids, use a backstroke with your legs downstream and feet near the surface. If your foot wedges on the bottom, fast water will push you under and hold you there. Get to slow or very shallow water before trying to stand or walk. Look ahead. Avoid possible entrapment situations: rock wedges, fissures, strainers, brush, logs, weirs, reversals, and souse holes. Watch for eddies and slackwater and be prepared to use them. Use every opportunity to work toward shore.

5. If others spill, *help the boaters first*. Rescue boats and equipment only if it can be done safely.

6. The use of rescue lines requires training. Never tie yourself into either end of a line without a reliable quick-release system.

V. UNIVERSAL RIVER SIGNALS

1. Stop. Arms extended horizontally or paddle held horizontally.
2. Help/emergency. Three blasts on whistle, or wave arm or paddle vertically above head.
3. All clear (come ahead). Paddle or arm held vertically.

RIVER ETIQUETTE

Etiquette on the river means treating other people as you would like to be treated, and keeping the environment as clean and natural as you would like to find it on your future trip. Landowners' rights, paddling and rowing etiquette, and camping conservation should be recognized and practiced. River-run descriptions make note of private land when it affects the river runner; pay attention to these warnings and respect private property rights. It is *possible* that historic granting of passage means the private property is okay to use until misused—in other words, use can be withdrawn at any time.

Private landowners have rights to the middle of the river adjacent to their land on rivers that are not designated navigable by the state of Oregon or the U.S. Army Corps of Engineers. Many of the rivers in this book are not "navigable" within the narrow river rights definition. The North Santiam River, for example, is not a "navigable" river. While free passage on an unnavigable river is assured, access to and use of the riverbanks can be withheld by private landowners. Landowners justifiably complain about mistreatment; beer cans, garbage, fishing tackle, fish guts, sandwich wrappers, and toilet paper are strewn over their land. Several California rivers have effectively been closed to boating because disgruntled landowners have closed the access. Keep Oregon rivers and riverbanks clean so the private landowners won't close us out too. Carry out not only the beer cans or other garbage that you bring in, but also any garbage that you may find along the way. Do not let Oregon rivers be closed.

Paddling and rowing etiquette involves all river craft. Kayakers who stop at surfing waves should be aware of and yield to other crafts paddling downstream. Rafters and drifters should be alert for smaller boats. Be courteous on the river.

Camping conservation is important. On long trips in fragile river environments, carry and use a fire pan if you have campfires. Pack out the excess coals and ashes. For less impact on the wilderness, use a gas stove.

Pack out your camping garbage, including bottle caps, cigarette butts, burnt aluminum foil, and orange peels. Buried human waste decomposes within 2 to 3 weeks, but toilet paper may last a year or longer, so pack out the toilet paper or burn it in your campfire. Do not bury it.

You river runners who are independent and enjoy wilderness, accept your responsibility.

Kim Hummer

RIVER PRESERVATION

Much has changed for river protection in Oregon since the printing of the second edition in 1986. Then, sections of only four rivers were included in the federal Wild and Scenic River system. In 1988 that all changed. Thanks to the vision and energy of Oregon Rivers Council founder Bob Doppelt, Senator Mark Hatfield, the forest planning process, and the popular support of the conservation community, Congress passed the 1988 Oregon Rivers Omnibus Bill. This unprecedented legislation included sections of forty Oregon rivers and encompassed more than 1,700 miles. Additionally, sections of five rivers were designated to be studied for future inclusion in the Wild and Scenic River system. For perspective, other than the Alaska Lands Act, the next largest river protection bill in history included only parts of three rivers in California.

More was yet to come. In November that year, Oregon voters added parts of eleven rivers to the State Scenic Waterways system, thanks to an initiative sponsored by fifty-five conservation, sporting, outdoor recreation, religious, and business organizations. This initiative doubled the river miles protected by the State Scenic Waterways system by adding 573 miles. Nearly $1,000 in proceeds from the sale of *Soggy Sneakers, Second Edition* was donated to the Oregon Rivers Council and the State Scenic Waterways initiative to help get these historic efforts off the ground.

Also in 1988, an historic ruling by the Oregon Supreme Court stated that the most important use for water in a State Scenic Waterway is for fish, wildlife, and scenic values. This decision affects the water rights to those streams and rivers. As a result, a process is underway for evaluating the minimum flows required in the State Scenic Waterways to protect their values.

Only recently was former President Bush's energy "plan" defeated. It had included incentives for low-head hydro-power development. Such developments can be devastating to river ecosystems while adding only small amounts of power to our nation's appetite.

The ill-conceived Salt Caves Diversion Project on the Klamath River is still being pursued. If this project is constructed, it will be against the desires of the citizens of Oregon as expressed through the State Scenic Waterways initiative, the Northwest Power Planning Council, and the Oregon administration (especially the Fish and Wildlife and Water Resources departments). There would be long-term economic damage for short-term gain by investors and the local economy.

Since 1990, under pressure from the Oregon Rivers Council, the U.S. Forest Service and other state and federal agencies have begun focusing on the concept of managing river basins instead of just river sections. This is clearly the way of the future. We must still work to protect stream segments using the Wild and Scenic Rivers Act and the State Scenic Waterways system as well as other tools at our disposal. However, it should be clear that no part of any river is protected or preserved if its upstream drainages are not protected. With the decline of the northern spotted owl and old-growth forest ecosystems as well as anadromous fish runs, it is becoming clear that only ecosystem-wide measures can protect an ecosystem.

It is fortunate that managers are finally looking at the big picture instead of attempting to manage and protect rivers piecemeal. Rivers receive their water from precipitation throughout their drainage basins. The character of a river, and its flows, vegetation, and wildlife, are dependent upon the entire basin. It is not enough to protect any one species or characteristic—they are all interconnected. We must continue to strive for the health of the entire system. To fall into the trap of saving only whitewater, an owl, or a flower would be a huge step backward.

Michael Becerra

A NOTE ABOUT SAFETY

Safety is an important concern in all outdoor activities. No guidebook can alert you to every hazard or anticipate the limitations of every reader. Therefore, the descriptions of roads, runs, and natural features in this book are not representations that a particular place or excursion will be safe for your party. When you follow any of the runs described in this book, you assume responsibility for your own safety. Under normal conditions, such excursions require the usual attention to traffic, road and river conditions, weather, terrain, the capabilities of your party, and other factors. Keeping informed on current conditions and exercising common sense are the keys to a safe, enjoyable outing.

The Mountaineers

NORTH COAST RIVERS

NEHALEM RIVER

1 Nehalem River
Spruce Run County Park to Nehalem Falls

Class: 3
Flow: 2,000–8,000 cfs
Gradient: 16 fpm, C

Length: 14 miles
Character: forested
Season: rainy

The Nehalem River flows westward from the northern Coast Range to the Pacific Ocean, and is among the largest rivers in the Coast Range. In earlier times many logs were floated down the Nehalem from the lush forests where they were cut. The terrain along the river is rugged, with very few inhabitants, and in places the hills rise 1,200 feet above the river. One freight train per day still makes the round trip from Portland to Tillamook on the coast, following a 1910 route along the Salmonberry and Nehalem rivers.

Spruce Run County Park, at the put-in, is a pleasant place with very few visitors during the winter and spring. Below the put-in, it is fairly straightforward for the first mile to Little Falls. At mile 7, the gradient increases and the river narrows in a long curve to the left through a gorge.

The next river mark is at mile 8 where the Salmonberry River enters from the left. A short distance farther is Salmonberry Drop, the

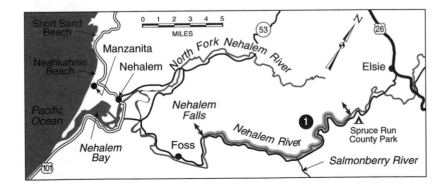

27

largest rapids on this section. Several more miles of good whitewater continue before reaching the take-out above Nehalem Falls in a small park by the same name. At moderate flows there are many play spots in the river. At high water, the hydraulics become powerful, and many of the play spots are washed out. Nehalem Falls (class 3–4, depending on water level) can be run as a finale.

Hazards. Little Falls, 1 mile below the put-in, should be scouted at low water. It consists of several shelves of 2- to 4-foot drops. At 8,000 cfs, it is hardly visible and can be run easily. The rapids can be seen from the road.

Salmonberry Drop, a short distance below the confluence with the Salmonberry River, should definitely be scouted. This drop cannot be seen from the road, but can be recognized from the river by a large rock at least 10 feet high on the right at the head of the rapids. At 8,000 cfs, some of the river flows to the right of the large rock. The main chute, at 5,000 cfs and less, has a stopper-keeper that is much more vicious than it looks, and should normally be avoided.

Nehalem Falls, just below the normal take-out, can be run at flows of 5,000 cfs and above, but scouting is required. Class 2 rapids lead into the main rapids and the runout is fast. At low water it becomes unrunnable.

Access. To reach the put-in, take US 26 west from Portland to the Nehalem River, 5 miles west of the highway summit. About 1 mile farther west, turn south on a secondary road or proceed another mile west on US 26 to Elsie and take the road south. In either case, Spruce Run County Park is about 6 miles beyond the turnoff.

The same road becomes rough and unpaved as it continues along the river to the take-out at Nehalem Falls Park. An alternate take-out for those who run Nehalem Falls is at the bridge, less than 0.5 mile downstream.

Gauge. Located near Foss. Contact the River Forecast Center in Portland. Flow is unregulated.

Rob Blickensderfer

KILCHIS RIVER

2 Kilchis River
Confluence of North Fork and South Fork to Little South Fork

Class: 2+(3)	**Length: 6.5 miles**
Flow: 300–800 cfs	**Character: forested**
Gradient: 45 fpm, PD–C	**Season: rainy**

Beautiful clear green water, small waterfalls cascading in from steep banks, moss-laden trees, and few signs of civilization characterize this scenic coastal stream. The run begins with several class 2 drops pushing around blind corners, with an abundance of eddies to catch. There are nice play spots and surfing waves in this section. Toward the middle of the run there are several 3-foot ledges. All of the obvious chutes are runnable, but be sure to check for logs in the drops before committing yourself.

At about mile 3.5 the gradient increases and the river becomes more constricted. This section cannot be seen from the road but can be lined or portaged. There are two good class 3 rapids in here that can be run without scouting by eddy hopping. Soon the gradient eases and the river splits around several islands. At about mile 5 there is a tricky drop. Here the river narrows and pours over a basalt ledge. The route seems clear, but should be scouted. A large diagonal hole at the bottom loves to give the unwary open boater a twist (and often a swim). The remainder of the trip is a pleasant class 1+–2.

Hazards. The ledge at about mile 5 should be scouted. Otherwise be sure to keep an eye out for logs. At high water this narrow run becomes a little more pushy, but new surfing spots appear, and the major rapids are no more difficult.

Access. Take US 101 North from Tillamook to Kilchis River Road. Drive upriver about 3 miles and turn right across the river. Continue on this road about 2 miles past the end of the pavement until it crosses a sizable creek (Little South Fork Kilchis River). The take-out is on the left just above the confluence of the Little South Fork with the Kilchis River. It's advisable to walk to the river to ensure recognition of the take-out on the way down.

To reach the put-in, drive another 6.5 miles up the bumpy potholed road to a fork in the road. Take the small road left down toward the river. Follow this road as far as you dare. Lower your boat down the steep slope to the river.

Gauge. None exists. Generally when the Wilson River gauge is over 5 feet, there will be enough water, but there is no consistent correlation. When the Wilson is too high to run, this stretch is a good alternative.

Alex McNeily and Paul Norman

WILSON RIVER AND TRIBUTARIES

3 Devil's Lake Fork Wilson River
Near Milepost 29 to Jones Creek Forest Camp

Class: 3+(4)   **Length: 5 miles**
Flow: 300–1,000 cfs   **Character: forested**
Gradient: 75 fpm, C   **Season: rainy**

This is a great little run, just an hour from Portland. It shares the emerald water and lush coastal forest that make this and the rest of the Wilson River runs so beautiful. Significant ledge-drops are mixed with steep continuous whitewater. Oregon 6 follows the Devil's Lake Fork and the Wilson and crosses the latter three times, but does not intrude.

Even if flows are too low on the Devil's Lake Fork, the flow on the Wilson may be sufficient. In 1991 a huge landslide went into Devil's Lake Fork, which made everything upstream of it unrunnable and inaccessible.

Put in at the normal put-in if there's enough water and you'll be rewarded with a fast continuous class 2–3 ride down to the confluence. If flows are too low, put in at the next bridge 0.5 mile downstream on the Wilson River, where the volume is approximately double. (The Devil's Lake Fork joins the South Fork to form the Wilson River just above this highway bridge at milepost 28.)

Once on the Wilson, the action picks up. First one encounters a class 3 rapids followed by class 3+ Elk Creek Drop. Elk Creek Drop is a ledge-drop with a boulder in the center and a rock wall at the bottom. Scout on the right and normally run on the right. Class 2+ water follows as one passes under the second highway bridge. The highway is on river right for the next 5 miles.

About 2 miles below the put-in, the river becomes braided into multiple channels. This area is clearly visible from the road. The middle channel is best. About 4 miles into the run is another multiple channel section. Avoid the far right channel, which is choked with trees. A short way downstream where a few homes are visible from the river is the start of the Lees Camp community. Keep off this private property. About 0.5 mile farther downstream the North Fork Wilson River enters from the right. The remaining 1 mile of the run includes mostly class 2 water, but there is one class 4 drop just above the take-out at Jones Creek Forest Camp. For a detailed descripton of this rapids, see run 4, North Fork Wilson River: Confluence with West Fork to Jones Creek Forest Camp. Take out under the Jones Creek Forest Camp bridge or 100 yards downstream on the right.

More adventurous boaters can put in 1.2 miles upstream from the usual put-in. This additional section adds some tougher rapids. Most notable are a series of rapids, visible from milepost 29 high above the river, which include unimaginatively named The Big One and The Little One. These are class 4+ at lower levels and class 5 at higher flows. Be sure to check for logs, and keep in mind that road construction has resulted in sharp rocks in these rapids. Run on November 26, 1977, by Ken Sharp and Kan Breznai.

Hazards. Both the class 3+ and the class 4 rapids should be scouted on each trip, since logs in the drops could be dangerous. Be especially alert for logs in the multiple channel sections of the river.

Access. The Wilson River Highway, Oregon 6, follows the river. The normal put-in is between milepost 28 and 29 on Oregon 6 at the bridge over the Devil's Lake Fork. The turnout is on the south side and a trail leads to the river. Alternate put-ins are 0.5 mile downstream at milepost 28 at the bridge over the Wilson River, or 1.2 miles upstream at the Drift Creek Bridge (from Oregon 6 between mileposts 29 and 30, take Drift Creek Road to the bridge).

To reach the take-out, continue downstream to milepost 23 where the Jones Creek Forest Camp road crosses the Wilson River. Parking is available on the north side of the river.

Gauge. Located at Tillamook. Contact the River Forecast Center in Portland. Because this section is so far from the gauge, the minimum gauge reading is about 7 feet if the river is dropping fast, and about 5 feet if it's dropping slowly. Flows in the Wilson change fast, so don't rely on two-day-old gauge readings.

Laurie Pavey, Alex McNeily, and Paul Norman

4 North Fork Wilson River
Confluence with West Fork to Jones Creek Forest Camp

Class: 3(4)   **Length:** 3 miles
Flow: 500 cfs   **Character:** forested
Gradient: 80 fpm, C   **Season:** rainy

If you are looking for continuous action with the biggest drop at the end of the run, the North Fork Wilson River is a good choice. The flow is fast, so the run can be completed quickly on cold snowy days, but abundant play waves, holes, and eddies invite a longer stay.

Boaters can extend the run by putting in farther upstream on either the West Fork or the North Fork. The North Fork is more interesting and has more gradient (estimated at 140 fpm). Scout the river from the road to decide whether you want to do this, and pay particular attention to logs, which are a major hazard in this narrow upper section. There is an interesting plunge drop, which deserves a scout, about 0.3 mile above the confluence with the West Fork. The upstream landmark for this drop is a smaller plunge drop.

About 1.5 miles below the West Fork confluence, after a nice waterfall comes in from the left bank, there are several ledges that deserve caution, because rocks and trees regularly slide into the river from the steep right bank. It's possible to scout and portage on the left. After the ledges you pass the houses of Lees Camp. This is a private area with a private road and is not an alternate access. Watch out for a nasty midstream boulder on a right turn.

Below Lees Camp the North Fork merges with the main Wilson River, which then splits into channels where the positions and status of logs and debris are subject to change. It is 1 mile to Jones Creek Rapids and the take-out.

Power lines cross the river just above the Jones Creek Rapids, which should be scouted from the take-out on river right. The left side is private property. If scouting from the river, the best view is from the brushy island on the right. To portage or take out, carry your boat across the island and ferry across the narrow channel. Below Jones Creek Rapids is a good take-out path a little below the bridge on river right.

Hazards. Watch for strainers at the ledges halfway through the run, and scout Jones Creek Rapids, where lots of good boaters have had less than perfect runs.

Access. The road to Jones Creek Forest Camp, the take-out, is at milepost 23 on Oregon 6. The road to the camp crosses the Wilson River and you can see Jones Creek Rapids from the bridge. This is the take-out; leave shuttle vehicles at the parking area across the bridge, or a short distance downstream on the road along river right.

To reach the put-in, continue on Jones Creek Road 0.2 mile and take the first right turn. The North Fork road roughly follows the river, but you won't always see it. Take a left at the first fork (at 1.4 miles) and a right at the second (1.7 miles). It's 3 miles to the put-in from the take-out. Sometimes there are directional signs at forks and intersections to help you find your way, but don't count on them.

Gauge. None exists. If it looks like enough water at the confluence with the West Fork, it's probably runnable. If the Wilson gauge is over 6 feet, there is probably enough water, but a gauge reading over 7 feet is usually better.

Linda Starr

5 Wilson River
Jones Creek Forest Camp to Milepost 15

Class: 2+; 3; 4	**Length: 8 miles**
Flow: 1,000 cfs; 2,300 cfs; 7,000 cfs	**Character: forested**
Gradient: 35 fpm, PD	**Season: rainy**

On this run, the Wilson River is relatively narrow as it winds between basalt rock walls. At medium flow, most rapids are pool-drop, and eddies directly below major rapids are turbulent with eddies of their own. The river curves frequently, pushing curling rapids off rock walls. Many small tributaries and cascading streams join the Wilson on this run, so the volume increases as the run progresses.

The usual put-in is directly under the Jones Creek Forest Camp bridge, or about 100 yards downstream along a dirt road with campsites on river right. About 100 yards above the bridge at the third possible put-in is the class 4 Jones Creek Rapids, described in the previous run (see run 4, North Fork Wilson River: Confluence with West Fork to Jones Creek Forest Camp). Some boaters carry to the head of the rapids and run it without warm-up. The first several miles have warm-up class 2 rapids. At about mile 2.5 an island divides the river and the riverbed has changed over recent years. Since 1992 most of the water flows in the right channel and pours over a steep jumbled outfall. Scouting the outfall from the road is advised.

Below the island, the river narrows into a gorge. This section is extremely turbulent at high water and excitingly turbulent with good drops at medium levels. Several log bridges cross the river at the beginning and end of the gorge section (at miles 3 and 4.8). After the second

Wilson River (photo by Nancy MacDonald)

log bridge, Jordan Creek enters on the left. At medium levels, play spots are common throughout the gorge and below. The take-out is on a rock ledge on the left, before a right bend in the river. Look for parked shuttle cars.

The Wilson is a popular winter steelhead fishing stream; boaters should attempt to minimize their contact with the many anglers along this section. Do not play in their fishing holes!

Hazards. The river can rise from a mild run to a hair-raiser within 3–4 hours, so beware of a fast runoff. The gorge section consists of several blind corners with no place to land or to scout from the river. Therefore, check the gorge from the road during the shuttle. Check for logs jamming the drops.

Access. Oregon 6 parallels the Wilson River throughout this run. The put-in at Jones Creek Forest Camp is at milepost 23 on Oregon 6. The road to the forest camp crosses the Wilson.

The take-out is opposite milepost 15 on Oregon 6. Park on a small turnout overlooking a rocky ledge. The carry from the river is not too difficult.

Gauge. Located at Tillamook. Contact the River Forecast Center in Portland. Several daily papers report the gauge reading.

Kim Hummer

6 Wilson River
Milepost 15 to Milepost 8 Boat Ramp

Class: 2+(3); 3(3+); 3+(4)　　**Length: 7 miles**
Flow: 900–1,000 cfs;　　**Character: forested**
　　　1,200–2,300 cfs;　　**Season: rainy**
　　　2,600–7,000 cfs
Gradient: 26 fpm, PD

The river flows through some beautiful sunless canyons where spectacular hues of green and yellow lichens cover the trees and rocks. The clean white bark of the young alder trees contrasts with the large green Sitka spruce and red maples. In the spring before the trees have foliage, young saplings and flowers can be seen growing from the thick moss of the tree limbs. This beauty can be enjoyed by boaters drifting in the glassy reflective pools and flat water between the rapids. The highway, never more than 0.5 mile from the river, and the homes overlooking the river do not detract from the scenery. One does not realize that the drifting speed is 4–7 mph until one looks through the crystal-clear water to see the colored rocks flashing by. This run becomes more difficult as the flows increase above 1,500 cfs.

The put-in has a set of nice waves that are perfect for warming up. After about 0.5 mile of short class 2+ rapids, the river begins to drop more steeply. This is a good time to stop and scout for logs in the Narrows—class 3+ at moderate flows—because a swim at the first drop might mean a swim through the narrow slot that is only about 6 feet wide. Scout and/or portage on the right.

About 1 mile downstream from here a small creek enters on river left near a wonderful ledge play wave that is about 20 feet wide. Just below is the second major rapids on this run. Here you'll find a rock garden with room-size boulders scattered across the river (one of which had a kayak wrapped around it for several weeks in 1988). About halfway through this rapids you may eddy out on river right to scout the steeper part of the drop. The usual run at moderate flows is in the middle-right channel to avoid the large hole at the bottom right. Beyond here the river is filled with fun play spots interspersed with quiet water.

At the midpoint of the run, mile 3.5, one passes under the Oregon 6 highway bridge and enters an especially scenic part of the canyon. Farther along a nice chute occurs between narrow rock walls spanned by a small bridge. Below, a gauge is located on river right just above a small boulder garden. A half mile below here look for a red log cabin on the right followed by boat skid rails, the take-out.

Hazards. The Narrows should be scouted every trip because logs in the slot would be a major problem. The big boulder rapids should be scouted at least the first time down.

Access. The Wilson River Highway, Oregon 6, follows the river. The put-in is opposite milepost 15. Park on a small turnout overlooking a rocky ledge.

The take-out is located just west of milepost 8 at a wide turnout with a drift-boat skid launch. An alternate take-out can be found at a county park farther downstream.

Gauge. See run 5, Wilson River: Jones Creek Forest Camp to Milepost 15.

Lloyd Likens and Laurie Pavey

7 Jordan Creek
Headwaters to Wilson River

Class: 3
Flow: 150–500 cfs
Gradient: 70 fpm, C

Length: 5 miles
Character: forested
Season: rainy

Anyone who has run the Wilson River has driven by Jordan Creek. This tight technical creek can be run after a good rain or when the Wilson is over 7 feet. Lots of maneuvering and tight turns are required. Many of the drops are blind and rather precipitous, and possibly blocked by logs. About halfway through the run is a technical ledge-drop of about 4 feet that goes left under a bridge and then over another 4-foot drop. The lower drop has two slots. The left slot might scrape a boat along the wall, so take the right one. Take out at the confluence with the Wilson, or continue down the Wilson for a few more good rapids.

Hazards. The biggest hazard is overhanging brush and logs. The most technical rapids, about halfway through the run, is clearly visible and can be scouted from the road.

Access. From Oregon 6, which runs along the Wilson River, proceed upstream along Jordan Creek on good gravel and dirt logging roads, crossing the creek several times and paralleling the entire run. Keep driving until there's not enough water to float a boat, and put in.

Take out on Oregon 6 where Jordan Creek meets the Wilson River, or continue downstream along the Wilson a few miles.

Gauge. None exists. The Wilson River gauge should be above 7 feet.

Alex McNeily and Paul Norman

TRASK RIVER AND TRIBUTARIES

8 North Fork Trask River
North Fork of North Fork Trask River to Steel Bridge

Class: 2+; 3
Flow: 500 cfs; 1,500 cfs
Gradient: 48 fpm, C

Length: 8 miles
Character: forested valley
Season: rainy

The North Fork Trask River flows through second-growth coastal forest draining an area of steep ridges punctuated by high rock walls, canyons, and frequent waterfalls. The upper half of this scenic run contains most of the significant rapids, including drops at 2.5, 2.9, and 3.1 miles. The drop at mile 2.9 is through a riverwide basalt ledge with the flow pouring over the right side. A significant boulder garden occurs at mile 4.5. Rock gardens and small play spots are plentiful. While rapids are less frequent on the lower half of the run, the road and river part company, providing a sense of isolation as well as a difficult hike out if problems arise.

Canoes on the Trask River (photo by Steve Cramer)

The 4.3-mile section from the take-out to Trask Park was not run by the authors but has been run by others. The gradient is 37 fpm, continuous. About 0.4 mile upriver from Trask Park is a difficult 8-foot drop through basalt that should be scouted on the shuttle if this section is to be run. It is marked by a basalt outcropping above the road on river right and follows a sharp right bend in the river.

Hazards. All the significant rapids can be scouted from the river.

Access. Roughly 1 mile south of Tillamook on US 101, go east on Long Prairie Road for 3.2 miles. Immediately after crossing the river, turn right on Trask River Road. (Boaters traveling west on Route 6 from Portland can turn south onto Trask River Road 2 miles before reaching Tillamook.) Proceed 10 miles upriver to the North Fork Road, 0.2 mile before Trask Park. Turn left and travel 3.5 miles on this dirt road to a prominent fork. The take-out is reached by traveling 0.6 mile down the right fork, crossing the steel bridge, and going upriver 100 yards.

To get to the put-in, return to the fork and travel 7.8 miles upriver on the left fork. A second fork is encountered; bear right and go several hundred yards to the put-in at the confluence of the North Fork of the North Fork Trask River with the Middle Fork of the North Fork Trask River.

Gauge. None exists. The minimum recommended flow corresponds roughly to 5 feet on the Tillamook gauge of the Wilson River.

Steve Cramer, Cliff Ryer, and Craig Colby

9 Trask River
Fish Hatchery to Upper Peninsula Boat Ramp

Class: 3   **Length: 6.7 miles**
Flow: 1,000 cfs   **Character: forested; residential**
Gradient: 30 fpm, C   **Season: rainy**

The run begins just below the hatchery on the East Fork of the South Fork Trask River and passes through a lightly populated valley. The gradient is steepest in the first 2 miles, with several tight twisting drops. The last of these is recognized by the remains of a log bridge hanging over the river 50 yards downstream. The drops should be scouted for debris.

After the confluence with the North Fork at mile 2.2, the gradient lessens but still provides interesting rapids and play spots. At mile 3.5 a busy class 2 rapids on a left bend leads immediately to a class 3 ledge-drop with a reversal that must be punched. Kayaks or decked single canoes (C-1s) should not be surprised when they briefly disappear in this hole. The remaining run is enjoyable class 2 water.

Several more miles of whitewater downstream from the take-out have been run in open canoes. The rapids are lesser except for a very tight class 3 chute, known as Dan's Hole, that should be scouted or portaged on the right, and is visible from the road. An alternate skid-rail launch is available to drift boats about 1.5 miles above the Upper Peninsula boat ramp.

Hazards. Drops at roughly 0.5 and 2 miles should be scouted. The drop at 3.5 miles can be seen from the road.

Access. About 1 mile south of Tillamook on US 101, go east on Long Prairie Road for 3.2 miles. Immediately after crossing the river turn right on Trask River Road. (Boaters traveling west on Route 6 from Portland can turn south onto Trask River Road several miles before reaching Tillamook.) The take-out is 6.1 miles upriver at the Upper Penninsula boat ramp on the right.

To reach the put-in, continue upriver 6.1 miles, passing Trask Park and the North Fork Trask River, to a fork in the road. Take the road on the left over the South Fork of the Trask. The put-in is located several hundred yards up this road just before the fish hatchery. Elk are frequently seen near the road during the shuttle.

Gauge. None exists. The minimum flow for running this section corresponds roughly to 4.5 feet on the Wilson River gauge at Tillamook.

Steve Cramer and Cliff Ryer

NESTUCCA RIVER

10 Nestucca River
Rocky Bend Campground to Blaine

Class: 3(4, 5)   **Length: 8 miles**
Flow: 1,000 cfs   **Character: forested; private property**
Gradient: 50 fpm, C   **Season: rainy**

Classified as a State Scenic Waterway, the Nestucca River drops relentlessly through a lush scenic forest into a small valley where a few small farms are squeezed in. Some stretches are quite uniform in gradient, others are pool-drop. Much of the river can be seen from the road.

On this run, the river flows through about half national forest lands and about half private lands. The rights of property owners along the river became a major issue in 1991 when kayakers were arrested for trespassing while scouting the class 5 rapids. The issue is not yet resolved. *Do not use private lands to scout or portage around the rapids.*

At the put-in at Rocky Bend Campground, the gradient is nearly uniform. At 1.5 miles below Rocky Bend, after a curve to the right, is Silver Falls, where the river drops over and through a jumble of boulders (class 5). Immediately following is a class 4 rapids in which the river flows around some boulders and over a shelf. A fast rock garden then leads to a log bridge that is an alternate put-in. Enjoyable class 2 and 3 water continues for the remaining 6 miles to the take-out on river right.

Hazards. The two rapids 1 mile below Rocky Bend Campground are by far the most difficult and are on private land. The landowners do not want boaters scouting or portaging—or even going down the river. The first rapids, Silver Falls, has been run at high water (not by the author). At moderate water, it is deemed inadvisable to run, because the arduous portage on the left requires the prospect of trespassing on private lands. Immediately after running the first rapids scout the next rapids (class 4), but avoid landing on private property to do so. The first of these two difficulties can be seen from the road where it is highest above the river and curves to the left when driving upstream.

Access. The Nestucca River may be reached from the coast on US 101 at the town of Beaver, about 16 miles south of Tillamook. At Beaver take paved County Road 858 east along the river. The take-out is

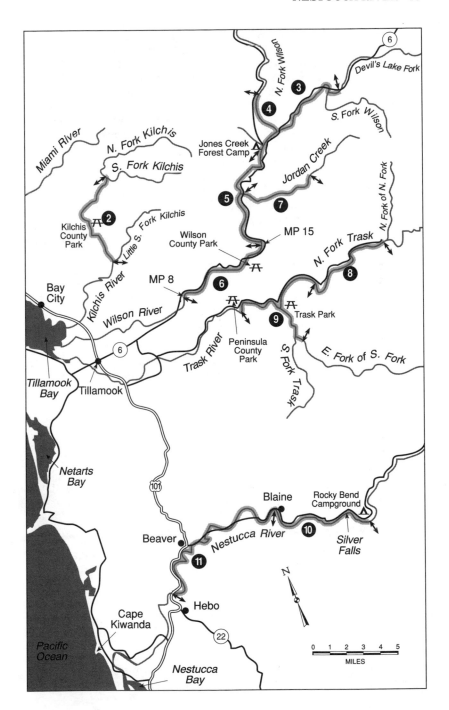

6.3 miles from Beaver near the community of Blaine. Look for a parking turnout where the road is quite near the river. There is a large school-like house across the road nearby.

To reach the put-in, continue upstream to either the old log bridge, 6.6 miles upstream from the take-out, or Rocky Bend Campground, 8 miles upstream.

The river may be reached from the Willamette Valley by driving west on the paved road out of Carlton, which is on Oregon 47 north of McMinnville. After 13 miles, pass Meadow Lake, the headwaters of the Nestucca River, and continue to the desired put-in.

Gauge. Located about 2 miles below Beaver. Contact the River Forecast Center in Portland. Several local newspapers list the gauge reading during the winter steelhead fishing season. A reading of 4 feet is too low; 6 feet or so is good.

Rob Blickensderfer

11 Nestucca River
Blaine to Hebo

Class: 1(2) **Length:** 14 miles
Flow: 500–2,000 cfs **Character:** rolling hills; rural
Gradient: 25 fpm, PD **Season:** rainy

This run on the Nestucca River starts in the sparsely populated coastal mountains and continues through the rolling hills and dairy farms of Tillamook County. The first several miles below Blaine are the steepest. Between Blaine and Beaver there are numerous riffles and a couple of ledge-drops. Below the confluence with Beaver Creek, just past the curving concrete bridge outside the town of Beaver, the river character changes. Here it becomes wider and flatter, yet it still contains riffles. The lower Nestucca River to Nestucca Bay is described by Philip N. Jones in *Canoe Routes of Northwest Oregon* (see Bibliography).

All of the drops are short and can be easily scouted from a boat. Many can be viewed from the shuttle road. At low water, technical maneuvering is required to avoid exposed rocks. Low levels also produce several good surfing spots with nearby eddies. Higher flows provide additional play spots and make most of the drops more straightforward, but increase the difficulty of the ledge-drops. Throughout the run the river splits into channels. All appear to be runnable if there is enough water and there are no logjams. The run is suitable for open boaters with class 2 experience. Sweepers are present at several spots and extra caution should be taken at higher flows. During certain times of the year anglers abound. Remember to be courteous.

Hazards. There are none in particular, except rocks at low water.

Access. US 101 and County Road 858 follow the Nestucca River and make multiple crossings of it throughout this section. Many of the bridges on County Road 858 have boat launches, thus allowing boaters to change the length and difficulty of the run. The lowermost take-out is located on US 101 1 mile north of Hebo at the steel bridge. Turn east onto Evergreen Drive at the south end of the bridge and park at the pullout. An alternate take-out is a wayside boat ramp on US 101 1.2 miles north of the steel bridge.

To reach the put-in, drive north on US 101 to Beaver and turn east on County Road 858 toward Blaine. The Blaine put-in is 6.3 miles from Beaver at a wide pullout next to the river and across from a large school-like house. Blaine is 0.3 mile farther upstream. Six bridges cross the river between Beaver and the Blaine put-in, offering alternate put-ins and take-outs. Mileage from Beaver to each bridge: first bridge, 0.3 mile; second bridge, 0.9 mile; third bridge, 1.5 miles; fourth bridge, 2.5 miles; fifth bridge, 3.6 miles; sixth bridge, 4.8 miles.

Gauge. See run 10, Nestucca River: Rocky Bend Campground to Blaine. A reading of 4 feet is about the minimum desirable level.

Kathy Sercu

SILETZ RIVER AND TRIBUTARIES

The free-flowing Siletz originates in the coastal mountains near the former logging community of Valsetz, and empties into the Pacific Ocean 4 miles south of Lincoln City. A paved road, Oregon 229, more or less follows the river from its mouth up to the town of Siletz; a paved road continues up to Moonshine County Park, and a poor gravel road continues upriver on private timber land. The upper sections, described below, contain excellent class 2, 3, and some 4 whitewater. Below Moonshine Park, the river unwinds from class 2 to class 1. Below Sam Creek, the class 1 sections are described in Supplement 1. The lowermost 22 miles are described by Philip N. Jones in *Canoe Routes of Northwest Oregon* (see Bibliography).

12 North Fork Siletz River
Boulder Creek to South Fork Siletz River

Class: 3(4, 5)   **Length: 5 miles**
Flow: 700 cfs   **Character: forested**
Gradient: 65 fpm   **Season: rainy**

The North Fork Siletz River might be more trouble than it is worth, but it does exist as a fun run worth trying if one is seeking another class 3 river in the area. All major drops can be easily portaged and can be seen from the road. This is a popular fishing section.

A mile from the put-in is a smooth ledge that can develop a riverwide keeper hydraulic. It is normally run on the right. Ten minutes later is Bombshell, a class 4 mini-gorge on a hard right bend next to the road. Check for logs during the shuttle. Several miles farther is a narrow chute that drops into an even narrower chute between two badly undercut walls. A portage is recommended. The remaining mile to the confluence with the South Fork is class 1 and 2.

Hazards. The three above-mentioned rapids present some difficulties. Logs could be present.

Access. From Falls City, near Oregon 223 west of Salem, take BLM route 34 toward the Valsetz townsite. Continue on this road past the townsite to a bridge across the South Fork Siletz River. Several hundred yards farther the road crosses the North Fork. This is the take-out.

To reach the put-in, proceed back up the South Fork and turn onto the first road on the left. Go 5.3 miles upstream to the locked gate and the confluence of Boulder Creek with the North Fork, the put-in. The road is bad and the drive is long, so allow plenty of time for the shuttle.

Gauge. None exists. The Siletz gauge at 6 feet is satisfactory.

Eric Brown and Arthur Koepsell

13 Siletz River
Elk Creek to Buck Creek

Class: 3; 4   **Length: 4.5 miles**
Flow: 1,000 cfs; 3,500 cfs   **Character: forested; roadless**
Gradient: 20 fpm, PD   **Season: rainy**

The river canyon here is extremely beautiful, remote, and unlogged. Once on the river, a boater has no contact with the road. The diversity of the rapids on this class 3 run gives intermediate boaters the chance to experience some interesting paddling. There are short ledge-drops, fast constricted chutes, and broad "V"-slicks leading to standing waves below.

This run begins anywhere one can get a boat to the river below Valsetz Falls. At the falls the river squeezes through a basalt plug and plunges 70 feet within a few hundred yards. This awe-inspiring section of the river is absolutely unrunnable, but fun to look at. Therefore, this run description begins 1 mile below Valsetz Falls, at Elk Creek. Boaters choosing to put in between the falls and Elk Creek will find a class 5 put-in, and two rapids that are class 3 and 4 at medium flows. Below Elk Creek the gradient drops and allows boaters to enjoy the plentiful play spots, solitude, and scenery. Take out at the Buck Creek bridge.

Many boaters combine this run with parts of the next run (see run 14, Siletz River: Buck Creek to Moonshine Park) for a longer day's paddle. The bridge above Silache Rapids offers a possible take-out for those not yet ready for class 4 Silache Rapids.

Hazards. The first two rapids are the trickiest. The remoteness of the river dictates caution, since a broken paddle or boat would lead to a tough hike out.

Access. From US 101 in Newport, take US 20 7 miles east to Toledo. Turn north on OR 229 to Siletz. Proceed 8 miles east on Upper Siletz Road to Logsden. From the Willamette Valley, Logsden is reached by taking US 20 west from I-5 near Albany to Blodgett; at Blodgett, turn north on Summit Highway and continue through Summit to Nashville. In Nashville, turn rught on Rock Creek Road and pro-

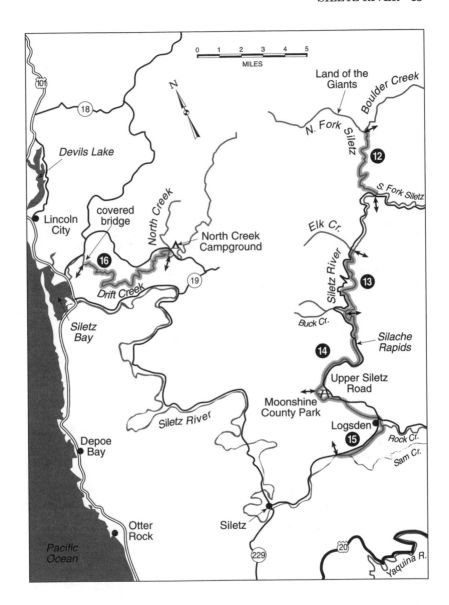

ceed to Logsden. From Logsden, head north on Upper Farm Road. About 10 miles upstream, the road crosses the river at the head of Silache Rapids. Two miles farther upstream, the road forks. The right fork leads to the take-out at Buck Creek.

To reach the put-in, return to the fork and take the left fork. Continue upstream for about 6 miles to the first and only place where the road meets the river, at Elk Creek bridge. This is the best put-in and avoids Valsetz Falls upstream.

To have a look at the falls, continue up the road for 1 mile. A small road to the right leads to the falls. At the head of the falls there is cable across the river, but there is no "last eddy" for unsuspecting boaters floating downstream to the falls.

Gauge. Located at Siletz (see run 14, Siletz River: Buck Creek to Moonshine Park). A level of 4 feet provides adequate water. At 7.5 feet the rapids are faster and more plentiful, but no more difficult.

Lance Stein

14 Siletz River
Buck Creek to Moonshine County Park

Class: 3(4); 4(5)	**Length: 6.5 miles**
Flow: 1,600 cfs; 4,500 cfs	**Character: second-growth; canyon**
Gradient: 40 fpm, PD	**Season: rainy**

Of the 50 or more miles of boatable water on the Siletz River, this stretch has the most whitewater. Several possible put-ins vary the distance for the run from 3 to 12 miles. At flows above 8 feet on the gauge, the river is swift, and a 12-mile run from Elk Creek to Moonshine County Park is an easy day. Buck Creek is the normal put-in and provides about 2.5 miles of warm-up class 2 rapids before the boater reaches Silache (Sil-at-chee) Rapids, the most difficult stretch on this run.

The steel bridge about 2 miles from the put-in marks the beginning of Silache Rapids. The hardest parts of Silache can be seen from the road on the way to the put-in. At low water, Silache is a class 3–4 rock garden with very distinct pools between drops. At moderate levels of 6–8 feet on the gauge, the pools become shorter and Silache turns into a long class 4 rapids that requires a boater to dodge rocks and holes. Above 8 feet on the gauge, Silache becomes a mile-long rapids with big waves and complex currents. The route through Silache straightens out, but the holes are large and the hydraulics powerful. As the flow increases, fewer and fewer eddies are available. At flows above 10 feet, expect the river to carry you through huge breaking waves and into big holes. Staying upright at high flows becomes very important, as there is little time to adjust your line. Joe Guide, a local expert, once flipped his raft in Silache and went for a mile-long swim before kayakers could get the raft to shore.

Good surfing spots are plentiful on the section below Silache. The rapids again tend to be pool- and ledge-drop. Two locations should be noted. About 2 miles above the take-out there is a gravel quarry on the side of the road opposite the river. At this spot the river narrows into a rock-sided gorge, called Quarry Drop. At the beginning of Quarry Drop there are several holes on the right. These holes can be challenged, or be avoided by keeping left. The last hole is the biggest, but is not noticeable from upstream. The second location to note is about 1 mile below the second bridge where the river is divided by a gravel island. The left channel has the most water and, although rocky, is the normal route. The right channel falls over about a 4-foot ledge.

The finale to the run is a group of beautiful surfing waves on the left at the beginning of Moonshine County Park. Although you may be tired from the lovely play spots upstream, you will be thoroughly worn out after playing at Moonshine County Park. At flows above 6 feet on the gauge, this spot contains some of the nicest play waves and holes around. At 8 feet, play boaters could easily spend an entire day here. The take-out is about 100 yards below these wonderful waves. At low flows you will see many steelhead anglers on the river. Please be courteous to them. Run in spring 1975 by John and Rob Blickensderfer, Chuck Leach, and Ed Trione.

Hazards. The boater is encouraged to scout the Quarry Drop near the gravel pit about 2 miles upstream from Moonshine County Park, Silache Rapids, and a few of the ledge-drops. This can be done during the drive to the put-in.

Access. The shuttle road follows the river along most of this run. Follow directions to Logsden given in run 13, Siletz River: Elk Creek to Buck Creek. From Logsden, follow Upper Farm Road upriver about 5 miles to the entrance to Moonshine County Park. Turn left and go 0.5 mile to the park, the take-out.

To reach the several optional put-ins, follow the gravel logging road that parallels the Siletz River. Please be careful on this road. It is a private road and continued access for boaters and anglers is dependent upon responsible use. Some boaters put in at the bridge marking the start of Silache Rapids or below Silache. The usual put-in is under the bridge over the Siletz River near Buck Creek. To reach that bridge, drive about 7 miles upstream from Moonshine County Park. Just after the road crosses Buck Creek, take the right fork and continue 400 yards to the bridge over the Siletz River.

Gauge. Located at Siletz. The flow can be obtained from the River Forecast Center in Portland, the weather radio, or local newspapers. Minimum flow for boating is about 4.5 feet; 6 feet is very nice.

Kim Hummer and Rick Starr

15 Siletz River
Moonshine County Park to Sam Creek Bridge

Class: 1; 2	**Length: 7 miles**
Flow: 400 cfs; 2,000 cfs	**Character: rural; roaded**
Gradient: 12 fpm, C	**Season: rainy**

This is a pleasant run for beginning kayakers and intermediate open canoers. It is usually runnable in the late spring or early fall when most of the other coastal rivers are too low to navigate. Numerous small rapids, shallow riffles, eddies, and a few small surfing waves provide easy boating with enjoyment. An occasional tree in the river is usually included. The river passes under the highway bridge about midway through the run. The second bridge (concrete) locates the take-out with a boat ramp on the left.

Hazards. At high water, the large standing waves that develop in some places could swamp an open canoe.

Access. The take-out is upstream 5.5 miles from the town of Siletz on Upper Siletz Road (for directions to Siletz, see run 13, Siltez River: Elk Creek to Buck Creek). At Sam Creek Road, cross the river and park on the left in the lot adjacent to the boat ramp.

For the put-in, see the directions to the take-out for run 13, Siletz River: Elk Creek to Buck Creek. From the parking area, it's a short carry to a nice pool put-in.

Gauge. See run 14, Siletz River: Buck Creek to Moonshine County Park.

Rob Blickensderfer

16 Drift Creek (Siletz River Tributary)
North Creek to Covered Bridge

Class: 3(4) T, P   **Length: 8 miles**
Flow: 400 cfs   **Character: forested; canyon**
Gradient: 31 fpm   **Season: rainy**

Drift Creek is a small Coast Range stream that flows through a scenic forest, including 5 miles of old timber, and into Siletz Bay. The river is very beautiful, with large trees draped in moss and lichens, and with many huge boulders, some as large as a house. In places the channel is very narrow—just enough to get a boat through.

The run starts out in a small valley with a fairly gentle gradient, but soon flows into a steep-sided, narrow canyon with a gradient of 95 fpm. This is followed by a lower-gradient section below the canyon, which is followed by another steep, narrow canyon. There is always the need to be alert because logs could block almost any drop. If the water is much higher than 400 cfs, some of the channels and drops might be easier, but it would be much more difficult to scout from a boat, and some of the very narrow slots would be very difficult to negotiate. There are no signs of civilization until the last mile or so, which reveals a few buildings and fields and a view of the road. The last mile is flat water. Run in March 1991 by the authors and others from WKCC.

Hazards. There are several twisting, rock- and tree-choked rapids that are not runnable at 400 cfs. The first one was totally blocked by a logjam in 1991. Some of the others might be runnable at higher water, but would probably become class 4 or class 5. Portages are difficult. There are many short, sharp technical drops that require careful scouting. This is a strenuous run in an isolated, steep canyon. Climbing out to the road would be difficult.

Access. Get a Siuslaw National Forest map or the *Oregon Atlas and Gazetteer!* Traveling north on Highway 101, a couple of miles south of

Lincoln City, take a right at the sign for Drift Creek. Go a little over 1 mile to a "T" intersection and take a right, continuing about 0.3 mile (past a fork to the left), to a bridge adjacent to an abandoned covered bridge. There is a small park here, which is the take-out.

To reach the put-in, go back and take the fork passed just before the bridge. Stay on USFS 19, an all-weather gravel road (keeping to the right wherever there is a choice), for about 8 miles. Follow signs to Drift Creek Camp. Just before getting to the turnoff for Drift Creek Camp, there is a turnoff to the right to North Creek Campground. Turn here, and park near the confluence of North Creek and Drift Creek, the put-in.

Gauge. None exists. With the Siletz gauge at 5.1 feet, Drift Creek was estimated as 400 cfs.

Al Grapel and Bob Metzger

ALSEA RIVER AND TRIBUTARIES

The Alsea River carries water from the crest of the Coast Range to the Pacific Ocean at Waldport. The upper drainage consists of two forks, the North Fork and the South Fork. The North Fork drains the slopes of Marys Peak, the highest Coast Range peak in Oregon at 4,097 feet, and offers an exciting upper run, including a waterfall. The South Fork also offers good whitewater in its upper reaches but has been accumulating downed trees in recent years. It joins the North Fork at the town of Alsea. From there the main stem continues another 45 miles to Alsea Bay, known for its treacherous bar. Oregon 34 follows the lower river for many miles where it is well known for winter steelhead fishing. When driving the road in the winter, one usually sees anglers trying to catch one of the 8- to 20-pounders. Many anglers use McKenzie River-type boats for their 6 to 8 miles of drift fishing. Several fishers' conservation organizations have been responsible for constructing several boat landings and also for cleaning up litter along the river every year.

Rob Blickensderfer

17 South Fork Alsea River
Hubert McBee Memorial Park to Rock Quarry Weir

Class: 2; 3　　　　**Length: 6 miles**
Flow: 400 cfs; 1,000 cfs　　**Character: forested; logging**
Gradient: 45 fpm, PD　　**Season: rainy**

The South Fork Alsea River is a narrow stream runnable only during or shortly after substantial rains. It runs through the scenic coniferous forests of the Coast Range, although recent logging and road building have encroached upon its beauty. Many logs in, above, or under the water have accumulated in recent years.

The upper 2 miles, down to the third concrete bridge, is a leisurely class 2 run with several small play spots at higher water levels. Around the corner below the third bridge is a drop that begins a 0.5-mile stretch of fairly continuous rapids. This stretch is a technical class 3 at lower water and a dynamic class 3 with chutes and twisting turns at high flow. The last third of the run flattens out somewhat, but is punctuated by three steeply sloping ledges and several play spots.

Hazards. Since the South Fork is a small seasonal stream, boaters must constantly be on the lookout for brush, low-hanging trees, and sweepers. Many trees occur in the river. The weir remnants just below the take-out should be avoided because large broken concrete blocks with exposed reinforcing rods may be encountered.

Access. From the town of Alsea, located on Oregon 34 about 25 miles southwest of Corvallis, turn south on the paved road with a sign pointing toward Lobster Valley. One mile from Alsea, turn left on South Fork Road toward Alsea Falls. At 2.9 miles from Alsea, remnants of a weir cross half of the river, near a small quarry. The take-out is in the pool above the weir.

Continuing upriver, approximately 6.5 miles from Alsea, the road crosses the river. This is the bridge mentioned in the description as the third from the top, and is an optional put-in. The put-in at Hubert McBee Memorial Park is 8.7 miles from Alsea. This park may also be reached by driving west from Alpine, which is just west of Oregon 99W near Monroe. A look at Alsea Falls, a short distance upstream, is always interesting.

Gauge. None exists. A reading on the main Alsea gauge at Tidewater can be used for a rough guide. A reading of 7 feet (which corresponds to about 400 cfs on the South Fork) is minimum for an acceptable run. A reading of 7.5 feet and above provides a delightful run. The upper gauge limit has not been established. The Tidewater gauge reading can be obtained from the River Forecast Center in Portland. Several local papers also carry the gauge reading, but the time of the reading should be noted since the river level can change rapidly.

Dan Valens

18 North Fork Alsea River
North Fork Bridge to Mill Creek Park

Class: 1	**Length: 6 miles**
Flow: 400–1,500 cfs	**Character: wooded**
Gradient: 15 fpm, C	**Season: rainy**

This is an enjoyable trip with attractive forest scenery, but without significant whitewater. About 0.2 mile below the put-in bridge, Crooked Creek enters from the left, adding about 25 percent more water. At the first bridge at mile 0.6 is Clemens County Park, a very pleasant place. After another 1.5 miles is a second bridge, and then a third bridge at mile 4.0 in the town of Alsea. After another 0.5 mile the South Fork

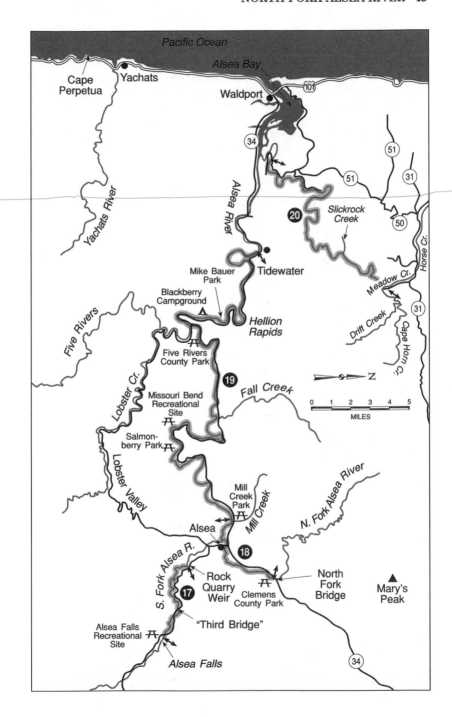

Alsea River enters from the left. One-half mile farther Mill Creek enters from the right and from thence it is a short distance to the take-out boat ramp at Mill Creek Park.

Hazards. The class 1–2 rapids that can be seen from the bridge at the put-in is the most difficult on this stretch. A certain amount of rock and brush dodging is required on the remainder of the run; consequently it is not recommended as a beginner's first trip.

Access. The put-in is at the upstream side of the bridge over the North Fork Alsea River at milepost 43 just above Crooked Creek on Oregon 34. This is 20 miles west of Corvallis.

The take-out is at Mill Creek Park on Oregon 34 west of Alsea 1.7 miles, at milepost 38.3.

Gauge. None exists. The flow at North Fork Bridge is about one-fourth of that in the Alsea River at Tidewater.

Rob Blickensderfer

19 Alsea River
Mill Creek Park to Tidewater

Class: 1(2)	**Length: 32 miles**
Flow: 500–2,000 cfs	**Character: rural**
Gradient: 7 fpm, PD	**Season: rainy**

The main stem of the Alsea River provides a number of runs that are used by the numerous drift boat anglers as well as beginning canoers and kayakers. In the summer the river usually becomes too low to negotiate in anything but a swimsuit and inner tube. Any of numerous possible runs can be designed between the river access points described below. The milepost markers are along Oregon 34; river distances are greater than the road miles.

The 9 miles from the put-in at Mill Creek Park (milepost 38.3) to Missouri Bend Recreation Site (milepost 31.2) include several surfing waves at high water and rocks at low water. The 12 miles from Missouri Bend to Five Rivers is the most isolated section. It is relatively flat except for a class 2- technical rapids about 1 mile below River Edge Recreation Site (milepost 23.1). At milepost 26.7, Fall Creek, a major tributary, enters from the right. At Five Rivers Junction (milepost 20.1), Five Rivers, the largest tributary of the Alsea, enters from the left.

The next 5 miles include a nice combination of class 1 drops, eddies, and pools. Opposite Blackberry Campground (milepost 17.7) is a small rocky shelf. The deepest slots are along the right third. At milepost 15.6, Rock Crusher Rapids has a fast class 1 lead-in on a right curve, followed by a clean chute with waves at the bottom. Part of the river flows left at the head of the lead-in. Stay in the right channel.

The biggest rapids on the Alsea, Hellion Rapids (milepost 14.9), class 1–2, has swamped unwary drift boaters. The rapids tends to push boats to the right onto exposed rocks. Below the bridge on a side road at milepost 13.2, the river is fairly flat and makes a 3-mile loop away from the highway. The last access is just above the town of Tidewater (milepost 10); the tidewater continues to Alsea Bay and Waldport.

Hazards. There are no particular difficulties on this run.

Access. From I-5 near Albany, take US 20 or Oregon 34 west past Corvallis to Philomath, and take Oregon 34 to Alsea. The first put-in is 2 miles west of Alsea at the boat ramp in Mill Creek Park, in Benton County, at milepost 38.3.

To reach the lowermost take-out, continue west on Oregon 34 to 0.4 mile before the town of Tidewater. The take-out is at a "ROAD TO RIVER" sign at a side road at milepost 10.4 that provides access at the head of Tidewater.

Other accesses include Campbell Park (milepost 34.7), Salmonberry Park (milepost 33.1), a bridge on a side road (milepost 30.7), an unimproved boat ramp (milepost 20.5) a short distance above Five Rivers Road Junction that is a good place to launch paddle craft, a Siuslaw National Forest boat ramp (milepost 19.4), the bridge at Mike Bauer Campground, a possible access for paddle craft (milepost 16.5), an unimproved access at Rock Crusher Rapids (milepost 15.6)—the driveway entrance is at an opening in the guardrail and leads to a parking area below—and a bridge on a side road (milepost 13.2).

Gauge. At Tidewater, a reading of 3 feet is adequate to cover most rocks; 5 feet is plenty of water.

Rob Blickensderfer

20 Drift Creek (Alsea River Tributary)
Meadow Creek to Lower Bridge

Class: 2(3)   **Length: 17 miles**
Flow: 700 cfs   **Character: wilderness**
Gradient: 23 fpm, C **Season: rainy**

Drift Creek flows through the Drift Creek Wilderness Area in one of the most remote regions of the Siuslaw National Forest. It is rare to be able to paddle through a magnificent wilderness surrounded by the hush of an old-growth forest and return home the same day. There is farmland only along the last 5 miles. Because the gradient is continuous and low, there are no real surprises, but there are steady class 2 rock gardens for the first 12 miles. These become easier at higher water, especially for open canoes. Starting at Meadow Creek, the next 5 miles are totally within the wilderness area. One sees evidence of logging several decades ago, including several log bridges that threaten to become part of the stream structure in the near future, and one that already has done so, requiring a portage. Around mile 11 is a fairly straightforward class 3 drop through a narrows that looks worse than it is. Shortly thereafter, the river flows under a private bridge at which the owners are unwilling to allow a take-out. The take-out is at the next bridge, a flat 5 miles downstream. Run in February 1984 by nine WKCC members.

Hazards. The remoteness makes this an inappropriate run for unskilled boaters. Expect one or more portages.

Access. Bring a Siuslaw National Forest map and Oregon Gazetteer for both the put-in and take-out vehicles. It is easy to get lost here. Go to the take-out first. From US 101 in Waldport, at the north end of the bridge over Alsea Bay, take Bayview Road eastward. After 4 miles turn left on Drift Creek Road and follow it to its intersection with Route 51. Continue on Drift Creek Road to a fork, then take the May Road to the take-out bridge, a total of 3.2 miles. The take-out is on national forest land. Most of the other land in this region is private.

To reach the put-in, return to the intersection with Route 51 and take it for 6.7 miles to Route 50. Bear right on Route 50 for 0.1 mile, then left on Route 50 for 6.5 miles to Route 31. Turn right onto Route 31 for 4.5 miles; it follows Horse Creek. When Route 31 forks to the left at Flynn Creek, continue straight along Meadow Creek for another mile to the confluence with Drift Creek, the put-in. Slickrock Creek, an alternate put-in, shortens the run to 13 miles.

Gauge. None exists. With the Alsea River gauge at 5.5 feet and the Siletz River gauge at 5.3 feet, there is adequate flow in Drift Creek.

Carl Landsness and Rich Brainerd

SIUSLAW RIVER AND TRIBUTARIES

21 Siuslaw River
Milepost 3 to Swisshome

Class: 1+(2+)	**Length: 8 miles**
Flow: 2,500 cfs	**Character: forested; logging**
Gradient: 16 fpm, C	**Season: rainy**

The Siuslaw River makes a 20-mile loop from Turner Creek to Mapleton away from Oregon 126. The upstream section of the loop constitutes this run. It is in a narrow valley flanked by a one-lane gravel road, a working railroad, and a few houses. Few of these intrusions of humanity are noticeable from the river, and the run has a pleasant, rural character. The paddling is easy, the current is strong, and small creeks and waterfalls are frequent.

However, be prepared for three class 2+ rapids. Each is conveniently marked by a railroad bridge. The first is a sloping drop under the first railroad bridge at 2.5 miles. A short quiet section is followed by a sweeping left bend and class 2+ rapids under the second railroad bridge at 2.8 miles. The third is at 6.5 miles, about 0.3 mile below the third railroad bridge. A cliff overhanging the road and a large rock on river right mark the rapids. The remainder of the run is relatively easy. The take-out is a boat ramp on river right 1 mile below the fourth railroad bridge at a left bend in the river marked by cliffs and a high waterfall on the right.

Hazards. Scout the three class 2+ rapids during the shuttle. The

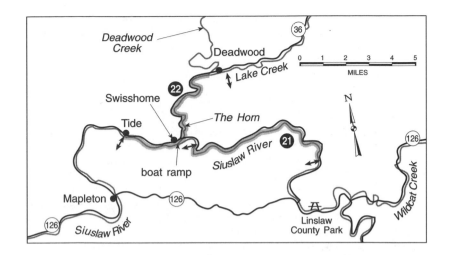

second rapids has a broad clear channel on the left. The center bridge piling hides the main drop from view. The third rapids has a hole at the bottom that becomes large at 2,500 cfs and takes much of the flow. This rapids can be portaged more easily on the left.

Access. Oregon 126 is near the put-in and Oregon 36 is near the take-out. From Oregon 126, 19 miles west of Noti, drive to an intersection approximately 1 mile below Linslaw Park. Turn right, go 150 yards, and cross a concrete bridge. Turn left onto Stagecoach Road/ Richardson Upriver Road, and go 3 miles downriver to the put-in, a rough boat ramp at mile marker 3.

Continue driving downriver to the take-out, which is 1 mile below the fourth railroad bridge and 0.7 mile above the intersection with Oregon 36 at Swisshome.

Gauge. Located at Mapleton. Contact the River Forecast Center in Portland.

Steve and Sandy Cramer

22 Lake Creek
Deadwood Creek to Tide on Siuslaw River

Class: 2+(3); 3(4)   **Length: 8 miles**
Flow: 1,600–5,000 cfs; 10,000–31,000 cfs   **Character: rural**
Gradient: 26 fpm, PD   **Season: rainy**

Lake Creek is an excellent big-water run immediately after or during a major storm. At lower flows, it is a superb class 2+ river with good action and lots of surfing waves. Lake Creek is named for Triangle Lake in the Oregon Coast Range. Emerging from the lake, the creek meanders a few hundred feet, turns a swift corner, and drops over several unboatable falls into impassable logjams and unrunnable rapids. A common put-in is

10 miles downstream at Deadwood Creek, which still gives the boater a chance to warm up for The Horn! Boaters who prefer a less ominously named put-in or a longer run can put in at any of the unimproved county parks 1–3 miles upstream.

The first few miles of the run have several small holes, innumerable waves to play on, and wide-eyed anglers who watch boaters go by. After turning a corner, the boater is engulfed in a series of drops and big waves leading to The Horn. The Horn is a unique rapids, formed by a hard volcanic formation. The rapids starts with small waves and keeps building up to bigger waves and holes. The last set of gigantic waves forms below a monster rock that bisects the river. When running the rapids, keep far left. Once in the rapids, stay upright. A large wave near the bottom crashes down on boats and can even stand decked double canoes (C-2s) on end. At low flows The Horn is class 3 and has been run by expert open canoers.

Below The Horn, where the river bends right, a significant shelf produces a very wide unfriendly hole. It is easy on the right. The 4-mile run from The Horn to the take-out continues with big waves and holes. The last few miles are on the Siuslaw River, which continues to provide many surfing waves, some of them extending more than halfway across the river. When boats are dragged out at the small town of Tide, the question is always the same: "Did you run *the Horn?*"

Hazards. The Horn should be scouted from the road during the shuttle. Run the rapids on the left. About 1 mile above the take-out, where a small tributary comes into the Siuslaw River, is a man-made structure on the left bank. It is often submerged at higher flows and should be avoided.

Access. Oregon 36, which connects the Eugene area with Florence on the coast, parallels this section of river. About 7 miles west of Triangle Lake, the upper put-in is found at one of the small county parks on the south side of the road. Other put-ins can be found along the road, including the popular one at the confluence of Deadwood Creek. Five miles downstream from Deadwood Creek, Lake Creek flows into the Siuslaw River.

The take-out is 3 miles farther down at the small park in the town of Tide. There is a boat ramp about 1 mile below The Horn on the south side of the Siuslaw.

Gauge. The gauge reading for the Siuslaw River at Mapleton is given in several daily papers or can be obtained from the River Forecast Center in Portland. A level of 7 to 8 feet is the minimum; 12 feet is optimum for surfing, and 20 feet is big water. The flow of Lake Creek at Deadwood is approximately one-third that of the Siuslaw at Mapleton.

George Ice and the authors

SOUTH COAST RIVERS

WEST FORK MILLICOMA RIVER

23 West Fork Millicoma River
Henrys Falls to Stonehouse Bridge

Class: 3(4)   **Length: 6.2 miles; 9+ miles**
Flow: 400–2,000 cfs **Character: canyon; forested**
Gradient: 44 fpm   **Season: rainy**

This run is enhanced in its upper end by numerous small play holes, which are derived from the wide, shallow, and ledgy character of its sandstone bedding. At moderate levels only two significant rapids interrupt its class 3- serenity. They can both be car scouted, although the road does not parallel most of the river. Flowing beneath a canopy of maple, cedar, fir, and aromatic myrtle, the river attracts many new sweepers annually.

Henrys Falls, a class 4 10-foot drop, occurs 1.6 miles into the run. It is scouted left, run in the chute, or easily portaged river right. This encounter is always stimulating. In another mile is a low-water river crossing. After 4.8 miles into the run is Girl Scout Triple Drop, named for the old facility below. It is located 0.5 mile inside the Elliot State Forest boundary; look for sweepers here during the shuttle. Girl Scout Triple Drop begins with a turbulent chute into a small pool, directly above a 5-foot diagonal ledge-drop. This is a tough portage. There is an ender wave after the "S" turn below. Drift another 1.1 miles to a 6-foot ledge, which is usually run right. Take out right in another 0.3 mile; higher flows permit continuing about 3 miles through another class 3 rapids, near some cabins, and on to Stonehouse Bridge, or even beyond. Run in 1977 by Ward Crane, Richard Dierks, Bernie Eskeson, David Taylor, and Craig Thurber.

Hazards. The easy portage to the right of Henrys Falls can be difficult to reach after scouting on the left because of the lead-in class 3 rapids. The keeper hole in the center below grows at higher flows. Its recirculation is powerful and forces one's support paddle to dive. At flood, Henrys is a huge, riverwide hole, and the rest of the run is class 4–5-.

Access. From south Coos Bay, turn east off US 101 toward Allegany/Coos River; begin counting mileage. Cross Isthmus Slough bridge and stay left. At Boyd's market, mile 1.1, turn right onto Coos

River Highway. Cross Ross Slough bridge at 2.1 miles and continue to the green steel bridge, 3.4 miles from US 101. Cross over the bridge, stay right, and follow the road for 10.4 miles, where it crosses the West Fork bridge into Allegany, 13.8 miles from US 101. From here to the East Fork, continue straight. Restart your mileage at the West Fork bridge and proceed left up the West Fork Millicoma River for 4.8 miles, to Stonehouse bridge, and park the take-out vehicle here. Check the river flow here (see Gauge, below). If necessary, continue 5.3 miles to Deans Mountain junction, stay right, and drive to the lower-flow take-out at mile 8, where there is a river access road behind a locked steel gate. There's not much room here, so park off the road opposite the gate.

To reach the put-in, continue upstream; at mile 8.7, note the spur road, which accesses the river above Girl Scout Triple Drop, and which can cause confusion on the return shuttle. Continue another tortuous

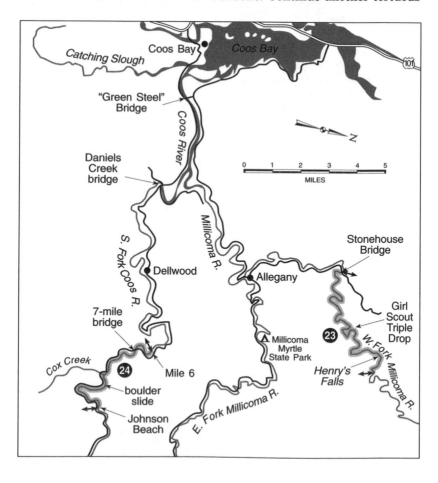

mile to an overlook, 260 feet directly above Henrys Falls, to look down for sweepers, and to experience a feeling of amazement at the anglers who regularly hike down to the pool below the falls. It's another 1-mile drive downhill to the put-in, next to the river among tall red cedars, 10.9 miles from Allegany. The old Vaughn Ranch gate a little farther confirms your location. The turnaround is quite small.

Gauge. None exists. Use the top edge of the concrete abutment on river right under the Stonehouse bridge (see Access, above). At 2 feet below the abutment, expect an abrasive run. Water near the top edge of the abutment indicates great fun for the advanced boater. Water over the abutment and up on the pillar indicates pushiness and sticky holes. This river requires an amazing amount of rain to come up, and it drops very quickly afterwards.

Richard Dierks

SOUTH FORK COOS RIVER

24 South Fork Coos River
Johnson Beach to Mile 6

Class: 3	**Length:** 6.1 miles
Flow: 500–3,000 cfs	**Character:** private land; forested; canyon
Gradient: 23 fpm, C	**Season:** rainy

This is a nice beginning and intermediate run. The sections above and below this can be run, too, but are shallower. The sandstone riverbed is wide and strewn with small to medium-size boulders. It becomes quite muddy and laden with wood during heavy rains, due to logging activity. Regeneration of streamside clear-cutting is beginning to improve the appearance of the corridor. The Coos River can be run only on weekends because the Weyerhaeuser Company restricts access during the week.

From the Johnson Beach put-in, 12.1 miles above Dellwood, it is 1.1 miles to the remnant of the splash dam, which was used to flush logs downstream years ago; while it poses no obstacle to boaters, swimming is discouraged.

On January 19, 1989, at milepost 9.5, a boulder slide crushed the car of a passing family of four, killing the mother. Forty-ton boulders still clog the river below, creating a class 3 pool-drop where previously there was only flat water, 2.6 miles from the put-in.

Cox Creek enters left of the halfway point, mile marker 9, and is a convenient start and/or end point for shorter runs. Less than 1 mile before the take-out, the 7-mile bridge crosses overhead, followed by a long class 3 rock garden. The road turnout at river right after 6.1 miles indicates the usual take-out, although some may want to continue on into the pool below.

Hazards. The new rapids, easily observed from the road at milepost

9.5, drops about 4 feet through a reversing wave. The large boulder in the rapids moved in 1991 and may move again, so beware.

Access. From Coos Bay on US 101, follow shuttle directions given for run 23, West Fork Millicoma River: Henrys Falls to Stonehouse Bridge, as far as the green steel bridge, 3.4 miles east of US 101. Follow the Coos River toward Dellwood by passing under this bridge, and at mile 4.4 cross over the concrete Daniels Creek bridge. At mile 8.7 turn right into Weyerhaeuser Company's Dellwood log dump/truck shop, and stop at the guard shack. You will not be permitted through on weekdays. Drive 0.5 mile through the facility and proceed upriver to the take-out at milepost 6.

To reach the put-in, continue upstream. At mile 8.4 the junction right leads to the upper end of the North Fork Coquille River; Cox Creek is at mile 9 and the put-in is at the turnout just past milepost 12.

Gauge. None exists.

Richard Dierks

SOUTH FORK COQUILLE RIVER

25 South Fork Coquille River
16-Mile Bridge to Milepost 3.2

Class: 4(5), T; 4+(5)	**Length: 12.9 miles**
Flow: 400 cfs; 3,000 cfs	**Character: forested; gorge; canyon**
Gradient: 60 fpm, PD; C	**Season: rainy**

Deeply cut into sedimentary formations of the coastal mountains, the South Fork Coquille River offers some of the finest technical whitewater in Oregon. Historically, this is timber and mining country but, surprisingly, the excellent scenic quality of the corridor has been maintained. Campsites are available at China Flat, Daphne Grove, and Myrtle Grove. The run is divided into four sections in acknowledgment of the varied gradient and character of the river. At medium flows the upper three sections are usually run together, but a more demanding combination is provided by Sections 3 and 4. During low water, only Section 3 is enjoyable. High runoff provides a fast, turbulent run from the top to Coal Creek.

Section 1: 16-Mile Bridge to Kelly Creek, 3.6 miles. Put in at the bridge or 100 yards upstream. Beware of rebar. The whitewater is technically demanding class 4 with a gradient of 86 fpm involving boulder gardens that are difficult to scout or portage. Most of it is not visible from the road and sweepers are abundant. About 2 miles below the put-in, 0.5 mile after passing under the concrete bridge at Daphne Grove Campground, is an 8-foot vertical drop followed by a boulder garden. The 8-foot drop can be scouted from the road 0.7 mile up from Kelly Creek at the gravel turnout. The take-out is 0.2 mile below Kelly Creek. Run in March 1985 by Richard Dierks, Brent Parks, and Don Wells.

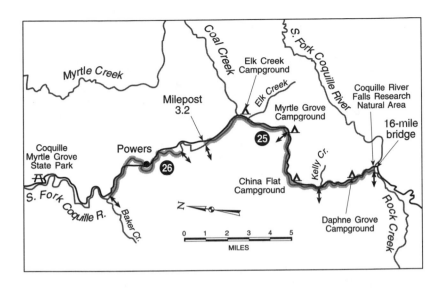

Section 2: Kelly Creek to Myrtle Grove Campground, 4 miles. The action slows down as the gradient decreases to 33 fpm. This class 2 cool-down section is a good place for intermediate boaters to join the run. An easier put-in is at China Flat Campground, 1.5 miles below. The section ends at Myrtle Grove Campground with a class 3 rapids.

Section 3: Myrtle Grove Campground to Coal Creek, 3.1 miles. Deep within vertical canyon walls, beautiful side-stream waterfalls exceed 100 feet, aromatic myrtle trees crowd the channel, and beaver sign is plentiful. The narrow class 4 pool-drops are more demanding than the gradient of 45 fpm implies. Immediately below the put-in is a series of blind drops followed by a short flat section. As the river sweeps back to the road, it begins an exciting descent into Roadside Narrows, which should be scouted from the road. Hole-in-the-Wall is next, featuring a dangerous outlet among the boulders on the left of the pool. Note the ender hole below. Nearly continuous whitewater continues to Coal Creek, which enters through two large culverts on the right. Because of its narrowness, this upper section remains runnable at lower flows than the others. Run in 1978 by Fred Mullinex, Craig Thurber, and David Taylor.

Section 4: Coal Creek to Milepost 3.2, 2.2 miles. Even more demanding rapids lie a short distance below Coal Creek as the gradient increases to 111 fpm for the first mile. It begins with a steep and narrow portion that narrows into a boulder field that has captured many logs. The canyon then tends left and constricts into a class 5 jumble, which is scouted and run or portaged right. Negotiating the approach through the reversal and around the large boulder can be tricky; there is no safe route to the left. It is located at Milepost 5 on the road high above. More rapids and 1 mile of flat water follow. The take-out is at the gully-washed site of an old footbridge, following a nice cliff exposure of shale. Run in 1985 by Richard Dierks and Franz Helfenstein.

Hazards. Sweepers are always a problem and must be aggressively scouted. Section 1 is quite technical at intermediate flows. At high flows the rapids become easier, except for the 8-foot drop, which forms a class 5 keeper hole. At high flows, most of the drops disappear. In Section 3, below Myrtle Grove Campground, Roadside Narrows and Hole-in-the-Wall become class 5 at high water. Hole-in-the-Wall is dangerous because of the person-size outlet among the boulders on the left of the pool. Section 4 below Coal Creek requires increasingly advanced abilities as the water levels rise. At high water the canyon becomes 1 mile of wild froth with major log hazards. The first walk may come after a short distance, in order to avoid a reversal. A second portage will avoid the riverwide log barricade. About halfway through, the class 5 rapids must be scouted or portaged.

Access. To reach Powers, see run 26, South Fork Coquille River: Powers to Baker Creek. Several accesses are available along the road upstream from Powers. The lower take-out is at milepost 3.2 at the end of the field on the right. An overgrown trail leads to the river. Parking is available, clear of the gate, a couple of hundred yards before the trail.

Continuing upriver, the road becomes NF 33. Accesses are available at Coal Creek, 5.4 miles above Powers; Myrtle Grove Campground at 8.5 miles; China Flat at 10.8 miles; Kelly Creek at 12.5 miles; and Daphne Grove at 14.3 miles. The upper put-in is at the bridge 16 miles above Powers, with parking at the Coquille River Falls Research Natural Area.

Gauge. None exists. Use the river-right pillar on 16-Mile Bridge. When the water just touches the pillar, the reading is 0 feet. Low is 1.5 feet, medium is 3 feet, and high is 5 feet. The maximum flow recorded at Powers is 48,000 cfs. When the water is up to the pillar (0 feet), section 3, Myrtle Grove Campground to Coal Creek, is the only one runnable. A gauge of 1.5 feet indicates that section 3 is runnable with only some class 4, but section 4 is tight and technical. Three feet is probably the premium level for all sections.

Richard Dierks

26 South Fork Coquille River
Powers to Baker Creek

Class: 2+(4)   **Length: 6.5 miles**
Flow: 400–1,500 cfs   **Character: wooded; rural**
Gradient: 12 fpm, C   **Season: rainy**

The upper 2 miles of this run are wide and shallow, and the scenery is open and pleasant. As the South Fork Coquille River meanders through Powers, high riverbanks hide the town, but the scenery is occasionally contrasted by washed-out bridges and Powers' dual solution to old automobile disposal and riparian erosion. Farther on, the river enters a scenic canyon, flows over a new fisheries weir, and offers some class 3 activity and then a 10-foot class 4 drop. After 1 mile, take out on the right just upstream of the next bridge.

Hazards. Beware of man-made hazards such as rebar. The class 4 rapids can be seen from the road during the shuttle by driving 0.8 mile up from the Baker Creek junction and looking down into the canyon. Although there is a pool above the drop, beginners should take note of the lead-in class 3- activity. Run the drop right, off the pillow, or portage through the boulders on the right. The new weir can be seen from the Forest Service station, just before Powers.

Access. The Powers Highway joins Oregon 42 at the confluence of the Middle and South Forks Coquille River, 4 miles southeast of Myrtle Point. The community of Powers is 17.5 miles upstream on the Powers Road. To reach the take-out, drive 15.5 miles toward Powers, turn right at the Baker Creek turnoff, and proceed 0.3 mile to the boat ramp, river right, just upstream of the bridge across the river.

For the put-in, continue upstream through Powers—following the signs to China Flat, Illahe, and Agness—to the parking area at milepost 2, just past Orchard City Park.

Gauge. None exists. See run 25, South Fork Coquille River: 16-Mile Bridge to Milepost 3.2.

Richard Dierks

ELK RIVER

27 Elk River
Blackberry Creek to Elk River Hatchery

Class: 4(5)	**Length: 15.8 miles**
Flow: 400–3,000 cfs	**Character: canyon; gorge; forested**
Gradient: 43 fpm, PD–C	**Season: rainy**

The Elk River is a beautiful pool-drop stream of advanced technicality. The green waters carve narrow passages beneath tall timber and large trees bridging the river. Nearly all of the run can be scouted from the road. High flows last only as long as the storms producing them.

Section 1: Blackberry Creek to Panther Creek, 5.6 miles. Although the gradient is 39 fpm, it is not difficult. It is fairly continuous class 2 except for a class 3+ slot, and it may be easily portaged. Run in 1987 by Sally Boyer, Richard Dierks, David Taylor, and Craig Thurber.

Section 2: Panther Creek to Slate Creek, 3.5 miles. Although the gradient continues at 39 fpm, it is punctuated by a few technical rapids. After an 0.8-mile warm-up, scout the long, high-gradient, class 5 rapids from the boulder left of the initial drop. Note the large boulders, transverse currents, and parked trees below. Run center to right, or easily portage left. From the road, only the long runout of this rapids can be seen in the distance. At high flows, powerful hydraulics minimize the probability of avoiding sweepers. Class 3+ and flat waters follow. Run in 1978 by Ward Crane and Craig Thurber.

Section 3: Slate Creek to Elk River Hatchery, 6.7 miles. The first 1.5 miles is active class 3 and 4 and drops at 60 fpm. Successive rapids intensify and merge with higher water. Run right against the boulder at mile 0.2 to avoid a submerged rock at low flows. At 1 mile, the turbulent, nose-bending, class 4 sluice beneath the drooping-top hemlock is a bit rowdy at lower flows. Portage left, on the road to quite a distance past the rapids. This fine upper series ends at mile 1.4 with a drop through a strong reversal into a turbulent pool exiting hard right. The next 3.6 miles is class 2 and 3. At 3.8 miles into the run, there is a tight "S"-turn around a boulder. At flood, a big class 4 with large reversing waves appears just down from here. About mile 5, begin the 0.3-mile class 4 lower gorge, dropping 150 fpm. Not easily scouted from the water, the final class 4 is a couple of hundred yards farther, and is usually run right. Paddle another mile, and take out left on the gravel bar past the hatchery gates and trolley cable crossing. Or one may take out below the next rapids, a low dam for the fish hatchery.

Hazards. Sweepers are the major hazard; they can be difficult to spot from the water. Scout all major drops from the road during the shuttle. Bent bows and sprained ankles occur during low-water runs. In very high water, inundated streamside vegetation discourages anything but rapid center transit, except where a few holes should be avoided. The upper 1.5 miles becomes class 5, with the remainder a continuous class 4.

Access. Between Langlois and Port Orford, 47 miles south of Coos Bay, turn east onto the Elk River Road (US 101 milepost 297.5). Drive

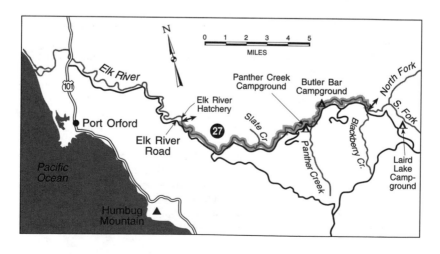

upriver 7.5 miles to the Elk River Hatchery, which is the take-out and the gauge location.

The paved road upstream parallels the river for 6.5 miles to the Section 3 put-in at Slate Creek bar. Take care not to block access with vehicles. En route is Laird Lake Campground, 10.5 miles above Slate Creek, beautiful even by Oregon standards.

Gauge. Located at the end of the parallel concrete fish returnways at the most downstream part of the hatchery. A low-runnable reading is 4.5 feet. Above 7 feet or so, the river begins to pump. When water laps at the steel grating above the gauge, which corresponds to 12 feet, it is well into flood. Call the Elk River Hatchery (541-332-7025) for the level.

Richard Dierks

CHETCO RIVER

28 Chetco River
Chetco Gorge

Class: 3(4, 5), P	**Length: 8.7 miles**
Flow: 500–3,000 cfs	**Character: forested; canyon**
Gradient: 27 fpm, C	**Season: rainy**

The Chetco River provides the only drainage outlet for the interior of the Kalmiopsis Wilderness Area. The run begins as a wide shale- and gravel-bedded stream not far outside the wilderness boundary. The initial rapids are class 2. About 3 miles into the run, the river gravels give way to colorful boulder outcroppings and some class 3 and 4 rapids develop as the gradient temporarily jumps to 90 fpm. These can be easily portaged, if desired. The next couple of miles are easy but are again compensated for at Chetco Gorge, where two class 5 rapids occur in close sequence. Portage on the right. A few hundred yards farther the river again disappears. This is Conehead, named for the monolithic centerpiece into which the torrent descends. Portage on the right. The remaining 2 miles are fairly flat. Nice ender spots are found at medium flows, one at the first bend below the put-in and the second at the take-out. Run in 1983 by Ward Crane, Craig Thurber, Bernie Eskeson, and Richard Dierks.

Hazards. The class 3 and 4 rapids at mile 3 and the class 5 rapids 1 mile below the steel bridge can be scouted or portaged. Conehead, below the class 5 rapids, should be portaged. It has been run on the right when clear of logs.

Access. From US 101 in Brookings, go east on Curry County 784, along the north shore of the Chetco River. After crossing the river the road enters Siskiyou National Forest and becomes NF 1376. Sixteen miles from Brookings, cross the South Fork Chetco River and go left on NF 1407 for 0.6 mile. Turn left on NF 170 and go 0.5 mile to "CHETCO

GORGE TRAIL," a washed-out bridge, and the take-out.

From here, some attention to road numbers is required if you want to reach the put-in before nightfall. Back at NF 1407, head upstream for 0.1 mile, then turn right onto NF 1917. After 3.1 miles, turn left onto NF 060. Stay right at the unmarked (as of 1992) junction that is at another 2.8 miles. After 1.5 miles turn left onto Primitive Road 067, and go a final 1.5 miles down to the river. The driver who is careless at the bottom may need a four-wheel drive vehicle to get unstuck.

Gauge. None exists. Observe the abutment of the former bridge at the take-out. A vertical distance of 5 feet from the river to the top of the wooden cross-beam indicates a lower-medium flow. At 3 feet expect an upper-medium flow.

Richard Dierks

29 Chetco River
Upper Summer Bridge to Loeb State Park

Class: 1	**Length: 10 miles**
Flow: 300–1,500 cfs	**Character: forested; logging**
Gradient: 12 fpm, PD	**Season: year-round**

The Chetco River is a famous southwestern Oregon stream noted for fine fishing and crystal-clear water. This is not a big whitewater run, but makes a pleasant easy-going trip. The trip is mostly flat water with a couple of riffles along the way. As the riverbed is all gravel, riffles and rapids change from year to year. Two miles from the put-in, the South Fork Chetco River enters on the left. Just below Little Redwood Campground, where the road becomes visible from the river again, is a large rock on the left with an ideal swimming hole below. This area makes a good lunch spot with a nice gravel bar on the opposite side of the river.

The next section, down to the concrete bridge, contains many fine swimming holes and beaches for lunch stops. The swimming hole un-

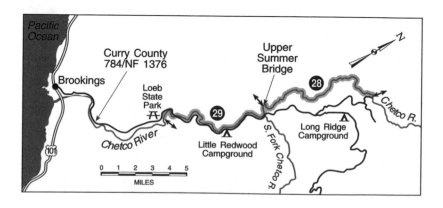

der the concrete bridge is probably one of the most popular on the river. A very nice diving rock is on the right. Loeb State Park, a very large park with overnight camping, rest rooms, and a picnic area, is 2 miles farther. Below this take-out there are many houses within sight of the river.

Hazards. The river is gentle and easy to run, but expect logs, snags, or river channels that change from one year to the next.

Access. To reach the put-in, drive up the North Bank Road of the Chetco River from US 101 (south of Brookings) to the South Fork Chetco River. This is an alternate put-in that shortens the run by 2 miles. Upper Summer Bridge, a plank bridge that can only be used at low summer flows, is located down a road to the left, approximately 1.5 miles beyond the South Fork bridge. This point is about 18 miles (including 1 mile of unpaved road) from Brookings.

The first reasonable take-out is at Little Redwood Campground. The 5-mile section from the first swimming hole at Little Redwood Campground to the concrete bridge has numerous access points. None of them are marked. Loeb State Park is a preferred take-out because afternoon winds, which blow off the ocean every day when the weather is good, make the paddling tough.

Gauge. The flow is unregulated. The river can be run spring, summer, or fall.

Ron Mattson

SMITH RIVER AND TRIBUTARIES

If there were ever a movement to appropriate the best whitewater rivers just outside Oregon, the North, Middle, and South Forks Smith River in northern California should be first on the list. In addition to terrific whitewater rivers and spectacular scenery, this area offers the Pacific Coast and beautiful redwood forests. At Jedediah Smith State Park you can camp on the river among 15-foot-diameter trees.

With torrential coastal rains falling on porous serpentine soil, river levels can go up and down like a yo-yo. Although the gorges on the Middle and South Forks are runnable with as little as 1,000 cfs on the gauge at Jedediah Smith State Park, it is not uncommon for a good winter storm to bring the water up to 40,000 cfs overnight. When it stops raining, the river often drops to 20,000 on the first day and to 10,000 on the second, giving it a "half life" of a day. Water levels dramatically affect both the character and difficulty of all the runs on the Smith River. High water means big hydraulics and extreme turbulence, even in some innocent-looking places. Good paddlers have taken bad swims here; be careful!

Bo and Kathy Shelby

30 North Fork Smith River, California
13 Miles above Gasquet to Gasquet

Class: 3; 5 **Length: 13 miles**
Flow: 800 cfs; 12,000 cfs **Character: wilderness; clear water**
Gradient: 45 fpm, PD **Season: rainy/snowmelt**

This is a run of rare isolation and beauty. Even at high levels the water is crystal clear, like a river of bubbling champagne. Although the authors have run this stretch in as little as 1½ hours at high water, it is best to start early and plan a long day. Hiking out after dark would really take out all the fun!

There are many distinct drops as well as a couple of small gorges on this run, but the entire trip is less severe than the Middle and South Fork gorges, ranking between them and the stretches above them in terms of difficulty. Big (but generally friendly) hydraulics develop at high water.

Hazards. This is a long run with a long shuttle, so give yourself plenty of time. The isolation makes walking out or getting help difficult, so plan to be self-sufficient.

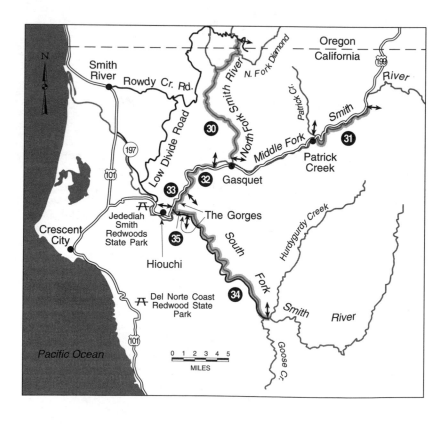

Access. The take-out is in Gasquet, California, at the confluence of the North Fork with the Middle Fork Smith River. Gasquet is on US 199 east of Crescent City, which is on US 101. To drive to the take-out, take Gasquet Flat Road from the east end of town and drive about 0.2 mile to the bridge over the Middle Fork. Just over the bridge, walk left down a dirt road about 200 yards to the North Fork Smith River. From the river, the confluence and large rock outcropping on river left is obvious. An alternate take-out is the put-in for run 32, Middle Fork Smith River: Gasquet to Oregon Hole Gorge.

To reach the put-in for this run, take US 199 to Left Bank Road. Turn right onto Low Divide Road. Keep straight at all intersections on Low Divide Road. At 14 miles from Left Bank Road, turn on County Road 308. After about 5 miles County Road 308 ends where it joins County Road 305; continue east on County Road 305. This shuttle route climbs several thousand feet and then winds back down, but don't lose heart; County Road 305 crosses the North Fork Smith River about 25 miles from US 199. Put in at the bridge. The area around this bridge is private land. Stay on public land by walking down the steep bank on river left just upstream of the bridge. Although the shuttle from Gasquet takes about 1½ hours one way, the road is well maintained.

Gauge. Located at Jedediah Smith State Park, which is on US 199 west of Gasquet. The flow is approximately 33 percent of the flow at the gauge.

Bo and Kathy Shelby

31 Middle Fork Smith River, California
6 Miles Above Patrick Creek to Patrick Creek

Class: 4(5) **Length:** 5–6 miles
Flow: 500–2,000 cfs **Character:** canyon; forested
Gradient: 65 fpm, PD **Season:** rainy/snowmelt

This run, which is seldom done, has a spectacular but very tight gorge. The authors ran it when the Jedediah Smith State Park gauge read about 8,000 cfs, a good level. The most difficult parts of the gorge can be scouted by walking along US 199 for a mile or so above Patrick Creek. The remainder of the run is not visible from the road. Other drops need careful consideration from the river.

Hazards. The gorge itself, most of which is visible from the road, is the major difficulty. Scout for trees and logs.

Access. Patrick Creek flows alongside US 199. Take out where Patrick Creek enters the Smith River.

To find a put-in, drive approximately 5.7 miles upstream on US 199. Just look around for a place to scramble down the bank.

Gauge. Located at Jedediah Smith State Park. The flow is approximately 17 percent of the flow at the gauge.

Bo and Kathy Shelby

Middle Fork Smith River, California
Patrick Creek to Gasquet

This class 3–4 section is described by Dick Schwind in *West Coast River Touring* (see Bibliography).

32 Middle Fork Smith River, California
Gasquet to Above Oregon Hole Gorge

Class: 2+; 3	Length: 6 miles
Flow: 1,000 cfs; 22,000 cfs	Character: clear water
Gradient: 20 fpm, PD	Season: rainy/snowmelt

This delightful run on the Middle Fork Smith River provides a good warm-up for the more demanding runs on the Smith. There are several good rapids and play spots.

Hazards. There are no particular difficulties.

Access. At the downstream end of the town of Gasquet on US 199, put in at the first place where the river is right next to the highway. There is a laundromat, trailer park, and a wide spot in the road. The obvious put-in is on private property, but look for a spot that isn't on private land.

The take-out is approximately 5 miles downstream. During the shuttle, look for a highway warning sign that says "SLIPPERY WHEN WET," where a small dirt road angles down to the river (the river is not visible from the road here). Walk down and scout the take-out; it is not obvious from the river.

Gauge. Located at Jedediah Smith State Park. The flow is approximately 55 percent of the flow at the gauge.

Bo and Kathy Shelby

33 Middle Fork Smith River, California
Oregon Hole Gorge

Class: 4; 5	Length: 1.5 miles
Flow: 500 cfs; 22,000 cfs	Character: gorge; clear water
Gradient: 50 fpm, C	Season: rainy/snowmelt

The only thing wrong with this gorge is that it is over too soon! The character of the run changes dramatically with the water level. At low water the drops are steep but distinct, requiring some tricky moves around big boulders. At high water the gorge becomes an awesome, turbulent flush in which eddies are hard to find. Oregon Hole Gorge is also known as Middle Fork Gorge.

Hazards. Most of the gorge is visible from US 199, but the road is several hundred vertical feet above the river, luring the unsuspecting

A low-water run on the Oregon Hole Gorge, Smith River (photo by Al Kitzman)

paddler into an inappropriate complacency. Be sure to take the time and effort to scramble down to river level and scout carefully; the water is bigger and faster than it appears from above. The last major rapids in the gorge is just barely visible downstream; it can be scouted from river left.

Access. Put in either at Gasquet on US 199 or just above the gorge (both access points are described in run 32, Middle Fork Smith River: Gasquet to Above Oregon Hole Gorge).

Take out at the bridge where the South Fork Road crosses the river (paddle under the bridge and land on river right at a small gravel beach). A steep trail leads up to a parking area where the South Fork Road takes off from US 199.

Gauge. See run 32, Middle Fork Smith River: Gasquet to Above Oregon Hole Gorge.

Bo and Kathy Shelby

34 South Fork Smith River, California
Upper Bridge to South Fork Gorge

Class: 3(4)	**Length: 10 miles**
Flow: 1,000–20,000 cfs	**Character: forested; canyon**
Gradient: 35 fpm, PD	**Season: rainy/snowmelt**

Most of the drops on this run are gradual and straightforward, with the exception of the sharp drop visible from the road several miles up from the gorge (past the point where the road climbs away from the river and then returns).

Hazards. The sharp drop mentioned above develops a nasty hole at some water levels; it can usually be avoided by running river left.

Access. Take the South Fork Road off of US 199 about 1 mile northeast of Hiouchi Hamlet. Cross the Middle Fork and the South Fork, then turn left and go up the South Fork. The take-out is about 1 mile above the South Fork bridge (2 miles from US 199). There is a large pullout (75 yards long and 40 yards wide), with trails leading down to the river. The river is not visible from the road at this point. Scout the take-out if you don't want to run the gorge; it isn't obvious from the river.

To reach the put-in proceed upstream, crossing the river twice on bridges high above the river. The put-in is at a bridge about 10 miles up. The river is generally visible from the road. It is possible to shorten the run by putting in farther down.

Gauge. Located at Jedediah Smith State Park. The flow is approximately 45 percent of the flow at the gauge.

Bo and Kathy Shelby

35 South Fork Smith River, California
South Fork Gorge to Bridge

Class: 4; 5   **Length: 1.5 miles**
Flow: 500 cfs; 9,000 cfs   **Character: gorge; clear water**
Gradient: 60 fpm, PD   **Season: rainy/snowmelt**

This gorge is a bit longer than the Oregon Hole Gorge, but it still isn't nearly long enough! Although the South Fork Road follows the river, the water is generally out of sight. With persistence and scrambling it is possible to scout most of this stretch from the road; do this before committing yourself to the run. This is one of the most beautiful gorges anywhere, complete with all the classic gorge characteristics: steep blind drops, tough landings for scouting, and powerful turbulent water. This run is particularly difficult and potentially dangerous at high water levels.

Hazards. The run has several distinct drops, which vary markedly with the water level. Be prepared to do your own scouting and make your own decisions.

Access. Put in at any of the access points for run 34, South Fork Smith River: Upper Bridge to South Fork Gorge, or at the take-out for that run.

Take out at the South Fork bridge by paddling under the bridge and landing at the small beach on river right. A trail goes sharply up the bank to the end of the bridge.

Gauge. See run 34, South Fork Smith River: Upper Bridge to South Fork Gorge.

Bo and Kathy Shelby

REGION 3

SOUTHERN OREGON RIVERS

UMPQUA RIVER AND TRIBUTARIES

The South Umpqua River arises from the southern foothills of the Cascades, while the North Umpqua River originates from the high Cascade Mountains near Diamond Lake. After the two join near Roseburg, the main Umpqua River then flows northwest all the way to the coast at Reedsport. This is the northernmost river in Oregon that is able to cut its way from the Cascade Mountains, through the Coast Range, and into the Pacific Ocean. Because the headwaters of the South Umpqua River are at relatively low elevations, the flow becomes quite low during the summer. However the North Umpqua River, with its mountainous headwaters, provides some truly fine boating year-round. The numerous campgrounds and the road along the tree-lined river canyon are used by many anglers, campers, and picnickers.

36 South Umpqua River
Campbell Falls to Three C Rock

Class: 3(4+); 4(5)   Length: 12 miles
Flow: 600 cfs; 4,000 cfs   Character: forested
Gradient: 29 fpm, PD   Season: rainy/snowmelt

The South Umpqua River is born with emerald green waters near Jackass Mountain in the Rogue Umpqua Divide Wilderness Area. Even though the Rogue and the Umpqua rivers meet the sea more than 100 miles apart, the South Umpqua and Rogue originate within 15 miles of each other.

The run starts with a bang at Campbell Falls (named in honor of World War II pilot and war hero Robert Campbell), a 14-foot vertical drop into a pool with a narrow exit. There is a chute along the far left wall, but at most water levels the falls seems to be the saner route. An alternative put-in is 75 yards downstream on river right.

The major rapids downstream change from narrow chutes through rock outcroppings to powerful riverwide ledge-drops as the flow increases. The first major rapids, Diversification Drop, is located 1.9 miles down from the put-in. At low flows there are two distinct chutes. River left is fairly straightforward; however, the right chute requires a quick left turn just as you drop over the 5-foot falls. A half mile farther, Boulder Creek enters on the right, and 200 yards below is a drop similar to Diversification Drop. Both of these drops can be scouted from the road. Dumont Creek, with campground and rest rooms, is less than 1 mile downstream.

The third rapids worth mentioning, Triple Drop, is located about 8 miles farther down, just a couple of miles before the take-out. Three distinct drops in this 100-yard-long rapids give a great ride.

Hazards. Campbell Falls and the three other rapids mentioned above present difficulties. Scout or portage.

Access. The run is east of I-5 between Roseburg and Medford. From the north, take Route 227 at Canyonville and proceed 23 miles to Tiller. From the south, take Oregon 62 from Medford to Trail and Route 227 to Tiller. In Tiller take Douglas 46 upstream 5.4 miles to the take-out at the Three C Picnic Area.

The put-in is 11.4 miles farther upstream at Campbell Falls. Hike about 200 yards on a fairly good trail down to the river.

Gauge. Located at Tiller. Call the National Weather Service in Medford or the River Forecast Center in Portland.

Terry K. Wyatt and Jeff S. Wolfe

37 South Umpqua River
Three C Rock to Milepost 22

Class: 3(4)   **Length: 8.5 miles**
Flow: 1,500–4,000 cfs   **Character: wooded**
Gradient: 23 fpm, C   **Season: rainy/snowmelt**

Although most of this run is class 1 and 2 in nature, there are several class 3 and a class 4 rapids at high flows. From the put-in, the river flows at a nice tempo through a small canyon. After passing a concrete bridge at mile 1.6, it is another mile to a demanding class 3 rapids where most of the river pours against a large boulder. At mile 3.6 is a class 4 riverwide ledge that can be scouted from the right. The river passes under the Route 227 bridge in Tiller at mile 4.7. The last major rapids is at mile 7.2, near the downstream end of a recent major road cut. The river piles up against a huge boulder on the right bank as it makes a tight left bend. Part of the water flows upstream on the right to form a strong boiling eddy feeding through trapped logs and debris that should be avoided. Several hundred yards downstream are the remains of a log bridge and a concrete bridge swept away in past floods. It is about 1 mile to the take-out.

Hazards. The class 3 rapids at mile 2.6 should be run well left of center to avoid a large upstream pour-over hole on the right, followed by a massive rock in midstream with most of the water smashing directly into it. The class 4 rapids at mile 3.6 is a combination of a ledge with a sticky reversal followed by a hole of raft-flipping proportions. The class 3 drop at the road cut is potentially the most dangerous. It can be scouted and portaged on the left.

Access. The put-in for this run is the take-out for run 36, South

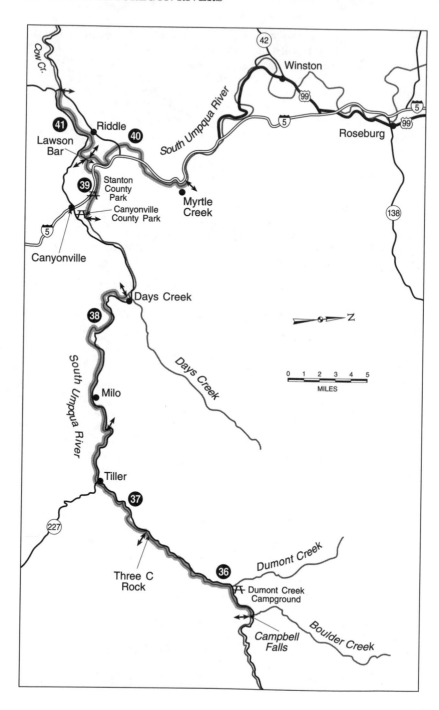

Umpqua River: Campbell Falls to Three C Rock.

The take-out for this run is at about Milepost 22.5 on Route 227, where the river makes a sweeping left bend close to the road through a broad area of low rock outcroppings. Parking can be found on the river-side shoulder of the road.

Gauge. Located at Tiller. See run 36, South Umpqua River: Campbell Falls to Three C Rock.

Steve Cramer and Rob Blickensderfer

38 South Umpqua River
Milepost 22 to Days Creek

Class: 2+(4)   **Length: 13.5 miles**
Flow: 1,500–4,000 cfs   **Character: rural**
Gradient: 13 fpm, C   **Season: rainy/snowmelt**

The scenery varies at almost every turn—low rock cliffs, volcanic tuff, extensive gravel bars, and rolling hills. The river has many pleasant riffles over gravel bars that become very fast and with big waves at higher flows. It passes under a covered bridge at mile 2.1 and from there it's only about 0.5 mile to the concrete bridge in Milo. At mile 3.6 there is a low ledge with a sticky reversal. After several miles of slow water, one hardly suspects the major class 4 rapids at mile 11.2, where the river slices through a low rock outcropping. Below this drop, the river bounces through delightful water with many play spots to the take-out.

Hazards. The class 4 rapids at mile 11.2 consists of a fast chute leading into a riverwide hole with a collapsing upstream wave that takes the full flow of the river. This rapids can be easily portaged on either side.

Access. The put-in for this run is the take-out at Milepost 22.5 for run 37, South Umpqua River: Three C Rock to Milepost 22.

The take-out is a boat ramp on river right located 50 yards upstream from the Route 227 bridge in Days Creek.

Gauge. See run 36, South Umpqua River: Campbell Falls to Three C Rock.

Steve Cramer and Rob Blickensderfer

39 South Umpqua River
Canyonville County Park to Lawson Bar

Class: 2(3)   **Length: 5 miles**
Flow: 600 cfs   **Character: rural**
Gradient: 12 fpm, PD   **Season: rainy**

A classic example of a pool-drop river can be experienced on this short run. After putting in at the pleasant Canyonville County Park, it is about 0.5 mile to the first drop, a straightforward class 2- rapids just as a bridge comes into view. A little farther along, a park is seen among large fir trees on the left. This is Stanton County Park on the road just north of Canyonville, and it offers an alternate access to the river. About 0.25 mile below the park is the most difficult rapids on this section, consisting of class 3 channels over ledges. It can be scouted or portaged on the left. A mile below here is a class 2 rapids with several channels through willows. The next rumble heard is not a rapids, but the traffic on the I-5 bridge overhead. Below the bridge are enjoyable small rapids among scenic rock formations. An extensive gravel bar on the left indicates the approach to the mouth of Cow Creek, on the left, followed by Lawson Bar on the right. One may take out on the right either above or below the class 2 rapids at Lawson Bar.

Hazards. The class 3 rapids mentioned above is quite technical at low flows.

Access. Canyonville is a short distance off I-5. To reach the put-in, go to the center of town and take Route 227 eastward toward Tiller for 1.1 miles. Turn left on Douglas 215, which leads directly to Canyonville County Park.

The take-out at Lawson Bar can be reached by returning to I-5 and proceeding northward. Take exit 102, turn west, and follow the sign to Lawson Bar (dead end).

Gauge. Located at Winchester. Call the River Forecast Center in Portland. The flow is about 25 percent less than at Winchester. A flow of 800 cfs at Winchester is adequate.

Rob Blickensderfer and Steve Cramer

40 South Umpqua River
Lawson Bar to Myrtle Creek

Class: 1+(2)	**Length: 9 miles**
Flow: 800 cfs	**Character: rural**
Gradient: 6 fpm, PD	**Season: rainy**

The pools are long and the drops are small on this classic pool-drop run. Lawson Bar, the put-in, is a very extensive gravel bar that provides the option of putting in either above or below the class 2 rapids seen here. After a short distance, the river parallels I-5 on a long sweeping curve to the left. As the river leaves the freeway, the only major rapids, class 2, is approached. At this rapids the water tumbles over and through a rock outcropping. The river continues for some distance on a scenic course among rock outcroppings. The latter half of the run alternates between rather long pools and short class 1 rapids. The last pool is about 1 mile long, followed by an easy class 1 rapids above the bridge at the take-out.

Hazards. The one class 2 rapids can be portaged if desired.

Access. For the put-in at Lawson Bar, see run 39, South Umpqua River: Canyonville County Park to Lawson Bar.

The take-out for this run is under the bridge that connects I-5 exit 108 with Myrtle Creek. The parking area is at the west end of the bridge, from which a steep path leads down to a gravel bar.

Gauge. Located at Winchester. Call the River Forecast Center in Portland.

Rob Blickensderfer and Steve Cramer

41 Cow Creek
Glenbrook Loop Bridge to Lawson Bar

Class: 1   **Length: 6 miles**
Flow: 300 cfs   **Character: rural**
Gradient: 9 fpm, PD   **Season: rainy**

Despite its unglamorous name, this is an ideal class 1 river, that is, there are plenty of class 1 rapids but nothing of greater difficulty and no mandatory portages. Cow Creek is among the largest creeks in Oregon, and surprisingly was not named Cow River. It's about the size of the better-known Alsea River. Enjoy the run. It's away from the road most of the distance. Upon approaching the mouth of Cow Creek, Lawson Bar can be seen on the other side of the South Umpqua River. To reach the take-out at Lawson Bar, it is necessary to ferry across the South Umpqua just above the class 2 Lawson Bar Rapids, or to go with the flow and run the rapids. The pool and eddy below the rapids provide the better take-out.

Hazards. Crossing the South Umpqua River from the mouth of Cow Creek, or running the rapids just below, is more difficult than the rest of the run.

Access. From I-5, about 20 miles south of Roseburg, take exit 102. Turn west and at the "T" intersection, follow the sign to Lawson Bar, the take-out.

To reach the put-in, return to I-5. Go south on I-5 to exit 101 and follow the sign to Riddle. On the outskirts of Riddle, turn left on Glenbrook Loop Road. Continue 4 miles, turn right, and cross the bridge over Cow Creek. The put-in is at the north end of the bridge. Alternatively, the put-in can be reached from the north of Riddle by taking exit 103 off I-5. Follow the Riddle Bypass Road about 6 miles, pass the Glenbrook Mine entrance, and continue another 0.5 mile to the Glenbrook Loop Bridge.

Gauge. None exists.

Rob Blickensderfer and Steve Cramer

42 Canton Creek
Upper Canton Creek to Steamboat Creek

Class: 3(5); 4(5)   **Length: 8 miles**
Flow: 300 cfs; 2,000 cfs   **Character: old growth; clear-cut**
Gradient: 93 fpm   **Season: rainy**

This run is usually good when waters on others in the area are too high. The scenery varies from beautiful old-growth timber to clear-cuts that extend all the way to the riverbank. The run offers surfing waves, sloping ledges, large ledge-drops, a couple of easy portages, and one spectacular 25-foot not-quite-vertical falls. Run in spring 1989 by David Gilmore.

Hazards. The major difficulty is the debris remaining from clear-cutting to the water's edge. The 25-foot falls should be scouted during the shuttle. The central 3-foot-wide chute has been run.

Access. The take-out is at Canton Creek Campground on Forest Route 38, 38 miles west of Roseburg, which is on I-5.

To get to the put-in, follow Oregon 138 to Steamboat Creek, and turn north onto Forest Route 38. At 0.5 mile, turn left onto Canton Creek Road and proceed 9 miles to the confluence of Pass Creek with Upper Canton Creek, the put-in.

Gauge. Located at Scaredman Creek Campground, 3 miles upstream from Steamboat. A reading between 1.3 and 5 feet indicates a good level. When the North Umpqua is about 5 feet and Steamboat Creek is about 2 feet, Canton Creek is good.

David Gilmore and Jim Reed

43 Steamboat Creek
Steamboat Falls to Canton Creek Campground

Class: 4(5)   **Length: 6 miles**
Flow: 600–2,500 cfs   **Character: forested**
Gradient: 40 fpm   **Season: rainy/snowmelt**

Steamboat Creek enters the North Umpqua River 1 mile west of Island Campground. Its feeling of isolation and good class 4 action make it worth dipping a paddle into.

The put-in is just below Steamboat Falls where the road is near the river. Steamboat Falls can be run, but it is not recommended because of cement and steel rebar at its base. A line down the center-right has been relatively clean for the author. One mile of easy play water allows a warm-up before a class 4 rapids. After 0.2 mile is a class 5 rapids that can be scouted or portaged on the right. The remaining portion of the run is class 2 and 3 with an occasional easy class 4. Little Steamboat Falls lies at the end of the canyon and ranges in difficulty from class 4 at moderate flow to class 5 at high flows. It makes an excellent take-out.

Hazards. At levels above 5 feet, the portage around the class 5 rapids becomes very difficult, as does the rapids. Check for logs.

Access. From Oregon 138 along the North Umpqua River, take Oregon 38 northward up Steamboat Creek. Canton Creek Campground, 0.5 mile upstream, is the take-out.

From the campground, drive 5.5 miles upstream. Put in where the road comes near the river. An alternate put-in is 100 yards up Steelhead Creek, which provides a short class 3 section.

Gauge. Located on Steamboat Creek just downstream from Canton Creek. A good low flow is 3.7 feet.

Eric Brown

44 North Umpqua River
Boulder Flat to Horseshoe Bend

Class: 2; 3	**Length: 7 miles**
Flow: 800 cfs; 2,000 cfs	**Character: forested**
Gradient: 39 fpm, PD	**Season: year-round**

Most whitewater boating on the North Umpqua River is done along the 32-mile stretch between Boulder Flat and Cable Crossing. As well as being a fine boating stream, the North Umpqua is renowned for its incomparable thrills for the angler. As a result, the Forest Service has established a few restrictions on boating in order to protect the best fishing areas. A copy of the guidelines can be obtained at the North Umpqua Ranger District Office at Glide. Restrictions affect boating from July through October, when river access is limited to 10:00 A.M. to 6:00 P.M. except between Island Campground and Bogus Creek, which is closed to boating. During September and October, Soda Springs to Wilson Creek is closed for salmon spawning. Please respect these closures. Anglers are our allies in protecting free-flowing rivers.

Most of this run can be scouted from the road. The river is characterized by swiftly moving water and fairly continuous activity in moderate-size waves amid numerous rocks and other obstacles. There are no really difficult rapids, though there are several spots where large holes and bigger waves are encountered. Snags are a hazard at times, and it is not unusual to encounter a tree spanning all or most of the stream. Just beyond the second bridge, a rocky ledge spans 80 percent of the river, creating a very narrow chute along the right bank. At lower water levels this chute is virtually the only runnable spot. A boater may readily get slammed into the wall on the right by the force of the current. It is a potential spot for lodged debris.

Hazards. The rocky ledge just below the second bridge should be checked for debris in the right chute. The ledge may need to be portaged.

Access. The put-in at Boulder Flat Campground is approximately 50 miles east of Roseburg on Oregon 138.

The take-out is at Horseshoe Bend Campground, also on Oregon 138.

Gauge. Located at Winchester. Contact the River Forecast Center in Portland. The optimum level is 2–5 feet. The river is dam controlled and runnable all year.

Kent Wickham

45 North Umpqua River
Horseshoe Bend to Steamboat

Class: 3(4); 4	**Length: 9 miles**
Flow: 800 cfs; 2,000 cfs	**Character: forested**
Gradient: 29 fpm, PD	**Season: year-round**

This run on the North Umpqua River can be described as pool-drop. Between Horseshoe Bend and Apple Creek campgrounds the river passes through a narrow gorge full of short, steep rapids that vary in difficulty. Most can be scouted from the road. Several of them require meticulous maneuvering between rocks and holes, especially Pin Ball Rapids, class 4. The pool-drop pattern of the river continues on to Steamboat. A boater should go slowly and get a look at the rapids that remain.

Hazards. Pin Ball Rapids is a boulder-choked drop not visible from the road. It is located about 0.3 mile below the bridge below Apple Creek Campground. Scouting is advisable. The rapids occurs on a right bend of the river with a large gravel bar just above it on the left. At water levels that allow for the bar to exist, it is possible to pull in at its base and scout from the left bank.

Access. Put in at any of the wide spots along Oregon 138 near Horseshoe Bend Campground. An alternate put-in is the small turnout 0.2 mile upstream from the Dry Creek Store, which is approximately 1.5 miles above Horseshoe Bend.

The best take-out is 0.2 mile below Island Campground and 1.5 miles above Steamboat.

Gauge. See run 44, North Umpqua River: Boulder Flat to Horseshoe Bend.

Kent Wickham

46 North Umpqua River
Steamboat to Cable Crossing

Class: 3(4)   **Length: 16 miles**
Flow: 1,500–3,000 cfs   **Character: forested**
Gradient: 21 fpm, PD   **Season: year-round**

This stretch, although highlighted by several of the North Umpqua's biggest rapids, is generally less technical than the upstream runs. Rapids are separated by long flat stretches.

Steamboat Inn marks the site of an exciting rocky rapids in the left channel, and a sometimes-runnable falls in the right channel. Do not trespass on Steamboat Inn property when scouting. Six miles below Steamboat is Wright Creek Bridge, which is followed in another 0.2 mile by Bathtub Rapids. At low water Bathtub deserves a scout.

Small fun drops continue for several more miles. A very large cliff rising from water's edge on the left is seen 200 yards above Island (or Staircase) Rapids, the North Umpqua's best ride. Several miles below Island Rapids, and marked by the Forest Service boundary sign at the side of the road, is Sleeper Rapids, a long sweeping turn ending in a troublesome hole. A notable rapids encountered at Susan Creek State Park is followed by a notoriously flat 4 miles. At Richard G. Baker County Park, a 5-foot falls known as Little Niagara helps to justify paddling the preceding flat stretch. Cable Crossing is the last convenient take-out above Rock Creek Falls. The run may be shortened by taking out at Susan Creek Picnic Area, although the motor home traffic may be heavy.

The mouth of Steamboat Creek is a holding area for migrating steelhead. From mid-July through October numerous anglers are encountered here. Confrontations have occurred in the past, and relations between boaters and anglers have been somewhat strained. Please be courteous. During fishing season it is a good idea to plan put-ins after 10:00 A.M. and take-outs before 5:00 P.M., to leave prime fishing time to the anglers. If there is an exceptionally high number of anglers, it is best to avoid the area altogether, and put in 4 miles down at Bogus Creek. With the exception of the rapids right at Steamboat, very few good rapids will be missed.

Hazards. Below the recommended take-out at Cable Crossing are two very demanding rapids, Rock Creek Falls and The Narrows. These rapids should be considered by experts only. Rafters might find it necessary to portage Bathtub at low flows due to the narrowness of the chutes. At Island Rapids the river divides into a broad, shallow left channel, which fizzles out to nothing, and a roaring right channel that approaches class 4. Island can be scouted from the road with difficulty. Sleeper is a long but rather innocuous rapids that starts out easy but requires a very tricky cut at the end to avoid a very large hole (a large rock at low flows). It can be scouted from the road.

Access. The best put-in is at the river access just below Island Campground on Oregon 138. Bogus Creek Campground is an alternative.

The take-out is at Cable Crossing, a poorly marked but very good access just up from Rock Creek Falls.

Gauge. See run 44, North Umpqua River: Boulder Flat to Horseshoe Bend.

47 North Umpqua River
Idleyld Park to Winchester

Class: 2+(3)	Length: 25 miles
Flow: 1,500 cfs	Character: rolling hills
Gradient: 11 fpm, PD	Season: year-round

This run is an unheralded gem, where the terrain makes its transition from forested mountain canyon to hilly pastureland. Near sunset, the hills of scattered oak become a breathtaking masterpiece of shadow and golden color. By June, the river is comfortably warm, yet mountain clear with plenty of flow, a rare treat for Oregon boaters. What's more, this run contains a fairly continuous offering of class 2 whitewater. All of these factors combine to make this one of the premier whitewater runs of western Oregon for open canoers and a very enjoyable one for novice kayakers.

Immediately after the put-in is Salmon Hole, a class 2+ straightforward drop with some big waves. In the 5 miles from here to Colliding Rivers, there are many class 2 and 2+ pool-drop rapids with fairly straight routes through 2- to 3-foot standing waves. At Colliding Rivers, the river is constricted by several large rock formations; it makes a sharp right turn after colliding head-on with Little River. A narrow

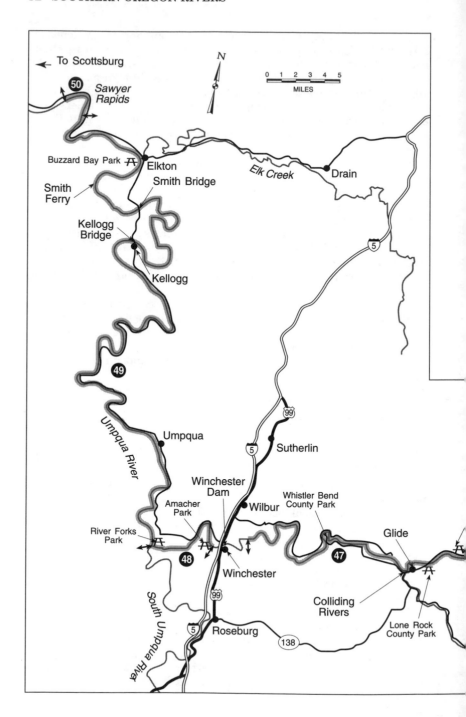

← To Scottsburg

N

0 1 2 3 4 5
MILES

50 Sawyer Rapids

Buzzard Bay Park 🏕 Elkton
Smith Bridge

Elk Creek

Drain

Smith Ferry

Kellogg Bridge

Kellogg

5

49

Umpqua River

Umpqua

99

5 Sutherlin

Winchester Dam

Whistler Bend County Park

Amacher Park

Wilbur

River Forks Park 🏕

🏕

48

Glide

47

Winchester

Colliding Rivers

Lone Rock County Park

South Umpqua River

99

5

Roseburg

138

class 4 drop makes a shortcut turn to the right. Don't be caught by it. The standard route is generally a class 3- with a rather tight right turn midway. This drop changes with the flow.

The river then starts its transition into open hills with a much wider streambed. The rapids take on more of a gravel bar nature with longer rapids (mostly class 2), but also longer flat-water stretches. The waves get smaller, but the drops get more technical, especially at summer flows under 3,000 cfs. Play spots are not as plentiful as on the first 5 miles.

About 6 miles below Colliding Rivers, the river makes a bend to the north, announcing Whistler Park Falls, a class 3- drop with several relatively turbulent routes. From here, the river makes a horseshoe bend around Whistler Bend County Park and begins the final 10 miles. About 4 miles down is Dixon Falls, a class 3- drop around the right side of an island. It starts with a slightly technical approach with poor visibility. The drop itself is a turbulent chute with side curlers, but it's a straight shot with a pool finish, so a swim is not too serious. The left channel around the island is a possible alternative, but it is very rocky and technical.

Another 2–3 miles downstream is a class 2+ straightforward drop. A curler big enough to swamp an open boat is followed by a whirlpool, which can help to flip a water-heavy boat. It can be skirted by those who don't enjoy swimming. After another 2–3 miles, the river makes a

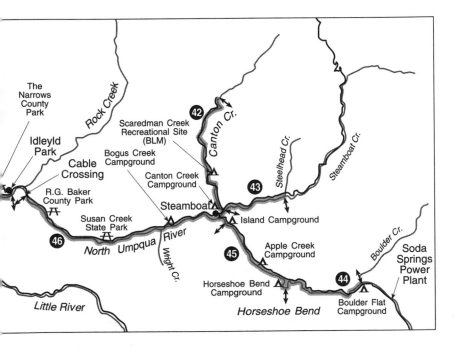

big horseshoe bend to the south, with Umpqua Community College visible high on the right bank. When the water slows to a halt due to the Winchester Dam, start looking for a small boat ramp on river left, the take-out.

Hazards. Colliding Rivers, Whistler Park Falls, and Dixon Falls are rated as class 3-.

Access. Put in just below The Narrows (class 4) at the end of the town of Idleyld Park on Oregon 138. It's a scramble down the bank. Another put-in is at a little park named Lone Rock, about 1 mile east of the town of Glide on Oregon 138. Most drift boaters put in at Colliding Rivers; just west of the Oregon 138 bridge, take the first dirt road to the north and put in over the bank. Whistler Bend County Park is a convenient access point about 7 miles west of Glide on County Road 223. Access is also available across the river from the park at Jackson Wayside on County Road 200.

The take-out is reached from Winchester, located on US 99 a few miles north of Roseburg. Take Page Road east out of Winchester along the south side of the river. There is a small boat ramp about 1 mile upstream.

Gauge. See run 44, North Umpqua River: Boulder Flat to Horseshoe Bend.

Carl Landsness

48 North Umpqua River
Winchester to River Forks Park

Class: 2   **Length: 6.5 miles**
Flow: 1,000 cfs   **Character: valley**
Gradient: 9 fpm, PD   **Season: year-round**

In this run the river makes another transition in character as it enters bottomland terrain and vegetation not unlike the Willamette River basin. There are surprisingly few houses, considering the proximity of roads. The frequency of rapids decreases, but those that exist have nice standing waves. This section is known as Roseburg's "beer and float" run. A warm summer day finds many Roseburg-area people leisurely rafting or tubing down to River Forks Park.

The first 4.5 miles to the Garden Valley Road bridge is intermittent class 1 and 2-. The mile following the bridge is locally known as "Sunburn Alley" to commemorate those who fall asleep without their suntan lotion on this notoriously slow and flat stretch.

Afternoon naps are abruptly ended by Burkhardt Rapids, a class 2+ ledge-drop that can be a nice jet ferry at higher water levels. Another class 2+ drop with moderate waves quickly follows. A little more whitewater brings you to the confluence of the North Umpqua and the South Umpqua rivers, with a nice beach on the right at River Forks Park.

Hazards. Burkhardt Rapids and several other class 2+ ledges present the only difficulties.

Access. Put in at Amacher County Park on the south side of the US 99 bridge in Winchester, beneath the I-5 high bridge.

To reach the take-out, follow Winchester Road west 5 miles. It becomes Wilbur–Garden Valley Road, and after 2 miles turn left and go 1 mile south to a sign indicating River Forks Park, the take-out.

Gauge. See run 44, North Umpqua River: Boulder Flat to Horseshoe Bend.

Carl Landsness

49 Umpqua River
River Forks Park to Scottsburg

Class: 1(2)	**Length: 84 miles**
Flow: 1,000–4,000 cfs	**Character: forested; agricultural; roaded**
Gradient: 4 fpm, PD	**Season: year-round**

From the confluence of the North and South Umpqua rivers west of Roseburg, the main Umpqua winds leisurely through the Coast Range to the Pacific Ocean near Reedsport. Numerous small farms and houses dot its banks, but many stretches show little development, and the development that one does see is fairly unobtrusive. Roads follow most of the river, but significant traffic is noticeable only on stretches below Elkton and along one short stretch near Kellogg. The predominant scenery is the forested hills of the Coast Range, enjoyable even with its considerable logging.

The Umpqua's riverbed is quite wide, capable of holding typical winter storm flows in excess of 50,000 cfs and the occasional 100,000+ flood. Yet summer flows are in the 1,000–3,000 cfs range. As one can guess from the low gradient, the Umpqua contains long stretches of slow or flat water interspersed with riffles and small rapids. As the river drops, it becomes restricted in places to narrow channels in the bedrock. Some of these develop into short class 2–2+ rapids, depending on the river level.

The Umpqua is runnable year-round by experienced boaters able to deal with the hazards of high-volume rivers. Newcomers should wait for summer with its lower flows and warm water. This combination provides a good setting for easygoing canoeists.

The numerous boat ramps along this 84-mile stretch allow boaters to choose any of numerous possible runs. Note the Bicycle Shuttler's Delight: A trip from Kellogg Bridge to Smith Bridge is about 14 river miles, mostly roadless, but the shuttle is just over 2 miles. *Warning*: the last rapids above Smith Bridge may be tricky.

Hazards. Although the rapids are few, they vary with water level and can still be tricky. Be prepared to scout. Inexperienced boaters can get into trouble if they do not stay alert.

Access. The uppermost put-in is the take-out for run 48, North Umpqua River: Winchester to River Forks Park.

There are many access points along the river (river miles differ from highway miles). The bridge on County Route 6 is near the town of Umpqua (rivermile 103); follow County Route 6 from River Forks Park or, from the Sutherlin/Oregon 138 exit—exit 136—on I-5, head west on County Road 9 to Umpqua. Bullock Bridge is on County Road 57 (rivermile 80); follow County Road 33 from the town of Umpqua, or follow Oregon 138 out of Sutherlin until it reaches the river (around milepost 13), or follow Oregon 138 south from Elkton on Oregon 38; one can cross the bridge and go upriver a couple of miles to a boat ramp, or follow Oregon 138 north about 1 mile to the Yellow Creek Boat Ramp. Kellogg Bridge is on Oregon 138 (rivermile 71), near milepost 6. Smith Bridge is on Oregon 138 (rivermile 57), near milepost 4. The bridge on Mehl Creek Road/County Route 67 is at rivermile 49; from the junction of Oregon 38 and Oregon 138 in Elkton, head south about 0.3 mile and turn right to cross the river; there is a boat ramp at Buzzard Bay Park on river left 0.3 mile below the bridge. The Oregon 38 bridge is at Scottsburg (rivermile 27).

Gauge. Located at Elkton. Call the River Forecast Center in Portland or see the *Eugene Register-Guard*. Typical summer flows are in the 3- to 4-foot range (1,100–3,000 cfs).

Dan Valens

50 Umpqua River
Sawyers Rapids

Class: 2+(3)	**Length: 2.3 miles**
Flow: 800–5,000 cfs	**Character: broad, wooded valley**
Gradient: 13 fpm	**Season: year-round**

This has long been a popular stretch when coastal streams are too low to run. Predictable flows allow instructional scheduling. After putting in, paddle immediately across the broad river to scout the class 3 chute from river left. Although revealed only during low flows, this narrow chute is turbulent, and novices often walk or swim it. The other class 3 rapids follows shortly, and is run down the middle. It does not flush at high water, but does develop a couple of play spots below on far right and left. Take out at the boat ramp on river right.

For a 3-mile flat-water warm-up prior to Sawyers Rapids, put in at Bunch Bar, milepost 30.

Hazards. The first chute at the put-in is a bit rowdy for beginners, but is easily portaged. High water means colder water and longer swims.

Access. The highway, Oregon 38, follows the river. The put-in is at the turnout at milepost 27, upstream and east of Reedsport between Scottsburg and Elkton.

Take out at Scott Creek County Park, near milepost 24.5.

Gauge. See run 49, Umpqua River: River Forks Park to Scottsburg.

Richard Dierks

ROGUE RIVER AND TRIBUTARIES

The Rogue River originates in the Cascades near Crater Lake and flows about 180 miles to the Pacific Ocean at Gold Beach. In 1968, 84 miles became part of the Wild and Scenic River System. The 35-mile section below Grave Creek is *the* world-renowned Rogue River. The lowermost section, not described in this book, is visited by hundreds of commercial jet boat passengers each week of the summer.

51 North Fork Rogue River
River Bridge Campground to North Fork Reservoir

Class: 3(4)	**Length: 5 miles**
Flow: 400–2,000 cfs	**Character: forested**
Gradient: 40 fpm	**Season: year-round**

This is a beautiful run, with massive fir trees and clear, cold whitewater. It is one of the few rivers in Oregon where you can have a combination of alpine boating and a hot summer sun, usually with enough water all summer. The rapids, though easier than the upper North Fork section, have some of the same characteristics: lots of ledgy mossed-over lava rocks and the constant potential for sweepers. Many of the rapids are fairly technical and require catching an eddy before threading the needle between the rocks. Many of the rocks are the nasty type that lurk just below the surface and grab your boat at unexpected moments. There are plenty of class 3+ drops in this short run. There are two or three class 4 drops in the second and third miles. The routes through the rapids are generally easy to see and, if not, scouting is always possible. After reaching the reservoir, continue paddling 0.3 mile to the take-out. Run in April 1990 by Margie and Hayden Glatte.

Hazards. Sweepers are a constant threat. The ledge rapids 1 mile below the put-in should be scouted. There are a couple of ledges that could form some sizable holes at flows over 1,000 cfs. Other rapids may also require scouting to check for sweepers.

Access. To get to the take-out, drive an hour north from Medford on Oregon 62 past Lost Creek Lake until you see signs for the turnoff to Prospect. About 0.5 mile beyond the first turnoff for Prospect, Oregon 62 crosses an aqueduct. The dirt road immediately on the left past the aqueduct and paralleling it is the take-out road. Turn left and drive 0.25 mile to the North Fork Reservoir, the take-out. (If you reach the Prospect Ranger Station on Oregon 62, you've gone too far.)

To reach the put-in, return to Oregon 62 and continue past the Prospect Ranger Station 3.8 miles to the sign "RIVER BRIDGE CAMPGROUND." Turn left and drive 1 mile to the river.

Gauge. The gauge is the total in-flow into Lost Creek Lake, which is predominantly made up of the North Fork and South Fork Rogue rivers. Generally this section of the North Fork is 50 percent of the inflow. It is runnable most of the year.

Hayden Glatte

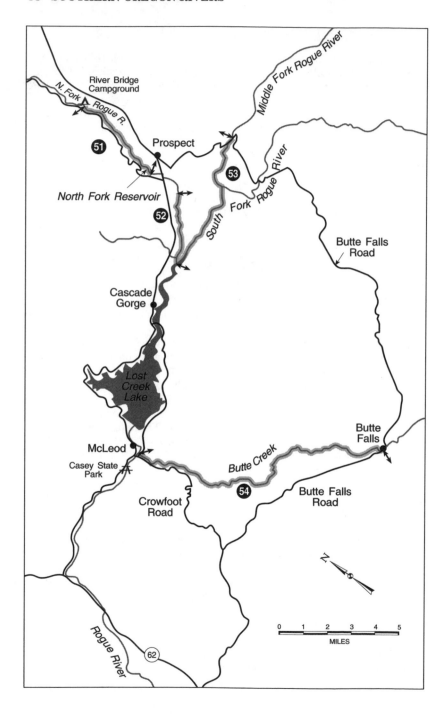

52 North Fork Rogue River
Mill Creek Falls to Lost Creek Lake

Class: 4+	Length: 3 miles
Flow: 500–1,000 cfs	Character: canyon
Gradient: 94 fpm, C–PD	Season: snowmelt

This short but beautiful stretch of river begins and ends with a 0.3-mile hike to the put-in and to the take-out. But the run is well worth the extra effort. Along the entire length are high canyon walls, waterfalls, and stands of old-growth trees. Allow a full day to do the portaging and scouting, and to enjoy the numerous play spots.

The put-in is just below the spectacular 173-foot Mill Creek Falls, which cascades into the middle of the Rogue. The run begins with a bang, with a gradient of 180 fpm. This translates into nonstop class 4+ action for the first 1.5 miles. Considerable scouting and possible portaging are necessary. The irregular basaltic rocks in the riverbed demand tight technical boating, and logjams are quite possible.

After mile 1.5, the discharge from the powerhouse on the right doubles or triples the flow. Below the powerhouse, the river becomes class 3 pool-drop in character for the second half of the trip. Once on the reservoir, paddle a few hundred yards down the North Fork arm to Skookum Creek, which enters on the right. A good trail leads uphill to Mill Creek Drive. Upper part run in May 1990 by Steve Albrathsen and Hayden Glatte.

Hazards. The first half, especially, requires scouting for routes and logs.

Access. To get to the take-out, drive north from Medford on Oregon 62. Go past Lost Creek Lake to Cascade Gorge, which is a store on the right where Mill Creek Drive begins. Go up Mill Creek Drive 1.7 miles, where you'll see a narrow turnout on the right with a sign that says "CAMPING PROHIBITED." An old-road-turned-trail leads to the North Fork arm of the lake.

To get to the put-in, continue up Mill Creek Drive 3.7 miles to Mill Creek Falls Viewpoint parking lot. Walk down the trail 0.3 mile to the actual viewpoint of Mill Creek Falls (a large map at the parking lot shows the trails). Near the viewpoint, a steep trail leads to the river.

Gauge. Call the Army Corps of Engineers (1-800-472-2434) for the flow into Lost Creek Lake. This flow includes the North Fork and South Fork Rogue rivers. Generally, the North Fork below the powerhouse is 70 percent of the total flow, whereas the North Fork at Mill Creek Falls is 20 percent of the total. It is usually runnable when the total is 2,500–5,000 cfs.

Hayden Glatte

53 Middle Fork Rogue River
Butte Falls Road to Lost Creek Lake

Class: 5
Flow: 400–800 cfs
Gradient: 88 fpm, PD

Length: 6 miles
Character: forested; gorge
Season: rainy/snowmelt

This is a steep run with the most difficult rapids in the first 2.5 miles on the Middle Fork and in the narrow gorge where the Middle Fork flows into the South Fork. Some of the gradient is 160 fpm. Brush, logs, and tight maneuvering provide ample opportunity for bridges, pins, and broaches, of which there have been plenty. Scouting and reasonable thinking carry the day.

After 2 miles of technical class 4 and 5 boating with some portages, the gorge appears; there is no mistaking it. The entire gorge should be scouted from the right before entering it. There are three serious rapids in it, one class 5. If any of these rapids are jammed with logs, the only options are to hike 0.5 mile around the gorge or to hike up and out to the road on the right slope. The upper half of the rapids leading to the gorge can be portaged on the right, while the lower half is run down into the gorge. The second rapids, class 5, is a longer one, beginning on the Middle Fork, colliding into the South Fork, and continuing another 50 yards. The third rapids is a short class 4. None of these is portageable due to the vertical gorge walls. Scout carefully before entering the gorge. It is no place for the faint of heart or the claustrophobic! Once out of the 0.5-mile-long gorge, the South Fork is class 3 to the lake.

On completing the run, paddle 0.25 mile out the South Fork arm of the lake and up the North Fork arm a couple hundred yards to where Skookum Creek enters on your left. A trail leads 0.3 mile up to Mill Creek Drive. Run a little later than March 1989 by Andy Cora, Hayden Glatte, and Bryan Tooley.

Hazards. This is an expert run. There are class 4 and 5 rapids leading up to the gorge and a class 5 in the gorge that cannot be portaged. The entire run requires scouting, including the 0.5-mile-long gorge before entering it. Attempting this run at flows under 400 cfs at the put-in is not recommended because many of the drops become unrunnable. A combination of rain and snowmelt is needed to provide enough water.

Access. To get to the take-out, drive north from Medford on Oregon 62. Go past Lost Creek Lake to Cascade Gorge, which is a store on the right where Mill Creek Drive begins. Go up Mill Creek Drive 1.7 miles, where you'll see a narrow turnout on the right with a sign that says "CAMPING PROHIBITED." An old-road-turned-trail leads to the North Fork arm of the lake.

To reach the put-in, continue up Mill Creek Drive to the town of Prospect and turn right at Prospect Hotel onto Butte Falls Road. Go 3.7 miles to where the road parallels the Middle Fork; this is your put-in.

Gauge. Call the Army Corps of Engineers for the total flow into Lost Creek Lake, which is predominantly made up of the North Fork and South Fork Rogue rivers. Generally, the South Fork carries 30 percent of the total flow and the Middle Fork about half of the flow of the South Fork, or about 15 percent of the total in-flow. Usually the Middle Fork is runnable when the gauge gives an in-flow of 3,000–4,500 cfs.

Hayden Glatte

54 Big Butte Creek
Butte Falls Picnic Area to Crowfoot Road

Class: 3+(4)   **Length: 12 miles**
Flow: 400–900 cfs   **Character: wooded**
Gradient: 66 fpm   **Season: rainy**

Beginning among firs and ending among oaks, this run cuts through some wonderful country. It is creek-type boating with the usual hazards of small riverbeds and heavy vegetation. Expect several portages around logjams. The upper stretch is fast, continuous class 2 and 3 water with a gradient of 120 fpm. There are some swift blind corners where very small eddies need to be caught. Butte Falls, a 15-foot runnable waterfall is located about 1 mile into the run. If waterfalls are not for you, the portage is on the right. Progressing downstream, the character becomes more pool-drop, mostly in the class 3–3+ range with an occasional class 4. All can be scouted or portaged at river level. Around mile 8 the gradient again becomes 120 fpm. Run in April 1990 by Steve Albrathsen and Hayden Glatte.

Hazards. Brush, logs, and the 15-foot runnable Butte Falls are the difficulties on this run.

Access. From Medford drive northeastward on Oregon 62 for 28 miles. Just past Casey State Park, turn right onto Crowfoot Road and go to any of the obvious take-out spots. The preferred take-out is 2.5 miles up Crowfoot Road to Netherlands Road, which crosses Big Butte Creek.

To get to the put-in, continue up Crowfoot Road to Butte Falls Road. Turn left and go just past the town of Butte Falls to Butte Falls–Prospect Road. After crossing Butte Creek, enter the picnic area, the put-in.

Gauge. None exists. The flow into Lost Creek Lake should be about 2,500–3,500 cfs. When judging the flow at the put-in, realize that about 100 cfs for irrigation is removed below Butte Falls.

Hayden Glatte

55 Grave Creek
6 Miles to Confluence with Rogue River

Class: 3   **Length: 6 miles**
Flow: 500–1,000 cfs   **Character: forested**
Gradient: 42 fpm, PD   **Season: rainy**

This is a small technical stream with short, twisting blind drops in the section not visible from the road. There are very few play spots, just nice scenery. The run continues down to the confluence with the Rogue River, and can even include Grave Creek Rapids.

Hazards. Possible hazards include low swinging footbridges and brush along the bank.

Access. The take-out is at the boat ramp beneath the Grave Creek Bridge across the Rogue River (see run 57, Rogue River: Grave Creek to Foster Bar).

To reach the put-in, take the road toward Wolf Creek from the northeast end of the bridge. Follow this for 4–6 miles to a point where it returns to Grave Creek after winding up the hill.

Gauge. None exists. Flow is flashy and depends on rainfall. The author made the run when the Rogue was running 4,000 cfs at Marial; however, it is unlikely that there is a dependable correlation between the Rogue and Grave Creek.

Karen Wilt

56 Rogue River
Above Nugget Falls to Gold Hill Boat Ramp

Class: 4- **Length: 2 miles**
Flow: 800–3,000 cfs **Character: forested; residential**
Gradient: 20 fpm, PD **Season: year-round**

This short run on the Rogue is gaining popularity because it provides enough good play spots and challenging rapids for an afternoon of boating. The put-in is in a short flat stretch, from which it is possible to paddle upstream to a rapids with some small play waves for warm-up. The first play spot downstream is at a broken weir, which has a hole in the right center. There is an excellent ender hole on the downstream edge of the broken weir, but use caution at lower flows, since some boats have been folded here.

Nugget Falls immediately follows. This is a class 3+ or 4 drop, which can be run down the middle of the left channel. It's a good idea to scout the falls on the first time down. Pull off on the left bank under the trees and take the trail to the rock bar. This is an easy scout, and the trail can also be used to rerun. There is a big surfing wave below the drop.

Nugget is followed by a fairly long flat stretch that ends at the dam above Powerhouse Rapids (class 4). There are two slots through the dam, both of which are right of center near the downstream bend in the dam. The best route from here follows the base of the dam downstream, weaves through some grassy clumps, and follows the channel through the main class 4 drop that is nearest the island on the left. For those wishing to avoid the maneuvers described above, there is a route on the far right side of the river where the dam joins the bank. This slot leads to a class 2+ route around the main drop.

Hazards. Nugget Falls and Powerhouse Rapids present some difficulties. Powerhouse can't be scouted from the river, so must be scouted from Upper River Road on the east side of the river. Upper River Road turns off of Oregon 234 east out of Gold Hill just after the road crosses the river. Go upriver about 1 mile to a pullout on the left. The last drop can be seen from here, but the entrance is hidden by some trees. It may be a good idea to run Powerhouse with someone who has been through before, since the entrance is tricky.

Access. Gold Hill is near I-5 between Medford and Grants Pass. Take Oregon 234 out of Gold Hill toward Sams Valley and Crater Lake. It's less than 1 mile to the take-out, a boat landing on the right.

A little more than 1 mile farther (in a long straight stretch), a gravel road turns off the main road and goes back to the river and the put-in. To make a longer trip, a class 2+ section can be added by driving a few miles farther up Upper River Road where there are a number of spots to put in along the road.

Gauge. Contact the Grants Pass Filtration Plant or the *Grants Pass Daily Courier*.

Garvin Hamilton

57 Rogue River
Grave Creek to Foster Bar

Class: 3+	**Length: 35 miles**
Flow: 1,200–6,000 cfs	**Character: protected; popular**
Gradient: 13 fpm, PD	**Season: year-round**

This run on the Rogue is one of the best-known whitewater runs in the United States. Flowing through the Siskiyou Mountains northwest of Grants Pass, it is classified Wild and Scenic, with the river preserved essentially in its natural condition. The banks vary from steep forested slopes to vertical rock walls. The river provides class 3 rapids connected by slower stretches and deep pools.

Recreational use of the Wild and Scenic section has a long and diverse tradition. Private lodges and cabins are located in several places, and many of these are reached only by boat or trail. Jet boats from Gold Beach originally delivered the U.S. mail, but later took passengers on popular excursions; these boats can be seen cruising at water-skiing speed along the lower 12 miles of the Wild and Scenic section. Drift boaters have long floated the river for the fine steelhead fishing. Zane Grey's writings were inspired by the solitude and wild setting of his cabin at Winkle Bar.

The scenery, rapids, easy access, and possibility of 2- to 5-day float trips make this a very popular run. Permits are required. They are selected by a lottery. Leftover or unclaimed launching dates sometimes become available. Permit information may be obtained from Siskiyou National Forest, River Permits (14335 Galice Road, Merlin, OR 97532; 541-479-3735).

The Wild and Scenic section is a forgiving and enjoyable stretch of water. Dam-controlled flows normally are above 2,000 cfs, and the river is runnable throughout the year. Warm summer weather, warm water, rapids ending in pools, and sandy beaches for camping make this a great place for a laid-back trip. One should expect to see lots of other people during the summer season, although the author's first trip was a cold and snowy one in February, when he saw no one else.

The Rogue River Map, available from the Forest Service, contains a handy blow-by-blow description, which to this writer seems unnecessarily replete with dire warnings. Follow it for the first few rapids and make up your own mind. Other accounts are given in *Wildwater Touring* by Scott and Margaret Arighi, *Handbook to the Rogue River Canyon* by Quinn et al., and *West Coast River Touring* by Dick Schwind (see Bibliography).

The campground at Almeda Bar is a popular put-in. The permit check-point, another common put-in, is 4 miles downstream at Grave Creek.

Rainie Falls, 2 miles below the Grave Creek put-in, is the first of the two major rapids on the Rogue. It is mandatory to scout or portage Rainie Falls. In the next 20 miles tributary streams, such as Russian, Howard, Big Windy, and Kelsey creeks, provide pools for swimming, nice camps, and places to scramble up the streambeds. There are numerous play spots for kayaks, including an ender hole at Black Bar Rapids. Take care not to hurry.

At Marial the river takes a sharp bend to the southwest and enters Mule Creek Canyon. The narrow canyon, with vertical walls, is one of the few continuous stretches of whitewater (about 0.5 mile). Blossom Bar, about 1 mile below Mule Creek Canyon, is the Rogue's second major rapids. Many rafts have been hung up or destroyed on the boulders in Blossom Bar. Tate Creek, about 7 miles below Blossom Bar, is a stop that should not be missed. About 0.2 mile up the creek is a pool with an exciting rock slide. Hiking above the slide is very beautiful.

Try not to be annoyed by the jet boats on the lower part of the river. This section also has lots of wildlife; it is common to see great blue heron, salmon, deer, otter, and bear.

Hazards. At Rainie Falls, a short portage trail is located on the left bank, and offers the best place to get a close-up view of the falls, which is always fun to look at. The falls has occasionally been run, but seldom right-side-up. Most people run the small fish-ladder channel on the far right bank, while the more adventurous run the steeper channel through the middle of the rock "island" between the fish ladder and the falls. Any run other than the fish ladder should be scouted.

In Mule Creek Canyon, the major problem is turbulence caused by constriction rather than large waves or holes. Everything seems to wash out of here eventually, but several places have been known to hold boats, spin them around, or push them into the walls. Swimmers are difficult to pick up until they get out of the narrow part of the canyon, but even they should look around to appreciate the scenery.

At Blossom Bar, stop on the right and clamber up the rocks to scout.

Gridlock at Mule Creek, Rogue River (photo by Phil DeRiemer)

The run starts on the left side in a channel that ends in a bunch of boulders, so the next move is to the right into a center channel. At low water this ends in boulders, so scout carefully and move fast. Dodge a few more rocks and that's it!

Access. The put-in at Grave Creek is reached by taking the Merlin exit off I-5, just north of Grants Pass, and proceeding westward through Merlin and toward Galice. A popular put-in is 3 miles below Galice at Almeda Bar. The Grave Creek put-in is another 3 miles downstream at the bridge.

The shuttle to the take-out goes back along this same road just past the town of Galice, then over the mountains and west toward Agness on USFS 23. After joining USFS 33 at the Rogue River, follow it downstream 1 mile, cross the river, and go upstream to Foster Bar. USFS 23 may be closed by snow early in the season, so check with the Forest Service or inquire locally. If the road is impassable, drive to Grants Pass, take US 199 south to Crescent City, then US 101 north to Gold Beach, and proceed upstream toward Agness. Shuttle services can usually be arranged at the Galice Resort.

Gauge. Located at Agness. Contact the River Forecast Center in Portland. The Galice Ranger District provides the Grants Pass reading.

Bo Shelby

58 Illinois River
Oak Flat to Oak Flat

Class: 4+(5)   **Length: 31 miles**
Flow: 500–3,500 cfs   **Character: forested; remote**
Gradient: 24 fpm, PD   **Season: rainy**

The Illinois, a crystal-clear tributary of the Rogue River, is one of the premier whitewater runs on the West Coast. In 1984 it received protection under the National Wild and Scenic Rivers Act. Flowing out of the Siskiyou Mountains south of Cave Junction, the Illinois runs in a northwesterly direction through the north end of the Kalmiopsis Wilderness Area. The canyons and mountains here are as steep and rugged as any found in Oregon. The area is largely devoid of topsoil, but Kalmiopsis, a plant in the heather family, grows here. Natural landslides and erosion are evident along the river. Look at the landscape and enjoy it, but treat it kindly. For a detailed description of the river, see *Handbook to the Illinois River Canyon* by Quinn et al. (see Bibliography).

The Illinois is truly a wilderness river that tests both the skill and strength of boaters. Once a trip on this river is undertaken, boaters are on their own. The only trail is miles from the river, and very difficult to reach except at Pine Flat. The whitewater is tough, even for the best boaters. Help is hard to get. Check the weather forecast, because a heavy rain can transform an 1,800-cfs trip into an 8,000-cfs nightmare.

The river is technical at levels below 800 cfs. Flows of 1,000–1,500 cfs seem to be the easiest, when most of the technical drops are flushed over enough to make them easier to run. Flows over 3,000 cfs turn the river into boiling holes and rapids.

The first 10–12 miles are typified by pools with very steep class 4 boulder-bar drops of up to 10 feet, or long rock gardens. Between miles 4 and 5 are three class 4 rapids, the third one, York Creek Rapids, being the biggest. Rivermile 7 brings the boater to an area called Pine Flat where the canyon opens into large meadows on both sides of the river. About midway through Pine Flat the river swings to the left, offering what appears to be two channels around a large rock in the middle of the river. On the left side is a class 2 route that can be run except at low water. On the right side is a chute with a raft-stopping hole at the bottom. Scout this one carefully from the right. The hole is tougher than it looks. Rafts and kayaks have been flipped end-for-end in it. Pine Flat makes an excellent campsite for the first night of a 3- to 4-day trip. Backpackers are sometimes seen because this is one of the few places where they have access to the river.

From Pine Flat down to South Bend the river continues in pool-drop fashion through beautiful deep green pools and many nice class 2+–3

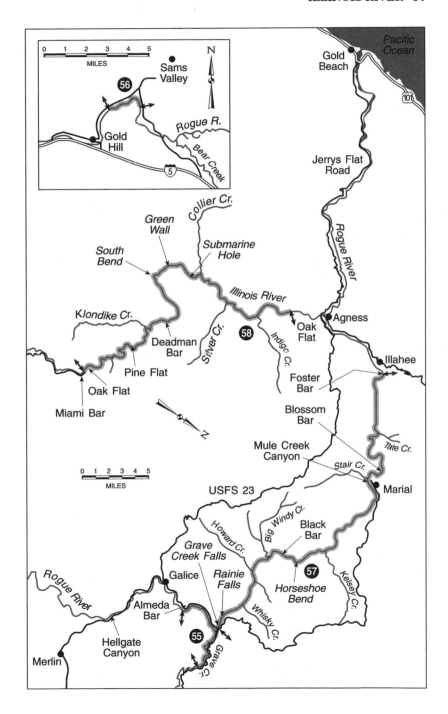

drops. Klondike Creek, named for the mining done along its banks, enters from the left about 2 miles below the last meadow of Pine Flat. Deadman Bar is a long straight bench on the right about 2 miles farther downstream. It is difficult to spot from the river because it is up a 35-foot rock bank. Several groups can share the grassy area without intruding on each other. Beware of poison oak when scrambling up the rocks, especially in the spring when it's not in leaf.

South Bend, at mile 17, should be called Last Chance, because it is the last chance to camp before Green Wall. South Bend Bar is located on the inside of a tight right turn in the river. A large creek cascades down the left bank; a large pink boulder on the right marks the spot. Sometimes this campsite gets washed away. The next 4 miles are the toughest of the trip. Immediately below South Bend is a good class 3+ drop, followed in 0.5 mile by Prelude, the class 4 rapids before Green Wall. Prelude doesn't look like much on the approach, but a sweeping rock garden leads to a solid 3+ drop that can't be seen from above. An eddy on the left next to a boulder at the bottom of the rock garden provides a good spot to scout the remaining portion of Prelude. There are two alternatives: one is the falls on the left, the other is the tricky "S"-turn on the right.

A short distance below Prelude is Green Wall, class 5. An innocent-looking rock garden leads into the main drop. Land left, well above the class 3+ lead-in rapids, or, if confident, catch the eddy on the left at the end of the lead-in rapids. A portage here is a tough 400 yards through a maze of truck-size boulders. Scout the class 3+ lead-in as carefully as the main rapids. Below the lead-in is a short section of relatively calm water followed by a drop of 7–8 feet. Take the middle or left channel; the right side is a keeper for all but the largest of rafts. Below here are more rapids with water rushing into the Green Wall itself on the right and a big hole in the middle. Stay off the right wall.

From Green Wall to Collier Creek the river has three class 4–4+ drops and six class 3–3+ drops that are quite technical and challenging. Don't hesitate to scout if in doubt. Submarine Hole, class 4+, 3 miles below Green Wall, can cause problems, especially for rafters. It is readily identified by the huge boulder in the middle of the bottom of the rapids. The right slots should be avoided. The canyon is steep and rocky through this 3-mile section, and there are no campsites.

The end of the major rapids is signaled by Collier Creek on the left at mile 21.7. About 100–200 yards below Collier Creek a campsite may be found up the left bank. Other campsites are located 2–3 miles downstream and less than an hour from the take-out. Most notable is a site high above the river on the right at Silver Creek. Land on the downstream side of the creek, climb 30 feet to the trail, and follow it upstream, across the bridge, and up to the top of the bluff.

From here to the take-out, the river flows placidly through country that is a feast for your eyes. Sit back and enjoy it. You're one of the lucky ones who have run the Illinois.

Just tuck the oars away on the Middle Chute at Rainie Falls, Rogue River (photo by Phil DeRiemer)

Hazards. Expect eight class 4–4+ rapids. Some of the named rapids are York Creek, Pine Flat, Prelude, and Submarine Hole. Green Wall, class 5, is considerably more difficult and longer. The 3-mile section below Green Wall has the greatest concentration of difficult rapids.

Access. To reach the put-in at Oak Flat, drive west on US 199 from Grants Pass to Selma. In the middle of town, turn west on Illinois River Road. This becomes NFD 4103. Drive 17 miles to Oak Flat at a broad gravel bar.

To reach the take-out, return to US 199 and continue to the coast, then go north on US 101 to Gold Beach. Drive up Jerrys Flat Road along the south bank of the Rogue River approximately 34 miles. After crossing the Illinois River, turn right onto Oak Flat Road, NFD 450, and continue 4 miles to a broad grassy area called Oak Flat, the take-out.

An alternate take-out is located 4 miles downstream from Oak Flat, past the confluence of the Illinois with the Rogue, at a public boat landing on the right just downstream from Agness. Shuttle service can usually be hired at the Galice Resort in Galice.

Gauge. Located at Kerby. Contact the River Forecast Center in Portland.

Ron Mattson

UPPER WILLAMETTE AND McKENZIE DRAINAGES

UPPER WILLAMETTE RIVER AND TRIBUTARIES

The Willamette River runs northward like a giant artery through the heart of western Oregon. It drains an immense valley in which more than half of all Oregonians live. In the latter 1800s and early 1900s riverboats plied the river, carrying goods and people. Thus the cities of Eugene, Corvallis, Albany, Salem, and Portland flourished. Perhaps because it is so much a part of Oregon life, this river enjoys a special place among Oregon rivers. Today, much of the river is protected by a Greenway Program that seeks to preserve the river corridor for public enjoyment. Numerous parks provide recreation and river access for boating. A multitude of tributaries arising from the foothills of the Cascade Mountains and the Coast Range provide numerous technical whitewater boating opportunities.

Even though the Willamette River traverses the heartlands and major population areas of Oregon, boaters see surprisingly little of the impact of civilization, especially on the upper and middle sections. The sharp-eyed drifter can observe a variety of plants and wildlife. Edible foods include red huckleberries, wild strawberries, blackberries, cherries, and apples. Do not pick produce from a farmer's field! Fish include trout, steelhead, salmon, sturgeon, sucker, carp, bass, and bluegill. Other wild animals and many species of birds, especially great blue heron, may be seen.

During the summer months, some sections of the river can be like a carnival, with a frenzy of inner tubers and paddlers. In contrast, during the winter the river is a place of solitude. It is perhaps the contrasts of the Willamette that are most striking. From the clear, wild, and free North Fork to the stately regulated Main Fork, the Willamette holds paddling opportunities for boaters of all skill levels and interests. For the curious, there are relics of abandoned bridges, dams, and old canals. This is a river to be explored!

The river may appear slow and calm, but many unsuspecting canoeists, both novice and expert, have misjudged the capacity for danger. Cable lines from a dredge can suddenly rise out of the river without warning. A lazily drifting canoe can hit a submerged log, and swamp.

High winds can blow upriver on a sunny afternoon and push boaters upstream. An inviting side channel can become blocked with debris after 1 mile or more. Water flowing fast through trees when the river is near flood stage can capsize a boat and leave boaters stranded in trees far from shore. Willamette Falls, an unrunnable 30-foot drop at Oregon City, looms after miles of flat water.

The upper two runs, beginning at Jasper Park and passing through Eugene, contain whitewater and are described in this guide. The mid- and lower Willamette are well suited for extended camping trips of several days. Beginners should take a few day trips on the river before attempting overnight trips. Some islands and camping spots have people, dogs, sheep, and cattle living nearby. Private property should be respected. For detailed information about the river below Harrisburg, consult the "Willamette River Recreation Guide" published by Oregon State Parks and Recreation. It is available from State Highway Division offices in towns along the river. Information concerning the Greenway Program can be obtained from the Oregon State Parks and Recreation Department in Salem.

Regulations on the Willamette require personal flotation devices for all passengers. Boats on the Willamette River are subject to laws and regulations enforced by the U.S. Coast Guard, Oregon State Police, and county sheriffs.

Ellen Oliver

59 Brice Creek
Upper Reaches to Champion Creek

Class: 4+; 5   **Length: 2.4 miles**
Flow: 300–700 cfs   **Character: forested**
Gradient: 215 fpm, C   **Season: rainy**

Brice Creek, a tributary of the Row River, drains a relatively uncut section of the Umpqua National Forest. Its clear water, beautiful scenery, and great rapids make it a creek worth paddling. Upper Brice Creek is a nearly continuous series of class 4 rapids, with long boulder gardens, big holes, and steep drops. Road scouting is the best way to see what this section offers, but beware: it is harder than it looks.

The first major rapids is a 12- to 15-foot drop followed by a tough gorge (be sure to check for logs). Bubble Trouble, an 8-foot ledge at milepost 10, should be scouted because it develops a nasty hydraulic at high flows. Several hundred yards below this ledge is a rapids that is usually portaged due to a pin spot and an undercut boulder. A group of three rapids starting 0.6 mile above Champion Creek bridge should be noted. Orthodontists' Nightmare is a steep and short boulder drop with tight twisty moves. A hundred yards downstream is another twisty drop with a false channel. Several hundred yards below this is Hop, Skip, Splat, which has pin spots and a terminal hole. It is normally portaged, but has been run on the left.

Orthodontists' Nightmare, Upper Brice Creek (photo by Jim Reed)

The run can be combined nicely with Lower Brice Creek.

Hazards. The run is very demanding. There are many locations where a boat could become pinned against a rock.

Access. The take-out is reached by taking exit 174 from I-5 near Cottage Grove and following Row River Road eastward to Disston. At Disston, take Brice Creek Road about 8 miles to Champion Creek Road and a bridge, the take-out.

The put-in is 2.4 miles upstream at the first bridge, or another mile at a trail where sight of the river is first lost.

Gauge. None exists. A flow of 2,500 cfs on the Row River gauge is adequate (see run 62, Row River: Wildwood Falls to Dorena Lake).

Eric Brown

60 Brice Creek
Champion Creek to Cedar Creek Camp

Class: 4(5)	**Length: 5.2 miles**
Flow: 300–1,000 cfs	**Character: forested**
Gradient: 60 fpm, PD	**Season: rainy**

This run is characterized by a narrow streambed with class 3 and 4 pool-drop rapids spiced up by several larger drops, all of which are easy to portage. Scout carefully.

The first mile is the most difficult. Several small ledges are followed by three big drops. The first is Trestle Rapids. Scout left. The best line is to skid-jump off the end of the "L"-shaped ledge on river left, although runs down the center have been made. Just downstream is Arthur's Ledge; scout or portage left. At low water, the right route is advised, but at high flow a nasty hydraulic develops. Downstream 50 yards is Pogo, a tricky drop that has been run by dropping through a slot just left of the bedrock island. Scout from this island. One-half mile downstream is Cheese Grater; scout from the left. Runs down the center have been made, but take care.

From here, fun class 3 and 4 rapids break up occasional class 2 rapids. Around mile 3 logs have been a problem. At mile 3.2 a large class 3+ rapids, named Fun (Gumdrop), splits around a house-size boulder; go left with enough speed to punch a sticky hole. The right is clogged with debris. Just downstream, on a sharp left-hand bend, is Not Fun, which should be checked for logs. Near the end of the run, at mile 5.2, a class 3+ rapids leads into Laura's Thighs, a 12-foot folding class 5 drop. Scout or portage on the right where a creek enters on the right. Just downstream from where this creek enters is Cedar Creek Campground, the take-out. One can extend this run 2 miles with class 2 and 3 rapids by continuing to the road bridge.

Hazards. Large drops occur over step ledges with dangerous holes at the bottom or rocks that can likely pin a boat.

Access. The take-out is reached by taking exit 174 from I-5 near Cottage Grove and following Row River Road eastward to Disston. At Disston, take Brice Creek Road 2.8 miles to Cedar Creek Campground, the take-out.

For the put-in, follow Brice Creek Road another 5.6 miles to Champion Creek Road. Put in just west of the bridge.

Gauge. None exists. The flow on the Row River should be 1,500 cfs minimum; 2,400 cfs is optimum. (See run 62, Row River: Wildwood Falls to Dorena Lake.)

Eric Brown

61 Layng Creek
Rujada Campground to above Wildwood Falls

Class: 3(4); 4(5) **Length: 5 miles**
Flow: 1,500 cfs; 5,000 cfs **Character: forested**
Gradient: 42 fpm, PD **Season: rainy**

This very exciting run is on a tributary of the Row River. It is normally class 3–4, but becomes a challenging class 4–5 run at flood stage. The entire run can be scouted from the road while running the shuttle. When nearby Brice Creek is too high or too low, Layng Creek can be a fun alternative. As usual, at higher flows the river is unforgiving to the unprepared. Just below the put-in is Rujada Falls, a 5-foot drop. Run left. About 0.5 mile downstream is The Plunger. At high water, it can be quite dangerous and should be scouted from the road. Below the confluence with Brice Creek is some of the most enjoyable whitewater of the trip. At high water, it is a fast, continuous flush, complete with large waves. Be sure to recognize the take-out just above Wildwood Falls. The falls have been run at high water.

Hazards. The Plunger and log strainers are hazards that should be checked from the road.

Access. Take exit 174 from I-5 at Cottage Grove and drive east on Row River Road, past Dorena Lake. Two miles beyond the town of Culp Creek, turn left onto Lower Brice Creek Road at the signs to Wildwood Falls. Follow this road for 0.5 mile to the fabulous 16-foot falls. The take-out is above the falls in Wildwood Park on river right.

To get to the put-in, continue upstream to the intersection with USFS 17. Turn left and go another 1.5 miles to Rujada Campground, the put-in.

Gauge. None exists. The inflow to Dorena Lake (503-937-3852) serves as an indicator. Optimum flow is 2,000–4,000 cfs.

Jason Bates

62 Row River
Wildwood Falls to Dorena Lake

Class: 3(4); 3+(4)	**Length: 5 miles**
Flow: 800 cfs; 4000 cfs	**Character: rural**
Gradient: 33 fpm	**Season: rainy**

This nice short run drops through little gorges, passes huge boulders, and skirts several houses. The class 4 drop is a falls near the end of the run just above a covered bridge. It is easily portaged on the left, but has been run by experts on the far right.

Hazards. The class 4 falls near the end presents the only difficulty.

Access. From I-5 take exit 174 at Cottage Grove. Turn toward Dorena Lake. Follow Row River Road 4.5 miles to the junction with Government Road, then turn right and pass Dorena Lake. After crossing the bridge over the Row River, turn left (on Row River Road again) and take the first left, which leads to the lake and the take-out.

To reach the put-in, return to Row River Road and head east toward Culp Creek and Disston. After 4.5 miles, at the junction with Lower Brice Creek Road, bear right and cross bridge over the Row River. Go 0.5 mile and turn left into Wildwood Park. The put-in is at the base of Wildwood Falls, river left.

Gauge. Located 1 mile above Dorena Lake (541-942-2491); call for flow.

Jason Bates

63 Row River
Dorena Dam to Scaling Station Bridge

Class: 3	**Length: 5 miles**
Flow: 300–1,000 cfs	**Character: rural**
Gradient: 35 fpm, PD	**Season: dam-controlled, rainy**

This run includes four major drops (4–6 feet each) and several minor drops, all of which make this a quick, exciting run. The first quarter of the run winds through some narrow channels where riverside brush can be a hazard. A point of information: Row rhymes with cow.

About 0.5 mile below the first bridge is a major drop. Watch for rocks in the middle of the river. Scouting this rapids is advisable, since considerable maneuvering is required to negotiate this drop, which is 50–75 feet long. At high levels (greater than 700 cfs) a right channel can be used. About 100 yards below the first drop is a second major drop and it also should be scouted. It is usually run on the left, although at high water an exciting channel exists on the right. Within the next mile is a third drop, again heralded by the presence of rocks in the middle of the river. This one is not of the same proportions as the first two but requires careful maneuvering. Start on the right and guide through the slot on the left, coming off the 3-foot drop at the bottom.

The last major drop is 0.8 mile downstream, right next to the road (to the delight of the passersby). Scout this rapids on the way up, and plan to hit the narrow slot. The remainder of the trip is less exciting, but is still fun because of the many ledges that traverse the width of the river and the sneaky rocks that inhabit the streambed.

Hazards. The first two class 3 rapids, at the 0.5-mile mark, should be scouted. The third major drop, 1 mile farther, and the fourth major drop 0.8 mile after that should be scouted on the first trip down the river.

Access. From I-5 take exit 174, the northernmost Cottage Grove exit. At the stop sign, turn toward Dorena Lake on Row River Road. Pass the Village Green Motel and continue on Row River Road about 1 mile to the first bridge just past the log scaling station, the take-out.

The put-in is just below Dorena Dam. Continue on Row River Road for 3 miles to a "Y" in the road. Take the right branch and travel another mile to the USFS Dorena Tree Improvement Center. Turn left and follow the road to the river. This is the upper section of Schmidt Park, a nice place to picnic before the river run. The gate to the park may be locked in the winter, necessitating a 0.2-mile carry.

Gauge. Located near the middle of this run. Because of variable releases, the flow can change by a factor of two within hours. Call recording at 541-937-3852 for flow. A flow of 300 cfs is probably the minimum flow that should be attempted. Summer flows can be as low as 100 cfs. Late fall, winter, or early spring are the most likely times to enjoy this run.

Larry Mooney

64 Coast Fork Willamette River
Cottage Grove to Creswell

Class: 1+	**Length:** 10.5 miles
Flow: 1,000 cfs	**Character:** rural
Gradient: 13 fpm	**Season:** rainy

The run starts on the Row River just east of Cottage Grove and ends on the Coast Fork Willamette River. The Row River section contains numerous enjoyable riffles and bends. The Row joins the Coast Fork Willamette at rivermile 2.5. One mile farther downstream is a rapids identified by the Bohemia Lumber Mill on the left. Run the rapids on the far right, being careful of the overhanging branches. The next mile has several good riffles before coming to an old rock wall ledge that should be portaged because of the nasty reversal at its base. Next comes the I-5 Rapids, which should be run on the left at most water levels. Continue to the bridge, the take-out.

Hazards. The rock wall ledge about 4 miles down from the put-in should be portaged.

Access. The take-out is reached by taking the Creswell exit, exit 182, from I-5 south of Eugene. Head east on Cloverdale Road for 1.2 miles. The take-out is the unpaved area by the bridge over the Coast Fork Willamette River.

The put-in is reached by returning to I-5 and exiting at Cottage Grove, exit 174. Head east for 1.5 miles on Row River Road. Put in at the small picnic area on the banks of the Row River behind the Masonic Lodge.

Gauge. None exists.

Herb Kielak and Mike Stevens

65 Salt Creek
Blue Pool Campground to Rigdon Road Bridge

Class: 3(4); 4(4+)   Length: 7.2 miles
Flow: 500 cfs; 1,200 cfs   Character: forested
Gradient: 99 fpm   Season: rainy/snowmelt

Salt Creek is a small tributary that enters the Middle Fork Willamette River just east of Oakridge. It is fed mainly by snowmelt after warm spells in the spring, but large winter rainstorms occasionally bring the creek to a runnable flow. Because of the randomness of the flow, bringing both skis and boats is a good idea. The continuous nature helps ease what many might call a steep gradient. Though play spots are few, the constant class 3 action creates an enjoyable cruising stream.

At mile 0.2, Luggage Inspector Rapids starts a series of class 3+ and 4 rapids. First-timers may want to scout on the right. At mile 0.3, Unclaimed Baggage Hole warrants a scout or portage on the right. At high flows the riverwide hydraulic gets gruesome, and a portage is recommended. For the next 1.3 miles, the river is an enjoyable 3+ roller coaster at high water, and technical class 3 at lower flows. Remember to scout whenever the river drops out of sight. Beyond mile 1.6 the river maintains a steady class 2–3 personality, but blind turns and logs should keep the attention of the boater.

Hazards. Logs are a constant problem, especially in the first and last miles. Be especially aware of a potentially dangerous logjam immediately below the put-in.

Access. To reach the take-out, take Oregon 58 east from I-5 just south of Eugene. Continue on Oregon 58 through Oakridge. Approximately 1 mile beyond Oakridge, turn right on Rigdon Road. Look for signs to Hills Creek Dam after 0.2 mile. Rigdon Road crosses Salt Creek at the take-out.

For the put-in, drive back to Oregon 58 and turn right. Proceed 5.4 miles to Blue Pool Campground. The campground is usually closed, so a short hike of 100 yards through the picnic area is usually necessary.

Gauge. None exists. Large winter storms do not always raise the flow. Spring runoff is more dependable.

Eric Brown

66 North Fork of Middle Fork Willamette River
Upper Section to the Gorge

Class: 4+(5) T; 5 T	**Length: 4 miles**
Flow: 300 cfs; 800 cfs	**Character: old growth; canyon**
Gradient: 150 fpm	**Season: rainy**

This very steep, very tight, very technical run is preserved as Wild and Scenic. After 0.3 mile of easy water, the bottom drops out. In the next mile between the two bridges, the gradient is 250 fpm. Eddies are small and difficult to catch. All except three drops can be scouted by boat.

Below the second island is Whoop-de-do, class 5. Scout or portage left. About 0.3 mile farther is a small, nearly invisible log on the right where several boaters have been pinned. Just around the bend below the second bridge is Dragon Slayer, a jumble of rocks in the river followed in 50 yards by a cliff on the right. The scout requires wading and gives boaters soggy sneakers. The bottom hole can cartwheel boats, suck boaters out of boats, or even pin them to the bottom. Below, where the river appears to turn right and plow into the canyon wall, is Spinal Compression. Portage left. The river flattens out for the next 1.5 miles before entering the class 4 gorge, described in the next run.

Hazards. The logs present in this very steep run are very dangerous. Several of the holes are also extremely treacherous.

Access. To reach the take-out, see run 67, North Fork of Middle Fork Willamette River: The Gorge to Westfir.

Continue upriver another 4 miles to where the road is close to the river, the put-in.

Gauge. The flow at the put-in is about half that at Westfir. See run 67, below.

Jason Bates and Jim Reed

67 North Fork of Middle Fork Willamette River
The Gorge to Westfir

Class: 4(5)	**Length: 9.5 miles**
Flow: 2,000 cfs	**Character: forested**
Gradient: 29 fpm, PD	**Season: rainy**

The North Fork offers exciting whitewater, superb scenery, and easy access. It flows into the Middle Fork Willamette River just below

Westfir, near Oakridge. Except for Ledges, all major rapids can be scouted on the drive to the put-in. The Gorge is a 0.5-mile section of class 4 rapids ending in a class 5 boulder garden. It is located between the two bridges on the main road. At high water the hydraulics in this section are very powerful. The Gorge has three main obstacles: a drop on the right, a very large curling wave that crosses the entire river about half-way through the Gorge, and a tight class 5 boulder garden at the end. The slots in the boulder garden are barely wide enough for boats. Scout very carefully.

The run below the Gorge is rated class 3, and has three noteworthy rapids: Shotgun, Bull's-eye, and Ledges. Shotgun is a twisting left turn with a small 3-foot drop that can be seen from the road. Bull's-eye can be recognized by a large rock that blocks the main channel on the left. Boaters may go either right or left of the rock, but some have been known to go straight over the top, giving it the name Bull's-eye! Ledges is difficult to scout from either the river or the road. It consists of a narrow channel on the far left that becomes apparent only at the top of the drop. Ledges can be recognized by a wall of rocks on the left at the start of the drop. It is located near the end of the run.

Hazards. The difficult Gorge section should be carefully scouted. Shotgun, Bull's-eye, and Ledges are class 3 rapids that present some difficulties. Ledges is difficult because it cannot be scouted.

Access. Take Oregon 58 eastward from I-5 south of Eugene. Proceed 32 miles to Westfir. At the covered bridge in Westfir, pass through the log storage yard on the road that follows the south bank of the river. A convenient take-out is at the weigh station located about 0.5 mile upstream of Westfir; from the river it is just around the corner from Ledges Rapids.

The normal put-in is just above the second bridge; this gives boaters a short warm-up for the Gorge. Those who do not wish to run the Gorge can put in at the bridge just below it.

Gauge. Flow can be estimated from the recording at 541-937-3852. Subtract the Hill Creek outflow from the Lookout Point inflow and divide by 2 to give the flow at Westfir.

Gene Ice

68 Fall Creek
Bedrock Campground to Fall Creek Reservoir

Class: 3(4)   **Length: 7.5 miles**
Flow: 800–3,000 cfs   **Character: forested**
Gradient: 42 fpm, PD   **Season: rainy**

Upper Fall Creek is one of the most exciting and beautiful runs in the Eugene area. The worst drawbacks of this run are the unpredictable flow, the cold water, and the difficult put-in and take-out. With the exception of two difficult rapids, intermediate paddlers can consider the run.

Within 0.5 mile of the put-in is the first class 3 drop. It starts out

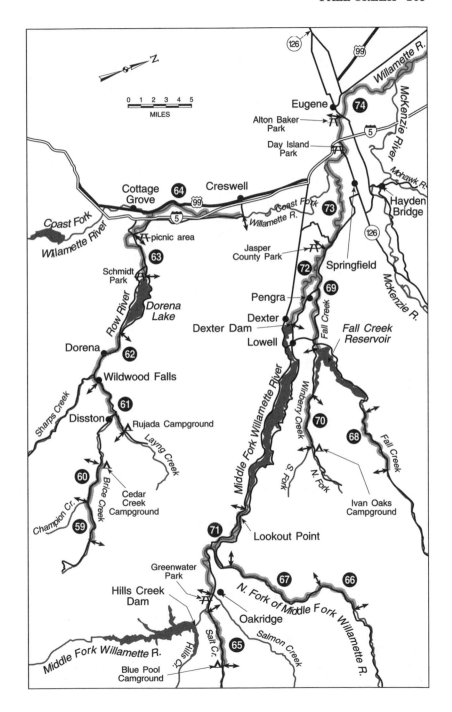

with a riverwide ledge, then narrows considerably. The water in this slot is turbulent and will flip an unwary boater. This drop is usually run best on the left. Below this rapids, the river has a series of ledges and pools. Several class 2 and 3 rapids are interspersed in this green Eden. The beauty of the stream's banks contrasts with the water, which is usually muddy at high flows.

Beyond the second bridge, begin preparing for Fish Ramp Rapids, which can be a very difficult and potentially dangerous rapids with a strong guard hole at the top. Scout this rapids during the shuttle. It can be reached by a short unmarked road leading down to a BLM boat ramp. This is the only road leading to the river above the open rural lower section of the run. Immediately above the turnoff for this road, the main road follows the river for a short distance.

Between the last bridge and the reservoir take-out lurks the second class 4 rapids. It is a 6- to 7-foot steep slide into a diagonal hole! Scout this drop before attempting to run it.

Hazards. Scout Fish Ramp Rapids and the steep slide between the last bridge and the take-out. Intermediate boaters may wish to portage around Fish Ramp Rapids. At flows above 2,000–2,500 cfs, this river is strictly for experts.

Access. From Oregon 126 in east Springfield, turn south on 42nd Avenue, which becomes Jasper Road. It passes through the town of Jasper and past Fall Creek Reservoir, on its north side. The put-in is at Bedrock Campground, 7.5 miles upstream from Fall Creek Reservoir on USFS 18. The trail just above the campground bridge leads to the river and sometimes looks more like a mudslide than a path. Be careful!

Boaters can take out either at Fish Ramp Rapids just downstream from the second bridge, at the last bridge, or at Fall Creek Reservoir.

Gauge. Contact Lookout Point Dam for Fall Creek Reservoir inflow.

Doug Tooley

69 Fall Creek
Fall Creek Dam to Jasper County Park

Class: 2(3)	**Length:** 9 miles
Flow: 1,000 cfs	**Character:** rural
Gradient: 10 fpm, PD	**Season:** dam-controlled

With the exception of the Willamette River and the McKenzie River at Hayden Bridge, this run on Fall Creek is the closest whitewater to the Eugene–Springfield area. It contains some excellent play spots that are good for beginners to try surfing. Because this portion of Fall Creek is not prone to flooding, fallen trees remain in the river, so keep your eyes open.

The first 0.5 mile of the run is the most interesting, with a nice series of short class 2 rapids. Throughout the run are many good play spots with eddies on both sides of the river. The run ends with a class 3 rapids located just downstream from the Pengra covered bridge. The class 3 rapids can be scouted easily from the bridge. Decked boaters should have no problems with this rapids. Open canoes risk swamping in the 3- to 4-foot standing waves. Boaters who do not wish to run the Pengra bridge rapids can take out on river left, at the base of the bridge.

Just around the corner from Pengra covered bridge, where Jasper Road bends near the river, is a possible take-out. It is also possible to paddle down to the confluence with the Middle Fork Willamette River and then continue to Jasper County Park for an additional 4 miles.

Hazards. Some boaters may opt to scout the class 3 rapids just below the Pengra covered bridge.

Access. From Oregon 126 in east Springfield, turn south on 42nd Avenue, which becomes Jasper Road. It passes through the town of Jasper, where the lower take-out on the Middle Fork Willamette is located across the river.

To reach the put-in, continue out Jasper Road to Fall Creek Dam access road and follow signs to the dam. The optional upper take-out at Pengra covered bridge is passed on the way to the put-in.

Gauge. Call Lookout Point Dam for Fall Creek Reservoir outflow.

Doug Tooley

70 Winberry Creek
Winberry Campground to Fall Creek Reservoir

Class: 3(4) P   **Length: 4.8 miles**
Flow: 300–1,000 cfs   **Character: forested**
Gradient: 45 fpm, PD   **Season: rainy**

Winberry Creek is perfect for an afternoon trip. It is one of the better runs of moderate difficulty that help one become accustomed to creek boating. The run can begin on South Winberry Creek, which includes a short class 3+ gorge, or at the confluence of the North and South Forks at Winberry Campground. Immediately below the confluence of the forks is a class 3 drop that should be scouted on the right for logs. Downstream 1.7 miles is Bloody Elbow, a class 3 rapids that twists under a small bridge. Another 0.4 mile below is a gorge section that can be scouted from the road. This 0.7-mile gorge section is class 3+, with some class 4 water. Two miles below the gorge is Bridge Over Troubled Waters, a class 5 drop that has been run, but which has a very dangerous pin spot. It can be recognized by a 3-foot ledge 50 yards upstream of a definite horizon line. Portage on the left. Take out at the bridge above Fall Creek Reservoir.

Hazards. The pin spot at Bridge Over Troubled Waters rapids is a severe hazard. Logs in this narrow, steep creek can be very dangerous.

Access. From I-5 south of Eugene, take Oregon 58 east to Lookout Point Lake at Dexter. Turn left at the covered bridge, go through Lowell and northward toward Unity. In Unity turn right onto West Boundry Creek Road. Proceed about 0.5 mile, turn right on Winberry

Creek Road, and go 5.5 miles to the first bridge over Winberry Creek, the take-out.

The put-in is 5.6 miles farther upstream at Winberry Campground.

Gauge. None exists. A flow of 1,200 cfs in Fall Creek is about the minimum desired.

Eric Brown

71 Middle Fork Willamette River
Oakridge to Lookout Point Lake

Class: 2+   **Length: 10 miles**
Flow: 1,000–3,000 cfs **Character: forested hills**
Gradient: 18 fpm, PD **Season: year-round**

This is a beautiful run for a sunny day in October when the discharge from Hills Creek Dam is increased, and before winter rains have brought up other rivers. The banks are lined with trees, so houses and roads seldom intrude upon the landscape. The current is fast, creating frequent class 1 and 2 rapids of all shapes and sizes. It is a challenging run for the novice, exciting for most open canoers, and nice and splashy for more experienced boaters. You will probably see a number of drift boaters and shore-bound fly anglers; be courteous by giving them a wide berth.

Immediately below the Greenwater Park put-in is a long class 2+ rapids, which has lots of waves and cross currents, but requires little technical maneuvering. At 3.5 miles, the river crosses under Oregon 58. There is a small Forest Service park, Ferrin Park, on river right just below the bridge. At 4.8 miles, there is a second bridge on the road that leads to Westfir. There is a good eddy and road access on river left, just below the bridge. Immediately below this is Hell's Gate Rapids, a rocky and technical class 2 at low water and class 3 at high flows. The remaining 5 miles to the take-out are similar to the first half of the run, except that the highway is more visible and audible. Depending on the water level in Lookout Point Lake, the last 0.2 mile of the trip may be flat.

Hazards. For novice boaters, there is no warm-up before the long, splashy class 2+ rapids near the put-in. Hell's Gate Rapids, just below the second bridge, is the most technically difficult of this section. It is easily scouted from the bridge on the road to Westfir.

Access. Take Oregon 58 east from I-5, just south of Eugene, and proceed upstream about 28 miles to the take-out at Black Canyon Campground, at the head of Lookout Point Lake. There is a boat ramp at the downstream end of the park. This boat ramp remains open later into the fall than the rest of the park.

To reach the put-in, continue east on Oregon 58 another 4–5 miles to Westfir Junction. To continue road scouting, take a left, cross the bridge, turn right toward Oakridge, and rejoin Oregon 58 in 1.3 miles, at the east end of the Oregon 58 bridge over the Middle Fork. The put-in is at Greenwater Park, at the upstream edge of Oakridge.

There is an alternate put-in 2 miles farther upstream near the base of Hills Creek Dam. This put-in appears to be popular with drift boaters, but this section has not been run by the authors. It is reputed to be class 2–2+.

Gauge. Contact Lookout Point Dam for Hills Creek Reservoir outflow. In dry years there may not be enough water released in July and August for a good run. If Hell's Gate Rapids, which can be viewed from the bridge, looks runnable, the whole run will have enough water.

Rob Blickensderfer and Rich Brainerd

72 Middle Fork Willamette River
Dexter Dam to Jasper County Park

Class: 1+
Flow: 2,000 cfs
Gradient: 14 fpm, C

Length: 8 miles
Character: rural
Season: year-round

The Willamette River makes its transition from the wild water of the upper reaches to the slower water found below Eugene on this and the next run described. The trip begins with fairly fast turbulent water from the discharge of Dexter Dam and continues at a brisk pace. The rapids are fairly small and straightforward, although at low water several exposed rock shelves require careful maneuvering.

About midway down is an area where trees have been deposited by high water and the river subdivides into several channels. The exact configurations of the channels and logjams can vary each year. Beyond here the river is a little less steep. Take out on the left at Jasper County Park, where picnic tables can be seen from the river, or 0.2 mile downstream at the Jasper bridge.

Hazards. There is a potentially dangerous section about midway on the run where the river splits into several channels and where there are logjams. At some flows a portage may be required. The casual boater without solid class 2 experience should not attempt this run on the Willamette.

Access. Dexter Reservoir is along Oregon 58 about 18 miles southeast of Eugene. It is easiest to drive first to the take-out at Jasper County Park. The park is 0.2 mile upstream from the Jasper bridge on the south side of the river. A more convenient take-out is under the southern end of the bridge.

To get to the put-in, follow the road along the north side of the river through Fall Creek to Lowell and thence to the base of Dexter Dam. The put-in is a bit of a scramble down riprap.

Gauge. Call Lookout Point Dam for Dexter Reservoir outflow.

Rob Blickensderfer

73 Willamette River
Jasper County Park to Alton Baker Park

Class: 2(3)
Flow: 2,000 cfs
Gradient: 16 fpm, C

Length: 14 miles
Character: residential; industrial
Season: year-round

Jasper County Park to Alton Baker Park is a popular summer run for Eugene residents and is the site of the annual Willamette River Race. Although racing boats try to finish this stretch in less than 1½ hours, the run is more often enjoyed at a leisurely float pace. Do not expect a wilderness run here; rather, enjoy a gathering of happy folks, especially during the summer when hot weather drives rafts, canoes, and crafts of all pedigree onto the water. Despite its popularity with novice paddlers, the river needs to be respected. During the summer the water is mild, but rocks are plentiful. During the spring, winter, and fall the water can be brutally cold.

The run begins on the Middle Fork Willamette River at Jasper County Park or under the Jasper bridge. The water is fast with a few surfing waves for the first 5 miles to Clearwater Boat Landing on the right. Below here the river splits around a rocky island, resulting in whitewater on both sides. About 4 miles below, look for the mouth of the Coast Fork Willamette River on the left. The railroad bridge and the two highway bridges at the west end of Springfield are the best watermarks. Below these bridges is Day Island with Day Island Park on the right, a possible take-out. Beaver are often seen near or below the park.

Just below Day Island the river offers Pizza Rapids, named for a local pizza establishment on the left bank. A flat section extends below this rapids to the weir at the head of I-5 Rapids. A sign posted on the riverbank warns boaters that the coming stretch is the most dangerous on the river. *Do not expect to see this sign from the river.* The weir is about 100 yards upstream of the I-5 bridge. At this point, boaters have a choice of two routes for the remaining 2 miles to Alton Baker Park:

1. For an easy paddle to Alton Baker Park, take out at the boat landing on the right above I-5 Rapids. Portage 200 feet to reach the Canoe Path, a pleasant canal that flows to Alton Baker Park.

2. To continue downstream, scout the weir and I-5 Rapids. They consist of a low rock wall and a broken weir with various slots, followed by a reasonably long rapids with a large wave at the bottom. The far right slot is the only safe route. Under no circumstances should any of the other slots be run, as debris and reversal action can make them unrunnable. Waves and holes become quite large at high water. Rafts are particularly prone to being trapped in the hydraulics behind the weir.

Below I-5 Rapids the river passes under two of Eugene's bike/footbridges. At the second one, about 1 mile below I-5 Rapids, there is a large standing wave in the main channel on the left. Boaters flock to this spot in the summer to do enders and prolonged surfs. The wave may be avoided by sneaking to the right. A mile downstream, the Ferry Street Bridge signals Alton Baker Park on the right and the end of the run.

A convenient circuit can be made by paddling from Alton Baker Park up the canal and down the Willamette. This loop obviates the need for a shuttle.

Hazards. The weir ahead of I-5 Rapids is dangerous at all water levels. Do not attempt to run any slot except the far right. The I-5 Rapids may swamp open boats at high water.

Access. Jasper County Park is on the south side of the Middle Fork Willamette River about 0.2 mile above the Jasper bridge. The town of Jasper is a few miles southeast of Springfield off of Oregon 126. There is good parking at Jasper County Park, but it is about a 50-yard carry to the water. An alternate put-in under the Jasper bridge has less desirable parking but a shorter carry to the water. Another put-in or take-out is about 5 miles downstream at Clearwater Boat Landing, on the road between Jasper and Springfield.

The take-outs are in Eugene on the north side of the river. The one above I-5 Rapids is off Centennial Boulevard east of the I-5 underpass. The Alton Baker Park take-out is near the junction of Centennial Boulevard and Coburg Road.

Gauge. The flow is regulated so that the minimum is runnable. Jasper gauge gives the flow for the Middle Fork; Eugene gauge gives the flow for the Willamette. Flows are available from the River Forecast Center in Portland.

Gene Ice

74 Willamette River
Alton Baker Park to Harrisburg

Class: 1(2)   **Length:** 21 miles
Flow: 6,000 cfs   **Character:** suburban; rural
Gradient: 5 fpm, C   **Season:** year-round

This run seems less popular than the previous one, perhaps because the water is a bit slower. However, the rural setting offers better scenery and interesting exploration of the riverbanks. An alternate route to Harrisburg begins on the lower McKenzie.

After the put-in at Alton Baker Park, the river immediately passes Skinners Butte Park and the Eugene Rose Gardens on the left. The first rapids is opposite the Rose Gardens, just above the Jefferson Street Bridge. Below the rapids the water is calm, and it is possible to paddle to the left for a closer look at the roses.

Below Jefferson Street Bridge the river passes Valley River Center and under a bike/footbridge. This section, although basically flat water, is interesting because of numerous small islands that divide the river into channels. Between Valley River Center and the Belt Line Bridge lies Marist Rapids, the most difficult rapids on this run. Marist

Rapids is fairly straightforward with large waves in the center. It can be scouted and/or portaged on the left, but watch out for slippery rocks! The next major landmark is Belt Line Bridge, a possible take-out. Below Belt Line, the signs of Eugene give way to rural Oregon. A few miles downstream on the right, the McKenzie River adds some cool water; however, it is easy to not notice this confluence.

The alternate put-in is at Armitage Park on the McKenzie River. It is 2.5 miles to the confluence with the Willamette River.

Two possible take-outs are located about midway between Eugene and Harrisburg (see Access, below). The second half of the river broadens and has fewer curves. The railroad bridge signals the approach to Harrisburg. After passing the highway bridge, land at the boat ramp on the right.

Hazards. Marist Rapids, between Valley River Mall and Belt Line Bridge, should be scouted on the left by open boaters or those unfamiliar with the rapids. Below Eugene, a section with downed trees normally exists. The resulting strainers can be extremely hazardous.

Access. Alton Baker Park, the put-in, is located on the north bank near the Coburg Road and Centennial Boulevard junction.

A possible take-out is located about halfway to Harrisburg at Christensen County Boat Landing. To find this take-out, follow Coburg Road north to Crossroads Lane. Another take-out is nearby on the other side of the river at Brown's Boat Landing. The boat ramp at Harrisburg is on the north side of town.

Gauge. The minimum flow is runnable.

Gene Ice

McKENZIE RIVER AND TRIBUTARIES

Of all the whitewater rivers in Oregon, few are more popular than the beautiful McKenzie. The river begins in the Cascades and flows in changing moods to the Willamette Valley. The upper McKenzie River Basin is historically and geologically fascinating. The basin was the site of frequent volcanic activity and the river has cut through numerous layers of tuff (consolidated volcanic ash) and basalt flows. A geologically recent basalt flow is responsible for the formation of Clear Lake, the origin of the McKenzie River.

The stark foreboding of the volcanic formations is in contrast to the dense forest stands that thrive in the soils. French Pete Drainage, above the South Fork McKenzie River, is a favorite hiking area for Eugene–Springfield residents. This area was recently established as a wilderness area. The H.J. Andrews Experimental Forest is located near the town of Blue River. This area is used by the U.S. Forest Service to research the impacts of logging activities on water quality and to monitor undisturbed basins. Filbert orchards, Christmas tree plantations, and other farmlands crowd the lower McKenzie Valley between the forests of the upper McKenzie and the confluence with the Willamette River. Whether one's interests lie in hiking, boating the main river, or paddling one of the exciting tributaries, the McKenzie truly has something for everyone.

Gene Ice

75 South Fork McKenzie River
Near French Pete to Cougar Reservoir

Class: 3; 4(5)   **Length: 8.5 miles**
Flow: 1,500 cfs; 3,500–4,500 cfs   **Character: forested**
Gradient: 81 fpm, C   **Season: rainy**

For most McKenzie River boaters, the South Fork is just another tributary that enters the main river unnoticed somewhere between Rainbow and Blue River. Above Cougar Reservoir, however, lies the free-flowing South Fork McKenzie River, one of the most interesting rivers of the Upper Willamette system. At flows above 2,000 cfs the South Fork is a superb experts-only run. At flows below 2,000 cfs the long rapids are no longer continuous, and the South Fork is suitable for paddlers with a dependable roll.

Although the South Fork McKenzie drainage is adjacent to the North Fork of Middle Fork Willamette River, it has greater fluctuations in flow. It is usually runnable only during or shortly after a hard rain. The spring snowmelt is undependable. Furthermore, one of the best rapids is exposed only during the fall and early winter when Cougar Reservoir is lowered.

Some rapids can be scouted on the drive to the put-in, but the South Fork is so continuous that it is impractical to memorize routes. The first part of the run is fairly shallow and rocky. Soon, however, side creeks begin to add volume and the gradient begins to pick up. Watch for logs! Below the confluence with French Pete Creek lies a long major rapids with holes and large waves. After French Pete Rapids the river quiets down for about 1 mile, to the bridge at the top of the reservoir. Below this bridge the river cuts deep into mud walls of the lowered lake and the second major rapids follows. This rapids has two 90-degree right turns that can be run to the inside. There are few eddies to catch for this 0.8-mile stretch. The rapids finally comes to an end in the lowered reservoir. The walk to the take-out is a bit muddy, but well worth the trouble. A welcome treat is a soak at the Cougar Reservoir Hot Springs on the way home. Run in 1975 by Bob Porter and Gene Ice.

Hazards. The run is very fast. The last rapids should be scouted.

Access. To reach the put-in, take Oregon 126 east from Springfield past Blue River and take the Cougar Reservoir exit on the right. Proceed to the top of Cougar Dam. (It is worthwhile to stop at the top of the dam to note the tremendous drop. We can only guess, with a shiver, at the rapids buried beneath the reservoir.) From the dam, drive along the west bank. Along the way are numerous creeks and waterfalls. Toward the end of the lake is a boat ramp on the other side of the reservoir; this is the take-out. Proceed over the bridge across the South Fork. The take-out is to the left.

The put-in is to the right, toward French Pete, about 8.5 miles upstream from the take-out.

Gauge. Contact Cougar Dam for the flow into Cougar Reservoir.

Gene Ice

76 Blue River
Quentin Creek to Blue River Lake

Class: 4(5) T   **Length: 4 miles**
Flow: 220–900 cfs   **Character: forested; logging**
Gradient: 91 fpm, PD   **Season: rainy**

Blue River is a technically demanding, high-gradient tributary of the McKenzie River located only 39 miles east of Eugene. Approximately 0.5 mile below the Quentin Creek put-in is a triple drop called Food for Thought. This drop has been run successfully, but may require a portage. The remainder of the river requires extensive scouting both from the road and the river.

Technical drops of 3–10 feet are numerous, as are extensive boulder

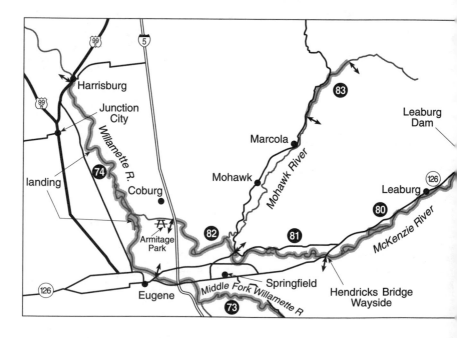

gardens that require precise boat handling. Due to logging activity in the area, boaters should be wary of log debris and sweepers. From Tidbits Creek, located 1 mile from the take-out, the river broadens and flattens, building up for one last boulder garden just before the take-out.

Hazards. This run is composed of a nearly continuous series of difficult chutes and drops. Beware of logs. Worthy of special note is the class 5 Food for Thought just below the put-in.

Access. Take Oregon 126 east from Springfield toward Blue River.

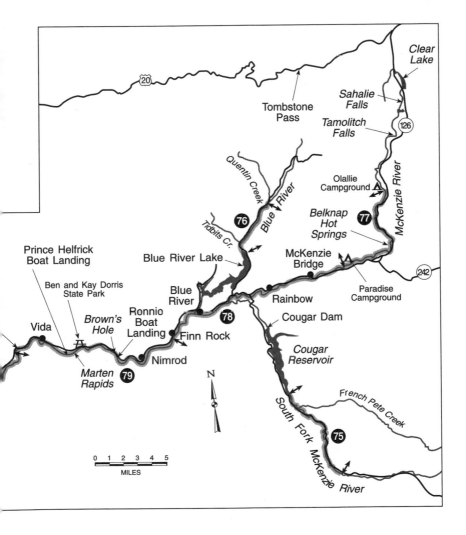

Two miles east of the town of Blue River, turn north from Oregon 126 onto USFS 15. The take-out is located at a boat ramp at the upper end of Blue River Lake, about 4 miles from the 126 turnoff.

The put-in is about 4 miles farther, at the confluence of Quentin Creek and Blue River. Put-ins for shorter runs are possible if low water warrants.

Gauge. Call Lookout Point Dam for the flow above Lookout Creek.

Ron Mattson

77 McKenzie River
Olallie Campground to Paradise Campground

Class: 3	**Length: 9 miles**
Flow: 700–2,000 cfs	**Character: forested**
Gradient: 60 fpm, C	**Season: year-round**

Within its tree-lined banks, the McKenzie rushes with almost non-stop rapids between Olallie and Paradise campgrounds. This continuous run has few play spots. The first few miles are a fun, bouncy ride. At the first bridge, there is a wave on the left that can be surfed at some water levels.

A few miles downstream lies Fishladder Rapids, class 3, the most difficult rapids on this run. It starts at a left turn just as you see power lines ahead across the river. To scout, land on the right. It is usually also scouted from the left during the shuttle. Pull off onto a dirt road at milepost 16, about 5 miles above Paradise Campground, and walk 100 yards to the river. Below Fishladder, the river continues to offer miles of interesting rapids. Just across from Belknap Hot Springs Resort, look for an eddy and plumes of steam arising on the right. The hot springs adds some welcome hot water to warm your cold hands during winter runs. Paradise Campground is a fitting name for the end of the trip. Take out on the left.

Hazards. Fishladder Rapids should be scouted by those unfamiliar with it.

Access. Drive east from Springfield on Oregon 126 to the take-out at Paradise Campground, located about 4 miles east of McKenzie Bridge. Paradise is partially closed during the winter. Take a close look at the take-out to be able to recognize it from the river. The highway bridge across the river at McKenzie Bridge and the covered Rainbow Bridge on McKenzie River Drive offer alternate take-outs for longer trips.

The put-in is at Olallie Campground, about 9 miles upstream on Oregon 126.

Gauge. Located at McKenzie Bridge. Call the River Forecast Center in Portland. The minimum flow is runnable.

Gene Ice

78 McKenzie River
Paradise Campground to Finn Rock

Class: 2+   **Length: 18 miles**
Flow: 700–2,000 cfs   **Character: wooded; cabins**
Gradient: 31 fpm, C   **Season: year-round**

A short distance below Paradise Campground the McKenzie loses some of its continuous nature and takes on a pool-drop character. A long boulder garden beginning at the town of McKenzie Bridge and ending above the covered Rainbow Bridge is one of the most significant rapids on this stretch. About 0.2 mile below Rainbow Bridge, where the river nears the main highway, is an "S"-curve that ends in a rocky stretch with a strong diagonal wave on the right.

Below this the river eases into a nice class 2 paddle for experienced open canoers with a good back-ferry. Play spots are few, but are highlighted by an excellent ender hole just across from the Redsides log

Helping dad scout the next drop (photo by Rick Starr)

scaling station, about halfway down. Even decked double canoes (C-2s) can do incredible enders on the wave on the right. Paddlers sometimes spend a whole day here seeking the perfect ender. Below Redsides the river becomes flatter.

Hazards. The class 2+ stretches at Paradise and below McKenzie Bridge are the most difficult.

Access. Take Oregon 126 east from Springfield to the rest area at Finn Rock. Kayakers can take out here, but rafters will find the gentle bank across the river easier. To reach this, cross the river on the concrete bridge and turn left on the gravel road and then left into the boat ramp.

The put-in is at Paradise Campground about 15 miles upstream on Oregon 126 (see run 77, McKenzie River: Olallie Campground to Paradise Campground, Access). Alternate put-ins are at the bridge at McKenzie Bridge and at the covered Rainbow Bridge, which is located off the main highway on McKenzie River Drive.

Gauge. Located at McKenzie Bridge and Vida. Contact the River Forecast Center in Portland. The minimum flow is runnable.

Gene Ice

79 McKenzie River
Finn Rock to Leaburg Dam

Class: 2(3)   **Length: 10–15 miles**
Flow: 900–3,000 cfs   **Character: wooded; cabins**
Gradient: 21 fpm, C   **Season: year-round**

When people speak of "The McKenzie" they usually mean the run from Finn Rock to Prince Helfrich Boat Landing. This run is one of the most popular day trips in Oregon. It offers rapids for paddlers of many skill levels, good scenery, and outstanding play spots. The run consists of long quiet stretches interspersed with exciting rapids and play spots. However, cold water is a danger to the unprepared.

Two miles below the put-in is one of the best play spots, Clover Point, just above and within sight of the bridge at Nimrod. It is identified by a large flat rock outcrop on the right bank. About 0.8 mile downstream is Eagle Rock Rapids, class 2, identified by the rock cliff on the left. The best ride is down the chute near the left side. A short distance below Eagle Rock is a long series of surfing waves along the left side. Pleasant class 1 and 2 water continues for several miles. Silver Creek Public Boat Landing is on the right at mile 4, followed in 2 miles by Rennie Public Boat Landing.

The most famous hole on the river, Brown's Hole, is next. It can flip a small raft or swamp a drift boat, but it can be easily avoided by staying to the right. Barely visible from upstream, it is located near the end of a straight section. A rock wall on the left about 30 yards upstream of a right jog marks Brown's Hole, about 15 feet from the left wall. For a thrill going downstream, kayakers can try to punch through the hole. If this is not enough, return to the hole and enter it from either side.

About 3 miles farther downstream, the river passes Ben and Kay Dorris State Park, with a boat ramp. Ahead is Marten Rapids, class 3, and an excellent hunting ground for scuba divers stalking watches, glasses, wallets, and other items "contributed" by unwary drift boaters, kayakers, and rafters. Marten Rapids can be a fun ride, but many people end up swimming through it. To run Marten Rapids, look for the largest boulder in the center of the river in the middle of the rapids; there is a good channel about 10 feet to the right of the boulder at most river levels. Beware of the large hole on the right toward the bottom of the rapids. This is a notorious ender spot, but should be approached only by competent paddlers. Most people take out 0.5 mile downstream at Prince Helfrich Boat Landing, marked by a suspension footbridge across the river. Boaters may continue on a few miles to any of several other accesses.

Hazards. Brown's Hole can flip a raft and be very sticky for kayaks at some water levels. It can be totally avoided by going on the right. Marten Rapids can be more violent than Brown's Hole, and contains some dangerous rocks. The water temperature, even in the heat of the summer, is always cool. A long swim through Marten Rapids with little on but a swimsuit (quite a common occurrence) can be quite dangerous, especially without a life jacket.

Access. Put in at Finn Rock on Oregon 126 east of Eugene, 2.7 miles beyond Nimrod. Cross the bridge and turn left into the unimproved Finn Rock boat ramp, provided by Rosoboro Lumber Company. Some boaters with limited time choose to put in at boat ramps located 0.5 mile and 1 mile below, or about 4 and 6 miles below at Silver Creek and Rennie boat landings, respectively.

The common take-outs are Ben and Kay Dorris State Park and Prince Helfrich Boat Landing, located at the end of Thomson Lane, on the south side of the highway 1 mile below Ben and Kay Dorris State Park. Other take-outs downstream are available at Goodpasture Road Covered Bridge, along the road beside Leaburg Reservoir, and the boat ramp at Leaburg Dam.

Gauge. Located at Vida. The minimum flow is runnable.

Gene Ice

80 McKenzie River
Leaburg Dam to Hendricks Bridge Wayside

Class: 2	**Length: 15 miles**
Flow: 900–2,000 cfs	**Character: agricultural**
Gradient: 14 fpm, C	**Season: year-round**

This run is fairly quiet compared to the upper runs, but is very enjoyable. The scenery is more typical of Oregon's agricultural countryside than the dense forests found upstream. The river meanders in deep pools around large islands and runs swiftly through sharp turns with tricky currents. Although some of the turns require careful attention, there are no major rapids until the very end. About halfway through the trip the river runs under the only bridge, then past a golf course and some farmland. Most of the channels around islands appear to be open, but close inspection for the best route is required, especially at low water. One of the channels to the right becomes an irrigation ditch.

Hazards. The most significant rapids is about 0.5 mile above the take-out, identified by the high ridge on the left that slopes down to river level. The river drops to the right, forms some high waves, and then runs swiftly out through some large rocks. In general, some of the turns are tight with brush at low water and require controlled back-paddling by open canoeists.

Access. To reach the put-in, take Oregon 126 east from Eugene to Leaburg Dam, cross the dam, and use the drift-boat slide just below the dam.

The take-out is at Hendricks Bridge Wayside, at mile 11.5 on Oregon 126.

Gauge. The flow is controlled by the Leaburg Dam. Contact the River Forecast Center in Portland.

Gene Ice

81 McKenzie River
Hendricks Bridge Wayside to Hayden Bridge

Class: 2
Flow: 900–2,000 cfs
Gradient: 11 fpm, C

Length: 15 miles
Character: agricultural; paper mill
Season: year-round

This run at Springfield's doorstep has much to offer and is an ideal run for beginning boaters. During the summertime the banks are lined with juicy blackberries and the cold water provides refreshing relief from the heat. Several surprisingly good rapids, including Hayden Bridge Rapids, are in store for paddlers.

The first few miles are quite calm and provide a good warm-up. In low water some rapids near the top can be scratchy, but things get better. About halfway down there is a tricky right turn, with strong eddies on both sides. This is a good place to practice ferrying. Watch the trees and sky; on several trips eagles have been sighted. Don't look skyward too long, however. There is a rapids with large standing waves. This is a fine place for surfing, but the waves can be easily avoided on the left.

The biggest rapids, Hayden Bridge Rapids, class 2, is at the end of the run. The rapids is below Weyerhaeuser Paper Mill with its highly visible smokestacks. Eugene paddlers often come to Hayden Bridge Rapids to practice. There are excellent eddies that allow a skillful paddler to work to the top of the rapids.

Hazards. Hayden Bridge Rapids is difficult. The best channels are to the left. The rapids climax in a sharp left turn. Statistics say this is one of the most dangerous rapids in Oregon! Certainly the power of the water is not the problem; it is the coldness of the water and the people who don't wear life jackets! Downed trees are usually present in the section above the rapids.

Access. Take I-105 east from I-5 in Eugene to Mohawk Road. Hayden Bridge is about 0.5 mile north on Mohawk Road. The take-out is a boat landing on the left bank next to a water intake station.

To get to the put-in, return to I-105, travel east to the junction with Oregon 126, and drive eastward to Hendricks Bridge Wayside, which has a paved parking lot and boat ramp.

Gauge. Located at Vida. Contact the River Forecast Center in Portland. The minimum flow is runnable.

Gene Ice

82 McKenzie River
Hayden Bridge to Armitage Park

Class: 1	**Length: 8 miles**
Flow: 900–2,000 cfs	**Character: agricultural; residential**
Gradient: 7 fpm, C	**Season: year-round**

This run makes an excellent canoe paddle close to Eugene and Springfield. There are very few rapids, but it is pleasant. The most difficult rapids are just above Armitage Park, but can be avoided if desired. One of the most enjoyable parts of this float is gliding by the Coburg Hills. After finishing the run, Armitage Park makes a fine spot for a picnic.

Those who want a longer trip can continue to one of the access points below the confluence with the Willamette. See run 74, Willamette River: Alton Baker Park to Harrisburg.

Hazards. There are none.

Access. See run 81, McKenzie River: Hendricks Bridge Wayside to Hayden Bridge, for directions to Hayden Bridge, the put-in for this run.

The take-out at Armitage Park is located on Coburg Road. From the north, take the Coburg exit from I-5, and turn south on Coburg Road. From the south, exit from I-5 onto Belt Line Road. Follow Belt Line west to the first exit, Coburg Road, and go north.

The shuttle may be run via I-105 or via the following back roads: cross Hayden Bridge and take an immediate left on Old Mohawk Road. After about 1 mile turn left on Hill Road and continue for about 0.5 mile. Turn left again on McKenzie View Drive, which intersects Coburg Road just across the river from Armitage Park.

Gauge. Located at Vida. Contact the River Forecast Center in Portland. The minimum flow is runnable.

Gene Ice

83 Mohawk River
Gate on Mohawk River Road to Hileman Road Bridge

Class: 2(3-) T   Length: 5.8 miles
Flow: 400 cfs   Character: wooded; residential
Gradient: 39 fpm, C   Season: rainy

The Mohawk River, a tributary of the McKenzie River, drains a small valley devoted largely to logging and farming. This run is meandering, shallow, narrow, and continuous in character, and has strainers. The river cuts through basalt for the first 2 miles, and then through alluvial deposits. The first mile has several ledges, including one 4-foot ledge (class 3-) and a sloping 5-foot ledge under a bridge and into a pool. A high waterfall cascades down to the river on the left within this first mile.

Downstream the river flows quickly between easy riffles. In 1991 two large logs and two low wires spanned the river in the section between miles 3.5 and 5. At about mile 5 the river pours over a log that forms a 2-foot drop.

Hazards. The ledges in the first mile provide the most whitewater difficulty. Downed trees are common and logjams may be encountered. Two wires cross the river near mile 3.5 in the vicinity of several geodesic dome homes. The first is only 4 feet above the water; the second is about 10 feet up.

Access. From the mid-Willamette valley, go to the put-in first. Take the Brownsville exit from I-5 between Albany and Eugene, and travel east on Oregon 228 to Crawfordsville. Turn south on Brush Creek Road 0.3 mile east of Crawfordsville. Go 8.2 miles to the intersection with Mohawk River Road. Turn left (east) and go 1.6 miles to the put-in at a locked gate.

For the take-out, return to Brush Creek Road (its name changes to Marcola Road) and continue south. The take-out is at the bridge on Hileman Road just east of Marcola Road.

From the Eugene area, follow Oregon 126 eastward, then take Marcola Road to the north. After crossing the McKenzie River at Hayden Bridge, go 15 miles to Hileman Road, and the take-out bridge.

To find the put-in, continue north on Marcola Road (its name changes to Brush Creek Road) to its intersection with Mohawk River Road. Turn right (east) and go 1.6 miles to the put-in at a locked gate.

Gauge. Located near Springfield, 20 miles downriver from the put-in. Contact the River Forecast Center in Portland. A flow of 1,000 cfs at the gauge is about 400 cfs at the put-in.

Steve and Sandy Cramer

MID-WILLAMETTE VALLEY

LONG TOM RIVER

84 Long Tom River
High Pass Road to Willamette River

Class: 1+ P   **Length:** 17 miles
Flow: 50 cfs   **Character:** rural; channelized
Gradient: 5 fpm, PD   **Season:** year-round

The Long Tom is for those who desire to float down a quiet stream away from the crowds. Elementary paddling skills can be practiced while maneuvering around rocks in slow-moving water. It is also an excellent river for novice poling practice. Much of the river channel has been lined with riprap. A narrow riparian vegetation strip separates the Long Tom from most of the agricultural activity in the area.

The river can be run at all levels except flood stage, but is best in late spring or fall. Many sections are rocky below 50 cfs; be prepared to hop out and wade in places. Caution is advised near each of the three dams. The first dam is just upstream, but within sight, of the second bridge (Ferguson Road), 2.5 miles below the put-in. The next dam is another 2.5 miles farther downstream. The final dam is at the Monroe mill, after another 3 miles downstream. All of the dams are more than 10 feet high and have very powerful reversals. Portage all three on the right. At the Monroe dam, take out about 100 feet past the US 99W bridge. Because of thick blackberries, there is no path closer to the dam.

For a shorter trip, the river can be reached at five of the six bridges along the way, the bridge at Stow Pit Road being the exception.

Hazards. The major problems are the three dams. Never try to run over a dam in any craft.

Access. The put-in is 9 miles south of Monroe, which is on US 99W between Eugene and Albany. Put in at the bridge on High Pass Road, which connects Junction City with the Monroe–Cheshire Road.

To reach the take-out from the put-in, go north on US 99W to 11 miles south of Corvallis and turn east from US 99W onto Eureka Road. Follow Eureka Road for 2 miles, crossing one bridge. Turn right onto another gravel road and go south to the take-out bridge. This bridge is within sight of a channel of the Willamette River. The take-out is a very steep pull up the right bank just past the bridge. (Note the upstream flow of water here on the Long Tom!)

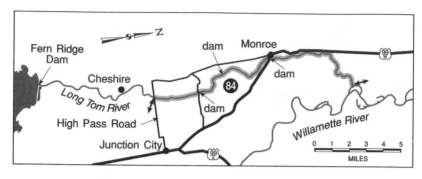

An alternate and much easier take-out can be reached by turning east off US 99W onto Old River Road, about 0.5 mile south of Eureka Road. Follow Old River Road to the take-out, which is on river left about 100 yards downstream of the Old River Road bridge. This is the third bridge below Monroe.

Gauge. Located at Monroe. The flow is regulated by the U.S. Army Corps of Engineers at the Fern Ridge Dam; call the Lookout Point Dam for flow. A minimum flow of 50 cfs is maintained except from July 1– September 30 when the flow drops to 30 cfs. In October the flow is greatly increased while Fern Ridge Reservoir is being drawn down for the winter.

Allen Throop

MARYS RIVER

85 Marys River
Blodgett to Philomath

Class: 1+(2)	**Length: 19 miles**
Flow: 400-900 cfs	**Character: wooded; rural**
Gradient: 10 fpm, C	**Season: rainy**

The Marys River flows from the Coast Range east to its confluence with the Willamette in Corvallis. It is a mild-mannered and isolated stream ideal for canoers and kayakers interested in scenery and mild whitewater. The rapids on the upper section are slightly easier and farther apart than those on the last 5 miles near Philomath. The exception is the class 2 series of shelves about 0.5 mile below the covered bridge in Wren. There are several options for put-ins and take-outs.

Hazards. The brushy banks and downed trees can be problems for novice boaters on this narrow stream. The class 2 shelves 0.5 mile below the covered bridge must be portaged at low flows.

Access. The uppermost put-in is about 1 mile downstream of the US 20 bridge in Blodgett, east of Corvallis (above here the river is choked with wood). A popular put-in is at the covered bridge a few miles upstream from Wren; take Marys River Road along the south side of the river.

Other access points are the US 20 bridge in Wren, and farther downstream at the Oregon 223 bridge in Wren. The lower take-outs are west of Philomath at the US 20 bridge or the Oregon 34 bridge, which is another mile downstream.

Gauge. Call the River Forecast Center in Portland.

Bill Ostrand and Richard Hand

CALAPOOIA RIVER

86 Calapooia River
Bridge 13 Miles Above Holley to Bridge 4 Miles Above Holley

Class: 3	**Length: 10 miles**
Flow: 740–2,500 cfs	**Character: forested; logging; residential**
Gradient: 48 fpm, PD	**Season: rainy**

The Calapooia is named after the Indians who once inhabited the Willamette Valley. It is a small river whose uppermost runs are within an hour's drive of many southern Willamette Valley communities. The river tumbles through forested land in the foothills of the Cascades. Winter storms augment the Calapooia's normally small flow.

The beginning of the run is swift, with sufficient gradient and rocks to immediately lead the boater into class 2–3 rapids. Spend a few minutes warming up by playing on the easier waves near the put-in. Within several hundred yards, a rock-strewn section sweeps past a point occupied for years by a logjam on the right. At mile 1.5 the river veers right with a rocky class 3 drop.

Bigs Creek enters on the right at mile 2, and a single cable marks mile 3.2. Below mile 4, the channel narrows and a ledge develops a tricky curl that can produce a tail stand or dump a too-complacent boater. Below is the Narrows with a rocky rapids. One mile downstream look for a small brushy gravel bar and a prominent culvert protruding from the road fill on the right. This marks a short class 2 drop and interesting play spot. Dollar Drop, named for the former town of Dollar, is at mile 6.5. It is 0.2 mile after passing beneath a bridge. Pull out on the right to scout the 4-foot drop over a ledge. Below here is class 1 and 2 water to the take-out. Run on Dec 26, 1977, by John and Rob Blickensderfer.

Hazards. Dollar Drop at mile 6.5 should be scouted. A hazardous reversal forms along the left half of the base. The runout is reasonably good, with a good eddy on the right.

Access. From I-5 between Albany and Eugene, take the Brownsville exit and turn east on Oregon 228. At the village of Holley, 4 miles upstream from McKercher Park, turn right on Upper Calapooia River

Class 2 on the Upper Calapooia River (photo by Rob Blickensderfer)

Road. Three take-outs permit runs of 8–10 miles. The take-out for the longer run is at the bridge 3.6 miles above Holley. This take-out requires a difficult carry up a steep embankment. Much easier take-outs are up the road another 1.3 and 1.7 miles at undeveloped parking areas near river level. One is below and the other is above a side-road bridge.

The put-in is where the road forks to the right before crossing the river on a concrete bridge, 12.5 miles from Holley.

Gauge. None exists. The flow is unregulated. An estimated flow of 700 cfs at Holley is low but good. Flow fluctuates widely and rapidly in response to rainfall. The flow does not correspond with that at the Albany gauge.

T. R. Torgersen

87 Calapooia River
Bridge 4 Miles Above Holley to McKercher Park

Class: 2
Flow: 400–1,200 cfs
Gradient: 18 fpm, PD

Length: 10 miles
Character: rural
Season: rainy

On this run, the gradient slackens considerably compared to the upper run. The relatively easy rapids and numerous riffles make it a good choice for open canoes. There are two rather rocky rapids within the first 0.5 mile. Along miles 2 and 3 the river winds its way through farmland, but maintains reasonable speed. The most difficult rapids is over a rocky shelf 0.2 mile below the double bridges at Crawfordsville.

Hazards. Widely fluctuating storm-influenced flows make sweepers and debris jams potential hazards. The class 2 rapids just below Crawfordsville may warrant scouting; land on the left.

Access. From I-5 between Albany and Eugene, take the Brownsville exit and head east on Oregon 228. At the village of Holley, 4 miles upstream from McKercher Park, turn right on Upper Calapooia River Road. The put-in is at the concrete bridge 3.6 miles from Holley on the Upper Calapooia River Road. There is a good parking place but the carry is a little steep. The bridge at McClun Road, 2 miles above Holley, is an alternate put-in.

The take-out is at McKercher Park, 5.8 miles east of Brownsville. A good landing can be made at the upstream end of the park. Be certain not to overrun the take-out, as there is a class 4 rapids a few hundred yards downstream.

Gauge. See run 86, Calapooia River: Bridge 13 Miles Above Holley to Bridge 4 Miles Above Holley. Recommended minimum flow is about 400 cfs.

T. R. Torgersen

88 Calapooia River
McKercher Park to Brownsville

Class: 1 P
Flow: 600–2,000 cfs
Gradient: 11 fpm, C

Length: 7 miles
Character: agricultural
Season: rainy

The gradient of this run is much less than that of the two upper runs. The river assumes a gentle, meandering course with occasional riffles, and flows through pastoral country. This is an ideal stretch for a gentle canoe run. The section from Brownsville to Tangent is unrunnable because of logjams and brush.

Hazards. There is a weir that should be portaged about 4 miles from the put-in.

Access. From I-5 between Albany and Eugene, take the Brownsville exit and head east on Oregon 228. McKercher Park is a quaint county park about 6 miles east of Brownsville on Oregon 228. The put-in is immediately below the falls at a small sandy beach. A good unloading point is the turnout at milepost 12, just after a bridge but before the park entrance. A short path leads down to the beach. The park offers picnic tables and rest rooms.

The take-out is on the right in the city park downstream from the bridge at Brownsville.

Gauge. Located at Albany. Flows of about 600 cfs indicate acceptable flows from McKercher to Brownsville.

T. R. Torgersen

89 Calapooia River
Oregon 34 Bridge to Albany

Class: 1+ C	**Length: 9 miles**
Flow: 300–1,000 cfs	**Character: agricultural**
Gradient: 3 fpm	**Season: rainy**

The Calapooia River follows a very serene and sinuous course on this stretch. Some of the meandering turns are nearly 360 degrees. The shores are heavily vegetated, so—despite the proximity to human activity—the river has few obvious encroachments by people. At high water, beware of the brush. Some nice sandy beaches become exposed at low water.

Hazards. Because of the heavy brush bordering the river, use reasonable care to avoid being swept into strainers. Small debris jams that require portaging are normal at low water.

Access. The put-in is under the bridge where Oregon 34 crosses the Calapooia River several miles east of Corvallis and 1 mile west of Tangent. A small access road on the south side of the highway, at the east end of the bridge, offers a put-in. Alternate put-ins farther upstream are available where Lake Creek Road crosses the river, about 2 miles west of Tangent, and where US 99E crosses the river, about 1 mile south of Tangent. These upper sections have more brush and downed trees, but provide a unique junglelike experience.

Several take-outs are available: where Riverside Drive crosses the river about 6 miles from the put-in; near the mouth, at Bryant Park; or at the confluence of the Calapooia and the Willamette behind the Senior Citizens' Center on Water and Washington avenues in Albany.

Gauge. Located at Albany. Call the River Forecast Center in Portland.

Allen Throop and Rob Blickensderfer

MILL CREEK

90 Mill Creek
Upper Bridge to Mill Creek County Park

Class: 3(4) T
Flow: 400–1,000 cfs
Gradient: 50 fpm, C

Length: 5.5 miles
Character: forested; hilly
Season: rainy

There are at least five Mill Creeks in Oregon; this one flows from the Coast Range northeastward to the South Fork Yamhill River. The stream is quite narrow and gives one a more intimate feeling with the water than any other river the authors know. From the put-in at the upper bridge, the water is fairly gentle for about 1 mile. Then comes the class 4 Triple Drop, which should be scouted on the drive to the put-in. This rapids has been run at estimated flows of 500–700 cfs; at lower flows it appears too steep and rocky.

Just below Triple Drop the river slows on a 90-degree curve to the left, then begins a 0.2-mile accelerating drop through The Gorge with a dynamic class 4 ending. Once a boater enters this fast water in The Gorge, there is almost no turning back or getting out. There are only a few small eddies for stopping, and the rock walls are too steep to allow one to climb. To scout, first look upstream from the road for the whitewater at the lower end of The Gorge. Check for logs. Then go up the road about 300 feet and climb down to the creek. Although difficult, there is a place to get down to creek level. Walk downstream as far as possible to see if the upper part of The Gorge is obstructed. The two major drops in The Gorge are bigger than they look from here. Below The Gorge, some stretches of the river are relatively quiet. After 0.5 mile, an island is passed, and later another island.

The next watermark is a bridge, below which the road is on river left. Straight downstream from this bridge is a fast, steep drop. After another mile is the second bridge and the road is back on the right. Just below this second bridge is The Claw, class 3. At low water The Claw has a large exposed rock area in the middle and the route must be picked. At high water, the rocks are covered. In either case, the bottom hole tends to reach up and claw at the sterns of boats.

The third and last bridge is 1 mile farther downstream and warns that you are near the take-out. The water picks up speed below this last bridge and leads to the final drop, The Twist, a 3- to 4-foot blind drop that is quite fast, with a turbulent runout. Take out immediately on the left, at Mill Creek Park.

Hazards. Triple Drop is aptly named. It can be seen from the curve in the road at a pullout about 1 mile below the put-in. The Gorge is a mandatory scout, since a log block here could be fatal. The Claw, class 3, is easier than The Gorge. It can be seen from the road just a short distance below the second bridge. The Twist, the last drop, is straightforward and can be observed from the take-out at Mill Creek Park, just opposite the parking lot.

Caution: Do not continue below Mill Creek Park. Within 0.2 mile is a steep, twisting, narrow class 6 logjammed gorge.

Access. Oregon 22 crosses Mill Creek about 22 miles west of Salem. Just west of the bridge, a crossroad runs along Mill Creek. Drive upstream 2.3 miles to reach Mill Creek County Park, the take-out.

Continue upstream another 5.6 miles to a concrete bridge, the put-in. Alternate put-ins can be found along the road downstream of The Gorge.

Gauge. None exists. The flow is unregulated. The run is best at high water after heavy or sustained rains.

Rob Blickensderfer and Steve Holland

91 Mill Creek
Buell County Park to Sheridan

Class: 2- T	Length: 10 miles
Flow: 500–1,500 cfs	Character: forested; agricultural
Gradient: 21 fpm, C	Season: rainy

This run on Mill Creek is quite enjoyable at high water when numerous class 2 surfing waves develop. After 7 miles, Mill Creek empties into the South Fork Yamhill River, but because there is no access nearby, the boater must travel 3 miles down the Yamhill to the take-out in Sheridan. The 3 miles of the South Fork Yamhill, with its gradient of 5 fpm, are uneventful; but when Mill Creek has adequate water, the Yamhill rolls along, making it only a 15- or 20-minute trip.

Hazards. Trees can block the entire river, but the alert boater will find it possible to land in time.

Access. Oregon 22 crosses Mill Creek about 22 miles west of Salem. Just west of the bridge an intersecting road runs along Mill Creek. Drive downstream 0.3 mile to Buell County Park, the put-in.

To reach the take-out in Sheridan, return to Oregon 22 and go westward 5 miles to Oregon 18. Turn right and proceed 5 miles to the Sheridan exit. The boat ramp is in downtown Sheridan, one block upstream of the highway bridge on river right.

Gauge. None exists. The flow is unregulated. This run is runnable after long or hard rains.

Rob Blickensderfer

SOUTH FORK YAMHILL RIVER

92 South Fork Yamhill River
Grand Ronde to Sheridan

Class: 2(3) T	Length: 15 miles
Flow: 700–3,000 cfs	Character: wooded; flat
Gradient: 10 fpm, PD	Season: rainy

The Yamhill and most of its tributaries flow rather slowly through the floor of the Willamette Valley. Draining the coastal mountainside of the Willamette Valley, the South Fork Yamhill River wanders through the foothills and then meanders through the valley. The boater has several options of put-ins and take-outs. Runs on the lower South Fork Yamhill are described by Philip N. Jones in *Canoe Routes of Northwest Oregon* (see Bibliography).

This run keeps open canoers busy and entertains beginning kayakers with many good surfing waves. Put in at the upstream right side of the bridge on Oregon 18. Only 0.2 mile downstream is a 3-foot ledge, class 2, followed by 1 mile of riffles. At about mile 2 is an old log bridge followed by a highway bridge. About 0.5 mile farther is a small ledge-drop. After another 0.5 mile is a second highway bridge. For the next 2 miles a secondary road runs along river left.

Five miles below the put-in is a modern concrete bridge and 1 mile farther is an old suspension footbridge. A half mile farther is a 1.5-foot ledge followed in 100 yards by a 2-foot ledge; then, 0.5 mile farther is another 2-foot ledge with a channel on the right. After another 0.5 mile the river passes under a very high concrete bridge, at Oregon 18, then an older concrete bridge, at Oregon 22, that provides reasonable access.

Just below here (mile 7.5) is another ledge rapids, class 2, with a maze of willows in fast water. After 0.5 mile is a steel bridge (which might be removed in the future; it is closed) near the town of Willamina. At mile 9, in the town of Willamina, Willamina Creek enters from the left. A mile downstream is The Ledge, class 3. A sawmill on the left bank is the landmark. Fast water leads to The Ledge. To scout, land on the left. The chute about a third of the way across the river from the right bank has been run at high water.

The river gradually slows as it approaches the town of Sheridan. A mile below The Ledge (at mile 11), Mill Creek enters from the right. A mile below Mill Creek is a maze of willows in medium-fast water. Two miles farther is the railroad bridge near Sheridan and the highway bridge in downtown Sheridan (mile 14). The boat ramp is on the right, one block upstream of the highway bridge.

Hazards. The Ledge, at mile 10, is difficult to scout because the riverbanks are so steep that it is hard to get out of one's boat. A fast riffle leading to The Ledge makes it difficult to get close enough in a boat to pick a safe route. Parts of The Ledge have potentially dangerous reversals. To scout, land on the left bank above the sawmill. The far left chute, and the chute about one-third of the way from the right bank, are feasible. Other ledges can be run by experienced boaters without scouting. Probably the second-greatest difficulty is willow trees growing in the river, especially at mile 7.5.

Access. Several accesses to the river are available and the choice depends upon the section to be run. The upper put-in is on Oregon 18 about 26 miles west of McMinnville (34 miles west of Salem), where a bridge crosses the river just east of the community of Grand Ronde. There is a parking lane and a good path to the river on the west side of the river, between the highway and the railroad trestle. Other accesses are available along the road that follows the river from miles 3–5, south of Oregon 18 and 22.

Another access, a good take-out for a shorter trip, is at the Oregon 22 bridge on the downstream left bank. The bank is fairly steep, but there is a good parking area above. In Sheridan, a boat ramp is located on the east side of the river, one block upstream from the highway bridge.

Gauge. Call the River Forecast Center in Portland. The flow is unregulated.

Rob Blickensderfer

SOUTH SANTIAM RIVER AND TRIBUTARIES

93 Canyon Creek
7-Mile Bridge to South Santiam River

Class: 5+ P	Length: 7 miles
Flow: 300–1,000 cfs	Character: forested; canyon
Gradient: 112 fpm	Season: rainy

Intense, steep, blind drops, giant logjams, and undercuts all describe this run. After a reasonable beginning, the gradient increases to 302 fpm for 2 miles of class 5+ steep creek boating. The lower 3 miles is enjoyable class 3 and 4 boating. Run in about 1980 by Ken Kenniston and Mark Wade.

Hazards. Day of Judgment and Terminator are the most difficult rapids. They contain a piece of steel guardrail, as seen when scouting from the road 500 feet above the creek and 5 miles upstream from the take-out.

Access. US 20, east of Albany and Sweet Home, follows the South Santiam River. East of Cascadia State Park 1.8 miles US 20 crosses Canyon Creek. Turn north on a short spur road that leads to the confluence of Canyon Creek with the South Santiam River, the take-out.

For the put-in, follow Canyon Creek Road (NFD 2022) along Canyon Creek for 7 miles to a fork, bear right, and put in at the bridge.

Gauge. None exists. A flow of 1,200–3,500 cfs on the South Santiam River at Cascadia means adequate flow. Call Foster Dam for flow.

Jim Reed

94 Wiley Creek
Upper Bridge to Middle Bridge

Class: 4(5-)	Length: 6 miles
Flow: 300–1,500 cfs	Character: forested; canyon
Gradient: 102 fpm	Season: rainy

Despite heavy logging, Wiley Creek remains one of the most beautiful creeks in the mid-Cascades. The moss-covered canyon has some fun

The beginning of the end at Terminator Rapids, Canyon Creek (photo by Rick Starr)

class 3 and 4 rapids. The drawback is a gate on the road about 4 miles from the put-in. The gate is sometimes locked. Still, the long hike makes this stream even more enticing. Once on the water, the boater soon forgets the hike. The upper part is very technical, with a gradient of 160 fpm. The lower mile, below Cascade Falls, is through a wonderful class 3 gorge.

Three drops stand out as steeper than the others. At 0.7 mile, the first drop, Ricochet, is a twisty 7-foot flume that can be recognized by a small footbridge at the first major horizon line. It is more difficult at lower flows, and may be portaged. One mile farther is a ledge named Taint Natural. It is a three-tiered drop featuring a man-made fish ladder on river left. At levels higher than 6 feet it is class 5. Scout on river right. In 3 more miles Cascade Falls drops 8 feet through another man-made fish ladder. Scout this during the shuttle, about 1.5 miles upstream from the take-out.

Hazards. Beware of large holes at flows above 4 feet. Logs are a problem at times.

Access. From I-5 at Albany, follow US 20 eastward to Sweet Home and cross the bridge over Wiley Creek. Turn right on Wiley Creek Drive and proceed 3.7 miles to a junction. Turn right and cross Little Wiley Creek, bear right at the fork and follow the road 0.7 mile to a bridge, the take-out.

The put-in is 6 miles upstream. Continue upstream along Wiley Creek for a mile and cross it again. Drive on the road along the east bank for 2 miles to a gate. If the gate is closed, a hike is necessary. Go

3.4 miles to a falls and a footbridge, a possible put-in. Upstream another 0.4 mile at a road bridge is the upper put-in.

Gauge. Located on the right, 100 yards before the end of pavement on Wiley Creek Road.

Eric Brown and Arthur Koepsell

95 Crabtree Creek
South Fork Bridge to Larwood Park

Class: 3 T; 4	**Length: 10 miles**
Flow: 700 cfs; 2,000 cfs	**Character: forested**
Gradient: 91 fpm, C	**Season: rainy**

Crabtree Creek is located between the South Santiam River and Thomas Creek. It is easy to reach, enjoyable to run, and interesting, as the river makes the transition from mountain to valley. The upper 2 miles are tight and rocky. About 1 mile from the put-in, just past the confluence of the North Fork on the right, is an interesting class 3 plunge, worth a scout. The river sieves its way through large cobble-bar rapids in the middle section of the run, and the lower section has several large bedrock ledges that spice up the end of the run. Some of the rapids are fairly steep, and seeing the bottom of each drop is often quite difficult.

A heavy rain is needed to bring up the river to a runnable level. At bank-full flows, rocks and eddies disappear on the upper section, and are replaced by large holes, great waves, brush patches, and trees. Cobble islands create blind channels that could dead end in alder stands or possibly contain sweepers. Play spots are found everywhere on the lower part.

Hazards. At high flows the speed of the water and brushy banks eliminate most eddies. Sweepers could be a problem in this narrow streambed.

Access. To reach Crabtree Creek, take US 20 east from Albany, and then Oregon 226 east from US 20. A few miles past the Crabtree exit look for Fish Hatchery Road. Turn east and continue about 7 miles to an intersection near Larwood Park. Go to Larwood Park, the lower take-out. To reach the upper, more common take-out, bear right (south) on Meridian Road just before reaching Larwood Park. After 0.5 mile bear left on East Lacomb Road, proceed another 1.8 miles, and then make a left onto Island Inn Drive. Head upstream following the river for 0.7 mile. The take-out is located at a pullout where the river is next to the road.

To reach the put-in continue upstream for 1 mile to the first intersection. Turn right, then immediately turn left onto the private logging road. After 1.2 miles, cross the river and continue up the road another 4.1 miles to a large parking area. Just past here, turn right and head downhill about 1 mile to the North Fork Bridge; cross it, and continue up and over the ridge and back down to the South Fork Bridge, the put-in.

Gauge. Located down a steep bank at a pullout about 0.5 mile up the private logging road toward the take-out. A reading of 3 feet is about the minimum runnable. Higher is better.

Lance Stein

96 Crabtree Creek
Larwood Park to South Santiam River

Class: 2-   Length: 15.5 miles
Flow: 600 cfs   Character: rural; wooded
Gradient: 14 fpm, C   Season: rainy

The lower river contrasts dramatically with the upper as Crabtree Creek empties into lightly wooded farmland. Larwood Park, where Roaring River meets Crabtree Creek, is an attractive place further enhanced by a covered bridge. This long stretch is divided into two sections.

Section 1: Larwood Park to Oregon 226 Bridge, 8.5 miles. With a gradient of 21 fpm, the first 6 miles provide steady class 1+ and 2- water with a few play spots. The last few miles to Oregon 226 are still swift but with only occasional class 1+ riffles. An alternate put-in (the upper take-out for run 95, Crabtree Creek: South Fork to Larwood Park) a few miles upstream from Larwood Park provides a class 3- rapids and additional class 2 action. The take-out is at the Oregon 226 bridge.

Section 2: Oregon 226 Bridge to Santiam River, 9 miles. With an average gradient of 7 fpm, the current slows dramatically and the river loses some of its open feeling as the bank vegetation thickens. Herons and beavers call this section home, and occasionally surprise an otherwise silent drift. A few miles below the put-in, a barbed-wire fence extends most of the way across the river. At mile 4, under a railroad bridge, there is a class 2 ledge-drop that has a clear path down the center. Take out at the bridge. Alternatively, one can continue a few miles down the South Santiam and then the main Santiam to Jefferson, thus adding 8 miles.

Hazards. The barbed wire fence across the river a few miles below the Oregon 226 bridge is dangerous.

Access. Take US 20 east from Albany, and then Oregon 226 east from US 20. A few miles past the Crabtree exit look for Fish Hatchery Road. Turn east and continue about 7 miles to an intersection near Larwood Park; go left to the park. The Oregon 226 Bridge, the take-out for the first section and the put-in for the second section, is between Crabtree and Scio.

To reach the take-out for the second section, go 1 mile west from Crabtree on Oregon 226, then 2.5 miles north on Gilkey Road toward Jefferson to the bridge across the creek near the South Santiam River.

Gauge. None exists, but this run is generally runnable throughout the winter and spring.

Carl Landsness

97 Thomas Creek
Hall Creek to 5-Mile Bridge

Class: 3(4) T
Flow: 800 cfs
Gradient: 68 fpm, PD

Length: 5 miles
Character: forested; logging
Season: rainy

Thomas Creek drainage is situated between the North Santiam River and Crabtree Creek. It is fed by winter rain runoff. The upper section of Thomas Creek descends in pool-drop fashion through a steep-sided river valley that has limited access by road. A scenic 40-foot falls is 1 mile upstream of the put-in. A half mile below the Hall Creek put-in is a nasty chute that plunges directly into a wall from a pool trapped by several very large boulders. Scout, and possibly portage, on the left.

The next 2 miles of river provide easy class 2 and 3 rapids. The river then enters a narrow, forested canyon and descends toward the take-out in pool-drop, class 3 rapids. The second major drop occurs at mile 3, at a constriction as the river bends right, away from a 20-foot vertical wall on river left. The last of the major drops is a ledge that extends across the full width of the river, with a reversal along the foot of the ledge. This last rapids can be seen on the drive to the put-in; it has not been run by the author.

Hazards. Three ledge-drops located at 0.5, 3, and 4.5 miles below the put-in should be scouted and possibly portaged—most easily on the left. Thomas Creek flows through clear-cuts and thickly forested areas, so all drops should be scouted for logs. A hazardous section occurs at mile 2.5, where a debris dam usually blocks part of the river.

Access. From I-5 near Albany, take US 20 east and then Oregon 226 east to 9.2 miles northeast of Scio. At the intersection of Oregon 226 and Thomas Creek Road, proceed 4.6 miles up Thomas Creek Road to a side-road bridge on the right, the take-out.

To reach the put-in, continue east along the north side of the river. Turn left (north) at an intersection 2.3 miles above the take-out and 100 yards downstream of another bridge. (This could be an alternate take-out for a shorter run.) From this intersection the road ascends the north side of the river valley and temporarily leaves the river. Stay right at all intersections until reaching the ridge-top intersection, 5.2 miles from the take-out, and stay left at this intersection. Make an immediate right at the next intersection, 5.4 miles above the take-out. Descend to the river, pass the first two intersections, and turn right on one of the short access roads 6–7 miles above the take-out, or continue on until the road ends just below Hall Creek, which joins Thomas Creek from the south.

Gauge. None exists. A high runoff is needed. The water level is easily determined from the old Jordan Power Dam, located where a bridge crosses Thomas Creek 8.2 miles northeast of Scio along Oregon 226. Water flowing over the top of the unbroken section of the dam indicates a sufficient water level.

Curt Peterson

98 Thomas Creek
5-Mile Bridge to Hannah Bridge

Class: 2+(P) T   **Length:** 9.5 miles
Flow: 500 cfs   **Character:** forested; logging
Gradient: 40 fpm, PD   **Season:** rainy

From the bridge at the put-in, the river moves right along. There are some rather steep rocky drops, but no blind drops as in the upper run. The rapids seen from Oregon 226 between Hannah Bridge and Jordan Bridge are typical of the difficulty of this run. The mean river gradient is close to 30 fpm for most of the river run; however, there are two sections where the gradient is much steeper. Between miles 3 and 4 above Jordan, the river drops 100 feet, and at the remnants of the Jordan Dam, the drop is about 20 feet.

Hazards. The old Jordan Dam and the chute below should be portaged. The main current sweeps under brush in several places. This run would undoubtedly become class 3 at higher flows.

Access. For the put-in, see the take-out for run 97, Thomas Creek: Hall Creek to 5-Mile Bridge.

Hannah Bridge, described in run 99, Thomas Creek: Hannah Bridge to Gilkey Covered Bridge, is the take-out.

Gauge. None exists. Judge it for yourself at the rapids along Oregon 226, between Hannah and Jordan bridges.

Mark Hower

99 Thomas Creek
Hannah Bridge to Gilkey Covered Bridge

Class: 1+ T   **Length:** 12.5 miles
Flow: 400–1,500 cfs   **Character:** wooded; agricultural; residential
Gradient: 15 fpm, C   **Season:** rainy

This run starts at a covered bridge, passes beneath a covered bridge, and ends at a covered bridge. The narrowness of the streambed, rocky banks, and overhanging tree limbs make the run technically challenging for open double canoers. Although it passes quite a few houses and goes through the town of Scio, the stream gives the general feeling of isolation.

The first 3 miles from Hannah Bridge to the concrete bridge on Oregon 226 are the steepest. There are no named rapids, but numerous short drops. Below the concrete bridge on Oregon 226 (an alternate put-in), the stream flattens somewhat, although some careful maneuvering is still required at low water, and some waves develop at high water. About midway between the concrete bridge and the town of Scio, the stream appears to run under a large red barn. Upon closer approach, it becomes Shimanek covered bridge, 130 feet long, on Richardson's Gap Road. The approach to Scio is heralded by a drop over a small ledge, followed by a sharp right turn. Below Scio the stream becomes broader and slower for the last 3 miles to the take-out at Gilkey covered bridge, on river right.

Hazards. The stream is very simple for experienced kayakers but could prove tricky for novice kayakers. It is relatively technical but not very dynamic for experienced open canoers. The first 3 miles are much more difficult than the small ledge-drop that can be seen from the road in Scio. For comparison, this run is more technically difficult than the main Alsea River.

Access. From I-5 in Albany, take US 20 east and then Oregon 226 east to 6.5 miles east of Scio, to Camp Morrison Drive. The put-in is at Hannah Bridge just off Oregon 226 on Camp Morrison Drive. An alternate put-in is the concrete bridge on Oregon 226, 3.5 miles east of Scio.

The take-out is at Gilkey covered bridge. From Scio take Oregon 226 0.5 mile south of the downtown bridge over Thomas Creek. Take Gilkey Road west, follow the zigzags for 3.2 miles, cross a railroad track, stop at the "T" intersection, turn right, and you will see Gilkey covered bridge. The take-out is between the covered bridge and the railroad bridge on river right. (The take-out can also be reached by county roads from Crabtree or Jefferson.)

Gauge. None exists. The flow is unregulated. Judge it at the small rapids in Scio.

Rob Blickensderfer and Mark Hower

100 South Santiam River
Mountain House to Foster Lake

Class: 4(6) P   **Length: 3–19 miles**
Flow: 800–3,000 cfs   **Character: forested; canyon**
Gradient: 45 fpm, PD   **Season: rainy/snowmelt**

The upper South Santiam is magnificent. This run can be made only after substantial rainfall or snowmelt. The rapids are pool-drop and all of the more difficult rapids can be portaged. The upper South Santiam can be divided into five short sections.

Section 1: Mountain House to Trout Creek Campground, 3 miles. This class 2 portion is somewhat of a rock scraper at lower water, but is much easier than what lies ahead. Run March 17, 1975, by Bob Porter and Rob Blickensderfer.

Section 2: Trout Creek Campground to US 20 Bridge, 3 miles. Some flat water and some nice warm-up class 2 rapids are found on this section. The highlight is Longbow Falls, an abrupt 3-foot drop with a fast entry. The runout from the falls is somewhat turbulent, but free of rocks. Run March 17, 1975, by Bob Porter and Rob Blickensderfer.

Section 3: US 20 Bridge to The Monster, 2 miles. This is the most exciting stretch of whitewater on the river. Most of these rapids are peppered with large rocks and require quick judgment and skillful maneuvering or a good roll and a strong boat. As in most high Cascade rivers, logs can be a problem. The Monster, at the end of this section, is class 6 and should be portaged. This conversation piece makes a nice lunch spot. Crawdad Rapids, a small twisty drop only 20 yards below The Monster, looks easy but munches a lot of boaters. Run March 17, 1975, by Bob Porter and Rob Blickensderfer; The Monster was run in 1976 by Bob Porter.

Section 4: The Monster to Cascadia State Park, 3 miles. A mile below The Monster is Tomco Falls, adjacent to Tomco Mill. This true waterfall has a 5- to 15-foot double drop. The height of the falls is usually about 8 feet; however, the estimate varies as the boater scouts it, goes over it, and looks back up at it. As the flow increases, the height of the drop decreases. The runout is turbulent, but free of rocks and other rapids. The easiest portage is on the left.

Shortly after Tomco Falls, a series of large haystacks is followed by a small drop with a tricky hole that throws boats against the left wall. Eddies exist on both sides above the hole. Catch the right eddy and sneak the hole on the right. Shortly after this hole the river narrows to less than 10 feet. The gap can be blocked by a log, hence the name The Plug. Below The Plug is a long gorge. On this most scenic stretch, the river runs for 1 mile between 30- to 50-foot-high rock walls. Notwithstanding the proximity of the road, the boater feels incredibly isolated. The rapids in the gorge are less violent than those upstream. The gorge section ends at Cascadia Park. A gravel bar on the right, upstream from the bridge, is the take-out. Stairs and a railed path lead to the parking lot. This lovely park is complete with rest rooms, picnic areas, and a soda spring. Run in 1976 by Bob Porter, Gene Ice, and Chet Koblinsky.

Section 5: Cascadia State Park to Foster Lake, 8 miles. After a few miles of relatively easy water is Tree Farm Rapids, class 4–4+. This maze of rocks and turbulence can be scouted from Tree Farm Park during the shuttle. Just beyond the rapids is a good set of play waves. The river continues several miles without any major rapids as it flows through a deep canyon before reaching Foster Lake. Run in 1976 by Bob Porter, Gene Ice, and Chet Koblinsky.

Hazards. Several rapids should be scouted before running: Longbow Falls, The Monster, Crawdad, Tomco, The Plug, and Tree Farm. The first three can be scouted from the road. The Monster (class 6) is seen from a right turn in the road (driving upriver) about 1 mile above Tomco Mill. Portage The Monster; portages can be made on either side and require some effort. Tomco is scouted from just beyond a deserted house in a cow pasture 0.5 mile above Canyon Creek; The Plug is scouted from just upstream of Canyon Creek; and Tree Farm is scouted from the riverbank inside Tree Farm Park.

Access. US 20 east of Albany follows the South Santiam River. The Mountain House Cafe is located at Upper Soda, about 24 miles east of Sweet Home. The uppermost put-in is along the road above Mountain House where the river is visible. Above this put-in the river makes a tumultuous 40-foot drop. The Trout Creek Campground put-in is about 3 miles downstream from Mountain House. There are other

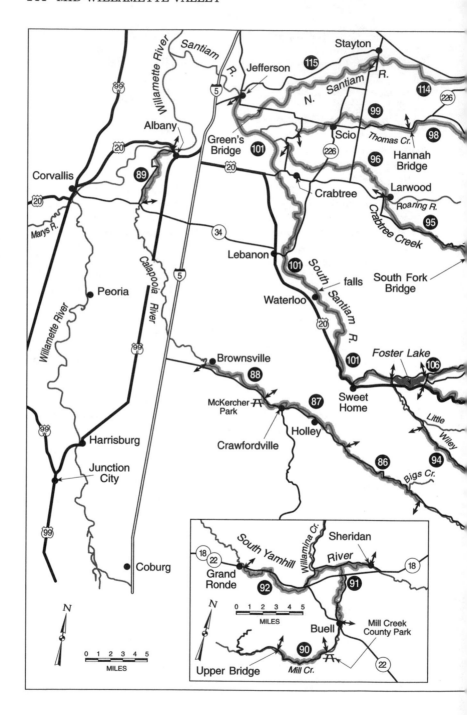

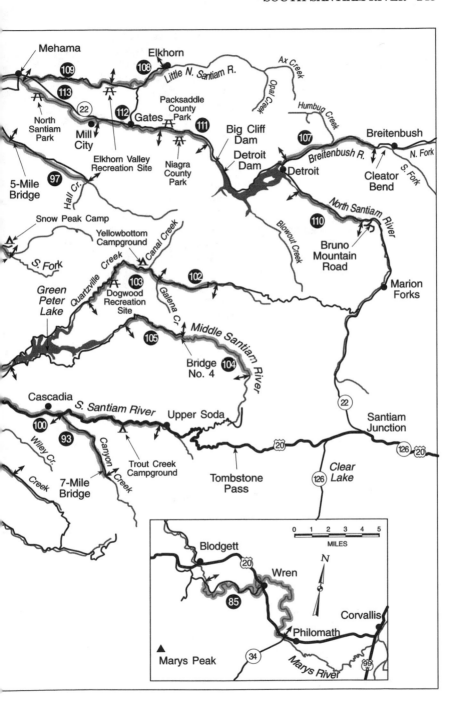

possible accesses where vehicles can be parked along the road.

The lowermost take-out is at Foster Lake on Quartzville Drive (just off US 20) just east of Foster. Alternate take-outs are on the left above Tree Farm Rapids or on the left 0.5 mile below Tree Farm Park.

Gauge. Contact Foster Dam for flow information.

Chet Koblinsky and Rob Blickensderfer

101 South Santiam River
Foster Dam to Jefferson

Class: 1 P; 2(4) P	**Length: 3–40 miles**
Flow: 900 cfs; 1,500–3,000 cfs	**Character: rural**
Gradient: 39 fpm	**Season: year-round**

Typical of rivers within the Willamette Valley are the tree-lined dirt banks, gravel bars, riffles, and sweepers on this run. The river flow is rather slow in most places, but the scenery is better than one might expect so near population centers. The run is divided into five sections that can each be run separately, each with its own put-in and take-out, or the sections can be combined as desired.

Section 1: Foster Dam to Sweet Home, 3 miles. This short section has the most action on this run, with small, evenly spaced class 1+ rapids at low flows. At high flows, canoers find an exciting class 2 run. At flood levels, kayakers find many excellent surfing waves. The put-in for this section is a pleasant park at the base of Foster Dam on river left. The most difficult rapids is the "S"-turn about 2 miles below Foster Dam. Just past the water intake for Sweet Home is a fine surfing wave as the river drops into a large pool. This is at the take-out for this section. The take-out is the boat ramp in Sweet Home on the south side of town near the bridge.

Section 2: Sweet Home to Waterloo, 11 miles. *Warning*: There is a falls at Waterloo. The put-in is the boat ramp in Sweet Home on the south side of town near the bridge. The only major rapids, Highway 20 Rapids, occurs 2 miles below Sweet Home as the river bounds off the highway embankment on the left. Large standing waves and strong eddies provide an excellent spot for practicing surfing and ferrying. Below here, there are only a few more small shelves before the river flattens out for the rest of the way to Waterloo Falls. Kayakers have run Waterloo Falls, class 4, at high water. But at low water, novices have become stranded on rocks, necessitating rescue by the county sheriff river unit. Unless you're prepared to run Waterloo Falls, take out on the left above the falls, in Waterloo Park. An alternate take-out is about 4 miles above Waterloo at the bridge on McDowell Creek Road. The nearby landowners do not want people on their property; therefore, take out near the bridge within the public right of way.

Section 3: Waterloo to Lebanon, 5 miles. The put-in is in Waterloo Park below the falls. The river flows nicely for the first 2 miles, then slows as gravel pit workings are seen and a dam is approached. The fairly difficult but *mandatory portage* of the 10-foot dam is on the right. Never attempt to run the dam in any type of craft, because the back-wash can hold bodies or rafts for hours or days. The take-out is on the left in the city park north of downtown Lebanon.

Section 4: Lebanon to Crabtree, 11 miles. Put in on the left in the city park in Lebanon. The river is class 1 at flows up to 3,000 cfs. It is characterized by flat water, gravel bars, and sweepers. A poor take-out with no boat ramp is at the bridge on Oregon 226 about 1 mile west of Crabtree. A good take-out on river left about 0.1 mile downstream of the bridge is available upon purchase of a permit from Linn County.

Section 5: Crabtree to Jefferson, 10 miles. Put in at either of the take-outs mentioned above for the previous section. This section is similar in character to the previous section. After 8 miles, the North Santiam River enters from the right and the volume increases for the last 2 miles on the Santiam River. The take-out in Jefferson is at a boat ramp on the right 100 yards downstream of the US 99E bridge.

Hazards. Rapids to watch for are those 2 miles below Foster Dam and Highway 20 Rapids. Waterloo Falls is normally portaged. The 10-foot dam below Waterloo *must* be portaged. *Never attempt to run the dam in any type of craft.*

Access. Put-ins and take-outs are given above for each section. The put-in for the entire run is a park at the base of Foster Dam on river left. From I-5 at Albany, take US 20 east to about 1 mile east of Sweet Home and follow the signs to the park, which is about 0.5 mile north.

The take-out for the entire run is in Jefferson just east of I-5 about 6 miles north of Albany. Take the Jefferson exit and look for US 99E; the take-out is at a boat ramp on the right 100 yards downstream of the US 99E bridge.

Gauge. Call the River Forecast Center in Portland or Foster Dam. The flow is controlled at Foster Dam. A minimum flow of 900 cfs is maintained during the summer.

Rob Blickensderfer

MIDDLE SANTIAM RIVER AND TRIBUTARIES

102 Quartzville Creek
Above Gregg Creek to Galena Creek

Class: 4+; 5	**Length: 6 miles**
Flow: 700 cfs; 2,000 cfs	**Character: forested; mining**
Gradient: 120 fpm, PD	**Season: rainy/snowmelt**

At the put-in the river is fairly flat and shallow, but 0.2 mile farther, around a right turn, the fun starts. The first 6-foot drop can result in a tail stand. About 100 yards downriver is a very technical lead-in to a 7-foot waterfall. These kinds of drops are typical of this run as it winds down through a steep, narrow canyon.

Quartzville Creek was first run by the author after extensive scouting from the road, which revealed a class 5 double drop consisting of two waterfalls separated by 25 feet. The two falls, named the Double Dip, give boaters something to think about while paddling the first 4 miles.

Hazards. The entire run requires scouting steep drops and looking for debris.

Access. From I-5 at Albany, take US 20 east to Sweet Home. Take the Quartzville road, which follows the river on its north side past Foster Lake to Green Peter Lake. From Green Peter Dam, drive toward Quartzville on USFS 11. The put-in is at a grassy wide spot on the left side of the road approximately 32.5 miles above the dam.

The take-out is by the bridge where Galena Creek enters Quartzville Creek, about 26.4 miles upstream from the dam.

Gauge. The flow is unregulated. Flow information can be obtained from Foster Dam.

Ron Mattson

103 Quartzville Creek
Galena Creek to Green Peter Lake

Class: 4; 5	**Length: 10 miles**
Flow: 800–3,000 cfs; 8,000 cfs	**Character: forested**
Gradient: 65 fpm, PD	**Season: rainy/snowmelt**

This lower run on Quartzville Creek is a good prelude to the upper run (see run 102, Quartzville Creek: Above Gregg Creek to Galena Creek). The lower run does not have quite the gradient and is not as intense as the upper run, but its pool-drop character still presents a challenge. Run in early 1979 by Gene Ice, Doug Tooley, Karen Wilt, Chet Koblinsky, Dave Coombs, and Ron Mattson.

At 800 cfs, stretches of relatively calm water culminate in 6- to 8-foot vertical or very technical drops; the whole run is quite rocky. At 1,500 cfs the run is at its easiest and play spots abound. Above 2,500 cfs, large waves and holes punctuate almost every rapids, but routes are fairly easy to find. At flows of 6,000–8,000 cfs, it is a hardy class 4. It has been run at 20,400 cfs, but was judged very dangerous.

Hazards. Two drops that are definitely worth scouting on the way to the put-in are at mile 24.4 and 24.8, just upstream from Yellowbottom Campground. Both have nearly vertical ledge-drops. Downstream, and within sight of the drop at mile 24.8, is another treacherous drop that should be scouted. A house-size boulder marks the spot. At low flows keep right and punch the hole between the boulder and the side of the cliff. At higher flows, a sneak chute on the extreme left is recommended.

Most of the other more difficult rapids can be scouted from the road during the drive upstream, except the several class 4 rapids below Dogwood Recreation Site that spice up this last pitch into the lake.

Access. From I-5 at Albany, take US 20 east. Driving east on US 20 past Sweet Home, take a left on the road to Quartzville at the upper end of Foster Lake. Proceed to Green Peter Dam, where the mileages start. Several put-ins are possible. The uppermost is at a bridge just upstream from the turnoff to the old Quartzville townsite. Another is at Yellowbottom Campground, just below the two ledge-drops at miles 24.4 and 24.8.

The take-out is at the first parking spot along the upper lake. For a shorter run, Dogwood Recreation Site is a convenient take-out, but some of the best rapids are between there and the lake.

Gauge. Flow can be obtained from Foster Dam.

Ron Mattson and Lance Stein

104 Middle Santiam River
Wilderness Run

Class: 3(4) T	**Length: 8 miles**
Flow: 700 cfs	**Character: forested; wilderness**
Gradient: 77 fpm, PD	**Season: rainy/snowmelt**

This is the most pristine river run in Oregon's Cascades and the only Cascade wilderness run. The trip begins in a broad basin with scenic views of neighboring mountain peaks. Initially, rapids are class 1, giving boaters a chance to take in the scenery. The tempo picks up at mile 3 with class 2 and 3 drops appearing frequently. There is a class 4 rapids, about two-thirds of the way through the trip, which is likely to have its main channel blocked with logs. After the class 4 rapids, the water is more consistently class 3.

The end of the wilderness is marked by a huge clear-cut that gives you a real appreciation of the unscarred vistas and huge trees you have just left behind. The last mile through the clear-cut contains some of the liveliest water on the run.

Hazards. There are many logs in the river and a few require portaging. The class 4 drop, because of its constricted nature, is likely to contain logs. Snow and mudslides make getting to the river difficult. Storms big enough to raise the river to a runnable level usually dump snow at Cool Camp, thereby closing roads. The Forest Service Ranger Station in Sweet Home (503-367-6108) usually knows about pass conditions.

Access. To reach the put-in, take US 20 east from Albany. Drive to Upper Soda on US 20, about 22 miles east of Sweet Home. Turn left on USFS 2041. Drive over the pass at Cool Camp (3,000 feet elevation) and down to the river. The final mile to the river was cut off by a soil slump in 1979. Park above the slump and carry down the slump to the put-in.

The take-out is located at Bridge No. 4, 7 miles upstream from the head of Green Peter Lake. (See the put-in for run 105, Middle Santiam River: Bridge No. 4 to Green Peter Lake.)

Gauge. None exists. See run 105, Middle Santiam River: Bridge No. 4 to Green Peter Lake.

Bill Ostrand

105 Middle Santiam River
Bridge No. 4 to Green Peter Lake

Class: 4   Length: 7 miles
Flow: 900–2,000 cfs   Character: logging
Gradient: 50 fpm, PD   Season: rainy/snowmelt

The Middle Santiam is a major water source for Green Peter Lake. This is a challenging run for advanced boaters. The character of the river changes according to flow levels. At 900 cfs, the rapids are continuous, featuring technically demanding boulder-dodging among steep twisting drops around blind turns. At 2,000 cfs, downstream visibility increases and scouting is necessary at only two places. This is not to say that the run becomes easier at higher flows. Boulders become holes, the speed of the river seems to double, eddies disappear, and twisting drops become screaming chutes of water dumping into waves or boat-eating holes. Scouting while driving along the river is very deceptive.

The river has several warm-up rapids for the first 0.8 mile, then action increases with a class 4 rapids that continues for 0.6 mile. More class 3–4 water follows. The 3-mile point is marked by a wooden bridge and the Ice Follies, a class 3 rapids named for Gene and George Ice, who took a swim here on the first descent.

At 4 miles, the river leaves sight of the road and enters a steep-banked gorge. This section should be scouted either on the way to the put-in or from the river. The first time that the gorge was run, a huge fir tree was jammed in the second drop. The river relaxes after the short gorge, giving boaters a chance to relax and lose some adrenalin from the bloodstream. Just above the third bridge (5.3 miles into the run), the pace briefly picks up to class 3. About 0.3 mile farther is a gauge and a good take-out for a shorter run.

The remaining 1.4 miles of river to the lake is mostly class 2. There is another short gorge (where the road swings away from the river), which has a class 3 lead-in rapids to a short steep ledge-drop. A good take-out is at the bridge where the river flows into the lake.

Hazards. The entire run presents difficulties.

Access. To get to the run, take US 20 east from Albany to Sweet Home. At Sweet Home, take a left on the road to Quartzville at the upper end of Foster Lake. Proceed to Green Peter Dam. Cross Green Peter Dam and continue along the lake to the river, 15 miles from the dam. The put-in is at the fourth bridge across the river (7 miles upstream from the lake).

Possible take-outs are at any of the three other bridges, the gauge 1.4 miles above the lake, or the bridge at the head of the lake.

Gauge. None exists. The flow is unregulated. Contact Foster Dam for the South Santiam reading at Cascadia. The Middle Santiam runs about 100–200 cfs less than the South.

Bill Ostrand

106 Middle Santiam River
Green Peter Dam to Foster Lake

Class: 4	Length: 2 miles
Flow: 2,000–4,000 cfs	Character: canyon
Gradient: 36 fpm, PD	Season: dam-controlled

This run, although short, offers some of the best whitewater available in the mid-Willamette area during the summer. Green Peter Dam has two generating turbines, each of which require 2,000 cfs. The flow from the dam is determined by electricity demand. When one turbine is in operation (also called one "unit"), the flow is up to 2,000 cfs. If both generators are operating, the flow can be up to 4,000 cfs. The water released comes from the bottom of the lake and is very cold even on a very hot day. Be aware that abrupt releases change the nature of the run very quickly.

The last three rapids—Swiss Cheese, Scrawley's Wall, and Concussion—are the major rapids on the run. Swiss Cheese consists of several ledge-drops that produce nice play waves at a flow of one unit. At two units the ledges produce many large holes. The right is the usual route. A short pool gives time for a party to regroup before the second drop, Scrawley's Wall, where the river forms standing waves and can push the boater very close to the left wall. Another short pool provides a second regrouping spot before Concussion, the grand finale. Concussion is formidable and has lived up to its name at both water levels. At one unit the central chute is recommended, but the right can be run with momentum. At two units the water is swift and turbulent. Boaters choose between trying to miss huge holes and turbulence on the right or huge holes and turbulence toward the center. The rapids ends abruptly in the slack water of Foster Lake. It's a short paddle to the take-out.

Hazards. Swiss Cheese, Scrawley's Wall, and Concussion present difficulties. Concussion can be scouted by parking 3.3 miles from US 20 and hiking down the steep bank to the river. Beware of abrupt releases from Green Peter Dam.

Access. From I-5 at Albany take US 20 east to Sweet Home. At Sweet Home take a left onto the road to Quartzville at the upper end of Foster Lake. The take-out is 2.6 miles from US 20 on the road to Quartzville. A wide turnout on the right near a gate in the fence that parallels the road gives access to the river.

To reach the put-in, continue up the road along the river toward Green Peter Dam. Park at the first road to the right, 0.5 mile before the dam. Because the gate is locked, boats must be carried down the road. At the second gate, climb the fence and continue 50 yards to the river.

Gauge. The schedule for water releases can be obtained 1–2 days in advance from Foster Dam.

Ron Mattson

NORTH SANTIAM RIVER AND TRIBUTARIES

107 Breitenbush River
Cleator Bend Campground to Detroit Reservoir

Class: 4 T	**Length: 8 miles**
Flow: 800–2,000 cfs	**Character: forested; canyon**
Gradient: 80 fpm, PD	**Season: rainy/snowmelt**

The Breitenbush starts from the crest of the Cascades north of Mount Jefferson and is one of the major tributaries of the North Santiam River. This run is typical of Cascade rivers, with high gradient, crystal-clear water, steep forested banks, and numerous logs. The Breitenbush has a short season, during the spring snowmelt or after a heavy fall rain. For most of the winter, the road and ground are covered with snow.

This run is rated class 4 because the drops are so closely spaced and require technical precision to run, although the individual drops are class 2 and 3. It might be said that the whole is greater than the sum of its parts. The pools are short and the route is often not apparent until the boater is almost at the brink of a drop, and sometimes not visible even then, thus the necessity for scouting. The run requires technical maneuvering and a reliable roll. This stretch can be divided into two sections: Cleator Bend Campground to the road bridge, and the road bridge to Detroit Reservoir.

Section 1: Cleator Bend Campground to Road Bridge, 6 miles. This upper section has tight and technical rapids, with many class 3 drops. There are short pools between the rapids and many eddies. Chutes are narrow, twisting, swift, and deep. More than half of the significant drops cannot be seen from the road, but all can be scouted from the river. There are several blind corners that should be scouted for logs by at least one member of the party. The author has run the first 0.9 mile below Cleator Campground only once, because two portages are required around large logs. To avoid these portages, put in just below The Slot, down a steep trail from a very small roadside rock quarry. Near the road bridge, the geology changes; the river becomes broader with frequent stretches of flat bedrock. The river volume and velocity increase significantly with the addition of Humbug Creek, 1 mile above the bridge.

Section 2: Road Bridge to Detroit Reservoir, 2 miles. In the first 2 miles there is one class 4 drop, Barbell, and numerous class 3 gems, including Woo-Man-Chew. Barbell Rapids should be scouted (not without difficulty) on the drive upriver, 2.4 miles above Detroit, since it is even more difficult to scout from the river. It is a complex, pushy, class 4 boulder garden, dominated by a huge barbell-shaped rock that lies parallel to the current, in the middle of the river. This rapids was blocked by a huge logjam in 1991. A half mile below Barbell is Woo-Man-Chew, a 5-foot waterfall into a deep pool. Scout on the left by landing at the low concrete structure. This drop can be seen at a distance by looking downstream from the road. The gauge is 2.3 miles below the bridge and marks the end of the difficult rapids. When Detroit Reservoir is full, the lake reaches just above the small unnamed Forest Service campground 0.5 mile below the gauge. When the reservoir is low, the rapids continue past the town of Detroit.

Hazards. This river requires a class 4 level of concentration and quick reactions. A quick reliable roll is mandatory. Logs are always a threat, especially in the narrower upper section, so be sure to scout all blind drops!

Access. From I-5 near Salem, take Oregon 22 east to the town of Detroit, at the east end of Detroit Reservoir. From Detroit, take USFS 46 east along the Breitenbush Arm. The take-out is at the marina or, preferably, at a Forest Service campground 0.5 mile upstream.

Continue up USFS 46 to one of the put-ins: the main road bridge 3.3 miles above Detroit; a dirt logging road that goes to the river 5.4 miles above Detroit; or a small quarry 8.1 miles above Detroit, where one can park on the left and put in down a steep bank just below The Slot Rapids. If there is sufficient water and no logs, the easiest put-in is at Cleator Bend Campground, 9 miles above Detroit.

Gauge. Contact the Detroit Dam or the River Forecast Center in Portland. Optimal flow is estimated at 1,000–1,200 cfs.

Rich Brainerd

108 Little North Santiam River
Salmon Falls to Elkhorn Valley Recreation Site

Class: 2(3) **Length: 6.5 miles**
Flow: 800 cfs **Character: forested; valley**
Gradient: 30 fpm, PD **Season: rainy/snowmelt**

The headwaters of the Little North Santiam River include the west slopes of the Bull of the Woods Wilderness Area, the Elkhorn Mining District, and the magnificent old-growth forest along Opal Creek. From these beginnings, this crystal-clear river pours over 25-foot Salmon Falls and into the Elkhorn Valley. From the put-in below Salmon Falls, it flows through much of the valley as class 1 with occasional technical class 2 rapids through rock gardens.

However, at rivermile 2.5 it enters the Slot, a 15-foot-wide entrance to a narrow basalt canyon. About 200 feet ahead of the Slot, the river divides around a steep gravel bar. The two flows converge at the Slot and roll off the cliffs with pulsating flows. At a low flow of 800 cfs, the Slot is class 3. At higher flows this rapids could be extremely difficult.

Below the bridge in Elkhorn at mile 3, the river slows as it passes through the broad Elkhorn Valley. The valley narrows at mile 5 as Elkhorn Valley Recreation Site appears on the left. For the next 1.5 miles the action picks up and includes two class 3 drops in the last 0.5 mile. These last two drops can be avoided by taking out at the campground on the left above the first class 3 drop.

Hazards. The authors know no boaters who have seen the Slot at high flows, but expect it to increase in difficulty substantially at flows of 1,000–3,000 cfs. It is not possible to portage the Slot because it requires a carry of about 0.5 mile around private homes and cliffs. The class 3 ledge- and boulder-drop at the end of the run can be scouted from the take-out. It is about 100 yards upstream from the entrance gate at the lower end of the recreation site.

Access. From I-5 near Salem, take Oregon 22 east to Mehama. Turn left at the flashing light 0.7 mile east of Mehama onto North Fork Road. The take-out is at the Elkhorn Valley Recreation Site, about 10 miles up this road.

Continue upstream to the put-in at Salmon Falls County Park on the right just below Salmon Falls, 3 miles above the bridge in the community of Elkhorn.

Gauge. See run 109, Little North Santiam River: Elkhorn Valley Recreation Site to North Santiam River.

Steve Cramer and Arnie Adams

109 Little North Santiam River
Elkhorn Valley Recreation Site to Mehama

Class: 3(4) T	**Length: 10 miles**
Flow: 750–2,500 cfs	**Character: forested; canyon**
Gradient: 39 fpm, PD	**Season: rainy/snowmelt**

This run offers a variety of rapids in crystal-clear water. The road appears only occasionally and there is a feeling of isolation on upper parts of this run, although many cabins stand along the lower section.

Before putting in at Elkhorn Valley Recreation Site, look at the two class 3 rapids visible from the campground road. Then decide whether to put in above or below. Class 2 rapids continue for 3 miles downstream to the concrete bridge, another possible put-in.

A half mile below the bridge, the river narrows and drops to the right. Just below the drop is a large rock wall extending almost to the left bank, which creates a large "S"-turn. This is easy in low water but formidable in flood.

Just downstream is the most difficult rapids on the run, affectionately known as Troll's Teeth, class 4. As the name suggests, this is a boulder garden with no clean route. At lower water levels, it is very technical and at flood becomes a mass of holes and keepers to eat you. Approach cautiously and stop to scout on the left before the river disappears among several large rocks. At least one tree or log is usually caught in this rapids. Portage if necessary along the left bank and put in about 100 yards downstream in a large pool. The normal route is to enter on the right and go far right behind the huge boulder and then to the left. Below Troll's Teeth is a steep, fast class 3 rapids.

The remaining rapids on this run are quite straightforward and can be run by an experienced boater without scouting. A particularly long and enjoyable section of rapids at the Little North Fork County Park is preceded by a large curving undercut cliff on the left, followed by a nice play spot with a fast "V" with green waves and generous eddies.

Downstream you'll pass under a bridge. At the next rapids the river narrows to the left and drops sharply in an "S"-turn. The large hole at the bottom of the drop is difficult to miss but usually can be punched. The rest of this run bounces pleasantly along until meeting the North Santiam River. Turn right here, please! and play on the nice surfing waves. It's only a short distance to the take-out boat ramp under the bridge in Mehama. Run in about 1970 by Scott and Margie Arighi and others.

Hazards. Everyone, regardless of experience, should scout Troll's Teeth. Logs and debris from floods frequently plug the channels.

Access. The river is about 18 miles northeast of Salem on Oregon 22. To reach the put-in, take Oregon 22 to Mehama and turn left at the flashing light 0.7 mile east of Mehama. Boaters can put in at Elkhorn Valley Recreation Site or at the concrete bridges over the river at miles 9 and 6, respectively, from the Oregon 22 turnoff. To miss the more difficult rapids on the upper section, put in at North Santiam Park or, better yet, at a bend in the river 1.2 miles above the park.

Take-outs include North Santiam Park and the boat ramp under the Lyons–Mehama bridge over the North Santiam.

Gauge. Call Foster Dam. Several days of good rain or snowmelt are needed. A good spot to check the flow is at the bridge on Oregon 22 over the Little North Santiam, 0.8 mile east of Mehama. Look downstream; the visible rapids indicates the condition of the shallowest rapids of the run. Also look at where the concrete arch joins the concrete base on the downstream west side of the bridge. The water should be within 1 foot of the joint, or higher.

Mick Evans

110 North Santiam River
Bruno Mountain Road to Detroit Lake

Class: 3(4); 3+(4)   Length: 7 miles
Flow: 1,000 cfs; 1,700 cfs   Character: forested
Gradient: 67 fpm, C   Season: rainy/snowmelt

With its headwaters in the Mount Jefferson Wilderness, this upper stretch of the North Santiam River is usually runnable from the time the snow begins to melt (usually late March or early April) until late spring. It may also be runnable after several days of hard rain during the fall or winter. It is not uncommon to tramp through snow at the put-in. In any season the water is always very cold.

Boaters find a continuous gradient that offers constant action throughout the run. Play spots are abundant. At 1,700 cfs the river is not very technical, but eddies are small. At 1,300 cfs the drops become more technical but eddies are more numerous. On a clear day spectacular views of Mount Jefferson reward boaters who turn around and look upstream.

The first 0.5 mile offers a good warm-up of class 2 and 3 water. The first major rapids, Ricochet, the most demanding of the run, is a class 3+–4 boulder garden, at mile 0.5 and can be scouted from the road during the shuttle. Some boaters prefer to put in below Ricochet Rapids at Whispering Falls Campground, another 0.3 mile downstream. The next 3 miles of river are class 2+–3. After the first bridge, which is about halfway through the run, the river becomes class 3+ with some significant drops and pushy water. Some good rapids occur at the lumber mill in Idanha, but the paddling and playing along this stretch are so much fun that one barely notices the mill. All the rapids can be scouted from the river by eddy hopping. The road is always nearby on river right, but it never seems obtrusive. Fun rapids continue to the take-out.

Warning: When the lake is low, a steep class 5 rapids between the take-out and the lake becomes exposed.

Hazards. Cold water, possible logs, and the class 4 rapids near the beginning are the difficulties to watch for.

Access. To reach the take-out, take Oregon 22 east from Salem and drive up to the head of Detroit Lake. Look for a log-scaling station on the right. Turn right off the highway here and drive downstream on a dirt road for about 200 yards to the primitive campground at the road's end.

To find the put-in, return to the highway and drive upstream 7 miles to Bruno Mountain Road, on the right. Put in under the bridge.

Gauge. Located 1 mile above the take-out. Call Detroit Lake for the flow of the North Santiam into the lake. A good level is 4 feet or about 1,500 cfs. The river has been run at 900 cfs, except Ricochet Rapids was too low to run. At flows higher than 2,000 cfs the difficulty may increase.

Laurie Pavey

111 North Santiam River
Big Cliff Dam to Packsaddle County Park

Class: 3(5) P	**Length: 5 miles**
Flow: 2,000–3,200 cfs	**Character: forested**
Gradient: 26 fpm, PD	**Season: year-round**

The North Santiam River is regulated by Detroit and Big Cliff dams above Gates. The numerous class 2, and several class 3 and 4, rapids make this run, known as Niagara, a fun and exciting stretch of whitewater. The two named rapids in this stretch are The Narrows and Niagara.

The Narrows, class 3+–4, is about 0.8 mile downstream from the put-in. It is preceded by a class 3 entry rapids with a large eddy on the right at the bottom. The current continues on the left side and funnels into The Narrows, a 100-yard-long constriction with a large drop. The upper section has a large wave across it, followed by a diagonal hole, very turbulent water, and a good pool at the bottom. The exposed rocks are covered at higher water. At low discharges, experts advise portaging this rapids. Scout this one before running.

Niagara is a twisting class 5 drop at Niagara County Park. The entrance, at which the river squeezes to a width of merely 5 feet, is followed by a swirling pool that leads into a turbulent snake of water and a drop into a huge, potentially dangerous boiling pool. The first time this rapids was attempted by a group of WKCC boaters, there was a log caught in the pool. Boaters timed their approach to miss the log as it circled. Boaters should be prepared for a difficult rescue if a person swims. The boiling pool recirculates along a cliff and makes self-rescue impossible. Niagara becomes more difficult at higher flows. Always scout Niagara.

There are several other memorable rapids and features in this stretch. Below Niagara, ender holes can be found at some discharges. About 2 miles below Niagara is Packsaddle Dam. The 12-foot dam is used to divert salmon and steelhead for capture to supply eggs for fish hatcheries. The reversal at the bottom is dangerous, and reinforcing irons are embedded at the bottom. This is a *mandatory portage*. Portage on the right. Just a couple hundred yards below the dam is Packsaddle County Park on the right.

Hazards. The Narrows and Niagara are technically demanding rapids that should be scouted. Portage around Packsaddle Dam.

Access. From I-5 near Salem, take Oregon 22 east past Mill City. The take-out at Packsaddle County Park is about 3 miles east of Gates on Oregon 22.

Proceed to the put-in at Big Cliff Dam about 5 miles east on Oregon 22. Stop at Niagara County Park to scout Niagara. About 1 mile east of Niagara there is an abandoned gas station on the left. The Narrows is found by scouting down the bank opposite this.

Gauge. Located at Mehama. Contact the River Forecast Center in Portland or Foster Dam for flow information.

George Ice

112 North Santiam River
Packsaddle County Park to Mill City

Class: 2+(3); 3; 4	Length: 6.5 miles
Flow: 750 cfs; 1,500 cfs;	Character: forested; residential
4,500+ cfs	Season: year-round
Gradient: 27 fpm, PD	

This run is one of the more popular boating trips in Oregon. Riffles immediately below the put-in can be used to warm up. Turning the corner, the riffles lead into a small rapids. Following a pool is a fun class 2 rapids that leads into a narrow chute. It has narrow eddies on both sides and can be very turbulent.

The next rapids finishes with an excellent play spot, referred to as The Swirlies. It is identified by rock formations on the left and a very large eddy on the right. The waves at this spot make excellent surfing. The runout is extremely turbulent, with small whirlpools and collapsing swirls. These Swirlies offer an excellent and difficult practice site for the ol' river roll.

After passing under the bridge at Gates, a series of mild rapids begins. At low discharges, the first rapids below the Gates bridge is rocky. A mile farther is Fake Spencer's Hole which, from upstream, looks quite like Spencer's Hole a short distance downstream. Both rapids give the appearance of big holes in the river between rocky shorelines. Spencer's Hole is one of the famous rapids on this river. At low flows it has an exposed rock in the middle of the drop; at higher flows a hole develops behind the rock and another hole develops farther down on the left. There is a pool below this drop, and occasionally boaters take out here. A short, steep trail leads to a road that goes to Gates.

About 0.2 mile below Spencer's Hole is Carnivore, hidden on the left side of an island. Jim Oliver named this small, twisting, frothy beast when it was hungry and "ate" him. There are several mild rapids and play spots between Carnivore and Mill City. A nice rapids that develops big waves at high water is located at the approach to Mill City. A big eddy on the right below the rapids offers an easy take-out, especially for drift boats. From here it is only 200 yards to Mill City Falls, which is usually scouted by walking out on the highway bridge before the trip begins. Otherwise, one can back-paddle while looking over the drop. The middle-left of the drop usually has a clear chute, and there is a slot on the far right. The take-out is at a boat ramp on the right below the bridge. Another take-out is at the boat ramp in Fishermans Bend Park, 1 mile downstream, but it is closed in winter.

Hazards. Spencer's Hole and Mill City Falls should be approached with caution.

Access. Oregon 22 east of Salem follows the North Santiam River. The put-in is at Packsaddle County Park about 3 miles east of Gates.

The normal take-out is at the small park (with changing rooms) in Mill City, at the north end of the bridge. The optional take-out above Mill City Falls is reached by driving through the paved parking lot at the north end of the bridge and continuing along a short dirt road to the turnaround. The third optional take-out is at Fishermans Bend Park, 1.5 miles downstream from Mill City.

Gauge. Located at Mehama. Call Foster Dam or the River Forecast Center in Portland. At 10,000 cfs, the maximum winter discharge desired by Big Cliff Dam, the current and rapids on the river require expert paddling. Summer levels of about 1,000 cfs are much less demanding. A flow of about 3,000 cfs is optimal for playing.

George Ice

113 North Santiam River
Mill City to Mehama

Class: 2; 3   **Length: 8.5 miles**
Flow: 1,000 cfs; 3,000 cfs   **Character: wooded; residential**
Gradient: 23 fpm, PD   **Season: year-round**

A pleasant trip is found below Mill City. The rapids are less demanding than those upstream, but should still be respected. Several broken dories, canoes, and kayaks have been observed along this stretch. The rapids tend to become rocky at flows below 1,500 cfs.

Several rapids have standing waves that can be surfed even at 1,100 cfs. A favorite play spot is at North Santiam Park, 2 miles below Fishermans Bend Park. A small ledge provides boaters with a good place to practice surfing, "S"-turns, and rolls. The ledge may be avoided by running far right. Near the end of the trip, John Neal Memorial Park, with a boat ramp, is seen on the left and the Little North Santiam River enters from the right. Along here excellent surfing waves develop at flows of 2,000 cfs or more. Then the river splits. The left channel has a nice wave for one last fling at surfing. The right channel is also runnable, with the current plowing into a low wall to produce a nice quick turn. As the channels rejoin, the Lyons–Mehama bridge at the take-out comes into view.

Hazards. The ledge at North Santiam Park is typical of the maximum difficulty.

Access. There are three optional put-ins, two in Mill City and one at Fishermans Bend Park, which are the take-outs described in run 112, North Santiam River: Packsaddle County Park to Mill City.

The take-out is under the bridge on Oregon 226, between Lyons and Mehama. This is about 0.5 mile south of the junction of Oregon 22 and 226. The take-out is reached from the southwest corner of the bridge. An alternate take-out is available at John Neal Memorial Park at 13th Street in east Lyons.

Gauge. Located at Mehama. The flow can be obtained from Foster Dam or the River Forecast Center in Portland.

George Ice

114 North Santiam River
Mehama to Stayton

Class: 2- P   **Length: 10.5 miles**
Flow: 1,000–2,000 cfs   **Character: agricultural**
Gradient: 20 fpm, C   **Season: year-round**

The coniferous forests found along the upper reaches of the North Santiam gradually shift to foothill and farmland vegetation along this run. After about 0.2 mile of smooth water below the put-in, the river begins a series of mild rapids. Following these rapids is a nice play spot on the left known as Beginner's Hole. A particularly troublesome chute for beginners occurs just before a group of three power lines comes into view. The chute flows from left to right directly into the bank and has a strong, swirling eddy on the inside of the turn. Another 0.2 mile below the power line is the largest rapids on this run, which should be run on the far left. Below this drop is the traditional lunch stop on the right bank. In the late summer wild blackberries can be added to the lunch menu.

Below the lunch stop are a number of class 1 rapids and riffles. Following a mild rapids, farmland fringed by bird boxes can be seen on the left bank. Below the bird boxes the river splits and there is a dam in the left channel. The right channel looks inviting but should not be taken because it becomes an irrigation canal with very brushy banks and no take-outs. The trip continues in the left channel below the dam, so a portage is required. At 1,100 cfs boaters can paddle to the far right of the dam and carry over it. At higher flows boaters should take out on the levee at the right of the dam. Salmon and steelhead can sometimes be seen jumping in the fish ladder or up the dam.

The rapids below the dam are rocky and swift. Beyond, the river becomes rockier and shallower. A few of the rapids have current moving into brush.

Hazards. Portage around the dam. The class 2 rapids below the power-line crossing is the most difficult.

Access. Take Oregon 22 east from Salem. The put-in is a boat landing located beneath the bridge that connects Mehama and Lyons, just off Oregon 22 on Oregon 226. During the summer this popular boat landing can be very congested with anglers, rafters, and drifters.

The shuttle to the take-out is along Oregon 22 to the Stayton turnoff; take this road and go south through Stayton. The take-out is at the boat ramp at the south end of the bridge that crosses the North Santiam in Stayton.

Gauge. Located at Mehama. Contact Foster Dam or the River Forecast Center in Portland.

George Ice

115 North Santiam River
Stayton to Jefferson

Class: 1+   **Length: 19 miles**
Flow: 1,200 cfs   **Character: rural**
Gradient: 17 fpm, C **Season: year-round**

Below Stayton, the North Santiam flattens as it winds through farmland and among stands of alders and cottonwoods. The scenery is very pleasant: wide gravel bars lined with trees, with almost no buildings in sight. At low water the banks could be characterized as class 1 with continuous lunch spots. There is little whitewater on this run, but a number of sharp turns, a few snags, and some turbulent water require boaters to pay attention. The relatively flat water and high frequency of eddies along the shore make this stretch excellent for beginning canoers and kayakers who can control their crafts.

The current is continuous through this run except for a long pool beginning about 2 miles above Jefferson. About 7 miles below the put-in the river splits and winds through many channels around a number of islands. This stretch has a well-earned reputation for becoming blocked by sweepers. There is an alternate access to the river at Green's Bridge, 14 miles below the put-in and 5 miles above the take-out. About halfway between Green's Bridge and the take-out, the South Santiam flows in from the left, and the river becomes the main stem Santiam.

Hazards. There are none in particular, but be alert for downed trees.

Access. All three accesses to the river on this run have well-developed boat ramps. To reach the take-out, take exit 238 off I-5 between Albany and Salem and follow US 99E 2.5 miles east to Jefferson. The take-out is about 100 yards downstream of the Jefferson bridge, on river right.

To reach the put-in, go back toward the Jefferson bridge and turn south on the road to Scio. About 2.5 miles east of Jefferson this road crosses Green's Bridge, under which, on river left, is an alternate access to the river. Continue on this road to Scio and take the road north from Scio to Stayton. The put-in is at the boat ramp on the southwest side of the bridge just south of Stayton.

Gauge. Located at Mehama. Contact Foster Dam or the River Forecast Center in Portland. The run begins to get a little bumpy at flows below 1,500 cfs.

John Westall

LOWER WILLAMETTE VALLEY AND CLACKAMAS RIVER

ABIQUA CREEK

116 Abiqua Creek
Abiqua Falls to Abiqua Road

Class: 2(3)   Length: 7.5 miles
Flow: 400 cfs   Character: forested; residential
Gradient: 80 fpm, C   Season: rainy

Abiqua Creek is in the watershed between Butte Creek on the north and Silver Creek to the south. All are tributaries of the Pudding River, which flows into the Molalla just before the latter reaches the Willamette. Abiqua Creek's gradient and drainage area are similar to both sister streams, but it doesn't have as much action as either of them. The gradient is fairly constant, with some pool-drop. Most rapids are rock gardens.

Above the recommended put-in, Abiqua Falls plunges over a 75-foot sheer drop into a pool. The gradient above the falls is steeper, up to 200 fpm, but there isn't a put-in far enough upstream to make the portage around the falls worthwhile.

The first 1.5 miles of this run are class 2, with a few strategically placed sweepers to liven things up. The first class 3, Hank's Mistake, has a large padded boulder near the bottom center. At the recommended flows, far right is advised, as the current pushes left all the way from the top. There are some nice holes and wave action just after the next island.

A mile later is Pink Bridge Rapids. Pinky is a long boulder garden with a left bend halfway through, where the bridge comes into view. A quick scout for logs is prudent. From here down, cabins and homes are occasionally seen, rapids diminish, and in one place the left bank consists of a huge pile of sawdust. About 1.8 miles below the recommended take-out (between mileposts 8 and 9), there's a dam that would be difficult to portage, mainly because of steep banks with barbed-wire fences at the top. Run on October 30, 1982, by Craig Colby, Hank Hays, and Murry Johnson.

Hazards. Getting to the put-in is probably the hardest part of the run. On the river, Hank's Mistake and Pink Bridge Rapids are the most difficult.

Access. From Oregon 99E in Salem, take Oregon 213 east to Silverton. About 3 miles north of Silverton on Oregon 213 is a blinking yellow light at Abiqua Road Northeast. Take Abiqua Road southeast about 6.25 miles east to a concrete bridge over Abiqua Creek. Just upstream is a rocky turnout that makes a good parking spot for the take-out.

To get to the put-in, continue upstream another mile to the end of the pavement at a green steel bridge. Proceed 2 miles from the green bridge, keeping right where the main gravel road swings left. In about another 0.2 mile, several driveways take off in all directions. Go straight on what looks like the main road. This is where the road gets bad. Three and one-half miles later, after a bone-jarring, oil-pan–crunching ride, is a grassy pullout on the right. From here a well-defined hiking trail takes off upstream, ending at the base of the falls in less than 0.5 mile. There are two short steep sections in the 0.25 mile down to the creek. You can continue up the road for a bit to the top of the falls, but the trails to it aren't as easy to find.

Gauge. None exists. If you don't mind the rockiness of the boulder garden at the take-out, go ahead and try the run.

Hank Hays

BUTTE CREEK

117 Butte Creek
Fault Line to Oregon 213

Class: 3(4-) T, P	**Length: 7.5 miles**
Flow: 200–800 cfs	**Character: forested**
Gradient: 60 fpm, PD	**Season: rainy**

This run on Butte Creek flows through scenic forested mountain foothills that are in abrupt contrast to the rural countryside found near Mount Angel and Woodburn. It has considerable variety for a small stream: ledge-drops, a few slots, "S"-curves, rock gardens, a gorge, one slide, a couple of logs, and two dams. An alternate take-out at the park in Scotts Mills shortens the trip by 2 miles.

At a bridge 1 mile below the put-in, there is a 5-foot drop. It's a nose cruncher at low water, but at higher water is less of a problem. A log directly below the bridge requires a difficult limbo. The local property owners let boaters walk this drop over their land on the left; in turn, boaters leave the log in place to form the locals' summer swimming hole.

One mile below the bridge is a difficult rapids that should be scouted from the right bank. The rock garden at the top leads into fast water that forms two large riverwide waves, funnels down to 20 feet wide, goes over a 4-foot drop, and bashes onto a rock on the right. The rock garden below is technical at low water. Boaters who choose to portage these two rapids should stay on the bank so as not to disturb property owners.

After another mile is a tight "S"-turn, first to the left, then right. A rock at the top splits the river; the right channel is recommended but beware of a log at the bottom. Otherwise, portage on the right. Scotts Mills Pond, 2 miles farther, is a good take-out for a short run. The dam is a *mandatory portage*. The fish ramp is class 3, but would only be class 2 if all the brambles hanging overhead were eliminated.

A rapids with numerous large holes can be scouted by looking upstream from the Scotts Mills bridge. Midway between the Scotts Mills bridge and Oregon 213 is a second dam with a fish ramp on the left that makes an abrupt right turn. The water smashes head-on into a raised ledge before connecting with the main channel. Those who feel they must run the fish ramp should intentionally miss the right turn, run sideways while keeping the bow pointed downstream, and high brace at the bottom off the ledge. Otherwise, portage on the left.

Hazards. The 5-foot drop at the first bridge, the 4-foot drop 1 mile farther down, and the "S"-turn rapids should be scouted or portaged. Two dams must be portaged or the fish ramps run as described above.

Access. From Oregon 99E in Salem, take Oregon 213 east to Silverton. The take-out is on Oregon 213 5.2 miles northwest of Silverton at Jack's Bridge. Alternatively, 4.5 miles from Silverton turn right onto Mount Angel–Scotts Mills Road and proceed 2.5 miles to the park and bridge at Scotts Mills.

From there to the put-in, drive 0.1 mile north of Scotts Mills bridge to Maple Grove Road, which runs east, and turn right. Butte Creek Road angles off to the right 0.1 mile later. Follow it 4.5 miles to a turn-off on the right by some houses. This road crosses a brook and looks down on Butte Creek after 0.5 mile. Use a throw rope to put in down the steep embankment. Local residents prefer that scouting be done from the creek rather than from the road. Please respect their wishes.

Gauge. Located at Monitor Bridge, on the downstream west bank. Minimum flow is 5.5 feet. Also have a look upstream from the Scotts Mills bridge. If these rocks are wet, the others upstream should also be wet. Usually 3 days of rain fill the creek to a fair level.

Andreas Mueller

MOLLALA RIVER AND TRIBUTARIES

118 North Fork Mollala River
Bridge to Molalla River

Class: 5 P, T	Length: 6 miles
Flow: 300–1,200 cfs	Character: gorge; logging
Gradient: 200 fpm, PD	Season: rainy

This river is on property owned by Cavenham Forest Industries. In April 1988, a strongly reinforced closed gate was installed less

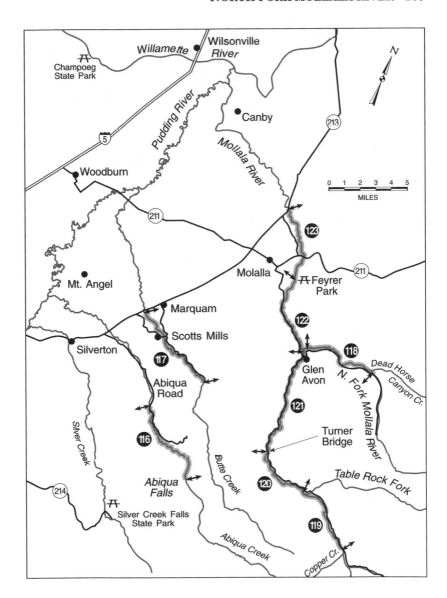

than 1 mile above the take-out. The property is patrolled by an armed security guard. Permission to enter must be obtained from Cavenham Forest Industries. Do not trespass.

Although the land has been logged in this magnificent canyon, the river has so much action that boaters don't notice the clear-cuts. This run should be made with someone who is familiar with the river, because there are many blind turns with technical and congested entrances and exits. In places the river is only about two boat lengths wide. The river consists of continuous class 4+ water, two rapids that are usually portaged, and blind turns that require scouting. The wild nature of the cliffs make scouting extremely difficult and time-consuming, if not impossible. The road high on the river-left cliff would be difficult to reach if a walk out were necessary.

From the put-in at the bridge, it is 0.5 mile to the first portage at a rapids known as Laughing Teeth of Death (LTD). The area around LTD can be scouted from the road on the way to the put-in. Just above LTD is a tricky drop around an island. Eddy out on the left for the carry around LTD. It is possible to put in below LTD by lining boats down the bank from the road.

The hardest rapids on this run is immediately below LTD. The rapids consists of three parts, with a pool below. The river then flows between several islands. The main drop is on the left, but is choked with boulders and followed by a log blocking most of the channel.

After two short drops is a rapids known as The Notches. This rapids is probably one of the most dangerous drops on any river because it looks innocent from above. There is an easy portage on the right. Be sure to eddy out high. The author does not know of anyone who has run this drop recently, although exciting adventures relating to this drop are told by early paddlers.

Following The Notches, the river eases to class 3 for about 1 mile, then without any transition resumes its class 4+–5- character. After several bends along cliffs, the river narrows into a canyon about two boat lengths wide. The water here is not difficult and the scenery is beautiful. One last big drop appears around a bend to the left. The remaining 4 miles to the main Mollala are runnable, but may be anticlimactic after the upper run.

Hazards. Portage LTD and The Notches and scout what you can't see.

Access. See run 121, Molalla River: Turner Bridge to Glen Avon Bridge. Shortly beyond the North Fork Mollala River crossing, turn left on Slais Road. Continue along this road, past the end of the pavement and an abandoned old gate. About 300 yards beyond this gate, park on the left where there is a blocked road that leads down to the river. The take-out is at this former bridge.

To get to the put-in, continue upstream to the locked gate. Obtain permission from the property owners before proceeding. From here it is about a 4-mile walk to LTD. Line boats down below LTD or continue to the first road to the left (about 0.3 mile), and cross the river in about 0.2 mile.

Gauge. None exists. The river is runnable only a few times a year after heavy rains, usually when the Feyrer County Park gauge on the Mollala River is between 3.25 and 4.75 feet. The gauge at Three Lynx on the Clackamas should be 3,000 cfs and rising or 4,000 cfs and falling.

Harvey Lee Shapiro

119 Mollala River
Copper Creek to Turner Bridge

Class: 3(4) T	**Length: 6.5 miles**
Flow: 500 cfs	**Character: canyon; forested**
Gradient: 60 fpm	**Season: rainy**

This run offers a variety of rapids winding through a deep canyon with pretty views of a moss-laden forest. Being near the upper reaches of the Molalla, this run is runnable only after several days of heavy rain. The put-in at Copper Creek Bridge offers easy access to the river. There are two rapids that need scouting and this can be done from the road en route to the put-in.

The first major rapids, Dungeon, is about 2 miles from the put-in. The longest rapids on the run, it consists of a boulder garden, several diagonal waves, and a tight "S"-turn with several well-placed holes. Scout this rapids from the road at a point where the road bank drops off several hundred feet. The next major rapids is about 0.5 mile downstream. Lightning Lonnie, named in memory of a firefighter who loved the river, has two distinct parts: a 6-foot falls, followed by a twisting drop along a wall. The falls should be negotiated by staying far right or far left, as the middle can cause a vertical pin. The next part of the run consists of several small boulder gardens that can be scouted at river level by eddy hopping.

After Table Rock Fork enters from the right, the flow nearly doubles and the river becomes the main Molalla. Stay on the river to the take-out, because this section is on private land. The take-out is reached at Horse Creek Bridge. One may wish to continue the 3 miles to the Turner Bridge take-out.

Hazards. The two major rapids need to be scouted for logs and other debris.

Access. To reach the lower take-out at Turner Bridge, see run 121, Molalla River: Turner Bridge to Glen Avon Bridge. The Horse Creek bridge take-out can be reached by taking the side road 2.7 miles above Turner Bridge.

To reach the put-in, continue on the main road going upstream. At 4.7 miles, take the right fork and continue up the gravel road about 5 miles to the next bridge across the river. This is the put-in, Copper Creek Bridge, with plenty of parking.

Gauge. Located at Feyrer County Park on the bridge pier. Minimum recommended flow is 5 feet. An ideal level is 6 feet.

Joe Gymkowski and Rick Kelley

120 Mollala River
Table Rock Fork to Turner Bridge

Class: 3(3+)   Length: 4.7 miles
Flow: 1,000 cfs   Character: forested; canyon
Gradient: 65 fpm, PD   Season: rainy

This scenic and playful run on the Molalla River is mostly class 2, with several class 3 drops near the middle of the run. This portion may be combined with upper portions of the next run to make a longer trip (see run 121, Molalla River: Turner Bridge to Glen Avon Bridge).

The put-in is on the Table Rock Fork of the Molalla. After paddling 0.2 mile, boaters reach the main Molalla and the flow doubles. The next mile is mostly class 2 and is a good warm-up. The first class 3 rapids is at the end of this mile and can be seen and scouted from the river by eddy hopping. Shortly below this rapids boaters pass under Horse Creek bridge. Horse Creek enters the river as a beautiful falls on the left. About 0.2 mile downstream from the falls is Horse Creek Canyon, where the river narrows to a boat length. This class 3+ drop is clean but turbulent. It's a good idea to check for logs before committing to this drop. The flat-water runout gives paddlers a chance to enjoy the beautiful, steep canyon walls. Less than 1 mile downstream, where the river makes a sharp bend to the left and then right, be alert for logs. The final couple of miles are class 2 with some nice play waves and ender spots to enjoy. A common day trip is to continue on down through the Three Bears and take out below Baby Bear (see run 121, Molalla River: Turner Bridge to Glen Avon Bridge).

Hazards. Horse Creek Canyon is very narrow at the steepest part of the drop. Logs may be a problem, so be sure to scout.

Access. See run 121, Molalla River: Turner Bridge to Glen Avon Bridge, to reach the take-out.

To reach the put-in, continue 4.4 miles upstream from Turner Bridge, just past the B Ranch residence, to a small turnout on the right. A short trail leads down to the river.

Gauge. Located at Feyrer County Park on the bridge pier. Minimum flow is about 3 feet. Flows higher than 4.5 feet are not recommended because scouting becomes a problem, eddies are few, and logs spanning the river could become a definite hazard.

Laurie Pavey

121 Mollala River
Turner Bridge to Glen Avon Bridge

Class: 3 T; 4   Length: 8 miles
Flow: 600–1,000 cfs; 2,000 cfs   Character: forested; canyon
Gradient: 55 fpm, C   Season: rainy

This run is known as the Three Bears Run. At the minimum flow of about 600 cfs, it is a technical class 3; at higher flows, it is a more enjoyable class 3; and at high water, it becomes big class 4. There are several 3- to 4-foot steep drops visible from the road on the way to the put-in. When running the rapids, some eddy hopping is necessary to pick the correct route. Many of the runouts are riffles leading to the next rapids.

For the first mile or so below the put-in, the water is fast but fairly straightforward. The first major rapids, Papa Bear, about 1 mile downriver, has two distinct parts. Another mile down is the most dificult rapids on the run, Mama Bear. The rapids starts with a boulder garden and some heavy water that leads into a fantastically picturesque gorge with moss-laden columnar basalt twisted into weird and wonderful shapes. The gorge is only 14 feet wide in places, and the water is deep, slow, and eerie. The next major rapids, Baby Bear, is another mile down. It consists of three separate drops.

After the Three Bears, there are about 4 miles of easier water, but don't forget about Goldilocks, probably the most dangerous rapids. It begins with fast water that is split by an island and can be run on either side. The left is easier, especially at low water. At the bottom is a blind turn to the right against an undercut rock that could entrap a boater. The final named rapids, Porridge Bowl, consists of an easier short, fast drop into a wall. A short distance below, Trout Creek enters from the right into a deep pool, followed by a house on the right. Take out on the right where the road is close to the river, about 0.2 mile above the Glen Avon bridge. Run in March 1980 by Rob Blickensderfer, Rich Brainerd, and Dan Valens.

Hazards. The Three Bears can be scouted from the road during the shuttle. Mama Bear, leading into the columnar basalt gorge, becomes solid class 4 at high water. Goldilocks cannot be seen from the road. It should be scouted on foot or by careful eddy hopping to check for logs and the undercut.

Access. From Oregon 99E or Oregon 213 between Salem and Oregon City, go east on Oregon 211 1 mile to the town of Molalla. Continue east on Oregon 211 and take the first right to Feyrer County Park. From Feyrer County Park, cross the river and turn right on Dickey Prairie Road. Go upriver and pass through the community of Dickey Prairie. Continuing upriver, Dickey Prairie Road crosses the North Fork Molalla and after 0.2 mile the Glen Avon bridge is on the right, crossing the Molalla River. Without crossing the river on the Glen Avon bridge, continue 0.2 mile to a wide area near river level, the take-out.

To reach the put-in, backtrack 0.2 mile and cross the Glen Avon bridge. Continue upstream 9 miles to Turner Bridge. Cross the Molalla and continue a little farther up to a roadside pullout on the right.

Gauge. Located at Feyrer County Park on the bridge pier. The flow is unregulated. The minimum runnable level is 2.5 feet. Good first-time levels are 3.2–3.5 feet. A more exciting level is 4–5 feet.

Rob Blickensderfer and Joe Gymkowski

122 Mollala River
Glen Avon Bridge to Feyrer County Park

Class: 2	Length: 6 miles
Flow: 1,000–2,000 cfs	Character: agricultural; rural
Gradient: 30 fpm, PD	Season: rainy

On this run, several straightforward class 2 rapids and good play spots alternate with class 1 stretches of fast water. The river is more interesting and not nearly as flat as it appears from the road on the way up to the put-in. Several houses are visible from the river. About 4 miles below the put-in, a private bridge crosses the river. The take-out is at the next bridge at Feyrer County Park, on the left. Depending upon the boater's skill and mood, this short run could be combined with either the previous run (see run 121, Molalla River: Turner Bridge to Glen Avon Bridge) or the next run (see run 123, Molalla River: Feyrer County Park to Oregon 213 Bridge).

Hazards. All of the largest rapids, class 2, occur in the upper half of the run. The waves can be relatively large, but the rapids are straightforward.

Access. See run 121, Molalla River: Turner Bridge to Glen Avon Bridge for directions to both the take-out and the put-in for this run. The take-out is at Feyrer County Park east of Molalla.

To reach the put-in from Feyrer County Park, continue to Glen Avon and its bridge across the Molalla River. Without crossing the river, continue 0.2 mile to a wide area near river level, the put-in.

Gauge. Located at Feyrer County Park, on the bridge pier. The flow is unregulated. A reading of 2.6 feet means ample water, estimated at 1,000–1,200 cfs.

Rob Blickensderfer

123 Mollala River
Feyrer County Park to Oregon 213 Bridge

Class: 1+	Length: 6 miles
Flow: 1,000–2,000 cfs	Character: rural
Gradient: 21 fpm, C	Season: rainy

This is an excellent run for a beginning kayaker's second river trip. It is relatively free of brush, and has numerous riffles and enough small rapids and speed to keep boaters interested. The first bridge, after 2 miles, is the Oregon 211 crossing. The second bridge, after an additional 6 miles, is the Oregon 213 crossing. Take out under the bridge on the left.

Hazards. There are none in particular.

Access. To reach the put-in at Feyrer County Park, see run 121, Molalla River: Turner Bridge to Glen Avon Bridge.

To reach the take-out, return to Molalla and continue west on Oregon 211 to the intersection with Oregon 213. Go north on Oregon

213 about 4 miles to the bridge over the Molalla River. The take-out is on the south side, river left.

Gauge. See run 122, Molalla River: Glen Avon Bridge to Feyrer County Park.

Rob Blickensderfer

CLACKAMAS RIVER AND TRIBUTARIES

The Clackamas system drains more than 930 square miles southeast of Portland. It offers a deep forested canyon, scenic sheer cliffs, excellent fishing, numerous campgrounds, and whitewater from class 1 to class 4. The river is one of the most used in Oregon. Estacada is the dividing line between the upper runs with reliable class 2–3+ whitewater and the lower sections with class 1 and 2 water. Bobs Hole in the upper section is one of the premier rodeo-riding holes in the nation. The lower Clackamas is part of the state Scenic Waterways System. Although the river is heavily used, especially in the summer, there are many miles of water available to capable boaters in search of solitude.

The proximity of the watershed to the state's largest population center has earned it the dubious distinction of claiming 109 lives between 1970 and 1980—a national record.

As is the case with most Cascade rivers, humanity's attempt to harness the river is significant, with six existing dams and several potential sites listed. During the 1964 flood, the Cazadero Dam broke and sent a wave of water down the river, exceeding the gauge at the river mouth with an estimated flow of 120,000 cfs.

Hank Hays

124 Collawash River
Bridge 5.5 Miles from Mouth to Two Rivers Picnic Area

Class: 4-; 4+(5)	**Length: 5.5 miles**
Flow: 900 cfs; 2,500 cfs	**Character: wooded canyon**
Gradient: 61 fpm, PD	**Season: rainy/snowmelt**

Enjoyable class 3 rapids and numerous play spots characterize most of this run, except for two difficult class 4 rapids. Both class 4 rapids are in the upper 2-mile section and can be avoided by using the lower put-in. From the bridge at the upper put-in, it is only about 0.25 mile to the first major rapids, Boulderdash, class 4, a 0.3-mile-long boulder garden complete with house rocks, narrow chutes, and a serious gradient. The entire rapids should be scouted from the roadside pullout 5.2 miles above the take-out. This involves some scrambling and peering through trees, but is well worth the effort. From the river, scout Boulderdash from the left bank. Most of the runnable slots are river left, with the exit near the center.

After 1.5 miles of class 2 rapids, the second class 4 rapids, Chute to Kill, is identified by the cliff on river right. Again, scout Chute to Kill on the way to the put-in from a roadside pullout 3.6 miles above the take-out. The run begins as a steep boulder garden followed by a large hole backed by a guard rock. A solid brace makes life more enjoyable here. A short pool leads into the last drop, a 5-foot plunge down a steep chute into a powerful hole on river left. A right side chute dead ends in a boulder jam, hence the name.

A quarter mile below Chute to Kill, the Hot Springs Fork enters from river left. This optional put-in allows 1 mile of easy warm-up before entering the class 3 section with its many nice play waves and holes. The final class 3, Up Against the Wall, comes at a right bend in the river, just past the only bridge, and marks the end of good whitewater.

Hazards. Boulderdash and Chute to Kill require skillful maneuvering and solid rolls at any flow. Scout both rapids on the way to the put-in. They are likely to become class 5 at higher flows. All of the class 3 rapids are visible from the road except Up Against the Wall, but it is an easier rapids than those upstream. Logs and trees create some potential hazards and should be noted on the way to the put-in.

Access. From I-205 southeast of Portland, take Oregon 212 east and then Oregon 224 south to Estacada. Continue about 23 miles upstream to Ripplebrook Ranger Station. Turn right on FS 46 and continue to FS 63; turn right on FS 63 and continue for 0.1 mile to the confluence of the Collawash and Clackamas. The take-out is in Two Rivers Picnic Area, at the confluence.

The lower put-in for the class 3 run is 3.4 miles upstream at the Hot Springs Fork confluence at Fan Creek Recreation Site. The upper put-in is another 2.1 miles upstream, where a bridge crosses the Collawash.

Gauge. None exists. Use the Clackamas Three Lynx gauge. Call the River Forecast Center in Portland. The flow is about 40 percent of that at the Three Lynx gauge. The authors made the run between 900 and 1,800 cfs (2,300–4,500 cfs at Three Lynx).

Jeff Bennett and Tonya Shrives

125 Eagle Creek
Fish Hatchery to Snuffin Road

Class: 3(6) T	**Length: 6 miles**
Flow: 300 cfs	**Character: forested; cabins**
Gradient: 62 fpm, PD	**Season: rainy**

Eagle Creek drains the Cascade foothills east of Estacada, and flows generally northwest into the Clackamas River about halfway between Estacada and Barton. It was named for the eagles that used to dip to catch the thousands of spawning salmon. The creek is small and seldom run, though anglers abound. Several bridges cross the creek, but paddlers catch only glimpses of the road, and then only in the vicinity of Eagle Fern County Park. The first settler in the area, Philip Foster, was part owner of the Barlow Road, the first real alternative to the dangerous rafting trip through the Columbia Gorge.

Warning: Several logjams have developed since logging activity in 1988. One jam is very large and very difficult to portage. At high water, eddies above it are almost nonexistent. The logjam is so large that it is not likely to wash out soon. The following description is from the 1986 edition of *Soggy Sneakers*, and readers should keep in mind the existence of more recent logjams.

At the put-in, the creek is narrow with overhanging shrubbery. If the water level is high, the current can be intimidating. Sweepers, logs, and blind turns make the upper part of this run quite interesting, although the rapids are usually not too complex. The logs spanning the creek and the logjams may change at any time. An unnamed creek enters on the right about 1.5 miles below the put-in. Two miles farther is a 15-foot waterfall. Watch for the 4-foot-high concrete fish ladder bypassing the falls. It's on the right bank past a sharp right-hand bend. Take out on the right in the slower-moving water well before the concrete wall. Portage on the trail or down the fish ladder.

It's about 1 mile from the base of the falls to Eagle Fern Youth Camp—a large open area on the left. Some of the best action on this run comes in the mile between the camp and the take-out. The creek goes around a right bend and into an interesting boulder garden. It gets worse near the bottom, after a left bend. There is a short respite, some more fun boulder gardens, then the bridge at the take-out.

Hazards. The falls, logs, logjams, water running into bushes, and boulder gardens between the youth camp and the take-out are the difficulties on this run.

Access. From I-205 southeast of Portland, take Oregon 212 east and Oregon 224 south to the community of Eagle Creek. Oregon 224/211 crosses Eagle Creek about 4.5 miles north of the stoplight in Estacada. Just north of the bridge, turn east onto Wildcat Mountain Drive, which is marked by a sign pointing to Eagle Fern County Park, the fish hatchery, and Dover District. Keep right at an immediate "Y" and then cross Eagle Creek Road. In less than 2 miles, turn right onto Eagle Fern Road. The entrance to Eagle Fern County Park is in about 2.2 miles. Snuffin Road comes in from the right in about 0.8 mile from the park entrance. Either the park or the Snuffin Road bridge can be used as a take-out. The take-out can also be reached from Estacada, on Oregon 224/211, by going east on Coupland Road (up the hill east of the high school) for 2 miles, turning left onto Currin Road, then right after another 2 miles onto Snuffin Road. Follow the signs toward George and Eagle Fern County Park.

To reach the put-in, return to the junction of Snuffin and Eagle Fern roads, and find George Road, which starts at this intersection. Follow

George Road about 4.5 miles to a right turn onto Rainbow Road. A sign on the left points toward the hatchery, 2 miles away and 600 feet down. There is a marked parking lot next to a private bridge across the creek. The easiest put-in is across the bridge on the downstream side. This is private property; get permission from the landowners before using it.

Gauge. None exists. Take a look from the Oregon 211 bridge.

Hank Hays

126 Eagle Creek
Snuffin Road to Eagle Creek Road

Class: 3+(6) P   **Length: 5 miles**
Flow: 300 cfs   **Character: forested; residential**
Gradient: 55 fpm, C–PD   **Season: rainy**

The character of the lower run on Eagle Creek is similar to that of the upper run (see run 125, Eagle Creek: Fish Hatchery to Snuffin Road).

About 0.5 mile below the put-in at Snuffin Road bridge is a low-head dam (1–2 feet). A shallow slide in the center of the dam makes an easy run. A mile below the put-in, the North Fork Eagle Creek emerges underneath a bridge at a left bend in the river. A half mile farther is "The Falls," preceded (by 200 yards, at least) by a sign on a cable across the river. (The sign may be missing as of 1991). There is plenty of action before the falls. Work toward the right after the sign and take out on the right in a very small eddy at the upstream end of the fish-ladder retaining wall. Portage and put in about 100 yards downstream.

There are 1.5 miles of boulder gardens below The Falls. The first 0.5 mile drops at the rate of 125 fpm. There are also some strategically placed logs, so scout blind corners before attempting a run. The first hard right bend below The Falls quite often has logs. Scout left.

About 0.5 mile below The Falls, a blind left bend around a small island also has several logs wedged between a rock and the left bank. Scout left, from the top of the island. Portaging would not be easy because the banks are sheer on both sides. This is the last really nasty spot, but there are many more interesting drops and boulder gardens for about the next mile. There are also a couple of automobiles in the creek.

The recommended take-out is the first concrete bridge. Land about 25 feet above it on the right for the easiest hike up to the road. The run could be continued down to the Dowty Road crossing, about 0.5 mile from the mouth, or even to Barton Park on the Clackamas.

Hazards. Difficulties include possible logjams, sweepers, steep-walled gorges, The Falls, and the rapids at the right bend and at the left bend after The Falls. There are usually many anglers in this section, so courteously avoid them.

Access. For directions to a put-in at Snuffin Road or Eagle Fern County Park, see run 125, Eagle Creek: Fish Hatchery to Snuffin Road.

A car can be dropped off at the take-out on Eagle Creek Road on the way in by taking a right onto Eagle Creek Road (the first crossroad after leaving Oregon 211), and parking in the pullout on the east side of the road before crossing the bridge. Please don't block the driveway.

Gauge. None exists. Look at the water level from the Oregon 211 bridge.

Hank Hays

127 Clear Creek
Oregon 211 Bridge to Redland Road Bridge

Class: 2+(3) T	**Length: 8 miles**
Flow: 500 cfs	**Character: forested; residential**
Gradient: 41 fpm, PD	**Season: rainy**

The main stem of Clear Creek drains the north face of Goat Mountain south of Estacada and flows into the Clackamas River at Carver. Because it's a small stream subject to logjams, take a peek around blind bends in the river before committing yourself. There are stretches of flat water with good current between drops. Most of the land along both banks is private except for two small sections of BLM timber and Metzler Park. Above the put-in, Clear Creek consists of several small feeders with no public access.

Just downstream from the put-in is a left-hand bend with some logs and rocks to dodge. At 0.5 mile, a footbridge crosses the river and Swagger Creek comes in on the left. Just below the footbridge is a small low-head dam that has a surfable roller at some water levels. The short rebar stakes in the shallow water below the dam present a hazard. Watch for more stream-spanning logs between here and Metzler Park, a little farther down. About 0.5 mile below the park, there is a good class 2+ rapids.

About 5 miles into the run a gravel logging road crosses the river. This marks the start of a 0.5-mile-long steep section that ends with a 3-foot rocky drop. The rest of the run is moving flat water, probably with logjams that require portaging. Take out at the Redland Road bridge. Below this bridge, the stream is runnable, but the land is used mostly for agricultural purposes, and boaters are likely to encounter fences crossing the river.

Hazards. Logjams and logs spanning the river are the main hazards. The low dam and the 3-foot rocky drop are the most difficult spots.

Access. The put-in is about 25 miles southeast of Portland where the Oregon 211 bridge crosses Clear Creek. This is about 5 miles south of Estacada or 15 miles northeast of Molalla. The put-in is river right on the downstream side of the bridge; all else is private property.

To reach the take-out at the Redland Road bridge, drive 3 miles north on Oregon 211 toward Estacada, turn left at the top of the hill onto Holman Road, and then take the first right onto Springwater

Road. About 5 miles farther, take Redland Road, the first left turn after the entrance to Milo McIver State Park. Proceed 1.5 miles to the
bridge over Clear Creek, the take-out.

Gauge. None exists. Clear Creek rises and falls abruptly. It has
been run when the Clackamas at Three Lynx was at 5,400 cfs. Check
the river level at the bridges described above.

Hank Hays

128 Clackamas River
June Creek Bridge to Collawash River

Class: 3+; 4   Length: 8 miles
Flow: 1,600 cfs; 5,000 cfs Character: forested; hot springs
Gradient: 77 fpm, PD   Season: rainy/snowmelt

Warning: This run is *too dangerous to make* because the USFS placed
logs in the river for fish habitat in 1991. The logs make an excellent way
of killing recreational boaters. The listing is included in hopes that the
river will again be runnable sometime in the future.

129 Clackamas River
Collawash River to Sandstone Road Bridge

Class: 4(6) P   Length: 8.5 miles
Flow: 1,000–3,000 cfs   Character: forested; roadless
Gradient: 43 fpm, PD   Season: rainy/snowmelt

This secluded and scenic run on the Clackamas River is also one of
the most dangerous. A perfect roll, reliable equipment, and a competent
leader are prerequisites. Boaters should always be wary of logs.

The first 2 miles have class 2 and 3 rapids, with short drops and fun
waves. The pace picks up during the next 2.5 miles. Gates Rapids, a
line of big boulders blocking the river, is the first major rapids. Just
downstream is Hole in the River, a large hole on the left. Several blind
corners, which could require scouting, follow. About 4.5 miles below the
put-in is Rocky's Rapids, where the river bends right after slamming
into a wall. Alder Flat Campground, just below, is the easiest take-out
before the nasty stuff begins downstream. From the trail on the right,
it is about 1 mile to the road and Ripplebrook Ranger Station, with a
pay telephone.

Immediately below Alder Flat Campground is a pushy class 4 rapids
called Drop Stopper, named for the large midstream boulder at the bottom. Twice in the next 0.5 mile, the river bends right after slamming
into high rock walls. Prelude Rapids, two narrow slots, is just to the
right of the second wall. The authors recommend scouting from above
Prelude, because Killer Fang, class 6, is 150 feet downstream and out
of sight. After running Prelude, land on river right for the *mandatory
portage* around Killer Fang. At flows under 1,100 cfs, all the water in
Killer Fang goes under three mega-boulders, into dead-end siphons.
Logs are visible in the underground chutes.

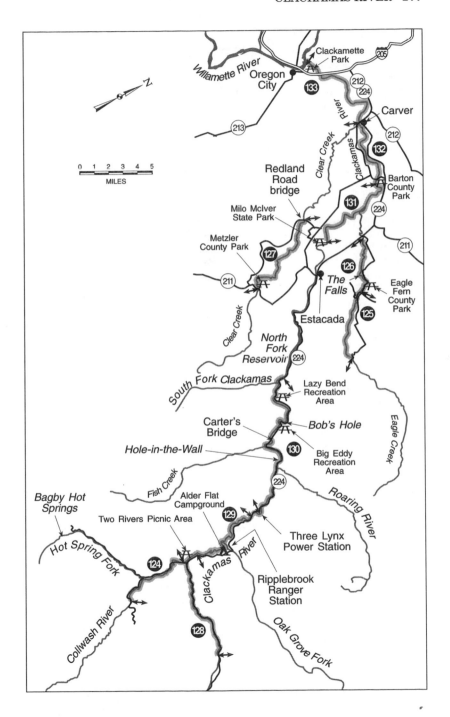

Note: In 1991 a slide below Killer Fang dammed the river sufficiently to raise the water level over Killer Fang. Since then, Killer Fang has been run at high water, but it could change again as the slide changes and the old Fang reappears. Also, the rapids through the mudslide may become harder.

Do not relax after Killer Fang. The next mile has two class 4 rock gardens. The first, Sieve, has some undercut rocks left of center, so scouting is advisable. Next comes River's Revenge, where some fancy eddy hopping is required to maneuver through the narrow slots between large rocks. Class 2 rapids continue for about 1 mile to the take-out.

Hazards. Due to the narrow slots and tight turns on this run, logs pose a real threat on any of the rapids. As always, scout if the bottom of a rapids is hidden from view. Definitely scout Drop Stopper, Prelude, and Sieve. Killer Fang is a *mandatory portage* at any water level.

Access. From the north, from I-205 southeast of Portland take Oregon 212 east and Oregon 224 south to Estacada. From the south, from Oregon 99E northeast of Salem take Oregon 211 east to Estacada. Follow Oregon 224 southeastward from Estacada, past Three Lynx Power Station 0.25 mile to Sandstone Road. The take-out is on river left just upstream of the bridge where Sandstone Road meets Oregon 224/USFS 46.

Continue up Oregon 224/USFS 46 toward the put-in. Turn right on USFS 63 toward Bagby Hot Spring. After 0.3 mile, cross a bridge and turn left into a little forest camp where the Collawash River meets the Clackamas. An alternate put-in, located 1 mile downstream at Riverside Campground, skips the beginning flat water.

Gauge. Located at Three Lynx. Call the River Forecast Center in Portland.

Roger Van Zandt and Hank Hays

130 Clackamas River
Three Lynx Power Station to North Fork Reservoir

Class: 3(4)   Length: 13 miles
Flow: 750–3,000 cfs   Character: forested; popular area
Gradient: 43 fpm, PD   Season: year-round

This scenic Cascade river has taken a great number of lives. Proper training in boating skills, safety, and rescue are needed for a safe run. Most people who get into trouble on this stretch are inexperienced boaters in unsuitable craft. These people have often been drinking alcohol. The river can be unforgiving.

A number of put-ins and take-outs are available on this stretch, but the run usually falls into a combination of three sections, with famous Bob's Hole on the lower section.

Section 1: Three Lynx Power Station to Carter Bridge. The upper put-in is at the bridge above Three Lynx, in which case the two large drops above the power station should be scouted. The first one splits around an island; the right channel is recommended, but has a midstream boulder near the bottom. The second drop bounces off a headwall. Boaters can also put in at the bridge below Three Lynx. Immediately below Three Lynx Power Station are several class 2 rapids that build to class 3 at the narrows about 0.2 mile down. Roaring River Rapids is the next major rapids, located just above the confluence with the creek for which it is named. The cleanest channels are to the left.

The notorious Hole-in-the-Wall follows 0.2 mile downstream. It has been called the Toilet Bowl by the Forest Service and rescue squads in

Portaging a log, a common problem on Oregon rivers (photo by Phil DeRiemer)

the past, and local boaters refer to it as the Head Wall. The "real" Toilet Bowl is farther downstream. Rescue teams are trying to standardize the name by calling this one Hole-in-the-Wall. The Hole-in-the-Wall is by far the most dangerous rapids on this run. Many lives have been lost here. At the approach, most of the water is forced to the left, where it forms a fast chute. This chute flows directly into the wall. Most of the water moves right and downstream, but a large portion of the flow turns left into a very turbulent and powerful eddy that can circulate logs, boats, or people for hours. The eddy is easily avoided at higher levels by running right. At lower levels, the right becomes too rocky. The common low-water route is to run the left chute and move quickly right before reaching the wall. The walls of the eddy are undercut and a submerged swimmer could be swept under the wall. The rock walls that border the eddy are too steep to climb, except where the walls form a corner. A metal ladder was installed to enable swimmers to climb out. Needless to say, this self-rescue plan must be reviewed while scouting the rapids, not while swimming in the eddy.

The next few miles are playful, with many class 2 rapids. Downstream of the second bridge, just after Fish Creek enters from the left, the river splits around an island. Usually both channels are runnable, but the left channel has a sizable hole in the center that surprises many boaters. A quarter mile below here is Carter Bridge Rapids, class 4. It is located just upstream of the third bridge on the run. Scout it during the shuttle. The route next to the left shore is the easiest. A take-out is possible at Carter Bridge.

Section 2: Carter Bridge to Bob's Hole. After some easier water below Carter Bridge, boaters drop into Big Eddy at Big Eddy Recreation Site, another access point. The exit rapids is fairly steep and very rocky, with pinning potential, especially on the right at low water. The Toilet Bowl, a class 3 rapids, located 0.2 mile downstream of the Big Eddy, presents probably the biggest waves in the Oregon Cascades. There is an access point just below Toilet Bowl. One quarter mile downstream is Bob's Hole, with access along the road nearby.

Section 3: Bob's Hole to North Fork Reservoir. This favorite play hole is the site of the nationally famous Bob's Hole Whitewater Rodeo, held every spring. The event, sponsored by the Oregon Kayak and Canoe Club (OKCC), draws expert hole riders and hundreds of spectators. It is located near the road, 13 miles east of Estacada. Bob's Hole was named after Bob Breitenstein, who, in his early kayaking years, always insisted on trying to run through the hole, but always got knocked over.

Bob's Hole consists of several play spots. The uppermost wave is Jim Bob. It becomes a hole below 2,000 cfs. The next three waves are called Jack Wave, Queen Wave, and King Wave. These are followed by Billy Bob Wave just above Bob's Hole. The best play level for Bob's Hole is 1,700–2,900 cfs. About 100 feet downstream on the right is Joe Bob's Hole, which may be played at flows of 2,500–4,500 cfs, but it can be quite

Championship style at Bob's Hole, Clackamas River (photo by Eric Larsen)

sticky and a lot of people swim out of it. (Flows are at Three Lynx gauge.)

The remaining 4 miles to North Fork Reservoir are class 2 and generally easier than the rapids above. There are a few ledges with pourovers that should be avoided at high water. Inexperienced boaters may tend to get pushed into the bank in several places. All of this lower section can be seen from the road. Slack water begins just after the South Fork Clackamas enters from the left.

Hazards. The Hole-in-the-Wall is by far the most dangerous rapids on this run. Many lives have been lost here. This rapids must be scouted. Should you find yourself out of your boat and swimming in the eddy, you're in for quite a ride. Keep cool. Take advantage of your life jacket and keep all parts of your body near the surface. Carter Bridge Rapids should be scouted as well.

Access. Oregon 224 follows the Clackamas very closely on this run and allows for many possible put-ins and take-outs. To reach Oregon 224, go to Estacada and take Oregon 224 southeast upriver. (To reach Estacada, see run 129, Clackamas River: Collawash River to Sandstone Road Bridge.) The two most common put-ins are at the bridges immediately above and below the Three Lynx Power Station.

Other accesses include Carter Bridge, Big Eddy Recreation Site, a road pulloff just below Toilet Bowl, along the road at Bob's Hole, Memaloose log-scaling station, Lazy Bend Campground, and, finally, North Fork Reservoir.

Gauge. Located at Three Lynx. Contact the River Forecast Center in Portland.

Bill Ostrand and Hank Hays

131 Clackamas River
Milo McIver State Park to Barton County Park

Class: 2+
Flow: 800–3,000 cfs
Gradient: 17 fpm, PD

Length: 8 miles
Character: park, lowlands
Season: year-round

This beautiful stretch of the Clackamas River may be run all year. The first 2.5 miles of the run are located entirely within Milo McIver State Park; for a short trip, boaters may take out at the lower end of the park. For those continuing on downstream, it is another 5.5 miles to the take-out at Barton County Park.

The put-in at the Milo McIver State Park boat ramp offers a view of the first and largest drop. A ledge across the river provides several good standing waves for surfing. The river twists through the park with more small rapids and goes into a rock garden. The rock garden is followed by a nice play spot with more standing waves and eddies on both sides. There are more bends and small rapids on the way to the optional take-out at Milo McIver State Park's lowest picnic area. From here to Barton County Park there are several more small rapids and play spots. It is mostly class 2 water and is fairly flat. Barton County Park also has both a boat ramp and picnic area.

Hazards. In high water, the first drop should be checked for the boat-eating hole that develops. There is a headwall below the play spot mentioned above that can circulate a swimmer at high water.

Access. Be prepared to pay an entrance fee at both parks. To reach the Barton County Park take-out, from the Portland area take Oregon 212 east and then Oregon 224 southeast. The park, about 7 miles from Oregon 212, closes at dusk.

The put-in is reached by driving upstream on Oregon 224 to Milo McIver State Park. Once in the park, follow the road down the hill. The put-in is at the boat ramp.

The optional take-out for the short 2.5-mile run is reached by driving to the lowest parking lot (and picnic area) within Milo McIver State Park.

Gauge. Located at Estacada. Contact the River Forecast Center in Portland. This run is runnable most of the year. Rocky runs have been made at levels as low as 750 cfs.

Bob Collmer

132 Clackamas River
Barton County Park to Carver

Class: 2
Flow: 800–3,000 cfs
Gradient: 14 fpm

Length: 5.5 miles
Character: residential
Season: year-round

This stretch of the Clackamas River is an excellent training area for beginners. There are many small class 2 drops, usually with eddies close by. The rapids are clean and have good runouts. The scenery is uncluttered, even though some areas have housing on the river's edge. The river class rises to the 2+ level in the spring and drops to the 2- level in the summer. It is runnable all year and is often run in the evening, when daylight permits.

Hazards. There are no major problem areas, although several rapids pick up speed and provide some bouncy places.

Access. To reach the put-in at the boat ramp in Barton County Park, which requires an entrance fee and closes at dusk, see run 131, Clackamas River: Milo McIver State Park to Barton County Park.

To reach the take-out, return north on Oregon 224 to Carver. The take-out is located at the boat ramp just upstream from the bridge in Carver.

Gauge. Located at Clackamas. Contact the River Forecast Center in Portland.

Bob Collmer

133 Clackamas River
Carver to Clackamette Park

Class: 2	**Length: 8 miles**
Flow: 800–3,000 cfs	**Character: residential**
Gradient: 9 fpm, C	**Season: year-round**

This stretch of river is a fine run for intermediate canoers. The rapids are characterized by turns with standing waves on the outside or the middle of the channel, with a nice soft eddy on the inside. The most difficult rapids are a pair of right bends followed by a pair of left bends. The second pair has a central rock to avoid. High rocks and a trestle bridge are next. There is an easy riffle here, but several 17-foot aluminum canoes have wrapped around the bridge piers. The run finishes with a nice long but not too tight "S"-turn. The waves here are irregular and can be fun. Clackamette Park is 0.8 mile farther down on the left. The Clackamas River then flows into the Willamette River.

Hazards. Canoers should know how to handle "S"-turns with high standing waves.

Access. The put-in is at the bridge that crosses the Clackamas at Carver. Carver is located on Oregon 224 4 miles east of Clackamas, which is near I-205 southeast of Portland.

To reach the take-out at Clackamette Park, go to the south end of the bridge in Carver and turn right on Clackamas River Road, which follows the south side of the river. At the intersection with Washington Street/Oregon 213, turn left. After 1 mile, turn right, cross the railroad tracks, and turn right again immediately after the tracks onto McLoughlin Boulevard. Continue north 0.5 mile to Clackamette Park.

Gauge. Located at Clackamas. Contact the River Forecast Center in Portland.

Kurt Renner

COLUMBIA GORGE

SANDY RIVER AND TRIBUTARIES

The Sandy River system is a major drainage of western Mount Hood. It offers a tremendous variety of boating opportunities, from steep mountain streams to the slower lower river. The high elevation of Mount Hood provides a good snowpack, which supplies the Sandy with water throughout most of the summer.

134 Zigzag River
Toll Gate Campground to Sandy River

Class: 3+ T; 4- T	**Length: 3.2 miles**
Flow: 300 cfs; 1,000 cfs	**Character: forested; cabins**
Gradient: 108 fpm, C	**Season: rainy/snowmelt**

The Zigzag River, a tributary of the Sandy River, is fed from the melting snows of Zigzag Glacier on the southwest side of Mount Hood. Cold and clear, the river zigzags its way through Mount Hood National Forest, rumbling along until it joins the Sandy River. The run starts at Toll Gate Campground off US 26, the site of the original Barlow Road tollgate. A plaque and wooden sign with a replica of the tollgate are displayed. Even the original wagon-wheel ruts are still visible.

A hike down the brushy embankment is required to begin this fast-paced run. The first section, to Still Creek, is fast-moving and steep with continuous rock dodging, yet it maintains a fairly consistent gradient of 145 fpm. There is a log across the river just downstream of Toll Gate Campground that is quite dangerous. This obstacle can be located by hiking along the riverbank 200 yards downriver from the Toll Gate Campground. A fast eddy out on the right is required to get around the log. Farther downstream, branches and limbs overhanging the right bank can present problems. A quarter mile below the US 26 bridge on a sharp left turn is a class 3 drop with some large holes at higher water. Another logjam is located on a left turn 1 mile downriver from the US 26 bridge. At higher water levels you can bypass it on the left. The next logjam is another 0.3 mile farther downstream on another left turn where the river splits around an island. The left channel appears to have a horizon line. In reality the river is pouring over a large log. Go right of the island.

If you don't feel comfortable running the upper section, you may put in at the US 26 bridge just west of Rhododendron, where Still Creek enters from the left and doubles the flow. From the US 26 bridge down to the confluence with the Sandy, the river gradient and pace decrease quite noticeably. Boaters sometimes continue down the Sandy River to the Wildcat Creek take-out; see run 137, Sandy River: Zigzag to Wildcat Creek.

Hazards. Because the gradient is steep and the rapids are continuous, particularly in the upper section, the main hazards are logjams.

Access. From the Portland area, head east on US 26 to the town of Zigzag, east of Gresham. Turn north on East Lolo Pass Road, east of the Zigzag Store. Proceed 0.2 mile to the Zigzag River bridge crossing. Turn right on East Zigzag River Road just after crossing over the bridge, the take-out. For the optional take-out on the Sandy River at Wildcat Creek, see run 137, Sandy River: Zigzag to Wildcat Creek.

To reach the put-in, backtrack to US 26. Turn left (east) on US 26 and proceed 2.8 miles to Toll Gate Campground. Turn right into the parking lot, the upper put-in. The alternate put-in is at the US 26 bridge over the Zigzag River just west of Rhododendron.

Gauge. None exists. Several days of good hard rain are needed to make this river runnable. The Sandy River gauge near Bull Run provides a rough guide. The Sandy gauge must read at least 11 feet. Best flows are between 11.5 feet and 14 feet. Over 14 feet, the upper section becomes more demanding.

Scott Harvey and Dan Anderson

135 Bull Run River
Bull Run Road Bridge to Dodge Park

Class: 3	**Length: 2.5 miles**
Flow: 700 cfs	**Character: canyon**
Gradient: 30 fpm, PD	**Season: year-round**

Portland's municipal water supply is drawn from the Bull Run River about 6 miles above the bridge at Bull Run Road. Consequently, the entire watershed is closed to public access. There is only a 2.5-mile section from this bridge to the confluence with the Sandy River that can be run.

The Portland General Electric (PGE) employees at the powerhouse just below the put-in have allowed gear to be left on their lot out of harm's way while boaters shuttle cars back to the take-out.

This brief run offers six class 3 drops beginning just below the bridge. The last of these drops is Swing-set, named for the cable and basket arrangement strung across the river just below the drop. The river mellows to class 2 for the final 0.5 mile or so to the confluence with the Sandy and the inviting take-out beach in Dodge Park.

Hazards. There are none in particular, with the possible exception of the very steep put-in. The passages are narrow at lower flows, increasing the difficulty slightly. At higher flows, Swing-set has an impressive wave.

Access. The take-out is at Dodge Park, east of Portland. Follow US 26 to the eastern city limits of Gresham. Turn left onto Powell Valley Road. Follow signs to Dodge Park, which is at the end of Dodge Park Boulevard.

To get to the put-in, go to the east end of the bridge at Dodge Park, head east and bear left on Lusted Road. Proceed 1.8 miles, then turn left again on Southeast Ten Eyck Road toward Aims. Turn left on Bull Run Road and descend to the bridge over the Bull Run River. Basically, take every paved road to the left after leaving the east end of Dodge Park bridge; the put-in bridge is within 3 miles.

Gauge. Not available. The flow is augmented by the PGE power-house at the put-in, with water diverted from the Sandy River at Marmot. Consequently, this section can be run most of the year.

Thom Powell

136 Sandy River
McNeil Campground to Lolo Pass Road Bridge

Class: 4+ T	**Length: 5.5 miles**
Flow: 600–800 cfs	**Character: wooded**
Gradient: 200 fpm, C	**Season: rainy/snowmelt**

There is only one rapids on this run on the Sandy. It begins at the put-in at the McNeil Campground bridge and ends 5.5 miles later at the take-out at the next bridge. It begins as a class 4, gets tougher around the middle (4+), and lets up a little toward the end. The run takes about 50 adrenalin-filled minutes to complete (barring unforeseen problems) and is among the steepest runnable river segments anywhere in the state. The rather continuous rate of drop makes a manageable run out of an otherwise outrageous gradient. This also makes the drops fairly uniform in difficulty, but occasionally a steeper or narrower passage is encountered. The first trip down this run is an unforgettable experience.

The class 4+ rating given to this run can be misleading. Much more than a reliable roll is needed here. It's the kind of place where you don't even want to think about tipping over. It's fairly tough to roll in most places, but it's even tougher to get a swamped boat ashore. In two instances, swimmers were able to get to shore quickly, but their boats traveled quite a way before being corralled.

It is important for boaters to keep their distance from each other. There's usually only one good channel and not much room to maneuver. Rescue is difficult because fellow boaters are usually too busy to be aware of anyone else's problems. The action demands total concentration and aggressive, continuous maneuvering. Also, protruding rocks in fast chutes provide countless opportunities to pin a boat, so boaters can almost never afford to get sideways to the current. If this discussion sounds discouraging, it should; this is expert-class whitewater.

This run has a remote feeling to it, but the Lolo Pass Road is usually less than 0.3 mile through the woods on river right. The alders and underbrush are quite thick, but anyone who is experiencing early difficulty should quickly opt for the nature walk, for the river gets tougher before it gets easier.

As of 1985, a log spans the river downstream of the McNeil Campground bridge, just out of sight. Paddlers should carry boats down the road for 400 yards or so and put in just below the log, on river right. The river begins with some very technical maneuvering and then eases up, giving one a false sense of accomplishment. Stay alert! The river picks up again shortly, only this time with more force. It is useless to describe the drops in detail since there are just too many of them. Eddies are very scarce, but they offer the only chance to catch your breath. There are no pools to speak of.

The river's channel is split by islands in several places. When in doubt about which way to go, take the left channel. In all cases, the left is freer of branches and obstructions.

Worthy of mention are the tree stumps that have been driven into the riverbed for some mysterious reason. They occur intermittently in the middle third of the run, and in two places they stand right in the middle of the river, appearing to block the channel. They look positively awful, jutting up out of the river with the water pillowing up against them. Experience indicates they can be outmaneuvered with decisive moves.

Near the bottom of the run, there are a couple of houses on river right. This is the start of a development called Zigzag Village. It is imperative that you use the left channels in the vicinity of these houses, for one of the right channels is completely blocked by a logjam.

Consider paddling past the take-out at Lolo Pass Road bridge and down to Wildcat Creek, another 9 miles. It is a bit anticlimactic after the race down from McNeil Campground, but the water is still quite swift and interesting.

Hazards. Logs are a concern on any river this steep and narrow. This is expert-class whitewater, very fast with almost no place to stop. Rescue is difficult. The action demands total concentration and aggressive, continuous maneuvering. It is important for boaters to keep their distance from each other; there's not much room to maneuver. Boaters can almost never afford to get sideways to the current. Where the current splits around an island, the left is the best choice in all cases.

Access. To reach the take-out, take US 26 east from Portland and turn north off US 26 at the Zigzag Store onto Lolo Pass Road. The take-out is about 1 mile down this road at the second bridge. (The first bridge crosses Zigzag River.)

To get to the put-in, continue up Lolo Pass Road. After 3.5 miles look for a sign that marks entry into Mount Hood National Forest. Just past this sign, turn right on USFS 1825, which leads to Ramona Falls. Continue up this road for 1 mile to reach the put-in at the bridge just before McNeil Campground.

Gauge. Located at Bull Run. Three days of heavy rain are needed, even in winter, to bring this run up to a runnable level. The only way to gauge the flow accurately is to check the water level against some logs that are built into the river-left bank just below the McNeil Campground bridge. When the water is halfway up the lowest log, it is a runnable flow, and if this same log is covered, it is too much. The river level drops rapidly as soon as rains subside, providing about a 3-day period to run the river before it gets too low.

Thom Powell

137 Sandy River
Zigzag to Marmot Bridge

Class: 2 T; 3	**Length: 7 miles**
Flow: 700–2,000 cfs; 2,000+ cfs	**Character: forested; residential**
Gradient: 70 fpm, C	**Season: rainy/snowmelt**

The river flows through a broad valley with an almost constant gradient. The sandy bottom gives the river its name, and the boulders give the river its rapids. Areas without boulders form fast-moving pools. The dynamic nature of this type of riverbed makes description of individual rapids pointless. Each minor flood changes the rapids somewhat and may change the locations of deep channels and the best paddling routes. A major flood may completely change the river.

The most difficult rapids are at the top of the run where the river is steepest. Farther downstream are more pools but still plenty of whitewater. After the confluence with the Salmon River (about 0.5 mile above Marmot Bridge), the volume increases greatly and the water takes on more "big-water" characteristics. There are many stationary, smoothly shaped waves in the lower rapids during medium and high flow levels.

At all levels, even at the highest runnable flows just short of flood, the river does not form dangerous features such as riverwide holes or exploding waves. The most difficult level is at medium-high flows when the river is high enough to form holes behind the large boulders. When the river is so high that rocks and boulders can be heard crashing together on the bottom, consider another form of recreation for the day.

Hazards. No rapids stand out as significantly more difficult or dangerous than the general pace of the river. Occasionally brush extending from the banks may cause problems.

Access. From the Portland area, take US 26 east to Zigzag. Turn north onto Lolo Pass Road, just east of the Zigzag Store. Continue to the second river crossing, the put-in.

To reach the take-out, return to US 26 and turn west. After 6 miles, turn north on Sleepy Hollow Road and proceed 0.3 mile to a road on the right that crosses the Sandy River on Marmot Bridge, the take-out.

Gauge. Located at Bull Run. This run is runnable most of the late fall, winter, and spring. Warm spring days during years of good snow-

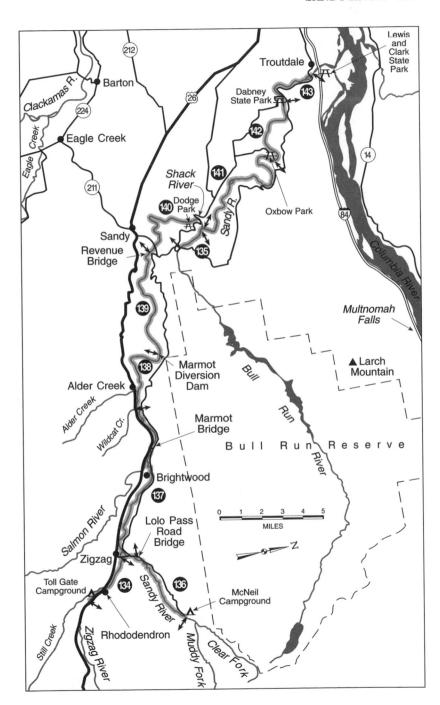

pack may yield excellent runoff when many other rain-dependent rivers are low. If the river appears too low at the put-in, consider putting in farther downstream.

Bill Ostrand

138 Sandy River
Marmot Bridge to Marmot Dam

Class: 2(4)	**Length: 6 miles**
Flow: 700+ cfs	**Character: forested; residential**
Gradient: 33 fpm, C–PD	**Season: rainy/snowmelt**

This run on the Sandy River provides a warm-up for boating the class 4 Sandy Gorge, which begins just below Marmot Dam.

The first 3 miles of this section begin with a series of class 2 rapids, followed after another mile by Alder Creek Rapids, class 4, recognized by an A-frame house overlooking the rapids from the left. Below Alder Creek the rapids become progressively easier until the water becomes completely flat at the impoundment behind Marmot Dam. The portage is on the right, along the public road. Follow it to the left across the aqueduct and down to the river. Continue boating 6.5 miles on the next run (see run 139, Sandy River: Marmot Dam to Revenue Bridge). Run in 1971 by Scott and Margie Arighi and others.

Hazards. Alder Creek Rapids can present a real challenge. The drop appears as a horizon line from upstream. An easy scout or portage is on the right. Marmot Dam is unrunnable. It is easily seen from above and is marked by a sign: DAM AHEAD. TAKE OUT ON RIGHT.

Access. From Portland, take US 26 east to the town of Sandy. The lower put-in is about 11 miles east of Sandy. Turn north on Sleepy Hollow Road. Continue about 1 mile to a road on the left that crosses the Sandy River on Marmot Bridge, the put-in.

To reach the take-out, see run 139, Sandy River: Marmot Dam to Revenue Bridge.

Gauge. Located at Bull Run.

Bill Ostrand

139 Sandy River
Marmot Dam to Revenue Bridge

Class: 3+; 4	**Length: 6.5 miles**
Flow: 1,200 cfs; 3,000 cfs	**Character: forested; roadless**
Gradient: 40 fpm, PD	**Season: snowmelt**

This run is also known as the Sandy Gorge. For almost the entire length of the gorge, the Sandy cuts a winding and often quite narrow canyon through a formation of compacted volcanic ash conglomerate. The walls of the canyon are deeply sculpted and sometimes overhanging, and rise 150 feet. A multitude of small waterfalls cascading down from both sides, plus lush vegetation consisting of both deciduous and evergreen trees and mosses and maidenhair ferns that cling to the ceilings of caves and overhangs, make this stretch of river among the most picturesque in Oregon.

In 150 yards below the put-in, a major rapids containing the remnants of a huge 1964 logjam should be scouted on the right. At moderate to upper levels, most people portage this on the right. It is possible to pin on any number of vertical logs about halfway down the rapids on the left, especially at lower levels. At the bottom, the current slams into the root system of a large downed tree on the right. If you decide to run it, start right and end up in the eddy on the left at the bottom. There are some holes about halfway down just to complicate the rapids a little.

For the next 3.5 miles the river drops with many short enjoyable rapids, and one longer class 3 rapids at about mile 2.5. In the last 2 miles there are four rapids that should be scouted: Boulder Rapids, Rasp Rock, Drain Hole, and Revenue Bridge. At Boulder Rapids, the canyon narrows dramatically, with a tremendous overhang and free-falling waterfall on the left and large boulders in the middle. It is almost impossible to portage. The right chute has a log that can be seen at lower levels. Normally boaters run the left chute, avoiding the huge undercut rock on the right. Eddy out under the overhanging left wall to avoid the big hole along the canyon wall, which usually cannot be seen when scouting.

The difficulty of the next two rapids, Rasp Rock and Drain Hole, varies dramatically with water level. Rasp Rock is a furious 50-yard drop over conglomerate boulders with some big holes interspersed throughout. It is shaped like a funnel with a huge hole at the beginning of the neck and two big boulders at the end. This hole tends to surf boaters into the left wall. Scout or portage. Check for logs in the narrow chutes at the bottom before committing yourself. Any of the three possible chutes are narrow enough for a boat to wedge crosswise, so if you flip anywhere near the bottom, a wet exit might be preferred to a delayed roll.

Drain Hole looks like the end of the river. A rock jumble forces the water left, and it appears to be dammed by a line of three mega-boulders. The water slams into the left boulder, which is dangerously undercut. There are logs in some of the other narrow chutes. The chute between the right-most rock and the canyon wall is usually open. Scout on the right. Even most expert paddlers portage this one at moderate to high levels.

Revenue Bridge Rapids is recognized by glimpses of the bridge through the trees when rounding the bend. One can try scouting from the cliff on the right shore, but it is difficult to see much of the beginning of the drop. The last half is easily scouted from the rocks on the left. The usual plan is to go far right against the cliff and then eddy out on the left before the two big holes near the bottom. Take the first one on the right and try to get left for the second riverwide stopper. At lower levels it can be run anywhere, but boats should be pointed straight downstream to avoid problems. Take out almost under Revenue Bridge on the left. A steep trail winds up to the road. Run on February 3, 1974 by Rod Kiel, Paul Ho, and Ted Ragsdale.

Hazards. The most dangerous rapids is about 1 mile below the dam. It is marked by large logs protruding from the river. Four other rapids—Boulder Rapids, Rasp Rock, Drain Hole, and Revenue Bridge Rapids—should be scouted or portaged. Logs in several of the rapids require great skill and care to avoid (a kayaker was drowned under one of these logs a few years ago).

Access. From Portland, head east on US 26 to Sandy. From the junction of US 26 and Oregon 211 in Sandy, head east for several blocks and turn left toward Bull Run and Oral Hull Park on Ten Eyck Road. This road switches back down into the Sandy River Canyon (take a hard left at the first "Y") and goes across Revenue Bridge, the take-out.

The put-in is that for run 138, Sandy River: Marmot Bridge to Marmot Dam.

Gauge. Located at Bull Run. To approximate the flow on this run, deduct 600 cfs from the Bull Run gauge. Looking upstream from Revenue Bridge, one sees a rock halfway between the bridge and the bottom of Revenue Bridge Rapids. The flow is ideal when enough water splashes over this rock to create a good visible souse hole.

Hank Hays and Rod Kiel

140 Sandy River
Revenue Bridge to Dodge Park

Class: 2+   **Length:** 5 miles
Flow: 1,200–3,000 cfs   **Character:** residential
Gradient: 40 fpm, C   **Season:** rainy/snowmelt

This run starts at Revenue Bridge with a crawl down the hill to the river. The upper part of the run is class 2 with many small rapids. Things pick up where a long slide area is visible on the left. Below here drops are steeper, more frequent, and sometimes rocky. This is a pretty run, but a little more open and populated than the next runs.

Hazards. The lower drops should be run with caution. Follow the main current and be careful of rocks in the drops. At very high water, this is a hazardous run because the water goes into snaggy banks and eddies disappear. There may be logs in the river at high water.

Access. From Portland drive east on Oregon 26 to Sandy and turn north on Ten Eyck Road. Follow the road downhill, across Cedar Creek, and over the ridge until it crosses the Sandy River at Revenue Bridge, the put-in.

The take-out is at Dodge Park (for directions to Dodge Park, see run 135, Bull Run River: Bull Run Road Bridge to Dodge Park).

Gauge. Located at Bull Run. Call the River Forecast Center in Portland.

Bob Collmer

"Otter in" at the put-in (photo by Phil DeRiemer)

141 Sandy River
Dodge Park to Oxbow Park

Class: 2+(3)   Length: 8 miles
Flow: 1,200–3,000 cfs   Character: forested; roadless
Gradient: 23 fpm, PD   Season: rainy/snowmelt

The Sandy River is very beautiful in this area. It is mostly wooded canyon and is a designated scenic river. It is pool-drop, with most of the drops clean and many surfing waves scattered along the entire stretch. Pipeline Rapids, class 3, is 0.5 mile from the put-in and should be scouted for rocks. Pull off in the eddy on the left above the visible pipe across the river.

The scenery remains almost primitive in the canyon. The lower stretch opens up somewhat, but remains wooded and remote. Wildlife is often seen. About 3 miles into the run is a long rock garden. The run ends at Oxbow Park boat ramp and there is always the feeling of a great trip. The run is nicest on a sunny day but neither rain nor snow hurt this run. Spring is best but the river is runnable usually through July.

Hazards. Pipeline Rapids should be scouted for rocks. There is always the possibility of trees in the river after heavy runoffs.

Access. The put-in is reached by driving to Dodge Park (for directions to the park, see run 135: Bull Run River: Bull Run Road Bridge to Dodge Park.)

The take-out is the boat ramp at Oxbow Park, which has an entrance fee during the summer. After leaving Dodge Park on Dodge Park Boulevard, go 2 miles to Hosner Road. Turn right (north) and proceed 2 miles to the Oxbow Park entrance. After entering the park, continue to the farthest upstream boat launch.

Gauge. Located at Bull Run. Call the River Forecast Center in Portland.

Bob Collmer

142 Sandy River

Oxbow Park to Dabney State Park

Class: 1+   Length: 4.5 miles
Flow: 700+ cfs   Character: wooded; roadless
Gradient: 8 fpm   Season: rainy/snowmelt

This mild run is a favorite among rafters for summer outings. The majority of the rapids are within Oxbow Park. No rapids are more difficult than class 1+ and there are plenty of eddies to catch. Beginning kayak classes often use the river section between the boat ramps within Oxbow Park.

Beyond Oxbow Park are a few more rapids and a number of riffles. Continued opportunities to view wildlife add to the pleasure of this trip. Sightings include osprey, bald eagle, great blue heron, and various species of waterfowl. The gentleness of the river and the beautiful scenery beckon many boaters to the river.

Hazards. A potential hazard occurs near the end of the run. There is a sharp right turn and the current tends to trap trees on the outside of the bend.

Access. Dabney State Park, the take-out, is located on US 30 (the Columbia River Highway, often called "the old scenic highway") east of Portland. Follow Stark Street east from Portland and take a right after crossing the Sandy River. The park is located approximately 0.2 mile from the bridge. For an optional route to the take-out, follow I-84 east from Portland to the Lewis and Clark State Park exit, and then follow the road along the river to Dabney State Park (about 3 miles).

The put-in is at Oxbow Park. From Dabney State Park, cross the bridge over the Sandy and follow the signs. After entering Oxbow Park, continue to the farthest upstream boat launch. There is an entrance fee during the summer. You may also put in on the north side of the river. To reach this put-in, continue east on the Columbia River Highway from Dabney State Park and turn right onto Hurlburt Road. Follow Hurlburt Road and turn right onto Gordon Creek Road. There is a sign at the parking area.

Gauge. Located at Bull Run. Call the River Forecast Center in Portland.

Sarah Ostrand

143 Sandy River
Dabney State Park to Lewis and Clark State Park

Class: 1	**Length: 3 miles**
Flow: 500 cfs	**Character: canyon; residential**
Gradient: 6 fpm, PD	**Season: year-round**

This is one of the most frequently floated segments of river in the state. Anglers float the river all winter and rafters and inner tubers drift during hot summer days. The run is not completely flat; there are several class 1 riffles.

Hazards. As with most Oregon rivers, the water is extremely cold. Most of the year, boaters encounter anglers in drift boats or along the shore, so look out for lines in the water.

Access. From Portland, take I-84 east to Troutdale. Just east of Troutdale, take the Lewis and Clark State Park exit and follow signs to the park. The take-out is at the boat ramp within the park. To reach the put-in, follow the Columbia River Highway along the river upstream to Dabney State Park.

Gauge. Located at Bull Run. Call the River Forecast Center in Portland.

Bill Ostrand

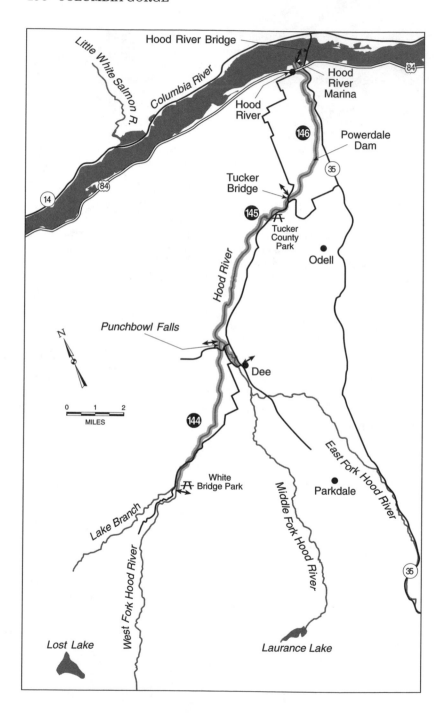

HOOD RIVER AND TRIBUTARIES

144 West Fork Hood River
White Bridge Park to East Fork Hood River

Class: 4(5) P   **Length:** 6.5 miles
Flow: 800+ cfs   **Character:** forested
Gradient: 100 fpm, PD   **Season:** rainy/snowmelt

This run is a solid class 4 at normal flows. At flows above 3,000 cfs, be ready for some class 5 water! The first 1.5 miles of this run are pool-drop with some nice play waves. But as Branch Creek flows in on the left, the river widens and the gradient increases. The most demanding drops are on the next section of the river. About 2 miles downriver from Branch Creek is a fish ladder, where there was once a beautiful 13-foot waterfall. The fish ladder is normally portaged on the left. The fish ladder has been run, but is now barricaded at the top. *Do not run the fish ladder*; it is illegal and dangerous to do so.

The next major rapids is a 50-yard-long boulder garden that is a technical rapids at low flows and a maze of holes at high water. It should be scouted on the right. The last drop, Punchbowl Falls, should be scouted from the take-out on the shuttle to the put-in. All of the water pours over an 8-foot ledge. Some good boaters get eaten here, so run the drop with plenty of momentum. The take-out is at the confluence of the West Fork with the East Fork, less than 0.5 mile downriver from Punchbowl Falls.

Hazards. The drops just after Branch Creek are more demanding than the rest of the run. The fish ladder should be portaged on the left. The boulder garden should be scouted on the right. The last drop, Punchbowl Falls, is a large powerful drop. At low water, scouting is possible from the ramp near the falls.

Access. From I-84 in the city of Hood River, take exit 62 (West Hood River–West Cliff Drive). Follow the signs to Odell and Parkdale, then follow the road toward Dee and Parkdale. Turn right at the sign for Dee–Lost Lake Road. After crossing the East Fork Hood River at Dee, turn right onto Punchbowl Road. Continue on Punchbowl Road, and take a right onto a road just before the bridge over the West Fork Hood River. This is the take-out. The river is about 500 feet down a trail. To scout Punchbowl Falls, continue across the bridge and up the road to a turnout on your right. A hike down the stairs brings you to the falls.

To get to the put-in, backtrack to the three-way intersection near the bridge over the East Fork Hood River at Dee; keep right at the intersection and follow signs to Lost Lake. Continue upriver on Lost Lake Road. After crossing the second bridge, continue upstream another 1.5 miles, then turn left into White Bridge Park, the put-in. The shuttle is 6.9 miles.

Gauge. Located at Tucker Bridge. Call the River Forecast Center in Portland. Two-thirds of the flow at Tucker is a good estimate of the flow on the West Fork. A reading of about 5 feet at Tucker is optimum.

John Karafotias

145 East Fork Hood River
Dee to Tucker Bridge

Class: 3(4); 4	Length: 7.5 miles
Flow: 700 cfs; 2,500 cfs	Character: forested; residential
Gradient: 66 fpm, PD–C	Season: rainy/snowmelt

The first 1.6 miles are on the East Fork, which is pool-drop and runs through a beautiful narrow canyon. At the confluence with the West Fork, the water volume doubles, and the gradient drops off and becomes more uniform. The main stem Hood River is wider, but no less challenging than the upper section. At lower flows the upper section is class 3, with a couple of technical class 4 ledge-drops. At higher flows it becomes continuous class 4.

Hazards. Two rapids should be noted. Approximately 0.5 mile from the put-in is a technical class 4 drop. Another class 4 drop occurs just above Tucker Park and is identified by an island with most of the river on the right.

Access. From I-84 in the city of Hood River, take the first or second exit and follow the signs to Parkdale and Odell on Tucker Road. After several turns, cross Hood River, where the take-out is on river right, under the bridge.

To reach the put-in, follow the signs up the river past Tucker Park toward Parkdale. Stay right on the paved road until the mill at Dee. Cross the bridge and enter a large parking lot on river left. The put-in is about 50 yards downriver, down a steep bank.

Gauge. Located at Tucker Bridge. A reading of 4.5–6 feet is ideal. Gauge information is also available from the River Forecast Center in Portland.

Stan Jacobs and Jay Nigra

146 Hood River
Tucker Bridge to Hood River Marina

Class: 3 P	Length: 5 miles
Flow: 800+ cfs	Character: forested
Gradient: 60 fpm, C	Season: rainy/snowmelt

At high water, above 8 feet, the run provides a fun day of class 3 hole crashing. The first part of the run provides fun, bouncy class 2+ rapids. At mile 1.5, Powerdale Dam necessitates a portage. Pull to the left shore the moment the dam comes into view and carry boats along the left bank. Below the dam, the river accelerates to class 2+–3 boulder gardens, occasional islands, and debris for the next mile, forcing some quick decision making. The next obstacle is a dogleg turn just beyond an orange railroad bridge. This requires a hard pull to the right bank to avoid a large boulder on river left. The remainder of the run is fast but flat. The take-out is at the footbridge located at the west end of the Hood River Marina.

Hazards. Powerdale Dam at mile 1.5 requires a portage. The rapids below the railroad bridge becomes class 3–4 at high water.

Access. From I-84 in the city of Hood River, take the Hood River/White Salmon exit and proceed north 150 yards to the Hood River Marina, the take-out. The marina is at the south end of the Hood River Bridge.

To reach the put-in, turn right as you exit the marina and follow Oregon 35 south. At mile 6.5 turn right toward Odell. Proceed straight through Odell to Tucker Road. Turn right onto Tucker Road and proceed 1.5 miles farther to Tucker Bridge, the put-in.

Gauge. Located beneath Tucker Bridge. Levels above 5 feet are excellent. Call the River Forecast Center in Portland.

Jeff Bennett

NORTH SHORE COLUMBIA RIVER AND TRIBUTARIES

The rest of this chapter consists of runs on the Washington side of the Columbia Gorge. Though these rivers aren't located in Oregon, they are very accessible to Portland-area and northern Oregon boaters. These runs are included because of their proximity and popularity.

The Klickitat River is a beautiful gem set in the ponderosa pine forests of south-central Washington. It extends 95 miles from the Goat Rocks Wilderness of Mount Adams to the Columbia River. The 51 miles described in these four runs extend from the Yakima Indian Reservation to 5 miles above the Columbia River. During the summer the river is fed primarily by glacier melt and springs. The large dirty glaciers of Mount Adams often make the river silt-laden. The Klickitat is very swift with an average gradient of 35 fpm. Many rafters start at the gauging station and float 48 miles to the take-out at rivermile 5. Rafts can run the river until the middle of July; canoes can run all year long from Summit Creek to rivermile 5—32 miles.

The camping options are one of the things that make the Klickitat special. Camping is allowed only above rivermile 21 (about 1.5 miles above the Little Klickitat); below is almost all private land. Please respect the property rights of these people. During fire season, fires are allowed only at developed campgrounds (Leidel, Stimpson Flats, and Gauging Station).

The fishing on the Klickitat is great and you can still watch the indigenous people fish with nets on narrow scaffolds below The Falls at rivermile 1.75. Help preserve this sparkling river and please be courteous to anglers. Drift boaters on the middle run and commercial rafters on the upper runs were the main users of this river until recently. Responsible private boaters are encouraged to use this mini Deschutes-like river.

Ernie Carpenter

147 Klickitat River, Washington
Yakima Indian Reservation to Klickitat Salmon Hatchery

Class: 3; 4	**Length: 13 miles**
Flow: 800 cfs; 1,800+ cfs	**Character: canyon; forested**
Gradient: 35 fpm, C	**Season: snowmelt**

The remote upper run begins near Mount Adams, which was called Klickitat by the Indians. The highest put-in is by the Yakima Indian Reservation boundary. Non-Indians are prohibited beyond here. The put-in is east of the road, down the slope and through the woods. The long, steep slope with loose soil and many fallen logs requires use of a short line for lowering the boat, because a runaway boat may not stop until reaching the bottom or crushing a companion. An alternate put-in, preferred by rafters, is located 3 miles downriver at Gauging Station Campground. Once on the river, boaters will not want to take out because the canyon is remote and mostly inaccessible.

The upper 3 miles is continuous class 3 boating at moderate levels. As flows approach 1,800–2,000 cfs during peak runoff, the river gets a big-water class 4 push to it. It is not technical but the continuous nature makes swims dangerous.

After this, the gradient decreases and the lower 10 miles are primarily class 2 with some class 3 headwall drops. At low water it is class 3 T. At high water it tends to wash out, but is fast. The middle one-third of the river is highlighted by immense vertical walls of columnar basalt that bend the river in long "S" turns. The river crashes into these walls, then runs alongside the gray cliffs, drawing dwarfed boaters' wide-eyed gazes upward. The bottom third of the river is mellow but is punctuated by a nice class 3 drop near the take-out at the Klickitat Salmon Hatchery. The weir at the hatchery should be scouted or portaged. Run in June 1980 by Dave Axelrod, Robert Frisbee, Bill Grey, and John McCracken.

Hazards. The upper put-in is tough. The upper river becomes continuous class 4 at high water when the push and continuous nature make swims dangerous. Watch for big holes at high water. The weir at the fish hatchery is potentially dangerous.

Access. From Oregon, cross the Columbia River at Portland or Hood River and take Washington 14 to Washington 141 near the town of White Salmon. Go north on Washington 141 23 miles to the town of Trout Lake. Then take the road east to Glenwood. Continue east 3 miles beyond Glenwood to the sign for "KLICKITAT SALMON HATCHERY." Follow the gravel road down to the hatchery. Park at bottom of the hill, before the buildings. Follow trail at far left to river, the take-out.

To reach the put-in, return to the pavement, and go back toward Glenwood a few feet. At the "Y" take the next gravel road to the right to the hatchery. The lower put-in is reached by going about 7 miles up this gravel road to road K1400, which goes to the right; take this road, then turn off onto K1410. (These road signs are small and almost concealed.) Proceed to Gauging Station Campground, the lower put-in. The upper put-in is another 4 miles up to the Yakima Indian Reservation sign on the right. Parking or driving beyond this sign is illegal.

Gauge. Located 3 miles below the put-in. Flows are usually available at the River Forecast Center in Seattle. The Klickitat is usually runnable if the White Salmon is over 1,000 cfs.

Frank Furlong, Bill Ostrand, and Jon Ferguson

148 Klickitat River, Washington
Klickitat Salmon Hatchery to Leidl Campground

Class: 3   **Length: 10 miles**
Flow: 700+ cfs   **Character: forested**
Gradient: 36 fpm, C **Season: snowmelt**

The first 5 miles below the fish hatchery consist of challenging technical rapids. At flows around 3,000 cfs, the rapids wash out and the run involves missing a few big holes and riding big waves. The first class 3 rapids can be seen from the fish hatchery dam. Two miles downstream is Wonder Falls, a spring-fed falls on the right and an alternate put-in. Other rapids along the upper section can be scouted from the road. However, about 1 mile below Wonder Falls is a difficult rapids that cannot be seen from the road. Scout or portage left. A long rocky class 2 rapids occurs 1.5 miles below Summit Creek bridge. This is followed by some big boulders and two headwalls with a deceptively vicious eddy on the right of the second wall. The lower 5 miles are relatively easier.

Hazards. The fast water gives the boater very little time to react to riverwide logjams. The dam just below the hatchery has reinforcing rods in the water that must be avoided; portage on left.

Klickitat River below the Fish Hatchery (photo by Nancy MacDonald)

Access. For the put-in, go to the take-out for run 147, Klickitat River: Yakima Indian Reservation to Klickitat Salmon Hatchery. To reach the alternative put-in, go north from Leidl Campground 1 mile toward Glenwood. Turn right on a dirt road near the logging station. Go 3 miles to Summit Creek Bridge. Cross Bridge, proceed upstream until the 30-foot Wonder Falls can be seen on opposite bank. Put in here or continue upstream another 0.5 mile to a fork; cross flats to a sandy beach put-in.

To reach the take-out from the fish hatchery, go south from the river to Leidl Campground. At Leidl Campground, turn right for the boat ramp take-out or left and go to end of road to a sandy beach.

Gauge. Located at Pitt. Call the River Forecast Center in Seattle (206-526-8530). For information on shuttles and logjams, call or visit the Shade Tree Inn in Glenwood (509-364-3471).

Ernie Carpenter

149 Klickitat River, Washington
Leidl Campground to Icehouse Public Access

Class: 2   **Length: 17 miles**
Flow: 500–3,500 cfs   **Character: wooded canyon**
Gradient: 24 fpm   **Season: year-round**

This is a run for those who want to see beautiful basalt cliffs and ponderosa pines, not for those who want wild whitewater. The forty class 1 rapids and a few class 2 rapids offer plenty of action for open canoers and beginning kayakers. The canyon is nearly 2 miles wide and 1,500 feet deep. The first 12 miles are on Washington State land, but from 1 mile above the Little Klickitat on down is private land. Because there are plenty of logs on this river, practice log recognition and log dodging elsewhere before attempting this run.

The put-in is at Leidl Campground, rivermile 33, at the boat ramp below the bridge or at a sandy beach 0.3 mile upstream. The river is braided with many channels for the first 7 miles. The first class 2 rapids is 2.5 miles below the Leidl bridge along a low rock wall on the left. Sneak, scout, or portage right. A half mile farther is Stimpson Flats Campground, an alternate river access point. There is a good shaded campground on the right at rivermile 28 and an abandoned homestead on a bench to the west. At rivermile 24.5, a four-wheel-drive road comes down to the river. About 5 miles downstream is a series of waves and holes that can be avoided by staying left.

Next, the Little Klickitat River enters from the left, at rivermile 19.5. A half mile farther is a class 2 rapids identified by a cliff on the left and boulders on the right. Two miles farther, at rivermile 17, is the most difficult rapids on this section, the second rapids below the second bridge, class 2. It has a pointed rock in the middle. Scout or portage right. It is normally run left of the pointed rock. The take-out at

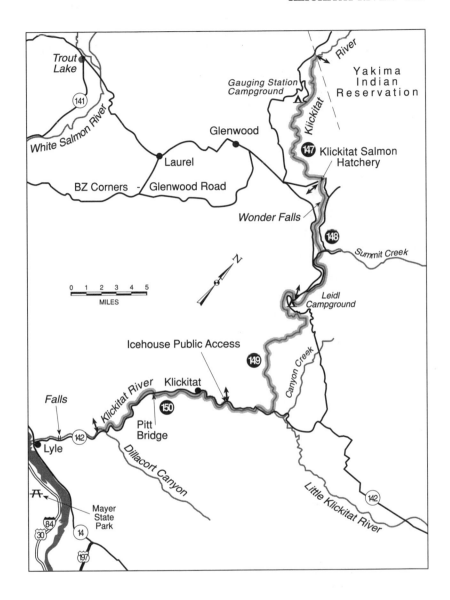

rivermile 16 is preceded by the large 1880s icehouse on the right used to store dry ice made from carbon dioxide produced from local wells. Take out on right at the concrete boat ramp.

Hazards. Ever-present logs and possible logjams are the greatest danger. Scout if in doubt. At rivermile 29, below Stimpson Flats Campground, the right channel is blocked with logs (1991) and the left channel flows through many sweepers. The class 2 rapids at rivermiles 30.5 and 17 are the most difficult.

Access. From Oregon, cross the Columbia at Portland or Hood River and take Washington 14 east along the Columbia River to Lyle. Here take Washington 142 north to the town of Klickitat. Continue 2 miles on Washington 142, cross the abandoned railroad tracks, turn right, pass the old icehouse, and go to the public boat ramp, the take-out.

To reach the put-in, return to Washington 142 and continue north along the Little Klickitat River toward Goldendale. After the road leaves the river and reaches a flat summit, turn left on the road to Glenwood. Before reaching Glenwood, cross the Klickitat at Leidl Campground and turn left to the boat ramp or, alternatively, turn right to a sandy put-in at the end of the road.

Gauge: Located at Pitt. Call the River Forecast Center in Seattle (206-526-8530).

Ernie Carpenter

150 Klickitat River, Washington
Icehouse Public Access to Rivermile 5

Class: 2+; 3	Length: 11 miles
Flow: 500–1,000 cfs;	Character: forested; roaded; residential
1,500+ cfs	Season: year-round
Gradient: 20 fpm, PD	

Fun rapids and good surfing waves are on found on this run. The river is pool-drop with some long rock gardens that can be seen from the road. The last 5.5 miles of the run are in the Columbia Gorge National Scenic Area. Some of the land is private and is posted. Do not land or stop for lunch on private land. Some of the rapids can be scouted during the shuttle.

The rapids 0.3 mile above the take-out is the most difficult; scout or portage river left. At low water (1,000 cfs) scout by walking up from the take-out, but prepare to get soggy sneakers! It's a difficult scout from river right at high water. Scout or portage the dam at the Klickitat Mill on the right. There is also a difficult drop about 1 mile below the Pitt Bridge; scout or portage left. Beware of the class 6 waterfall 2.5 miles below the take-out.

Hazards. Logs are not as common as upstream, but keep an eye out for the possibility. The rapids in this run get more difficult at higher water.

Access. From Oregon, cross the Columbia River at Portland or Hood River and take Washington 14 east to Lyle; at Lyle turn north on Washington 142 and proceed 4 miles upstream along the river to the take-out, a public access on the left with no boat ramp.

To reach the put-in, continue upstream about 8 miles to the town of Klickitat. The Icehouse Public Access put-in is on the right, about 2 miles past Klickitat (see run 149, Klickitat River: Leidl Campground to Icehouse Public Access). An alternate put-in is another 2 miles upstream, 0.5 mile past the bridge across the river (4 miles above Klickitat) on the left side of the road. Alternate take-out (or put-in) is the dirt road about 0.25 mile downstream from the Pitt Bridge.

Gauge. Located at Pitt. Call the River Forecast Center in Seattle (206-526-8530).

Ernie Carpenter

WHITE SALMON RIVER AND TRIBUTARIES

151 Trout Lake Creek, Washington
Guler Road Bridge to River Road Bridge

Class: 3(4)	**Length: 2.8 miles**
Flow: 400+ cfs	**Character: wooded; agricultural**
Gradient: 60 fpm, C	**Season: snowmelt**

This short but enjoyable run is a nice change if you happen to be in the area. The first 0.5 mile contains many brushy class 2 rapids that culminate in an exciting series of class 3+–4 ledges. The ledges can be scouted ahead of time and avoided by using a lower put-in.

After the ledges the river winds through farms and class 2 rapids for about 1 mile. The next rapids appears above the Old Creamery Road bridge, where the river drops over a few small ledges in a tight channel. After 0.6 mile the river passes beneath a covered bridge and enters a mini-gorge. By this point, Trout Lake Creek has entered the White Salmon River and the flow has doubled. The gorge contains fast water and many small waves. The trip ends where River Road crosses the river. Just below the take-out, the river drops over a 2- to 3-foot weir. The author has not explored the 1-mile section from the take-out down to the next run.

Hazards. Scout the ledges in the upper section and portage them, if desired. Brush and trees are potential hazards.

Access. For directions to Trout Lake, see run 147, Klickitat River: Yakima Indian Reservation to Klickitat Salmon Hatchery. At Trout Lake turn right on Guler Road and put in next to the bridge at the end of this road. To find the optional lower put-in, take the right fork of the road at the south end of the town of Trout Lake. Go 0.2 mile to the put-in beneath the bridge.

To find the take-out, return to Washington 141 and follow Little Mountain Road southeast out of the south end of town. The take-out is 1.6 miles down this road at River Road bridge.

Gauge. Located at Northwestern Lake. The run is good during heavy snowmelt from April to June, or when the gauge at Northwestern Lake is above 1,200 cfs.

Jeff Bennett

152 White Salmon River, Washington
Warner Road Bridge to Green Truss Bridge

Class: 4(5) P	**Length:** 5.1 miles
Flow: 800–1,500 cfs	**Character:** forested canyon
Gradient: 60 fpm, PD	**Season:** snowmelt

This run can be much more intense than the 60 fpm gradient indicates. It contains numerous class 3 and 4 rapids, and some sharp ledge-drops of 5–15 feet. Since the river is so narrow, a small change in flow creates big changes in difficulty. When flows exceed 1,400 cfs, the run contains continuous whitewater and powerful hydraulics; below 1,000 cfs the run becomes enjoyable pool-drop with large recovery pools. The run can be done year-round, but is best during spring runoff.

After 0.5 mile of warm-up, the river descends into a steep-walled canyon and drops 200 feet in the next 2 miles. It first drops over two 4-foot ledges and enters a narrow 100-yard-long chute with turbulent hydraulics. The second ledge, Sidewinder, can force kayakers uncomfortably close to an undercut ledge on river left at medium flows. A short pool occurs 0.9 mile later before dropping over—or through—The Faucet. Above 1,300 cfs, this is a vertical 15-foot waterfall with a runnable tongue near the right bank. At low flows a unique lava dam appears in which all the water funnels into a 3-foot hole and emerges again in the river below. There is an easy portage on the right bank.

The Faucet is followed by 0.5 mile of pool-drop rapids that become pushy at high water, then the canyon opens up and the gradient tapers off considerably. The next 2 miles are mostly class 2 rapids with an occasional class 3. At low flows this section is very shallow and rocky.

Around mile 4 the river picks up again, then disappears over Off Ramp, a marginally runnable 12-foot ledge. Portage this along the left bank. The run ends below the Green Truss Bridge. Save some energy for the strenuous take-out, or put in early and continue all the way to BZ Corner. Run in May 1980 by Dave Axelrod, J. Housby, and Robert Frisbee.

Hazards. The first 2.5 miles become very powerful and nearly continuous above 1,400 cfs. At low flows, the middle section is shallow and rocky. The take-out requires a throw rope to hoist the kayaks up the cliff.

Access. The put-in is at the Warner Road bridge, past BZ Corner. For directions to BZ Corner, see run 155, White Salmon River, Washington: BZ Corner to Husum. From BZ Corner, drive 8 miles north to Warner Road and turn right. Follow Warner Road about 1 mile to the

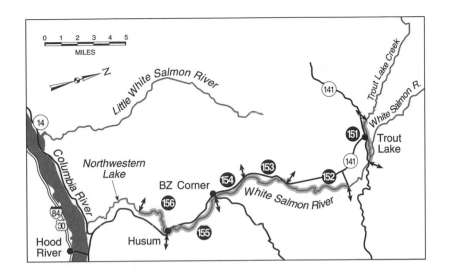

first bridge. The put-in is on the northeast side of the bridge.

For directions to the take-out at the Green Truss Bridge, see run 153, White Salmon River: Green Truss Bridge to Zigzag Canyon.

An alternate route allows boaters to scout two major drops during the shuttle: Turn right off Highway 141 6.6 miles north of BZ Corner onto Sunnyside Road. The Faucet is beneath an alder stand 0.6 mile up this road (find a small ledge to peer into the canyon), and Sidewinder is found at a wide spot 0.9 mile upstream.

Gauge. Located at Northwestern Lake, many miles downstream. This reading can be obtained from the River Forecast Center in Seattle (206-526-8530). Flows may be 40 percent lower than at the gauge.

Jeff Bennett, Doc Loomis, and Curt Knight

153 White Salmon River, Washington
Green Truss Bridge to Zigzag Canyon

Class: 4 T, P; 5- P **Length: 2.7 miles**
Flow: 400 cfs; 1,000 cfs **Character: forested canyon**
Gradient: 135 fpm, PD **Season: snowmelt**

The upper Upper White Salmon is always at least a solid class 4, even in early fall when the snowfields on Mount Adams have nearly melted. When every other good run in summer has dried up, this run is still guaranteed to keep the adrenalin bubbling, with some drops so concentrated that it is like boating down a flight of wet stairs. This water is absolutely for experts only. Walking out at any point between the put-in and take-out is extremely difficult. At high water during spring runoff, pools disappear and the run becomes a mad dash downhill with three class 5 rapids and one *mandatory portage*. When the water is down it's not as pushy, but boaters get more tail stands. First-timers should boat the river at low water in early fall to become familiar with the portages.

A half mile below the put-in, at a point where the guard rail from Washington 141 is visible, there is a double "S"-curve that goes from right to left to right to left. Eddy hopping down, rather than running it in a straight line, lessens the risk of plowing into the boulder at the bottom. In 1992 a tree blocked the channel halfway down. A quarter mile below the "S"-curve is Bob's Falls. It is about 10 feet high and has an enormous boil. At high water, nothing short of a hanglider would allow a boater to sail over the falls and land downstream of the boil. Portage on the right. At low water, Bob's Falls can be run or portaged on the left. The pool below is plenty deep, according to Bob's underwater darkness and inner-ear–pressure tests. An eighth mile below this is an unrunnable 30-foot falls. Get out at the pool on the left side, and portage up the embankment and across the plateau. Use a rope to get down the next ravine at the base of another falls similar in appearance to Bob's Falls. This falls is runnable.

Below the waterfalls, the river eases up and changes character down to Zigzag Canyon, the take-out. You'll need to line your boat up the steep embankment on the right at Zigzag Canyon.

Hazards. This water is absolutely for experts only.

Access. Because the take-out in Zigzag Canyon is on private land, it is imperative to get permission from the landowners before making this run; otherwise, continue downstream to BZ Corner, run 154. To reach the take-out, go to BZ Corner (for directions to BZ Corner, see run 155, White Salmon River, Washington: BZ Corner to Husum). From BZ Corner, go 2.1 miles north on Washington 141 and turn right on a dirt road with overhanging brush. Go 0.15 mile to the end of this dirt road; it first turns left and then sweeps right 180 degrees, to parallel the river.

To reach the put-in, return to Washingon 141 and drive 2.6 miles farther north (4.7 miles above BZ Corner). Turn right down a paved road and drive 0.1 mile to the Green Truss Bridge. A leaking water pipe crosses the river on sagging supports just upstream and parallel to the bridge. Line your boat down the west embankment less than 50 yards from the bridge. Eat your Wheaties; there is no warm-up.

Gauge. Located at Northwestern Lake. The White Salmon receives considerable ground water and therefore runs more at the take-out than at the put-in. Stop at Husum Falls on your way to the put-in and have a look. As a general rule, only about 40 percent of the water cascading over Husum Falls is flowing at the put-in. Flow information is available from the River Forecast Center in Seattle (206-526-8530).

Andreas Mueller

154 White Salmon River, Washington
2 Miles Above BZ Corner to BZ Corner

Class: 4+ T, P	**Length: 2.2 miles**
Flow: 900 cfs	**Character: forested canyon**
Gradient: 90 fpm, C	**Season: snowmelt**

Boaters must recognize their abilities and limitations when considering this run, as well as those upstream. If, after numerous trips on the run below this one (see run 155: White Salmon River: BZ Corner to Husum), a boater feels the need for real challenge, there are excellent opportunities on this run. Not only does this run offer some class 4+ water, but also a somewhat annoying put-in and one significant portage. Boaters also need to know the road location in case a carry-out is necessary.

Two rapids are definitely more difficult than the rest. The first is just below the put-in, and should be scouted on the left. Precise boat handling is mandatory on this rapids. The second major drop appears less than 1 mile below the first; scout on the left. Although this drop is not as technical as the first, the penalty for a swim here is much more severe, because less than 200 yards downriver is a 14-foot waterfall, the only portage on this short run.

Hazards. The falls that lies two-thirds of the way down should be portaged on the right. It is identified by a sweeping right turn. The two most difficult rapids should be scouted.

Access. To reach the take-out near BZ Corner, see run 155, White Salmon River, Washington: BZ Corner to Husum. From BZ Corner, continue north on Washington 141 about 0.2 mile and turn right at the sign indicating the access point. This is private land, which you are permitted to use after paying a fee to the landowner; knock on his door.

The put-in is also on private property. It is imperative to get permission from the landowner before making the run. To reach the put-in, return to Washington 141 and drive north 1.8 miles on Washington 141. Look to the right for a small roadside turnout. Park here and begin the walk to the river. When you reach what is left of an old log bridge, lower or carry your boat to the water. This is best done with some rope and a few friends.

Gauge. See run 155, White Salmon River: BZ Corner to Husum.

John Karafotias

155 White Salmon River, Washington
BZ Corner to Husum

Class: 3+(4)	**Length: 5 miles**
Flow: 900–2,000 cfs	**Character: forested canyon**
Gradient: 90 fpm, C	**Season: year-round**

On a hot afternoon, the cold, clear water, nice lunch spots, and good ender hole draw rafters and kayakers to this river canyon. The rapids are fairly continuous, especially during the first few miles. The river is very narrow and one must move from one side of the river to the other and back again. If, at the end of the run, you decide to run Husum Falls, you might receive the added pleasure of running the slalom course for the Husum–White Salmon Slalom and Wildwater Race, an annual event held here in July.

This exciting class 3+ run has two class 4 drops that can be portaged. The first drop, BZ Rapids, is the most difficult and can be scouted on the right while putting in. It can be portaged on the right by carrying boats down the rock shelves to the last possible put-in area. The last drop, Husum Falls, is a 15-foot vertical drop generally run right of center. Scout Husum Falls from the take-out in Husum. Take out about 150 feet before the falls on river right to avoid the plunge.

Hazards. The first and last drops are by far the most intense. If you can't see through an entire drop, scout it first. Also, keep a sharp eye for logs spanning the river.

Access. To reach the take-out, from the Portland area take I-84 east to Hood River. Cross the Columbia River at the White Salmon Bridge, turn left onto Washington 14, then turn right onto Washington 141 just before crossing the mouth of the White Salmon River. Follow Washington 141 north, following the signs to Husum. The take-out is on Washington 141 at Husum, either 500 feet below the falls on river left or 150 feet above the falls on river right.

To get to the put-in, continue north on Washington 141 to BZ Corner, go past the town about 0.2 mile, and turn right at the sign indicat-

The Faucet on the White Salmon (photo by Jason Bates)

ing the put-in. This is private land which you are permitted to use after paying a fee to the landowner; knock on his door.

Gauge. The flow should be approximately equal to the release from the Pacific Power and Light station at Northwestern Lake, which is downstream from Husum. Flow information is available from the River Forecast Center in Seattle (206-526-8350).

John Karafotias

156 White Salmon River, Washington
Husum to Northwestern Lake

Class: 2
Flow: 900–2,000 cfs
Gradient: 25 fpm, PD

Length: 3 miles
Character: shallow canyon
Season: year-round

The very scenic lower run on the White Salmon winds its way through a shallow, wooded canyon. It is short, but beginning boaters enjoy the class 1–2 rapids and may even stop to play at a few spots. The upper end of the run has opportunities for practicing eddy turns and surfing small waves. The lower end of the run near the take-out is flat—great for "paddle-in-a-straight-line" practice.

Hazards. At high water some of the play spots develop good class 3 holes. The water is always very cold.

Access. For directions to Husum, the put-in, see run 155, White Salmon River: BZ Corner to Husum.

The take-out is back down Washington 141 from Husum. Take the first road to the right that crosses a bridge; go over the bridge and turn left into a small park on Northwestern Lake. There is usually a landing fee charged during the summer.

Gauge. See run 155, White Salmon River: BZ Corner to Husum.

Bob Collmer

WIND RIVER

157 Wind River, Washington
Stabler to High Bridge

Class: 5
Flow: 300–1,500 cfs
Gradient: 90 fpm, PD

Length: 6 miles
Character: forested gorge
Season: rainy/snowmelt

This river has an extremely long season, from the start of the rainy season until late May or June. The river flows through beautiful scenery approaching that of a rain forest. One has the feeling of being deep in an isolated gorge. However, the road is always relatively close on river left and is accessible from almost anywhere along the run. At medium level the river is calm at the take-out, and at the put-in the river appears to have minimum water.

Because of the power and pushiness of the water, and the continuity of the rapids in the 2 miles below Rock Creek, the author believes this run is one of the more difficult in the area. There are stories about long dangerous swims and unexpected winter overnight camping. It is strongly advised that boaters new to this river run it with those who are familiar with it.

Put in at Stabler and enjoy the 0.8 mile of technical class 3- warm-up. An optional put-in is on Trout Creek for 0.6 mile of very technical water before reaching the Wind River. The biggest rapids on the Wind are in the first third of the trip and are close together. The first big rapids is Initiation, identified by a house on a cliff on the left and the confluence of Trout Creek on the right. This long rapids can be scouted from river left. Following Initiation are four tightly spaced rapids, which become a single mile-long rapids in medium-high water. Just past here, eddy out on river left to scout the next major drop, Ram's Horn. Below this rapids is the first real pool since Initiation.

Looking downstream from the pool, boaters can see a 30-foot waterfall entering the Wind River on the right. Several drops of moderate difficulty follow, then Climax, the biggest drop on the river, is reached. At levels above medium-high, careless paddlers have been uncomfortably recirculated for extended periods of time. Fortunately, at these levels Climax can be sneaked on the far right, which is also the side on which to scout or portage. After Climax, the rapids ease up. Take a breather on the second half of the run and enjoy the scenery!

Hazards. Initiation, Ram's Horn, and Climax are the most difficult and are all within the first third of the trip.

Access. The Wind River is near the town of Carson, Washington, which is off Washington 14 about 7 miles east of Bonneville Dam. From Carson drive north on Wind River Road. To get to the take-out, turn left onto High Bridge Road, which is about 300 yards south of High Bridge across the Wind River. There is a sign for a log-scaling station on the right just north of High Bridge Road. From High Bridge Road make the first right onto Old Detour Road and follow this dirt road down to the river and the take-out.

To reach the put-in, return to Wind River Road, turn left, cross the Wind River, and continue north to the town of Stabler. Make a left onto Hemlock Road and immediately cross the Wind River. Put in at this bridge or make the first right and then bear right for an alternate put-in.

To get to the Trout Creek put-in, continue west on Hemlock Road from Stabler and turn at the first left, which is Trout Creek Road. Follow this road south until it crosses Trout Creek, the put-in. (Alternately, continue on Hemlock Road and put in about 1 mile higher on Trout Creek. There are no significant rapids on this mile.)

Gauge. Located near Carson. No known correlation exists. The river is usually runnable when the Three Lynx gauge on the Clackamas reads 1,900 cfs or more. To approximate the level, look at the pilings from the ramp at the take-out. If six or seven tops are showing, the level is medium to low. If four or five are showing, the river will be quite pushy.

Harvey Lee Shapiro

158 Wind River, Washington
High Bridge to Columbia River

Class: 4(5)	**Length: 5 miles**
Flow: 800 cfs	**Character: forested gorge**
Gradient: 50 fpm, PD	**Season: rainy/snowmelt**

The first 0.5 mile of this run is class 1 and 2 water for warm-up. In the more difficult water below, the pool-drop nature allows easy scouting. The excitement begins as High Bridge comes into view. High Bridge Rapids is a long complex class 4 boulder garden that becomes quite pushy at higher flows. Another 0.5 mile downstream, the river backs up before crashing through The Flume. This class 5 rapids creates an obvious horizon line and can be scouted or portaged on river right.

Beyond The Flume, the Wind River continues to demand concentration and sound judgment. The next big rapids, Beyond Limits, a steep falls that slams onto a rocky keeper, is usually portaged along the fish ladder on the left. Next, Shepherds Falls creates an unrunnable obstacle that demands a strenuous portage on the left. Eddy out far enough upstream to allow a safe hike along the fish ladder, then portage over and down the cliff on the left bank. A throw rope comes in handy here. The final mile to the Columbia River is normally class 2. The take-out is on the Columbia River at a boat ramp near the Washington 14 bridge.

Hazards. The Flume, class 5, at mile 1, should be scouted or portaged on the right. Beyond Limits rapids, about another 0.5 mile down, is usually portaged. Shepherds Falls is a *mandatory portage*. Although the lead-in to the falls is only class 2, use the utmost caution and catch an eddy. Never cross a horizon line before scouting.

Access. In Oregon, take I-84 to Bridge of the Gods at Bonneville Dam, and cross the Columbia River to Washington 14. Follow Washington 14 east for 7.8 miles. Shortly after crossing Senator Al Henry Bridge, turn left on Old Hatchery Road and proceed 0.4 mile to a developed boat ramp, the take-out.

To get to the put-in, return to Washington 14 and head west. Immediately after crossing Senator Al Henry Bridge, turn right onto Hot Springs Avenue. At mile 1.9, turn right at the four-way stop onto Wind River Road. In 1.9 miles reach High Bridge Road and turn left. Finally, 0.1 mile later, turn right onto Old Detour Road. Follow this road to the river. The take-out before the last mile of class 2 water is up a long, steep trail to Carson Hot Springs Hotel, which is 1 mile up Hot Springs Avenue from the take-out.

Gauge. See run 157, Wind River: Stabler to High Bridge.

Jeff Bennett

WASHOUGAL RIVER AND TRIBUTARIES

The Washougal River system is not large, but its proximity to the Portland metropolitan area makes it popular. It offers some steep runs that include a number of waterfalls. Because the drainage area is not large and is at relatively low elevations, substantial rains are needed for boating.

159 West Fork Washougal River, Washington
West Fork Bridge to Washougal River

Class: 4+ P	Length: 7 miles
Flow: 400 cfs	Character: wooded canyon
Gradient: 100 fpm, PD	Season: rainy

The West Fork Washougal River is an exciting, steep, and technically demanding run for expert boaters. In addition to countless class 3–4 rapids, the run boasts a gradient often in excess of 100 fpm, and five narrow falls that require precise boat handling or portages.

At the put-in, the West Fork appears to be a shallow rock-strewn stream, but constant feeder streams quickly increase the flow. Within 1 mile of the put-in, the river begins to display its true character as it disappears over a horizon line at Teakettle Falls. This 16-foot double drop has been run on river left, but a strong diagonal wave above the last drop makes the final moves very difficult. At normal flows some of the falls drop into chutes only 3–4 feet wide, and therefore must be portaged. Save some energy for the near-perfect play hole that forms at some flows on the main Washougal shortly below the confluence with the West Fork. The take-out is on river left about 0.5 mile below the confluence.

Hazards. The steep gradient, falls, and potential for sweepers produce a difficult run that mandates constant scouting. Some portages may require steep scrambles through thick brush.

Access. Cross the Columbia River in Portland and take Washington 14 east to the town of Washougal. From the town of Washougal, follow Washington 140 8.4 miles upstream. When Washougal River Road and Washington 140 split, turn right across the bridge. After 75 yards, turn right again onto Sportsman Road and follow it 300 yards to the Washington Game Department Public Access Area, the take-out.

To reach the put-in, return back across the bridge to Washougal River Road and go 0.5 mile farther upstream. Turn left on Skye Road and proceed 3.7 miles. Turn right on Northeast 412th Avenue/Skamania Mines Road and go 2.6 miles to the stop sign. Turn left on 1200 Road and stay left at the first fork. The put-in is 0.7 mile from the stop sign at a turnoff just before the bridge over the West Fork Washougal River. There is an alternate put-in at a bridge about 1 mile down Skamania Mines Road.

Gauge. None exists. However, there are two visual indicators on the main Washougal. Both are beneath the bridge near the take-out where Washington 140 and Washougal River Road split. First, look at the fence posts on river left. The river should be between the fifth and sixth post counting up from the river. Second, look at the steel base plate for the bridge support girder on upstream river right. Water should be lapping on the steel portion of this support. Either cue indicates adequate flow on the North Fork.

Jeff Bennett

160 Washougal River, Washington
Doc's Drop to Dougan Falls

Class: 5+	**Length: 2.6 miles**
Flow: 1,500 cfs	**Character: forested**
Gradient: 55 fpm, PD	**Season: rainy**

This run is a favorite for thrill-seekers who like to run waterfalls in catarafts, self-bailing rafts, and kayaks. Because the run is short and quick, it can be added to the next run (see run 161, Washougal River: Dougan Falls to Salmon Falls).

From the put-in, the action begins immediately with Doc's Drop, a 10-foot drop on a boulder ledge. A half mile downstream is Reeder Falls, a 4-foot drop just above the bridge. It is easiest to approach Reeder Falls from the right. Just below the bridge is Naked Falls, a 15-foot drop over a few ledges, which should be run right of center—left is suicidal. The 1.8 miles of class 1 and 2 water that follow allow time to think about Dougan Falls, the grand finale, a 15-foot drop over two ledges. Dougan Falls is normally run close to the right bank.

Hazards. The four named falls are rated as class 5–5+. Each can be scouted during the drive to the put-in. Scout Dougan Falls at the take-out. Drive 1.9 miles upriver to scout Naked Falls. Upriver 0.1 mile, Reeder Falls can be scouted from the bridge. Scout Doc's Drop at the put-in. Remember, if in doubt, stay river right.

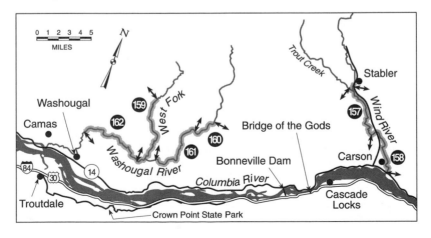

Access. Cross the Columbia River in Portland and take Washington 14 east to Washougal. From Washougal, follow Washington 140 upstream 8.4 miles; when Washougal River Road and Washington 140 split, continue straight on Washougal River Road (Washington 140 turns right). Go 7.2 miles to the take-out at the bridge below Dougan Falls. The put-in at Doc's Drop is 2.6 miles upstream.

Gauge. None exists. The flow is unregulated. Several days of hard rain are required. If the flow looks too low to run Dougan Falls, don't run the rest.

Val Shaull and Jeff Bennett

161 Washougal River, Washington
Dougan Falls to Salmon Falls

Class: 3-(4) P; 5 P   Length: 6 miles
Flow: 700 cfs; 2,000 cfs   Character: wooded; fishing
Gradient: 42 fpm, PD   Season: rainy

Although it is less than an hour from the Portland–Vancouver area, the upper Washougal is not often run. This apparent lack of popularity may be due to the dramatic changes in character of the river over this 6-mile stretch. In the upper section, long stretches of flat water, with occasional class 2 or 3 rapids, appeal to intermediate boaters; but the gorge presents class 4 water and is difficult to portage. Remember that the banks are private property above the high-water line. Be respectful of private property.

There is a concrete weir 1.5 miles from the put-in and just downstream from a short class 3 drop. It is marked by a wire across the river. Portage right. A wooden dam lies just beyond the highway bridge. From December 1 through September 15, sections of the dam are removed for migrating salmon, and it can be run on the left. Otherwise, portage on the right. Both portages can be scouted on the way to the put-in.

The beginning of the difficult water at rivermile 4.5 is marked by a green trailer on a hill on the right where the bank is washed out. Just downstream is a class 3+ entrance rapids. If the class 4 water below is to be portaged, it is necessary to get out above this entrance rapids, on the right, and carry along the road high above. The return to the river after this portage involves a challenging hike through blackberry bushes. Below this entrance rapids, the river passes through a pool and then drops out of sight. Scout from the right bank at low to medium water, but from the left at high water. The rapids is about 200 yards long with several distinct parts at low water. At high water it is class 5 with huge holes and little room for error.

The river broadens again for the last mile before the take-out above Salmon Falls. Be sure to scout the landmarks here, because the falls comes up fast around a blind curve. Although Salmon Falls has been run at some levels, it has dangerous rocks and a keeper at the bottom. Run in 1977–78 by Rod Kiel, Dan Breznai, and Chuck Stanley.

Hazards. There are two dangerous but easily portaged obstacles in the first 3 miles: the concrete weir and the wooden dam.

Access. For directions to where Washougal River Road and Washington 140 split, see run 160, Washougal River: Doc's Drop to Dougan Falls. At the split, take Washougal River Road straight ahead (Washington 140 turns right across the river). Continue 1.5 miles from this point to the Salmon Falls Fish Hatchery. Pull off on the right side of the road near a dirt road that leads down to the river. This is the take-out.

To get to the put-in, follow the road upstream 5.7 miles to the second bridge. Dougan Falls is on the right. The put-in is on either side of the bridge or upstream from the falls.

Gauge. None exists. The flow is unregulated. It is runnable only after a heavy rainfall.

Maryann McCormick and Susan Seyl

162 Washougal River, Washington
10-Mile Bridge to above Washougal

Class: 3(4); 4	**Length: 7.3 miles**
Flow: 200–800 cfs;	**Character: forested; residential;**
1,000–5,000 cfs	**agricultural**
Gradient: 33 fpm, C	**Season: rainy**

This delightful run is close to Portland. It has several different types of rapids. A class 4 boulder garden, called Big Eddy, is about 2.5 miles below the put-in. A short distance downstream is a steep class 3 rapids with a large hole midstream. Many of the rapids are wide and clean.

Hazards. Big Eddy Rapids, the class 4 boulder garden, can be scouted from the road 4.7 miles above the take-out.

Access. Cross the Columbia River in Portland and take Washington 14 east to the town of Washougal. At the town of Washougal take Washington 140 north and go upstream approximately 2.5 miles to the take-out at an unimproved boat ramp.

The put-in is 7.3 miles farther upstream. Cross at the bridge, turn right, and proceed down a gravel road to a public access across the river from the store. There is an access point at a public area 1 mile above Big Eddy Rapids.

Gauge. None exists. The flow is unregulated. A flow of 1,500 cfs is excellent and occurs when the Twin Rocks in Big Eddy Rapids are barely exposed.

Stan Jacobs and Jay Nigra

REGION 8
CENTRAL OREGON RIVERS

DESCHUTES RIVER AND TRIBUTARIES

The Deschutes River, Oregon's second-longest river, drains the east side of the Cascade Mountains from Diamond Peak to the Columbia River. Near the source, the river has stretches of class 1 or easier water. However, the literal translation of the French name "Riviere des Chutes" (river of falls) should not be overlooked because there are some class 4–6 waterfalls. In Bend the river flows through lovely Drake City Park. From Bend to Lake Billy Chinook, the river level is normally quite low because much of the water is diverted into irrigation canals. Local boaters sometimes set up a class 2 or 3 slalom course in a canal. Two main tributaries, the Crooked and Metolius rivers, join the Deschutes in the upper arms of Lake Billy Chinook. Below the lake, the flow is regulated and always has enough water for boating. The Warm Springs River, which enters below Lake Billy Chinook, is no longer runnable because the Warm Springs Indian Council closed access to the river. The lower regions of the Deschutes have considerable class 2 whitewater, some class 3, and unrunnable Sherars Falls. The White River is the lowermost major tributary.

Rob Blickensderfer

163 Metolius River
Source to Lake Billy Chinook

Class: 3(4)   Length: 30 miles
Flow: 1,300–2,000 cfs   Character: forested; fishing
Gradient: 24 fpm, C   Season: year-round

This very unusual river originates in the Cascades beneath Black Butte. Within several hundred feet, the river wells up from the ground and becomes 30 feet wide. Within 0.5 mile, the river swells to an average flow of 1,500 cfs, from which it deviates little throughout the year. Because the water comes from underground, it is always frigid. The river level fluctuates so little that the banks are overgrown with heavy vegetation. At the first bridge in the community of Camp Sherman, visitors pause to look for the huge trout waiting to be fed. Throwing a few salmon eggs into the water makes the fish suddenly appear as the bait disappears. The character of the Metolius can be divided into two sections.

Section 1: Source to Lower Bridge Campground, 13 miles. This section has a resort atmosphere with private camps, forest campgrounds, and picnic areas. The source is on private land, fenced to keep the public out. The river flows through meadowlands for the first few miles, and put-ins are along the road. The bridge at the resort community of Camp Sherman, about 3 miles downstream, provides access, as do the improved campgrounds farther downstream. From the source to several miles below Camp Sherman, the river is swift and replete with snags, but has no significant whitewater.

The tempo increases below Gorge Campground, which is 3 miles below Camp Sherman and 6 miles below the source. The Gorge is a fast class 3 rapids about 1 mile below Gorge Campground. Along the right bank of The Gorge, a group of springs gush forth into the river. Because of the inaccessibility of The Gorge, very few people other than boaters have seen these lovely springs. Immediately downstream, the land on both sides of the river is privately owned, so stay off of it. One or more of the very low bridges may require a portage. Kayakers sometimes run low bridges "bottoms-up" and roll up once the passage is completed. Wizard Falls, just above a low bridge to Wizard Falls Fish Hatchery, is not a true falls but a turbulent region with narrow channels through lava bedrock. The 3 miles from Wizard Falls to Lower Bridge Campground are class 1. Because Section 1 has been designated for fly fishing only, it is a favorite area for anglers, so respect their space.

Section 2: Lower Bridge Campground to Lake Billy Chinook, 17 miles. This section contains premier crystal-clear whitewater in a primitive setting. The swiftness and uniform gradient of the water, and the thick vegetation, make eddies and landing spots hard to find. A swimming boater may float a long way before finding a landing spot. Because of the river's swiftness, these 17 miles can be easily run in a day.

Starting at Lower Bridge Campground, the tempo increases for 1 mile, then a long class 3 rapids begins. The lower end of this rapids cannot be seen from the top. Therefore, check for possible tree blockage from the dirt road below Lower Bridge. Numerous long class 2 and 3 rapids with truly beautiful whitewater continue. A very poor dirt road extends for 8 miles downstream from Lower Bridge and a gravel road extends several miles upstream from Lake Billy Chinook. Between the roads is wilderness with no access. Along the dirt road are numerous primitive camping areas with access to the river. In the inaccessible area, the water is similar to that along the dirt road except that it has the most difficult rapids on the river, an easy class 4 located about 2 miles below the end of the dirt road. It is in a straight section of river identified by boulders and large holes at the top, the most difficult part. The river continues at a fast pace to Lake Billy Chinook, where the change to flat water is like a gentle awakening from a pleasant dream. Take out on the right at Monty Campground along the river above the lake or paddle down the lake 2 miles to the first public campground.

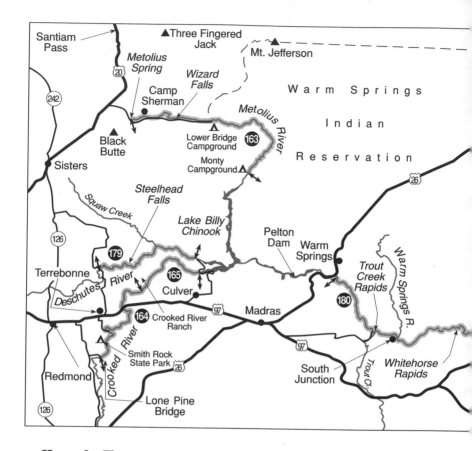

Hazards. The greatest danger is the potential of a large ponderosa pine completely blocking the river. A short distance below Gorge Campground is The Gorge, a relatively long, fast class 3 rapids requiring rock dodging. The second and longer fast class 3 rapids is located 1 mile below Lower Bridge. The most difficult rapids is an easy class 4 located about 2 miles below the end of the dirt road. Be prepared for very cold water, about 43 degrees Fahrenheit at most, year-round.

Access. From the west, take US 20 or Oregon 22 east across Santiam Pass, or from the east, take Oregon 22 west from Sisters toward Santiam Pass. The turnoff to the Metolius is 5.5 miles east of Suttle Lake. Follow the signs to "HEAD OF THE METOLIUS." This unusual sight is well worth seeing! The paved road from the Head of the Metolius essentially parallels the river on the east side to Lower Bridge Campground, where a poor secondary road continues along the east side for another 8 miles and dead ends at a trail.

Put-ins are available at any of the campgrounds along the road to Lower Bridge Campground. If you put in at Gorge Campground or Wiz-

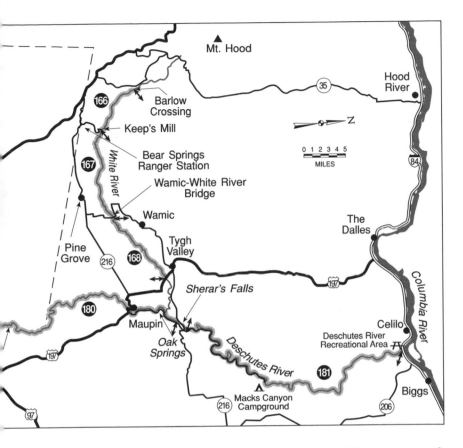

ard Falls, for example, the take-out can be at any of the unimproved camps below Lower Bridge Campground or at the end of the dirt road. If the take-out is at one of the unimproved camps, be sure to find a good landmark because this region all looks the same from the river.

The shuttle to the Lake Billy Chinook take-out is about 35 miles, mostly over gravel roads. From Lower Bridge Campground, go upstream about 0.5 mile on Route 14. Turn left onto NFD 1490 and climb Green Ridge. At the junction with NFD 1140 (Prairie Farm Road), head east on 1140. Farther east, Prairie Farm Road continues as NFD 1180 and then 1170 to its end at a blacktop road, Route 64, near the lake. Turn left, pass Perry South Campground, and continue another 5 miles to the Monty Campground on the lower Metolius, about 0.5 mile above lake water.

Gauge. Flow information is unnecessary because discharges range from 1,250–2,500 cfs with a 58-year mean of 1,500 cfs.

T. R. Torgersen and Rob Blickensderfer

164 Crooked River
Lone Pine Bridge to Crooked River Ranch

Class: 3(4); 4(5)   **Length: 18 miles**
Flow: 800 cfs; 4,000 cfs   **Character: inaccessible desert gorge**
Gradient: 40 fpm, PD   **Season: dam-controlled**

The Crooked River has many big rapids and runs through a spectacular gorge. There are few good put-ins or take-outs on this hair-raising run for advanced to expert boaters. Much equipment has been lost in the Crooked River gorge. The next lost paddle or boat could be yours if you decide to run this river! For rafters, the run requires quality river rafts and expert rowers able to run technical drops of 10–25 feet.

There are two possible put-ins for this run, one 4 miles above Smith Rock State Park and the other 1.5 miles above the park. The put-in 1.5 miles above the park immediately begins with 1.5 miles of continuous class 4 rapids. Then there is a long loop of very slow water around Smith Rock State Park. Rock climbers flock to this area year-round for some of the best climbing in Oregon. Boaters who paddle around Smith Rock hear cries of "crazy" from above. The "crazy" may well apply to the small speck hundreds of feet above the river.

About 1 mile downstream of the park is Number One, the first rapids in a series of rapids. Number One is a very steep, short drop with a boulder in the center and more boulders and big holes in the left channel. Scout right. About 1 mile farther is Number Two, which may be run on the left or right side of Lava Island. This drop has a difficult approach and should be scouted from the left.

The next rapids is a series of waves called The Bumps, located about 0.2 mile beyond Number Two. The Bumps are a prelude to Wap-te-doodle, a very long drop with powerful hydraulics and a very large hole at bottom center. It can be scouted from the left; note the log on the left. There are a couple of lesser rapids between here and the US 97 bridge that crosses high above.

From the bridge to the next major rapids, called No Name, the river is a very busy class 3–4. No Name is very long and rough, with many boulders and a large hole at the bottom. Scout on the right. Several shorter and easier rapids follow. The next major rapids is Chinese Dam, located at the end of a stretch of flat water along sheer cliffs. The dam was built for mining operations years ago. The river broke through the dam, leaving the center and the left of the riverbed very shallow and with sharp rocks. Scout. Chinese Dam can be quite difficult at lower levels.

It is possible to take out just above Chinese Dam Rapids on the left at the access road from the Crooked River Ranch. This take-out requires a very steep climb to the public access road. An easier take-out is about 200 yards below Chinese Dam. Public facilities are available at the ranch for camping. Run in April 1975 by Rod Keil, Ted Ragsdale, George and Gene Ice, the late Bob Porter, and several others.

Hazards. This run presents many difficulties that demand special attention. Retreat from the river due to equipment loss or injury is very difficult in most of the canyon.

Access. The put-in is 6 miles east of US 97 between Redmond and Madras. From US 97 at Terrebonne, go east 3 miles to Smith Rock State Park, and continue another 3 miles east to the Lone Pine Bridge, the put-in. An alternate put-in is 1 mile east of Smith Rock State Park at the aqueduct.

The take-out is at Crooked River Ranch, a resort community. The roads are public. From US 97 north of Terrebonne, follow the signs to Crooked River Ranch and the clubhouse. Drive past the clubhouse and turn right just before the little white church. Continue on the gravel road to a graveled lot. Drive through the gate on Hollywood Road, a very rough, steep (four-wheel-drive) road down 1.3 miles to Chinese Dam, or portage 1.3 miles to the canyon rim.

Gauge. It is runnable for only a short time each year, usually in late April. In years of low snowfall there may be no water released. For information on planned releases, contact the Oregon Department of Water Resources Watermaster in Bend or the Ochoco Irrigation District in Prineville (541-447-6449).

Ron Mattson and Scott Russell

165 Crooked River
Crooked River Ranch to Lake Billy Chinook

Class: 3(4) P **Length: 9 miles**
Flow: 1,000–5,000 cfs **Character: inaccessible desert gorge**
Gradient: 35 fpm, PD **Season: year-round**

This part of the Crooked River is not quite as intense, and only half as long, as the previous run. Still, there are some challenging rapids and boaters are a long way from help. With a flow of only 100 cfs at Prineville Dam, numerous springs increase the flow to 1,000 cfs within 5–6 miles, making the river runnable year-round. Boaters may opt to put in either above Chinese Dam Rapids, class 4, or about 200 yards downstream. At normal summer flows (low), Chinese Dam is not runnable. Put in below it.

One mile past Chinese Dam is The Wave, which, at flows above 3,500 cfs, has a steep "V"-wave that envelops boaters with water converging overhead. A rockfall (1990) from the left at the top makes low-water runs more difficult. The Wave is steep; at really low water, the left looks most promising, but it may not be runnable. It is rocky on top left and even worse on bottom right. At higher water, center to right is best.

Four miles farther is Opal Springs Dam, where the river disappears into a power tunnel. It is recognized by a concrete structure on the left. Portage right for 0.2 mile (beware of sharp and slippery rocks) and put in at the generator tail water. Below Opal Springs Dam is Opal Springs itself, followed by a gauge; both are on the right. Several easier rapids follow. The last whitewater before Lake Billy Chinook is long, with heavy whitewater and big holes. It is very likely to contain logs or trees. Scouting is highly recommended. The main chutes force boaters left where logs are most likely to be lurking. The recommended route is to work right as soon as possible and stay there. About 3 miles of lake paddling brings boaters to the take-out at the bridge over the Crooked River arm of the lake. Run in April 1975 by Rod Keil, Ted Ragsdale, Gene and George Ice, the late Bob Porter, and several others.

Hazards. The Wave, 1 mile below Chinese Dam, is steep. Opal Springs Dam must be portaged. The last rapids has big water. Logs or trees in the river may block channels at any time.

Access. For the put-in at Crooked River Ranch, see the take-out for run 164, Crooked River: Lone Pine Bridge to Crooked River Ranch.

The take-out bridge crosses the Crooked River arm of Lake Billy Chinook several miles west of US 97 near Culver, between Madras and Redmond. From US 97 south of Madras, go west a few miles to Culver. Follow signs to Cove Palisades State Park, about 6 miles west of Culver. Pass the park and continue to the bridge.

Gauge. Located below Opal Springs Dam, on right. It is not telemetered. At 2 feet the flow is nearly 1,200 cfs, and at 3 feet, it is 1,700 cfs.

Scott Russell and Hank Hays

166 White River
Barlow Crossing to Keeps Mill

Class: 3(4)	**Length: 6 miles**
Flow: 400–1,400 cfs	**Character: forested**
Gradient: 50 fpm	**Season: snowmelt**

This magnificent river starts on the east side of Mount Hood among the trees and often in snow, continues through a wilderness gorge, and ends in a desert. The change in scenery en route is spectacular. This upper run is seldom done because the next run, starting at Keeps Mill, is sufficiently long, interesting, and spectacular to keep most paddlers content. This upper run has accumulated many logs in recent years and is no longer very enjoyable.

The put-in is at Barlow Crossing, where the pioneers crossed the White River while traveling Barlow Road. The first 2.5 miles below Barlow Crossing are class 1+. The river gradient then increases and there are many blind turns. The first significant drop is 3 miles below Barlow Crossing. It consists of two big ledges, class 4, which should be scouted on river left. From here to Keeps Mill is a fast-flowing continuous class 3+ with lots of maneuvering required. A Mount Hood National Forest map, which shows the entire river and all shuttle roads, is indispensible.

Hazards. The numerous logs in the river make the run especially hazardous.

Access. From Portland take US 26 east; from eastern Oregon take

US 26 west from Madras on US 97. On the shoulders of Mount Hood, turn north onto Oregon 35. After a few miles, turn right on Forest Road 43, which crosses the White River at Barlow Crossing, the put-in.

To get to the Keeps Mill take-out, return to US 26 and follow the instructions for the put-in for run 167, White River: Keeps Mill to Wamic–White River Bridge. For runs from Barlow Crossing to Wamic–White River Bridge, shuttle on the north side of the river, turn right, and continue on Forest Road 48. One mile before Wamic, turn right, following signs to Smock Prairie Road, and continue (the road becomes dirt) to White River Bridge.

Gauge. None exists.

Harvey Lee Shapiro

167 White River
Keeps Mill to Wamic–White River Bridge

Class: 3+(4); 4–(4+) **Length: 12 miles**
Flow: 400 cfs; 1,400 cfs **Character: forested**
Gradient: 46 fpm **Season: snowmelt**

The water is always cold, but from January to March the air temperature is also cold within the deep canyon. Winter runs are therefore uncomfortably cold and not recommended. In May and June the air temperature is warmer and the steep canyon rocks radiate heat, resulting in very warm or hot air, especially in the lower half of this run. The character of the run is very similar to what you see at the put-in: continuous fast-moving whitewater over rocks, a few boulders, and an occasional logjam. The river is a continuous class 3+ with a beautiful rhythm of its own. There is one class 4 rapids. At medium levels, eddies and play spots are abundant. All drops are runnable and can be scouted by eddy hopping, except for the inevitable occasional logjam.

The most difficult rapids on the river is about 1.5 miles below Keeps Mill. It can be recognized by the highest cliffs on river left one or two drops above the rapids. It should be scouted by first-time paddlers. Problems in this rapids are unpleasant and result in an extremely long and difficult day in this wild canyon. Scout on the right from above before starting the easy lead-in, because there is no easy eddy immediately above the drop. Normally it is approached on river left and run right of center. About 8 miles below the put-in, a wire crosses the river, with hanging metal gates on each shore and several others in the river. These mark the Mount Hood National Forest boundary. A short way below here the river gains more volume, and at higher water levels becomes pushy and more memorable.

Hazards. Logjams that require portaging are likely. Most paddlers underestimate the speed of the current, which results in dangerous encounters with logjams on almost every trip. Scout the class 4 rapids 1.5 miles below Keeps Mill.

Access. From the Portland area take US 26 east; from eastern Oregon take US 26 west from Madras. At Oregon 216, turn east toward

Maupin. After 3 miles look for a small green sign to Keeps Mill/White River on the right side just as the road takes a long curve to the right. (If you see a sign for Bear Springs Ranger Station, you have gone 0.3 mile too far.) Turn left and continue on the main road down to the river. Follow signs to Keeps Mill. The road for the last 1.5 miles is dirt with rock slides. It is slow but passable and arrives at a primitive campground.

To reach the take-out, go back to Oregon 216, turn left on Oregon 216 and head east toward Maupin, and continue past Bear Springs Ranger Station to Pine Grove. About 3.5 miles past Pine Grove, there is a small green sign on the right that reads "VICTOR ROAD, WAMIC, WHITE RIVER." Turn left onto this dirt road and follow it as it jogs right and then left. Shortly after it turns right again, take the first road to the left. There is a sign to Wamic on the right side, if someone hasn't knocked it over. After making the left turn, note the sign about the road being extremely hazardous, especially in winter. Have faith and continue to the river and the take-out at Wamic–White River Bridge on river left.

Gauge. None exists.

Harvey Lee Shapiro

168 White River
Wamic–White River Bridge to Tygh Valley

Class: 3(4)   **Length: 11 miles**
Flow: 400–2,000 cfs   **Character: forested canyon**
Gradient: 40 fpm, PD **Season: snowmelt**

This is a beautiful run through some of the most delightful canyons in Oregon. Don't do this run just for the whitewater. Do it for the scenery and the possibility of seeing hawks, eagles, lynx, ouzels, vultures, mergansers, grouse, deer, deer flies, and butterflies. The river passes springs, caves, beaches, and creeks but, most of all, has a wonderful sense of isolation. The first half of this remote run has the easiest whitewater and the best scenery, where rock walls rise right out of the river. In the second half of the run, the steep canyon walls are farther from the river and the difficulty of the rapids increases. At low levels the run is very technical, especially the last two rapids. At higher flows, the first 9 miles provide fast-moving class 2+ rapids and the last two rapids are more open with greater choices, but are significantly pushier with bigger waves.

The run starts with a rocky or bouncy rapids just below the put-in. If boaters have trouble here, return to the vehicle, because the rapids on the lower part are significantly more difficult. About halfway through the run, an eroding multihued ash-and-dirt bank on river right signals the start of the more challenging whitewater. Logs frequently complicate this rapids, and all the others as well, so be prepared to dodge, duck, or portage at any time. The two long rapids above Tygh Valley are the most difficult. They start quickly, so pay careful attention and eddy out before entering these rapids. The first of these is a long, winding class 3+ log-choked rapids. The final rapids is rated as class 4- because it is very long and continuous class 3+ water in the wilderness.

Warning: Three miles below Tygh Valley is a 90-foot unrunnable waterfall. It can be viewed from White River State Park.

Hazards. Throughout this run, constantly watch for logjams, and use extreme care when approaching them. Be sure to leave room to stop for logjams. Do not underestimate the speed of the current. Consider scouting the last two rapids.

Access. To reach the put-in, follow directions to the take-out for run 167, White River: Keeps Mill to Wamic–White River Bridge.

From the put-in, continue on the north-side dirt road toward Wamic. Once you progress from dirt to paved road, stay on paved road. (As of 1991 there was a sign incorrectly pointing to Wamic via a dirt road.) Follow the paved road to the stop sign; turn right and continue through Wamic toward Tygh Valley. At the stop sign, turn right and follow this road to the Tygh Valley White River bridge. Take out on river right, above or below the bridge.

If boaters do not have to pick up a shuttle vehicle at Keeps Mill, they can return to Portland on the north side of the White River. Follow signs to Wamic. (Be careful to make the correct right turn in Tygh Valley toward Wamic. At the right turn, there are two roads; take the left one.) Follow this road through Wamic. About 1 mile beyond Wamic, turn right and follow signs to Sportsman Park and Rock Creek Reservoir. Continue straight on this road, which becomes Forest Road 48 and goes all the way to Oregon 35. Make a left on Oregon 35, which merges into US 26.

Gauge. None exists. A warm day on Mount Hood will raise the river. If the first rapids below the put-in is runnable, probably the entire run is runnable.

Harvey Lee Shapiro and Linda Starr

169 Deschutes River
Wickiup Dam to Pringle Falls

Class: 1(4)   Length: 9 miles
Flow: 500–1,000 cfs   Character: forested; osprey sanctuary
Gradient: 4 fpm, C   Season: dam-controlled

This is one of the author's favorite class 1 runs in Oregon. Many things combine to create a stimulating and often exhilarating experience; high mountain air, clear blue water, ponderosa pines, abundant camping sites, and great fishing are but a few. Perhaps the strongest asset of this region is the dense population of osprey. The sound of an osprey calling and the sight of a vertical dive to pull a 12-inch trout from the water near your canoe are experiences not soon forgotten.

The majority of boaters on this stretch take out at Wyeth Campground on river left. There are signs warning of upcoming Pringle

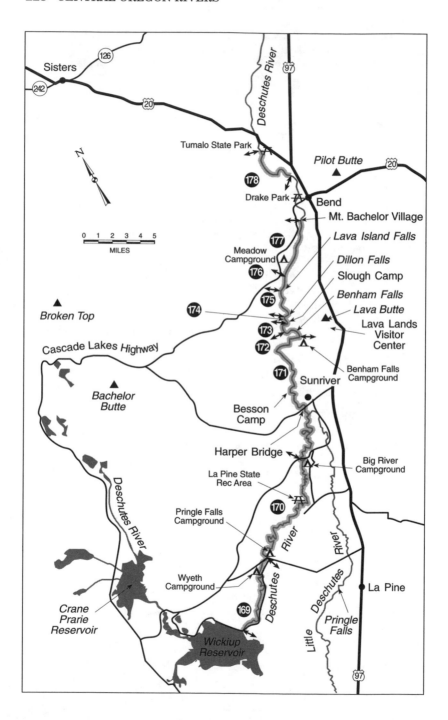

Falls, class 4, which lies just below here. Only expert kayakers should consider this drop, and only after scouting. It is definitely not a rapids for open canoes.

For those who wish to continue downstream without running the falls, a portage is possible. The portage around Pringle Falls is long but easy walking. From Wyeth Campground, follow the entry road to Forest Road 43; turn right and cross the river. Continue about 0.3 mile to the second road on the left and follow it to Pringle Falls Campground. The portage is about 1.5 miles long. Unfortunately, the land on both sides of the falls is private, thus necessitating the long portage.

The falls starts with 200 yards of class 2- whitewater above the NFD 204 bridge. Experienced class 2 boaters could eddy out on river right just above the bridge and save almost half the portage distance. The next 100 yards of class 3+ water lead into a class 4 drop with a potential keeper just above a footbridge. The remaining 200 yards are a bouncy class 3.

Hazards. The portage around Pringle Falls is difficult. Do not accidentally go over Pringle Falls.

Access. Most people reach this river section from US 97 between La Pine and Bend. About 2 miles north of La Pine, or about 4.5 miles south of the entrance to La Pine Recreation Area, turn west onto Forest Road 43 at a sign to Wickiup Reservoir. In 9 miles Forest Road 43 crosses the Deschutes River just above Pringle Falls. The first left after the bridge, Forest Road 4370, leads to Wyeth Campground, the take-out, with a boat ramp.

Reach the put-in at Wickiup Dam by continuing west on Forest Road 43 another 2.5 miles. Take a left onto NFD 4380, which runs to the reservoir levee. Turn left again to follow the levee to the put-in on the north (river left) side of the dam. There is a 200-yard carry from a locked gate to the water. The access is public; the gate is to keep vehicles out.

Gauge. Flow is regulated at Wickiup Dam. From late spring until early fall, the flow is generally consistent at 1,200–1,600 cfs. At other times the flow can be severely and abruptly reduced. For information on water release from Wickiup Dam, contact the Oregon Department of Water Resources Watermaster for the Bend region (541-388-6669).

Carl Landsness

170 Deschutes River
Pringle Falls to Big River Campground

Class: 1(2)	**Character: forested; marsh grass;**
Flow: 500–1,000 cfs	**waterfowl haven**
Gradient: 2.5 fpm, C	**Season: dam-controlled**
Length: 16 miles	

The first 7 miles of this run are similar to the pine-forested run upstream. Near the La Pine Recreation Area, the river begins to slow and meander through wide-open areas of marsh grass. The river is serene, disturbed occasionally by the sounds of fish and waterfowl. Views of the nearby hills and distant mountains further enhance this enchanting run.

Hazards. Tetherow Logjam blocks the river 4 miles below Pringle Falls. Several signs warn of its presence. The portage is an easy 200-yard walk along the right bank. It is often possible to sneak the logs along the right bank and then run 100 yards of class 2 waves.

Access. Put in at Pringle Falls Campground, below Pringle Falls on river right (see run 169, Deschutes River: Wickiup Dam to Pringle Falls, Access).

Reach the take-out by driving west on Forest Road 43 for 0.5 mile, and then going right onto Forest Road 4350 for 2 miles. Turn right onto Forest Road 42 and follow it 8 miles to Big River Campground.

To reach the take-out from US 97, drive 2 miles south of Sunriver, turn west onto Forest Road 9724, and follow it to Forest Road 42, and from there to Big River Campground. An alternate take-out is at La Pine State Recreation Area. Check the Deschutes National Forest map for details on this alternate access.

Gauge. See run 169, Deschutes River: Wickiup Dam to Pringle Falls.

Carl Landsness

171 Deschutes River
Big River Campground to Benham Falls

Class: 1(5+)	**Character: forested; residential;**
Flow: 1,000–3,000 cfs	**resort country**
Gradient: 1 fpm, PD	**Season: dam-controlled**
Length: 18 miles	

The first 7 miles to Harper's Bridge wander very slowly, with houses lining the banks for most of the length. The next 6-mile section passes Sunriver Resort with a noticeably stronger current and a large contingent of leisurely drifters. Below Sunriver, the Deschutes makes a rather dramatic geological transition as it passes around and over the many lava flows of this region. After miles of mirrorlike water, the river is suddenly and violently churned into a frenzy at Benham Falls, a spectacular series of class 5+ ledges, holes, and froth, cascading more than 100 feet in 0.5 mile (see run 172, Deschutes River: Upper Benham Falls). The normal take-out is on river right at the Benham Falls boat ramp, just above a footbridge over an impassable logjam.

Experienced boaters might save 0.2 mile of walking above the falls by attempting a quick but tricky portage around the upstream logjam and paddling the 0.2 mile to the falls. However, the take-outs above the falls on river left are small and tricky to catch. Do not miss them!

Boaters who wish to continue on downstream to the next run must portage the logjam and the falls. To portage, take out at the boat ramp, cross the footbridge, and follow a small jeep road 0.3 mile to the start of the falls. The portage leaves sight of the river and continues another 0.8 mile or so. Several paths lead down to the river. The exact put-in depends on the skill of the boater. About 200 yards from the base of the steepest part of the falls, the river becomes a series of class 3+ ledges and waves, flowing through several channels and continuing for about 0.5 mile. The final few hundred yards are class 2. Scout it, enjoy the view, and make your choice.

Hazards. Do not get into the logjam just below the take-out ramp. The optional portage around Benham Falls to the next run is 1.5 miles.

Access. Put in at Big River Campground, on river right, by the Forest Road 42 bridge (see run 170, Deschutes River: Pringle Falls to Big River Campground, Access).

Reach the take-out at Benham Falls from US 97 just south of Lava Lands Visitor Center. Take Forest Road 9702 west 5 miles to Benham Falls Campground. Alternate accesses are at Harper Bridge and Besson boat ramp, near the middle of the run. Refer to Deschutes National Forest map for roads and campgrounds.

Gauge. See run 169, Deschutes River: Wickiup Dam to Pringle Falls.

Carl Landsness

172 Deschutes River
Upper Benham Falls

Class: 5+
Flow: 700–2,000 cfs;
    1,500 not recommended
Gradient: 100–200 fpm, C–PD

Length: 1 mile
Character: forested canyon
Season: year-round

At low water, Upper Benham Falls is a series of class 4 drops to an eddy just above Lower Benham Falls, which is a class 5+ cascade. At high water, Upper Benham Falls is a series of class 5 drops to an elusive eddy just above the Lower Benham Falls. Scout the entire run before getting on the water. It is a lot bigger and pushier than it looks.

To portage from the previous run, see run 171, Deschutes River: Big River Campground to Benham Falls. The put-in is in the calm water 0.5 mile above the parking lot at Benham Falls Campground. The first drop is over a small tongue into a large hole on river left. The current moves to the right, to the second drop, a sharp lava pour-over. Stay right, then center, and move right through the next few drops; in the last series of drops, it is crucial to stay on line. Boaters must be to the extreme left side of the river to eddy out above Lower Benham Falls. Run by Sam East.

Hazards. This run is very dangerous; a swim from upstream makes it a life-threatening situation. This is a serious class 5+ descent. At high water the entire run is difficult; at low water the upper part of the falls is the most difficult.

Access. Reach the put-in at Benham Falls from US 97 just south of Lava Lands Visitor Center. Take Forest Road 9702 west 5 miles to Benham Falls Campground. One can also portage from the previous run (see run 171, Deschutes River: Big River Campground to Benham Falls).

The take-out below Upper Benham Falls is at the Benham Falls parking lot.

Gauge. See run 169, Deschutes River: Wickiup Dam to Pringle Falls.

Morgan William Smith

173 Deschutes River
Lower Benham Falls to Slough Camp

Class: 3+; 4-	**Length: 1.5 miles**
Flow: 400; 2,400 cfs	**Character: forested**
Gradient: 60 fpm, C	**Season: year-round**

This is one of the "unknown" fun runs. The put-in is at the base of Lower Benham Falls. Scout this thoroughly, as there are a number of quick class 3+ moves that need to be made. At the bottom of the rapids is a good play spot on the right. The next class 2 section is fun, but short. After a calm section and a right turn is a rapids that contains logs. Scout on the left. Below, it is calm to the take-out.

Hazards. Some logs require scouting. Rocks are numerous and sharp.

Access. From US 97 in Bend, drive toward Mount Bachelor on Century Drive. Turn at the first left after the Inn of the Seventh Mountain, onto Forest Road 41. Turn left at the Dillon Falls sign. Turn right at the next intersection. Continue until you see Slough Camp. Turn left and park next to the river, the take-out.

To reach the put-in, turn left as you leave the picnic area and proceed until the road ends at Benham Falls parking lot.

Gauge. Located at Benham Falls. Call the Oregon Department of Water Resources Watermaster at Bend for information. The *Bend Bulletin* reports flow information most of the summer.

Morgan William Smith

174 Deschutes River
Slough Camp to Dillon Falls

Class: 1(6)	**Length: 2.5 miles**
Flow: 1,000–3,000 cfs	**Character: forested meadows; lava flows**
Gradient: 2 fpm, PD	**Season: dam-controlled**

This short run can be a lovely diversion on a warm summer afternoon for boaters in the Bend area. The nearby resorts use this stretch heavily for their guests. Even though it's a short run, give it a try.

After 2 miles of easy water, several signs warn of Dillon Falls, a lava flow over which the river cascades. Don't miss the take-out on the left above the falls! At Dillon Falls the river careens over a 15-foot class 6 ledge, and continues for 0.5 mile of class 4 rapids. It is possible for advanced kayakers to put in at the base of the falls and run the class 4 rapids. Scout it first. The movie *Up the Creek* was filmed here. Some boaters portage the mile around the left of Dillon Falls to the next run.

Hazards. Don't miss the take-out; Dillon Falls is below.

Access. From US 97 in Bend drive west on Century Drive toward Mount Bachelor; turn south on Forest Road 41. After 1.5 miles, turn left on NFD 4120 and proceed 1.5 miles to Dillon Falls Campground. The boat ramp is the take-out.

To reach the put-in, continue on NFD 4120 about 2 miles along the river to Slough Camp.

Gauge. See run 173, Deschutes River: Lower Benham Falls to Slough Camp.

Carl Landsness

175 Deschutes River
Dillon Falls to Lava Island Falls

Class: 3	**Length: 2.5 miles**
Flow: 1,000–3,000 cfs	**Character: forested; rafting freeway**
Gradient: 16 fpm, PD	**Season: dam-controlled**

This is the famous "Big Eddy" run. The nearby resorts run an incredible number of visitors down this whitewater mini-run in the summer. One curler here has undoubtedly captured more rafts on film than any other in Oregon.

The trip begins with a quiet mile between Dillon Falls and Aspen Campground. Most people put in at Aspen Campground to avoid the 0.8-mile put-in walk at Dillon Falls. The next mile offers a few class 2 rapids before the river makes a sharp right turn through a quiet pool above Big Eddy. Big Eddy consists of several curlers. These can be great play spots or potential keepers, depending on the flow. Scouting is advised (left bank). One hundred yards farther downstream is a class 2+ drop with a nice play wave at the top. Catch the small eddy on river right in order to play here. For the ambitious, it's an easy 300-yard carry back upstream to do Big Eddy again.

The take-out is on river left above Lava Island Falls. It is clearly marked with warning signs. Lava Island Falls is 0.5 mile of class 4–6 rapids where several drownings have occurred. The portage is equally hazardous. Don't attempt either.

Hazards. Scout Big Eddy Rapids. Take out above Lava Island Falls; *do not run or portage the falls,* unless you are a Class 5 boater.

Access. To reach the put-in at Dillon Falls (an 0.8-mile walk), see run 174, Deschutes River: Slough Camp to Dillon Falls.

To reach the take-out, from US 97 in Bend, drive west on Century Drive toward Mount Bachelor; turn south on Forest Road 41. Turn left at the sign to Lava Island Falls. Refer to the Deschutes National Forest map for details.

Gauge. See run 173, Deschutes River: Lower Benham Falls to Slough Camp.

Carl Landsness

176 Deschutes River
Lava Island Falls to Meadow Camp Picnic Area

Class: 4–6; 6
Length: 1 mile
Flow: 700–2,000 cfs;
Character: forested;
   2,000 cfs not recommended
   lava canyon
Gradient: 125 fpm, C
Season: year-round

Although this run normally starts just below Lava Island Falls, the falls can be run in kayaks. Run in 1988 by Loren Hall, Linda Heisserman, and Morgan Smith.

For those not running the falls, paddle across the calm pool at the top of the falls. Portage on river right down the irrigation canal walkway. Put in at the bottom of the falls.

The action starts immediately, with no real warm-up. This first class 4 section, Cut Up, abounds with sharp rocks, holes, and waves, depending on water level. The current is very swift. Eddy hop down, watching for new logs at all times. There's some good play in this section, but look downstream first.

A long calm pool precedes the next difficult section. The river constricts to a small, narrow chute with canyon walls rising from the river. Scout here. A hundred feet downriver on the left is a big eddy and a mandatory scout. Directly below on both sides are small eddies from which boaters may scout. Do not try to run this drop without scouting. A portage here is an ugly undertaking, but a swim is much worse. Climb up above the river to scout this class 5 ledge-drop. There are logs on both sides of this drop. At high water you won't be able to see the logs between the large rock in the center and the right shore. Don't run right of the rock. If you do the run, stay left into the 5-foot pour-over—you'll understand the name "Barry's Back Ender." Start left, then thread the needle in the center and ski jump the rocks. If you go too far right you'll end up in "Loren's Lunch Stop" under some wood.

There's a great play hole, High Five, just below this drop. At high water it's big! Beware of the riverwide tree 100 yards downstream. This is also visible from the scout.

One drop past a dangerous logjam on the right, it's smooth sailing to the take-out on the left at the picnic area.

Hazards. The higher the water level, the more dangerous this run becomes. At high water it's a serious class 5+ with logjams. The second part has a class 5 ledge-drop with logs and an almost impossible portage. A swim here would be hazardous because of a riverwide log 100 yards downstream, followed by a logjam. The rocks are extremely sharp in this run. A swim could result in injury and loss of equipment.

Access. To reach the take-out, from US 97 in Bend, drive west toward Mount Bachelor on Century Drive; turn left at the Meadow Camp Picnic Area sign. Go to the end of the road, then upriver, and park.

To reach the put-in, return to Century Drive; turn left on Forest Road 41, past the Inn of the Seventh Mountain. Take the first left. Follow NFD 4120 to the Lava Island Falls shelter sign. Turn left and go to the end of the road. Put in at Lava Island Falls.

Gauge. See run 173, Deschutes River: Lower Benham Falls to Slough Camp.

Morgan William Smith

177 Deschutes River
Meadow Camp Picnic Area to Mount Bachelor Village

Class: 4; 5	Length: 5 miles
Flow: 700; 2,200 cfs	Character: forested canyon
Gradient: 125 fpm, C	Season: year-round

On this run, most of the riverbank is private property with no public access, so once you're on the river, stay on it. The run starts with 1 mile of flat water. After passing a house on the left next to the river, the action begins. Just past two log houses is a great play hole, and another smaller but good play spot. Around the corner is the first class 4 rapids, Play Time: continuous eddy hopping with some great play spots. In the middle of this section, Rollodex Hole provides rodeo side surfing. Other ender and play spots abound for the next 0.25 mile.

In the calm water above the diversion dam, get out and scout Darn It on river right. Scout down past the first drop, because the lateral wave below is a flipper. At most water levels this drop is run center; at higher flows it can be run left, then move center. Looking back upstream from the river below gives an impressive view.

The next major rapids is called Amazing. It is amazing at high water, and amazing if you can make it through the maze of rocks at low water. It is located at the river gauge on the right. Scout all the way down around the next corner because there is not a good eddy before the next big drop, which has a log at the bottom. Below here is one of the best play spots on the run, Frank's Fun Hole. Continuing downstream, boaters come to a logjam that looks like it completely blocks the river. Scout on the right. At the bottom, there's a rompin', stompin' rodeo-riding hole called Ride 'Em Roy. Hang onto your helmet!

The river continues through fallen trees used for fish habitat. Scout the last big drop of the run, where the river drops out of sight. Don't try to play in the big hole at the bottom. It is called 100 Percent because boaters are 100 percent guaranteed to hit a gnarly rock if they flip over. Continue down to the pump house on river left, the take-out.

Hazards. Logs are the biggest problem on this run. There are a couple of continuous class 4+ drops that need scouting. A swim in this stretch could result in injury and loss of equipment.

Access. From the city of Bend on US 97, follow Century Drive to the southwest and go toward Mount Bachelor Village. To reach the take-out, turn left at the Mount Bachelor Village sign and go 100 yards; then turn left onto a dirt road. Park at the blocked-off road leading down to the pump house on the river.

To reach the put-in, return to Century Drive and turn left. Go 3–4 miles and turn left at the sign to Meadow Camp Picnic Area. Follow the road to the end and park.

Gauge. Located at Benham Falls. See run 173, Deschutes River: Lower Benham Falls to Slough Camp.

Morgan William Smith

178 Deschutes River
Bend to Tumalo State Park

Class: 4; 4+	**Length: 5.2 miles**
Flow: 500 cfs; 1,700 cfs	**Character: canyon; residential**
Gradient: 60 fpm	**Season: rainy**

Many towns in Oregon claim that rivers flow in their backyard, but the city of Bend has a river that flows through the middle of a house. This run starts in the heart of town, but most of the run is down in a canyon. It is known as the Lava Canyon run. There is one drawback: the river is managed as an irrigation ditch with all but a trickle of water removed through a canal system, except during the winter. Boaters feel conspicuous in Bend with a kayak on the rig while others are laden with skis. But there are occasional warm days November through March that provide better boating than skiing.

The put-in at the Riverhouse Motel allows boaters to do some paddle twirls in the class 2 rapids there for the gawkers in the restaurant. The next 0.5 mile is fairly flat waterfowl habitat encroached upon by motels and houses adjacent to Sawyer Park. A mansion ahead on river left signals the beginning of the action. Two long class 3+ drops wind past the houses of Rimrock West. The third closely spaced drop, the Wright Stuff, is a tricky shallow ledge at low levels. It is run just right of the large midstream boulder. Downstream 50 yards, an island splits the river into the Flumes of Doom, class 4. Both channels are runnable but are narrow, long, and complex. Because pins have occurred, scouting is required. Near the bottom after the confluence of the channels is an ender spot; however, it can deposit a boat on the boulders.

The river stays very active with class 3 and 4 drops for the next 3 miles with a gradient of 80 fpm. Following a class 3 rapids with a narrow slot entrance, the river bends right and enters a rapids known as T-Rex. The lower end of this long rapids is guarded by a boulder fence best run on the far right. At high flows this becomes an ugly riverwide hole. The next 0.8 mile is a succession of twisting drops leading blindly into The Ogre. Pull out right by the big log on shore to scout. A house-size boulder at the bottom just as you plunge over the main drop makes things interesting. Swimmers should be aware of the ledges below. Many fun drops and several deceiving small side surf holes continue. The take-out is on the grassy lawn of Tumalo State Park.

Hazards. The named rapids should all be scouted. The narrow technical nature of the run always makes logs a threat. During rare high flows of 1,500 cfs and up, it is one continuous rapids from Rimrock

West to below The Ogre. Because of the 3,500-foot elevation, be prepared for cold conditions.

Access. The put-in is in the north end of Bend on US 97 by the bridge on the south end of the Riverhouse Motel.

The 5-mile shuttle to the take-out at Tumalo State Park is along O. B. Riley Road, which enters US 97 on the north side of the Riverhouse Motel. A bicycle shuttle is quite easy.

Gauge. There is a gauge on the bridge support at Sawyer Park, but its placement makes flow correlation difficult. Flow can be obtained from the Oregon Department of Water Resources Watermaster in Bend. Optimum flow is 800–1,200 cfs.

Carl Landsness and Jon Ferguson

179 Deschutes River
Lower Bridge to Lake Billy Chinook

Class: 4 P	**Length: 15 miles**
Flow: 500–1,000 cfs	**Character: inaccessible desert gorge**
Gradient: 39 fpm	**Season: dam-controlled**

This extraordinary run has been overlooked because of its short season, inaccessible gorge, and long paddle out. Magnificent canyon scenery, bountiful wildlife, and challenging whitewater await those who do attempt this run.

The river is essentially class 3 for the first 4 miles as it winds through brushy shallows and braided channels. However, at mile 1.5 an obvious horizon line marks Big Falls, an unrunnable 18-foot drop. It may be portaged either side. At mile 4 Steelhead Falls presents the next portage. It is marked by a class 3 entrance rapids, a steepening of the canyon, and a stone wall at the brink on river right. Portage along river left. For 2 miles below Steelhead Falls, the river meanders through class 1–2 rapids as the canyon walls steepen. Gradually, the gradient increases and some long class 4 boulder gardens present the first real challenges. After Squaw Creek enters from a huge canyon on river left, the flow increases, and class 4 rapids line up in quick succession. Great whitewater and breathtaking scenery combine for the last few miles to Lake Billy Chinook. The final 2 miles are on the lake.

Hazards. Big Falls at mile 1.5 and Steelhead Falls at mile 4 must be portaged. A rope could come in handy on either portage. Other difficulties include the shallows and brush in the first few miles.

Access. To find the put-in, drive to Terrebonne, on US 97 15 miles north of Redmond or 17.3 miles south of Madras. Just north of Terrebonne, turn west on Lower Bridge Road (marked by a Crooked River Ranch sign) and proceed 6 miles to the river. Put in at Lower Bridge. Kayakers can shorten the run by following dirt roads behind Crooked River Ranch to Steelhead Falls and carrying to the river.

The take-out is reached by turning west from US 97 toward Cove Palisades State Park, 24 miles north of Redmond or 7.2 miles south of Madras; follow signs to the park. Once at the park, continue south and west to the Upper Deschutes day-use area. Take out on the bridge upstream of the boat ramps.

Gauge. In low to normal water years, two gauge readings are required to predict the flow. First, obtain the flow at Benham Falls from the Oregon Department of Water Resources Watermaster in Bend; this should be at least 550 cfs. From November to March, the Benham Falls reading roughly equals the flow at Lower Bridge; from April to October, the upper stretch is usually dry.

Second, obtain a Culver gauge reading from the USGS (503-231-2018); this should be above 1,000 cfs. The Culver reading includes the increased flow from Squaw Creek (usually 500 cfs). In very-high-water years, greater releases from Wickiup Reservoir provides flows that result in some solid class 4 and class 5 rapids.

Jeff Bennett

180 Deschutes River
US 26 Bridge to Sherar's Falls

Class: 3	**Length: 53 miles**
Flow: 3,000–8,000 cfs	**Character: popular desert canyon**
Gradient: 12 fpm, PD	**Season: year-round**

The lower Deschutes runs through a large desert canyon with an active railroad along the river. Rattlesnakes, chukars, and deer live here. The bottom of the canyon can become oppressively hot in the summer. Stiff upcanyon winds are normal in the afternoon. This stretch is a designated Scenic Waterway. The river has numerous class 2 play spots, good sharp eddies, and several class 3 rapids. The water is clear, fishing is usually good, and campsites are plentiful—but watch out for poison oak. The Warm Spring Indians own the land along the left. The run from Upper Wapinitia, just above Maupin, to Sherar's Falls is a popular day trip. The tempo is faster on the section from Maupin to Sherar's Falls, one of the most popular rafting runs in Oregon during the summer.

The first 20 miles below the US 26 bridge (rivermile 98) are fairly flat with only one significant rapids, Trout Creek Rapids. For this reason most boaters put in at South Junction, 13 miles downstream. At rivermile 94, there is a gorge of dark basalt. At rivermile 89, there is a large island and the whitewater begins. A mile later, Trout Creek Rapids, class 2, begins on a right turn. The next 8 miles are open valley; there are dirt access roads on both sides. South Junction is on the right at rivermile 85; the Warm Springs River enters on left.

Whitehorse Rapids (rivermile 76), class 3, identified by a sharp pinnacle on the right and a steep bank leading up to the railroad on the right, is at the end of a stretch of slack water that ends in a short plunge. Land below here on the right to scout Whitehorse. The rapids begins on a sweeping right bend. A mile later, take the left channel, because the right channel runs onto rocks. There is enjoyable water through here. From Davidson or North Junction, where the railroad crosses to the left bank (rivermile 73), there's not much whitewater for

Whitehorse Rapids on the Deschutes (photo by Al Kitzman)

the next 10 miles. The river passes through the very scenic Mutton Mountains, with windows in colored stone, eroded by wind.

At rivermile 64, Buckskin Mary Falls is run straight down the middle for a fine roller-coaster ride. There is good whitewater for the next 3 miles. Upper Wapinitia Rapids (rivermile 55), can be spotted after a left bend, where a steel railroad bridge on the left crosses Wapinitia Creek. The rapids begins there on a right turn. Run right. A mile later, Lower Wapinitia Rapids, class 3, begins with an abrupt left turn, then curves right with a very fast current. Next is a ledge across the entire river, with a 2-foot drop on the left and a 4-foot drop on the right. A huge boulder with a dangerous hole behind it lies just below the ledge. Scout the first time through from either bank.

At Maupin, there is a possible take-out at the bridge at the city park on the right (rivermile 52). There is fine whitewater from here to Sherar's Falls. The big waves of Surf City (rivermile 48) provide popular surfing for many boaters. Oak Spring Rapids (rivermile 47.5), class 3, can cause problems. Look for green growth on the left side of the canyon and the mossy tanks of the Oak Springs fish hatchery. Whitewater begins 200 yards above the hatchery. The lower rapids is made difficult by the two ribs of basalt that divide the river into three channels. At high water the left channel can be run easily, but at low water the middle channel should be run. The big hole next to the rock, on the right, flips many boaters. The runout is shallow and rocky.

In 0.5 mile, the White River enters on the left with nice waves, followed in 0.3 mile by Upper Elevator. The Elevator (rivermile 46) provides a great wave train with good surfing. A long narrow eddy elevates boaters back up to the top. In 0.5 mile, a sandy beach on the right is a good take-out. Osborne Rapids (rivermile 45) is a 4-foot drop in a short distance. It is identified as the second drop below a protruding rock near midstream. In 0.5 mile, sight a shed and the road to Tygh Valley, both on the left. Land on the left as soon as the highway is reached and take out. Do not miss the take-out, 0.5 mile above Sherar's Falls, class 6, a 15-foot waterfall.

Hazards. Watch for overheating in hot weather, and beware of poison oak. There are several rapids that present difficulties. Whitehorse Rapids, class 3, drops 25 feet in 300 yards. Upper Wapinitia Rapids has probably the fastest chute on this run. Lower Wapinitia Rapids, class 3 (sometimes called Boxcar Rapids, where a boxcar fell into the river in the late 1940s), requires going over a 2- to 4-foot ledge and maneuvering around some large boulders. Oak Springs Rapids, a class 3 rapids that becomes more difficult as the water drops and rocks become exposed, is considered the most difficult on this run. Don't miss the take-out above Sherar's Falls; look for a lumber shed and a road approaching the river on the left.

Access. From US 97 in Madras, take US 26 northwest 11 miles. The upper put-in is at the east end of the bridge where US 26 crosses the Deschutes. An alternate put-in is at the end of the road from South Junction. From Madras take US 197 north 22 miles to the turnoff to South Junction. It is a fairly slow 12-mile drive over a dirt road to the river. Another alternate put-in, or take-out, is just below the US 197 bridge in Maupin on the right at City Park. Boaters may also put in at Upper Wapinitia Rapids by following a dirt road out of Maupin on the east side of the river.

The take-out at Sherar's Falls is above the falls on the left along Oregon 216 between US 197 and US 97. From US 197 in Tygh Valley take Oregon 216 east; from US 97 in Grass Valley take Oregon 216 west. An alternative take-out is at a sandy beach on river right about 1 mile above the falls. An alternate shuttle route is a paved road that follows the east bank from Maupin to Sherar's Falls.

Gauge. Contact the River Forecast Center in Portland. The flow is controlled by Pelton Dam, and adequate flow is maintained all year.

Rob Blickensderfer

181 Deschutes River
Sherar's Falls to Columbia River

Class: 3	**Length: 44 miles**
Flow: 3,000–8,000 cfs	**Character: popular desert canyon**
Gradient: 12 fpm, PD	**Season: year-round**

This run has more horseshoe bends and fewer rapids than the previous run, but the current is brisk. Allow 3–4 days to run this portion of the Deschutes River. The Indians have treaty rights to fish for salmon at the base of Sherar's Falls. During the spring and fall they stand on flimsy scaffolding to dip salmon from the maelstrom below. From early times, the Indians had a bridge across the narrow gorge below the falls. A possible put-in is just above the bridge on Oregon 216 at Sherar's Falls (rivermile 44), on the right bank. Bridge Rapids, class 3, is just below this put-in; it is more difficult in low water. A better put-in is 1 mile down the access road along river right past Buck Hollow (this road continues to rivermile 23). At Wreck Rapids (rivermile 39), class 3+, the extreme right is clean; the center is runnable but has some concealed rocks. There are no major rapids for the next 30 miles, but the river moves at 5 mph. Many small rapids are present.

At rivermile 31, at Cedar Island, a dramatic basalt cliff is seen near the end of a large horseshoe bend; there's a campground on the right. Sinamox Island, and the abandoned buildings of Hill's Ranch on both sides of the river, occur at rivermile 26. A mile later Ferry Canyon, with a railroad bridge over it, emerges on the left. At rivermile 20 there are two islands after a right bend in the river. Harris Canyon (rivermile 12) and an old water tank are seen on the right near tall overhanging reddish basalt cliffs. At rivermile 8.5, just below the powerline at Stecker Canyon, is Washout Rapids, class 3, formed in 1995; the run is clean on the right. Freebridge, with old piers remaining, and Kloan, a railroad shed, are seen on the left at rivermile 8.

At rivermile 6, Gordon Ridge Rapids, class 3, occurs after the river makes an abrupt right turn and drops over a 3-foot shelf, followed by heavy whitewater for 0.5 mile. Two miles later, Colorado Rapids, class 3, is on the right, identified by the old wooden trestle across the mouth. Colorado Rapids is a long series of large standing and breaking waves. Small rafts sometimes capsize here. In another mile, Green Narrows rapids is a maze of rock ridges covered with grass that divides the river into numerous channels; the right side is deepest. This leads directly to Rattlesnake Rapids (rivermile 3), class 3. This is the most powerful rapids on this run. The rapids can be scouted from either bank. Most of the river flows over a very narrow upper ledge. The fierce hole below must be avoided. It is normally run on the left. In 2 more miles, Moody Rapids, class 2, consists of standing waves where the fast Deschutes encounters the pool caused by The Dalles Dam. Take out in 0.5 mile on the right at Deschutes River State Recreation Area.

Hazards. There are six class 3 rapids. Bridge Rapids, just below the upper put-in, is difficult to see as it is approached; it can be avoided by using the put-in 1 mile downstream. Wreck Rapids is 4 miles farther. Four other major rapids—Washout, Gordon Ridge, Colorado, and Rattlesnake rapids—come within the last 8.5 miles.

Access. There are two possible put-ins near Sherar's Falls, where Oregon 216 crosses the Deschutes. The first is just above Sherar's Bridge on the right bank. The other is downstream along the right bank on a secondary road about 1 mile, then turn left to get to the boat ramp. See directions to the take-out for run 180, Deschutes River: US 26 Bridge to Sherar's Falls.

The take-out on the right is at Deschutes River State Recreation Area, just off I-84 between The Dalles and Biggs. The park is visible from the interstate. You can also take out at the boat ramp on the left.

Gauge. See run 180, Deschutes River: US 26 Bridge to Sherar's Falls.

Rob Blickensderfer

KLAMATH RIVER

182 Klamath River
Keno Dam to John C. Boyle Reservoir

Class: 3+	**Length: 6–7 miles**
Flow: 2,000 cfs	**Character: forested; agricultural**
Gradient: 50 fpm, PD	**Season: rainy**

The best points of this run are the large number of rapids in a few miles, relatively few flat spots, and accessibility to Ashland and Klamath Falls paddlers. Most of the rapids are wide open and can be run by eddy hopping behind boulders. Unfortunately, the water is very dirty from pasture runoff. This is not the river for making many practice rolls.

This seldom-run section of the Klamath is difficult to scout from the banks. The river leaves the road at the put-in and is hardly accessible until the take-out. A few logging roads go to the edge of the river's south side, and a dirt road from Keno is used by anglers on the north bank. None of these roads is easy to find.

The river flows below the dam for about 2 miles of short, busy rapids. Some of the best play spots are in the rapids immediately below the dam. Then an easier section culminates in a rapids with a sharp drop at the bottom. The next notable rapids has waves that pile up on a wall at the bottom and could become more of a face-wash in higher water. Next is a section of rocky, pebbly, wide river. The water gathers together again for one last rapids, a good play spot, before the reservoir. This last drop may require scouting, depending on the water level and the skills of the party.

Hazards. The last rapids before the reservoir may require scouting.

Access. From US 97 in Klamath Falls, take Oregon 66 west to Keno, cross the river, make an angled left turn before an overpass, and take the very next left to parallel the logging right-of-way. Continue to a stop sign where a road crosses the right-of-way, bear left (instead of crossing the right-of-way), and drive to a point below the dam where it is convenient to put in.

The take-out is a few miles west on John C. Boyle Reservoir, where Oregon 66 crosses the Klamath at a roadside rest area.

Gauge. None exists.

Karen Lewis

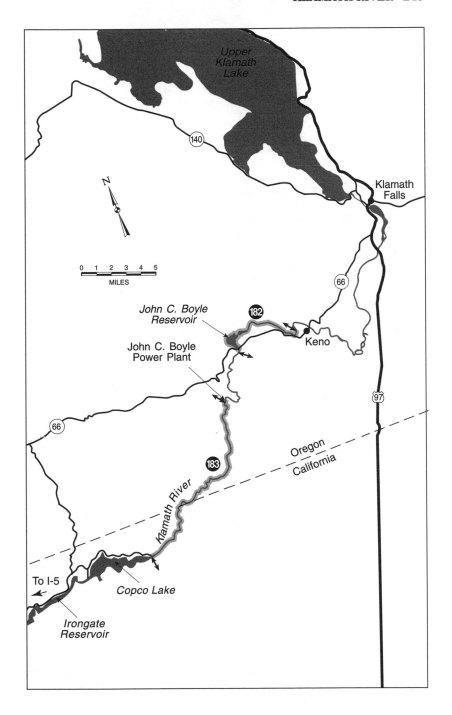

183 Klamath River
John C. Boyle Power Plant to Copco Lake

Class: 4(5)   Length: 15 miles
Flow: 1,500 cfs   Character: roadless
Gradient: 51 fpm, PD   Season: year-round

This dam-release run provides paddlers with some of the most exciting "brownwater" in the Northwest. Brownwater? The Klamath drains the warm, shallow Upper Klamath Lake, which supports an abundant growth of algae during the summer. The results are beautiful brownwater rapids and suds-filled slack water. Don't let that deter you from wetting your blades in this challenging river. The thick foam is only decaying algae from Klamath Lake. At the normal release of 1,500 cfs, it boasts two class 5, five class 4, thirteen class 3, and twenty-five class 2 rapids.

The length of the trip depends upon which of the six designated access points is chosen for the take-out. Access 6, the farthest upriver, provides a 10.5-mile trip. Access 1 adds about 4.5 miles of class 2 water. The take-outs are provided by the power company and farmers along the river. Respect their property rights and use only the designated access points. The access points are clearly marked from the road and river.

There are no camping areas at the take-outs on Copco Lake, but there is camping at Mallard Cove on Copco Lake about 2 miles west of Access 1 on the Copco–Ager Road. Camping areas are found between 3 and 5.5 miles from the put-in. The most popular of these is Frain Ranch, where several century-old log houses still stand. There are only a few marginal campgrounds in the canyon below. Camping is available at the BLM–State Line access. There is camping at the Topsy Grade USFS campground 1 mile south of milepost 44 on Oregon 66, between Keno and the power plant turnoff. There is no potable water at Topsy or along the river.

The run starts just below the John C. Boyle Power Plant, where the release from the turbines augments the minimum flow of 400 cfs. One unit (1,200 cfs) provides this pool-drop river with plenty of action for the expert paddler and the intermediate with a bombproof roll. An occasional release of two units makes it a respectable class 5 challenge. When the flow exceeds 3,400 cfs, it is deemed too dangerous to run.

The action begins immediately with 1.5 miles of class 2–class 3 warm-up rapids. The brownwater adds another aspect to reading the river, because waves and holes that look safe may conceal rocks just below the surface. After the warm-up stretch, the river flattens out for the next 3 miles, presenting an opportunity to enjoy the abundant wildlife: bald eagles, red-tailed hawks, cormorants, and herons.

Immediately below Frain Ranch the river is squeezed into a tight canyon, which begins the major excitement. Caldera, a 200-yard class 5 cooker, begins the nearly nonstop series of class 3, 4, and 5 rapids for the next 6 miles. Scout Caldera from either side. If you feel you may be in over your head, take the jeep road on river right that leads back to the put-in. With a gradient of 76 fpm, many of the rapids drop out of sight. Eddy hopping is very difficult and not recommended for first-time boaters. A mile farther is Satan's Gate, a class 4 rapids that drops on a right turn that leads directly into Hell's Corner, a 350-yard-long class 5 rapids. It can be scouted from the left. The last 50 yards of Hell's Corner is known as the Ego Bruiser and is best run far right to catch the eddy at the bottom before you are thrust into The Dragon, a fun class 4 with some big holes, waves, and obstacles.

A couple of rapids later, enter Dance Hall, a long shallow rock garden that sweeps right and then left. This leads directly into a 90-degree right-dropping turn known as Ambush, which has wrapped many a boat and embarrassed even those familiar with the river. A half mile farther, pass Salt Caves on the left. The action continues for another 3 miles to the Oregon–California border, identified by bridge abutments on both sides of the river, and followed immediately by a 4-foot drop known as State Line Falls. An optional take-out is available on the left just above the falls, and another (better) is 0.25 mile downstream. Both are on BLM land with lots of room for camping. This is Access 6.

The trip continues another 5 miles to Copco Lake. The canyon widens as you float along in class 1 and 2 rapids interspersed with some calm stretches. The river passes some working cattle ranches and the historic ghost town of Beswick. The take-out is at Access 1, on the left after 0.5 mile of lake paddling. An alternate take-out is another 0.5 mile along the lakeshore at Copco Store, which charges a small fee.

Hazards. The Caldera, Satan's Gate, Hell's Corner, and The Dragon are long, difficult rapids. The length of the rapids, the proliferation of holes and rocks, and the brownwater all add to the difficulty. The water moves fast enough to flush boats out of most holes, but the rocks are still hard.

Access. From US 97 in Klamath Falls, take Oregon 66 west to between mileposts 42 and 43. The road to the put-in heads south from Oregon 66 between these mileposts; it is marked with a sign to John C. Boyle Power Plant. Follow the road 4.5 miles to the power plant; continue another 0.5 mile to a steep switchback road that leads to the river's edge and the put-in.

There are two shuttle routes to the take-out; both require returning to Oregon 66. The shorter route takes about 2 hours, and should be considered only in good weather. Drive west on Oregon 66; between mileposts 25 and 24, look for a row of mailboxes, a dirt road, and a defunct signpost, all on the left. Turn left onto this road. At mile 2.5 take the right fork. Just beyond a group of houses and a farm at mile 8.5, take a right fork again. A mile and a half of very steep class 4 road starts near mile 10.7. At the junction with a better road near the bottom of the hill, take a left. From this point take every major left fork (Copco Lake should be on your right) until you reach the bridge across the head of the lake at mile 18.5. Cross the bridge and take another left. Access 1 is

0.5 mile upriver from the bridge. Follow the poor dirt road 0.25 mile to the river's edge, the lower take-out. For the upper take-out, cross the irrigation ditch, turn left, and follow the road. Access 6, the BLM–State Line Access, is another 5.5 miles upstream. Total mileage from the put-in to Access 6 is 49 miles.

The other shuttle route, although longer, is more commonly used because it is not so harsh on vehicles and drivers. Drive west on Oregon 66 to I-5, then south on I-5 to the Henley Hornbrook exit, 1 mile south of the California fruit inspection station. Go east 3 miles to the Klamathon Bridge, then right (south) 5 miles to Copco–Ager Road. Turn left and go east 16 miles to the bridge on the east end of Copco Lake. Continue 0.5 mile to Access 1 or 5.5 miles to the BLM–State Line Access. For shuttle service, call the Copco Store.

Gauge. Call Pacific Power and Light Company (800-547-1501) for a recording of expected releases from the John C. Boyle Power Plant. Releases of 1–9 hours' duration occur daily, except for a 2- to 3-week shutdown for maintenance usually starting the first Monday after July 4.

Lance Stein, Dan Valens, Mike Hale, and Noah Hague

EASTERN OREGON RIVERS

JOHN DAY RIVER AND TRIBUTARIES

The John Day's course of 280 miles from its headwaters in the Blue Mountains to its confluence with the Columbia River makes it the longest undammed river in the Pacific Northwest. Four of the longer scenic and more isolated runs are described below. These runs provide a good combination of moderate to easy whitewater and fine camping and hiking. The uppermost run on the North Fork is the most difficult and is not recommended for open canoes except for the very experienced and well prepared. The second run on the North Fork is considerably more difficult than the lower two runs on the main stem, which are excellent for open canoe and beginning kayak trips. The countryside changes from pine forests in the upper regions to semi-arid treeless desert, complete with small cactus, in the lower region. For the most part, the scenery is superb. The countryside is open range, and cattle visit the river for drinking water, especially in the lower runs. They are not a problem in camp if you don't mind "cow chips."

Come prepared. Most canoers carry about a half gallon of drinking water per person per day. Creeks in the lower segments are normally dry; if not, they are polluted. The sun can be very intense. Bring protective clothing and sun screen.

The John Day is fed primarily by snowpack in the Blue Mountains, so its flow is very seasonal. The peak flow is usually in April, and at Service Creek can be 20,000 cfs or higher, although the mean peak is 6,000 cfs. The minimum flow from August to October can be less than 200 cfs. The best time to run the North Fork is in April or May after the flow has peaked.

Although the lower stretches are runnable at the higher levels of around 6,000 cfs, the combination of cold and big water could become very serious for the ill prepared. Wetsuits or drysuits should be required for all persons in April and May. The lower runs are more enjoyable at flows around 2,000 cfs when the water and air are much warmer. At this time, usually in June, the river is one of the few in Oregon that swimmers can enjoy. Bass can also be caught then.

Additional information on this river can be found in *Wildwater Touring* by Scott and Margaret Arighi, *John Day River* by Arthur Campbell, and *Oregon River Tours* by John Garren (see Bibliography).

Rob Blickensderfer

184 North Fork John Day River
Route 52 Bridge to Dale

Class: 3+ (5)   Length: 41 miles
Flow: 800–1,500 cfs   Character: wilderness; placer mining
Gradient: 70 fpm, C   Season: snowmelt

This run high in the Blue Mountains passes through roadless terrain for 30 miles. Open canoes have run everything in this stretch except the short class 5 below Granite Creek and the logjams. The initial gradient is more than 100 fpm and completely free of pools and eddies. Fallen lodgepole pines block the narrow, shallow upper 7 miles about every 0.5 mile, requiring frequent boosting of boats over them. This water is class 1, 2, and 3 in roughly equal proportions.

Downstream the river becomes a real delight with mile-long stretches of exhilarating class 3 water in the next 20 miles. After 30 miles, the canyon then opens up and the gradient drops. There is evidence of mining along the entire river, with occasional miners' cabins, camps, and old placer mining operations. However, below Oriental Creek the river is less interesting because the 10 miles to Dale have been heavily mined and the scenery consists largely of tailings. Run in May 1987 by Alex and Nancy McNeily, Paul Norman, and Craig Colby.

Hazards. A short class 5 rapids that requires a moderately difficult portage on the right occurs just below Granite Creek. About 2 miles below Granite Creek is a class 3+ rapids where the river drops 50 feet in 300 yards. Because this rapids would be very difficult to portage or line, it sets the standard for boating ability.

Access. Take US 395 either south from I-84 in Pendleton or north from US 26 between Redmond and John Day to reach the take-out at Dale, on US 395 between Ukiah and Mount Vernon. The put-in is reached by taking NFD 55 east out of Dale, which follows the north side of the North Fork for roughly 6 miles and then goes overland an additional 12 miles to Route 52. Follow Route 52 east about 30 miles to the put-in at the bridge crossing the North Fork at the North Fork John Day Campground.

Gauge. Located at Monument. Contact the River Forecast Center in Portland.

Paul Norman and Alex McNeily

185 North Fork John Day River
Dale to Monument

Class: 2+; 3   Length: 44 miles
Flow: 800–2,500 cfs; 4,000 cfs Character: forested canyon
Gradient: 21 fpm, C   Season: snowmelt

This run marks the transition between the foothills of the Blue Mountains and the high desert country typical of eastern Oregon. The terrain is mountainous but not steep, with open forest of ponderosa pine and little evidence of civilization. Wildflowers are abundant in the spring, and walks into the hills above camp are well worthwhile. The open vegetation makes walking easy and enjoyable. Good campsites are common. The trip is usually done with two nights of camping.

From the put-in at Tollgate Campground to Camas Creek, the river is quite fast and has some holes. If there are problems in these first 3.5 miles, boaters should consider aborting their trip; three major rapids occur in the next 10 miles. The river gradually flattens out over the next 30 miles, but several long class 2- rock gardens and some large standing waves make it interesting all the way. At higher water the river takes on a class 3- character. At any water level the North Fork is definitely more difficult and much faster than the lower John Day.

About 6.5 miles below the put-in, the first of the three largest rapids occurs. Grandstand Rapids, class 2+, can be rocky and require some maneuvering. The rapids begins with a wide curve to left. To scout, land on the right at the curve and walk down the road. The straight, fast drop ends with a curve to the right as a wave rolls off a cliff on the left. A small pool below the rapids is followed by a fast class 1+ rapids.

A half mile after Grandstand, a frame house appears on the right (mile 7). One-third mile after this is a class 2 rapids (mile 7.3), followed in 0.2 mile by a cabin on the right (mile 7.5). One and a half miles after Grandstand Rapids is Surprise Rapids, class 2+ (mile 8). The approach is not obvious. Large waves are at the bottom of this relatively short rapids. A hole on river left near the small cliff or the big boil in the middle may surprise boaters.

Chainsaw Rapids, class 2 (mile 9.5), is 1.5 miles downstream from Surprise Rapids. A good eddy on river right, ahead of the rapids, provides a landing. The upper section of this rapids has large standing waves between relatively narrow, steep banks. A pool with an eddy and a cabin on the right precede the lower section, a straightforward 500-foot-long rapids. Shortly after Chainsaw is a small white house on the right (mile 10).

Four miles from Chainsaw is Zipper Rapids, class 2+ (mile 13.5). The approach is an "S"-curve. The main rapids, at the end of the "S"— quite similar to Grandstand Rapids but more demanding—can be scouted from either side. Two miles later, Stony Creek enters on the right (mile 15.5). In a little less than 2 miles, Upper Bridge Rapids, class 2- (mile 17.3), a 1,000-foot-long fast boulder garden, begins just as the bridge becomes visible. Next is Lower Bridge Rapids, class 2- (mile 18), another 1,000-foot-long boulder garden 0.5 mile below the bridge.

At mile 20, an old homestead with a log house is in a clearing on the right near a creek. One and a half miles later, Potomas Creek enters on the right at mile 21.5, followed by a concrete bridge in 0.5 mile (mile 22). Mallory Creek enters on the right in 0.5 mile (mile 22.5) and 2 miles later Ditch Creek enters on the right (mile 24.5). In another 2 miles there's a class 2- rapids (mile 26.5) on a gentle curve to the left. In 1.5 miles, Middle Fork John Day River enters from the left (mile 28); there are several campsites below here.

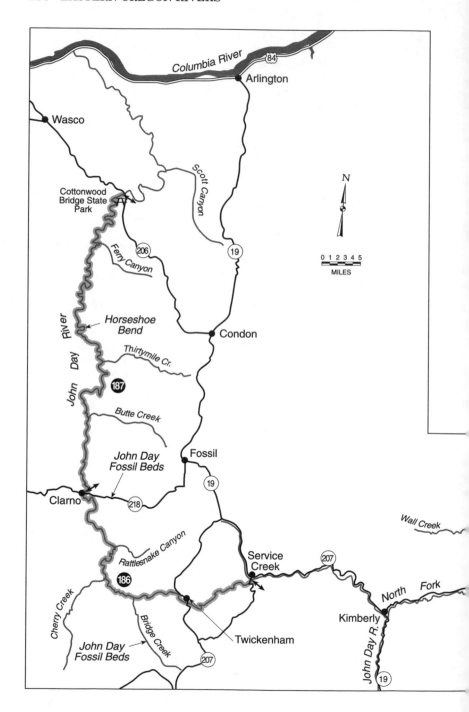

In 4 miles, Cabin Creek enters on the right (mile 32). In 2.5 miles a class 2- rapids (mile 34.5) runs in a narrow basaltic channel. A mile later, Two Cabin Creek enters on the left at mile 35.5, followed by a class 2- rapids. Shortly after, a barn, cabins, and a house are seen on the right at mile 37.5. Soon after, Wall Creek, a major tributary, is seen straight ahead before the river makes a sharp 180-degree turn to the left. Wall Creek enters from the right at mile 37.7. In 4–5 miles, take out on the right, 2–3 miles above Monument.

Hazards. The water is quite cold from the snowmelt, and the remoteness from civilization must also be considered. The weather can turn cold unexpectedly, with the possibility of frosty nights or snow flurries into June. Thus a smashed boat, lost gear, and cold weather could combine to threaten one's survival.

Access. There are several put-ins in the vicinity of Dale. To reach Dale, take US 395 either south from I-84 at Pendleton or north from US 26 at Mount Vernon, between Redmond and John Day. Several campgrounds are within a few miles of Dale. US 395 follows the north shore of the North Fork for 3 miles, from the bridge over the North Fork on the east, just north of Dale, and the bridge over Camas Creek on the west. The upper put-in is at Tollgate Forest Service Campground, reached from the US 395 bridge just north of Dale by driving upriver 0.5 mile on USFS 55 and turning right across another bridge over the North Fork. There are also several river accesses downstream along US 395. Lower put-ins can be reached from the west end of the Camas Creek bridge, where an unimproved road follows the north

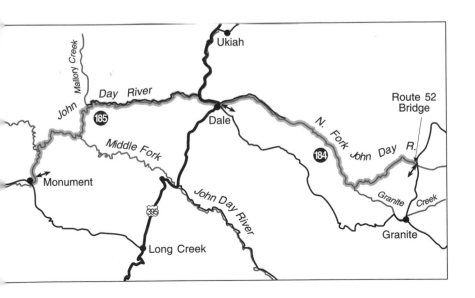

shore of the North Fork and provides a choice of put-ins on BLM land. Some of the land is private, so use only BLM areas. The unimproved road goes all the way to Monument, but is often impassable.

To reach the take-out, follow US 395 south from Dale for 26 miles to the town of Long Creek, then turn west onto the Kimberly–Long Creek Highway and proceed 21 miles to Monument. The land in Monument is private and getting permission to take out can be a problem; better to head for public land that is available 2–3 miles upriver from Monument on the unimproved road on river right.

Gauge. Located at Monument and Service Creek. Contact the River Forecast Center in Portland. The gauge at Monument includes the flow of the Middle Fork, which usually carries less than half as much water as the North Fork. The flow at Monument is normally 60 to 70 percent of the flow at Service Creek.

Rob Blickensderfer

186 John Day River
Service Creek to Clarno

Class: 1+(2)	**Length: 47 miles**
Flow: 1,200–6,000 cfs	**Character: desert canyon**
Gradient: 8 fpm, PD	**Season: snowmelt**

This stretch of the John Day is a favorite for open canoers, drift boaters, and beginning kayakers who want a fine desert wilderness experience. Although there are a number of ranches and cultivated fields at several places along the river, other sections are uninhabited and cut off from civilization by the towering walls of the canyon. Below the put-in at Service Creek, boaters have several easy class 1 rapids and riffles as they feel themselves slipping away from civilization. The sculpture of nature in the twisted basalt canyons presents forms never before imagined. The most beautiful stretch has been designated a Scenic River. The other stretches have seen ever-increasing pressures of humanity's relentless efforts to cultivate any land that has water available. Thus the many irrigation pumps flooding alfalfa fields leave boaters with the uneasy feeling that the river may be pumped dry before they reach the take-out.

Campsites are quite plentiful, often with sandy beaches below and juniper trees farther up. There are no campsites near the ranching area of Twickenham or along the last 8 miles to Clarno. The trip is normally done with two or three nights of camping on the river.

Six miles after the put-in at Service Creek, the boater encounters Russo Rapids, class 2. The approach is at a curve to the left. The rapids is straight, with a cliff at bottom left. A few miles below here, private land exists all the way to Twickenham. Do not camp on private land. The Twickenham Bridge is at mile 12. In 4 more miles is Wreck Rapids, class 2, with a side-breaking wave off the cliff on the right at the

Close inspection of columnar basalt on the John Day River (photo by Steve Cramer)

lower end. The approach is a slight curve to the right. Boaters can land on river left to scout or portage. Schuss Rapids, or Burnt Ranch Rapids, occurs in another 8 miles (mile 24). There is a large rock in the center at the head of the rapids at levels below 3,000 cfs. Boaters can scout from left or right.

In 3 miles, Cherry Creek enters on the left at mile 27. Some boaters take out here. In another 2 miles, the Big Bend region begins at mile 29.5; the river makes several sweeping bends in a beautiful deep canyon with fine beaches and campsites, and numerous class 1 rapids. Toward the end of the Big Bend Region, Rattlesnake Canyon can be seen on the right (mile 34.5); a back road comes in here. In 4 miles, a secondary road on the right at mile 38.5 connects to the highway near Clarno. In 8.5 miles is Clarno Bridge (mile 47). Take out on the right.

Hazards. Open canoers should scout the three class 2 rapids in this run, although kayakers with class 2 experience will not have difficulty. In places the river drives headlong into cliff walls. At high water the rolling waves off the cliff, as well as the eddy on the inside of the bend, can give the unwary boater problems. Afternoon upcanyon winds are normal and occasionally strong with erratic side gusts. Rattlesnakes and scorpions are present but seldom seen.

Access. The take-out is at Clarno where Oregon 218 crosses the river. Parking and a boat landing are located at the east end of the bridge. Oregon 218 is located between US 97 at Shaniko and Oregon 19 at Fossil (Oregon 19 can be reached from the north from I-84 at Arlington or from the south from US 26 near Dayville).

The put-in near Service Creek is about an hour's drive from Clarno via Oregon 218 east to the town of Fossil. From Fossil, take Oregon 19 south to Service Creek, which consists of a general store on Oregon 19. The Service Creek Trading Post will shuttle cars to Clarno. Service Creek is the junction of Oregon 207 and Oregon 19; Oregon 207 comes from the south from Mitchell, on US 26. At this junction, go south on Oregon 207 0.2 mile downstream toward Mitchell. The put-in is on river right 100 yards upstream from the bridge on Oregon 207.

Gauge. Located at Service Creek. Contact the River Forecast Center in Portland.

Rob Blickensderfer

187 John Day River
Clarno to Cottonwood

Class: 2-(3)
Flow: 1,200–6,000 cfs
Gradient: 11 fpm, C

Length: 69 miles
Character: desert canyon
Season: snowmelt

This run on the John Day is a favorite for open canoers, drift boaters, and beginning kayakers. Because the gradient here is steeper than it is in the preceding run, the river moves faster and has more wave action. There are fewer ranches and boaters feel more isolated in this stretch. It has been designated a Wild River under the Oregon Scenic Waterways System. Many magnificent canyon walls exist, unseen by all but river runners. Allow at least four nights of camping on the river. A very relaxed trip with swimming and side-canyon hiking may last 6–7 days.

Put in on the right at the Clarno bridge. In 3.5 miles, boaters encounter a large riffle with big holes in the middle at high water, and rocks at low water. In less than 1 mile, Clarno Rapids (mile 4.4) is marked by an island ahead of the rapids; take the left channel. Trees on the left bank are followed by an eddy on the left with a small landing spot just above the main chute. Heavy, fast water, class 2, leads around a left curve and into the main drop about 300 feet downstream. The rapids can be scouted from the left by landing above the class 2 drop. Most open double canoes swamp in Clarno Rapids, but they can be portaged about 150 yards over the rise on the left or lined with difficulty on the left. Lower Clarno, class 2, continues for 0.3 mile. It is rocky at low water.

On the right below Clarno Rapids is Mulberry Camp (mile 5.3), the last camp and beach not on private land for 6.5 miles. Around 6 miles downstream power lines cross the river, followed by old ranch buildings at mile 11.3 that signal 0.3 mile of class 1+–2- rapids. One-third mile later, Butte Creek enters on the right at mile 11.9. In 1.6 miles, buildings on the right at mile 13.5, visible straight ahead from far up-stream, are the watermark for nearing Basalt Rapids.

Basalt Rapids, class 2 (mile 15.9), is replete with basalt boulders. The approach is not obvious but can be identified by fast water leading around a slight curve to the right, with juniper trees on the right. Land right to scout. Below 3,000 cfs, the rounded black basalt rocks are exposed in the rapids and some maneuvering is required. The main rapids is fairly short and curves to the left. Lower Basalt Rapids, with large black basalt boulders in the river, continues for 0.5 mile, with some hole dodging and rock dodging. There are good campgrounds here and in Great Basalt Canyon for the next 4 miles. Arch Rocks (mile 20) has a large camp on the right.

Thirty Mile Creek enters on the right 5.3 miles later (mile 25.3), with an access road to civilization. In 8.2 miles, the river begins a sweep to the right (The Saddle, ahead, is only 300 feet wide), followed by Horseshoe Bend, a 320-degree, 2-mile turn to the left. In less than 2 miles, two springs emerge from the vegetation on the hillside on the left (mile 37.3), identified by a dirt bank on river left and distorted columnar basalt near the river on river right.

In 7.7 miles, Southbound Rapids (mile 45), straightforward class 1+, is headed due south, with a large gravel bar on the left. Landmarks are visible in 4.3 miles at mile 49.3: Hoot Owl Rock, a 6-foot-high "owl," is seen against the skyline about 200 feet above the river; a gravel bar is on the left; and Citadel Rock, a fairy-tale fortress of a rock formation, dominates the view downstream. The river makes a sharp 180-degree turn to the right around Hoot Owl Rock.

In 0.7 mile, Doomsday Wall is on the left at mile 50; the river seems to disappear under the wall. A good ferry is required here. Campsites arc less numerous and less desirable from here on. In 3.8 miles, Little Ferry Canyon comes in on the left at mile 53.8; two flat islands can be seen just downstream, and the red bluffs ahead on the left are The Gooseneck. The river first curves sharply right, then makes a long 200-degree curve left around The Gooseneck (mile 54.5).

In little less than 1 mile, Ferry Canyon (mile 55.5) comes in on the right, with Ferry Canyon Rapids, straightforward class 1+. In 4.5 miles, power lines first become visible on a distant ridge (mile 60). Almost no campsites can be found below here. It's another 9 miles to the take-out at the Cottonwood bridge (mile 69). Take out on the right, just below the bridge.

Hazards. In addition to the rapids described above, the terrain provides difficulties. Spring weather can range from snow flurries to sunny with temperatures above 100 degrees Fahrenheit within a few days. Beware of rattlesnakes, strong upcanyon winds in the afternoons, and the lack of potable water.

Access. The put-in is at the bridge in Clarno where Oregon 218 crosses the river. Parking and a boat landing are located at the east end of the bridge. Oregon 218 is located between US 97 at Shaniko and

Oregon 19 at Fossil (Oregon 19 can be reached from the north from I-84 at Arlington or from the south from US 26 near Dayville).

The take-out is at the Cottonwood bridge where Oregon 206 crosses the river. To get from Clarno to Cottonwood, follow Oregon 218 east to Fossil, then take Oregon 19 north to Condon, and then take Oregon 206 north to Cottonwood.

Gauge. Located at Service Creek. Contact the River Forecast Center in Portland.

Rob Blickensderfer

SNAKE RIVER AND TRIBUTARIES

The Snake, the largest tributary of the Columbia River, begins its westward journey at Yellowstone National Park. The upper stretches are very popular with anglers and rafters alike, especially those around Jackson, Wyoming, and the Birds of Prey area in southern Idaho. Farther westward, where it forms most of Oregon's eastern border with Idaho, rapids that were considered to be bigger than those in the Grand Canyon of the Colorado have been transformed into a series of reservoirs by Brownlee, Oxbow, and Hells Canyon dams.

Spared many times over from the U.S. Army Corps of Engineers' grandiose plans for dams, Hells Canyon is now protected as a National Recreation Area. Most boaters float through this mile-deep canyon in 4–6 days. Permits are required from the Friday preceding Memorial Day weekend through September 15. For permit information, contact Hells Canyon National Recreation Area (3620 B Snake River Avenue, Lewiston, ID 83501).

Hells Canyon, rich in cultural history, was inhabited by Shoshone and Nez Percé Indians because of the abundance of fish and game and the mild winters. In the late 1870s fertile streamside canyons and meadows were used to raise sheep, cattle, and hay while miners scoured the country for gold, copper, and other valuable minerals. After the canyon's classification as a national recreation area, the Forest Service acquired most of the remaining homesteads. For further reading see *Snake River of Hells Canyon* by Carrey et al. (see Bibliography).

The Snake is joined in the very southeastern corner of Washington by the Grande Ronde. The Grande Ronde and its main tributaries, the Minam and the Wallowa, drain about 4,000 square miles of northeastern Oregon. The drainage includes portions of the Elkhorn, Blue, and Wallowa mountains. Originating in the Elkhorns, the Grande Ronde River descends through nearly 50 miles of forest and rangeland. Near La Grande it changes abruptly into a pastoral river in a broad agricultural basin.

Past Elgin, the river strikes northeastward where it has carved a deep canyon through nearly 100 miles of forests and grasslands. At Rondowa the river is joined by the Wallowa River, and from there to the Washington state line is designated a Wild and Scenic River. The 8.5 miles of the Wallowa River above Rondowa is a State Scenic Waterway.

The canyon provides habitat for elk, white-tail deer, mule deer, black bear, and bighorn sheep. The riparian zone is also home for bald eagle, a diversity of waterfowl, otter, beaver, mink, raccoon, black bear, and cougar. A diverse flora exists here, and several rare and endangered plants grow in the protection of canyon wall and forest glade.

Recreationists use the river and its canyon for fishing, hunting, hiking, and berry picking. Several guide services hold permits to float the Grande Ronde River, and many local boaters use the river.

T. R. Torgersen

188 Grande Ronde River
Tony Vey Meadows to Red Bridge State Park

Class: 3(4+) T	**Length: 17 miles**
Flow: 250–800 cfs	**Character: forested**
Gradient: 54 fpm	**Season: snowmelt**

The put-in is near an old dam at the edge of Tony Vey Meadows, though the 8 miles above Tony Vey Meadows provide an easy and attractive float for open canoers and anglers. The river meanders through meadowlands in cattle country. There is a potential hazard of barbed-wire fences across the river.

The river changes character abruptly after Tony Vey Meadows and quickly becomes narrow, rocky, and swift. Fairly steep, well-timbered slopes and generally dense streamside vegetation border this section. There are several campgrounds and picnic sites affording comfortable rest stops. The Stygian Steps are a series of drops that require scouting. They can be scouted from the road during the shuttle, about 3.5 miles upstream from Utopia Campground. On the river, they are about 0.3 mile below the River Picnic Site.

Hazards. The generally narrow channel and rapid descent of this stretch create a run that is potentially hazardous; newly fallen trees may block the channel. At times a barbed-wire fence and collection of debris forms an obstruction at Starkey, about 2.5 miles below Bikini Beach Campground, and 2 miles below a former bridge site.

Access. Take the Hilgard Junction State Park/Oregon 244 exit off I-84 4 miles west of La Grande. Proceed 7.5 miles west on Oregon 244 to Red Bridge State Park, the take-out.

To reach the put-in, continue 5 miles southwest on Oregon 244 to Starkey Trading Post at the junction with Route 51. Turn left (south) on Route 51 and go 11.5 miles to the junction with NFD 200. This junction is the put-in.

Gauge. Located at La Grande, near Perry on river right, between the road bridge and the railroad trestle. A flow of 900–1,100 cfs on the gauge gives a boatable level.

T. R. Torgersen

189 Grande Ronde River
Red Bridge State Park to Hilgard Junction State Park

Class: 2; 2+   **Length: 8 miles**
Flow: 850 cfs; 5,000 cfs   **Character: forested**
Gradient: 22 fpm   **Season: snowmelt**

The river canyon broadens considerably on this run and is bounded by open forest and some rangeland. A modest gradient and easy riffles make this a fine float for beginners in almost any craft.

Hazards. Rapids constitute little hazard on this run, but beware of barbed-wire fences across the river. A rifle club shooting range is situated on the river about 4.2 miles below Red Bridge Park. A sign reading "CAUTION: ENTERING RIFLE RANGE IMPACT AREA," hanging on a wire crossing the river, warns the boater of potential hazard. Make your presence known to shooters who may be at the benches when you reach this spot!

Access. To reach the put-in at Red Bridge State Park, see directions to the take-out for run 188, Grande Ronde River: Tony Vey Meadows to Red Bridge State Park.

To reach the take-out, return to Oregon 244 and proceed 7.5 miles east to Hilgard Junction State Park, 4 miles west of La Grande and I-84. The take-out is on river left at Hilgard Junction State Park, either above or below the bridge.

Gauge. See run 188, Grande Ronde River: Tony Vey Meadows to Red Bridge State Park.

T. R. Torgersen

190 Grande Ronde River
Hilgard Junction State Park to Riverside City Park

Class: 2(3+); 3(4)   **Length: 9 miles**
Flow: 1,500–6,000 cfs; 7,000 cfs   **Character: road**
Gradient: 26 fpm   **Season: rainy/snowmelt**

This is a favorite conditioning and play run for local boaters. An annual raft race on this stretch attracts a flurry of floaters in every imaginable type of craft.

The river is wide and gentle at first. After a few miles of warm-up, a ledge called Snoose Falls nearly spans the river to form a good surfing wave. It also marks the beginning of intermittent rapids. The first significant rapids begin when the tall I-84 bridge comes into view. Below the bridge is a series of splendid standing waves as the river veers to the right. Two bridges beyond is Vortex, a fine play spot and well-known spectator vantage point to watch rafters and others get "eaten" in the curl. The last rapids, Riverside Rapids, is the most difficult on this run. Take out on the left immediately below the rapids. To avoid Riverside Rapids, take out on the right just before the Spruce Street bridge.

Hazards. Vortex, below the third bridge, can flip a raft. Riverside Rapids, known by kayakers as Baum's Swimmin' Hole, should be scouted before the run when parking the shuttle vehicle. On the river, the sound of the rapids and the presence of the Spruce Street bridge forewarn of the two closely spaced drops and the large curl at the bottom on river right.

Access. The put-in is at Hilgard Junction State Park near La Grande; the park is reached by taking the park exit from I-84.

The take-out is in La Grande at Riverside City Park. Take the La Grande exit, exit 261, off I-84. Proceed left toward town, and turn right at the five-way intersection regulated by a traffic signal. Travel one block and take another right onto Spruce Street and continue for about 1 mile to Riverside City Park. An alternate take-out that avoids the Riverside Rapids is on river right, at the Spruce Street bridge.

Gauge. See run 188, Grande Ronde River: Tony Vey Meadows to Red Bridge State Park.

T. R. Torgersen

191 Grande Ronde River
Riverside City Park to Elgin

Class: 1	**Length: 32 miles**
Flow: 600–5,000 cfs	**Character: agricultural**
Gradient: 4 fpm	**Season: rainy/snowmelt**

This gentle, slowly flowing stretch has appeal for leisurely day outings. The borders of the river abound with wildlife, including small mammals, waterfowl, and songbirds. In its meandering course through the broad, fertile Grande Ronde flood plain, the river is crossed intermittently by numerous county roads and lanes that grid the valley. This abundance of crossings permits an almost limitless variety of trip lengths.

Hazards. Be on the lookout for obstructing debris and barbed wire.

Access. To reach the put-in at Riverside City Park from I-84, take the La Grande exit, exit 261, and proceed left toward town. Turn right at a five-way intersection, go one block, and turn right on Spruce Street. Riverside City Park is about 1 mile farther on Spruce Street. The put-in is also accessible from Oregon 82 via either of the I-84 La Grande exits.

To reach the take-out in Elgin, take Oregon 82 north from I-84 in La Grande. The take-out is at the Oregon 82 bridge at the north end of town. The Wallowa–Whitman National Forest map shows road details for alternate put-ins and take-outs.

Gauge. Located at La Grande. Flows for this run may be difficult to estimate because of water diversions for agriculture.

T. R. Torgersen

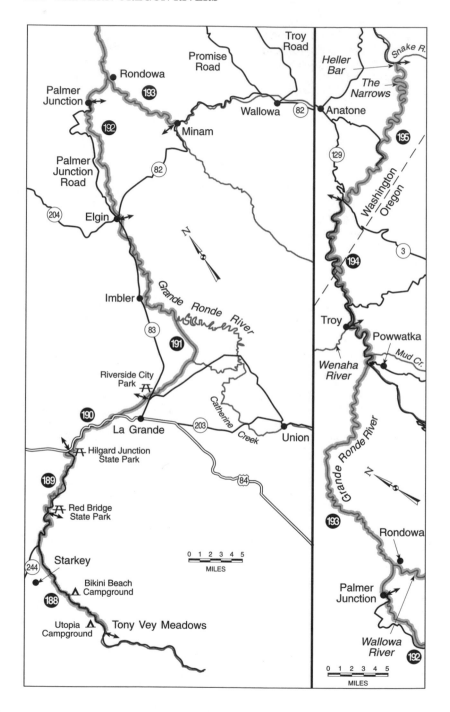

Troy Road

Promise Road

Rondowa

193

Palmer Junction

192

Palmer Junction Road

Wallowa

82

Heller Bar

The Narrows

Snake R.

Anatone

195

129

Minam

82

204

Elgin

Washington
Oregon

194

3

Imbler

Grande Ronde River

83

191

Troy

Powwatka

Mud Cr.

Wenaha River

Riverside City Park

190

La Grande

203

Catherine Creek

Union

84

Hilgard Junction State Park

189

Red Bridge State Park

Grande Ronde River

244

Starkey

Bikini Beach Campground

188

Utopia Campground

Tony Vey Meadows

0 1 2 3 4 5
MILES

193

Rondowa

Palmer Junction

Wallowa River

192

0 1 2 3 4 5
MILES

192 Grande Ronde River
Elgin to Palmer Junction

Class: 2(3); 2(4)　　　　　　　Length: 13 miles
Flow: 2,000–5,000 cfs; 8,000 cfs　Character: agricultural; hilly
Gradient: 21 fpm　　　　　　　Season: year-round

Initially this run retains the agricultural and rangeland character of the previous run from La Grande. Within 5 miles from Elgin, the river descends into a deeper, narrower "V"-shaped valley that characterizes the river's course for much of its remaining length to the Snake River. For a much longer trip, boaters may continue 3 miles to the confluence with the Wallowa River at Rondowa and from there another 36 miles to Troy (see run 193: Grande Ronde River: Minam to Troy). The former access at Rondowa is on private property and is not available.

Hazards. Andy's Rapids occur 4 miles from Elgin; scout this one. Portage or line on the left, or run the normal route on the right.

Access. To reach the put-in from I-84 in La Grande, take Oregon 82 north to Elgin. The put-in is at the Oregon 82 bridge at the north end of Elgin.

The take-out is reached by taking Oregon 204 north from Oregon 82 to the center of Elgin and going north on Palmer Junction Road. The take-out is about 0.5 mile below Palmer Junction at the campsite on river left.

Gauge. Use the La Grande gauge to estimate flows. The Rondowa gauge can also be used, but it measures flow for both the Wallowa and Grande Ronde rivers.

T. R. Torgersen

193 Grande Ronde River
Minam to Troy

Class: 2; 3　　　　　　　　Length: 46 miles
Flow: 1,200–3,800 cfs;　　　Character: forested canyon
　　　5,000–12,000 cfs　　Season: year-round
Gradient: 22 fpm, C

This is the popular wilderness run of the Grande Ronde. Boaters usually spend two or three nights camping on the river. Campsites are pleasant and abundant, except on Memorial Day and Fourth of July weekends when 200–300 boaters appear. This description is dedicated to Tuk-eka-kas and Hin-mah-too-yah-lat-kekt, who, along with their Nez Percé people, respected the land and had the wisdom never to abuse a river or wish that they could stop it from flowing. They called the Grande Ronde River Welleweah—"river that flows into the far beyond."

A rolling plateau makes up the canyon rim. The canyon walls present tiers of horizontal lava flows that occurred during the Miocene epoch. These stratified formations are the oldest exposed rocks in the canyon, and contain pillars, spires, window-holes, and caves. Abstruse dikes and columnar basalts add more geological variety.

This stretch is reasonably well suited to intermediate boaters except at high flows. It usually has enough water any month of the year. May normally has the highest mean flows, while September sees the lowest flows. In very low water (700–1,200 cfs), anticipate encounters with rocks and seemingly endless shoals. Rafters and drift boaters should be prepared to do a lot of pushing, tugging, and cursing. Flows of about 2,000 cfs are optimum for open canoes. Kayakers find flows of about 5,000 cfs optimum. From 10,000–15,000 cfs, eddies become rare, the current is fast, and large standing waves develop into great rides for dories, rafts, kayaks, and expert canoers. At these volumes swimmers would experience a long, cold endeavor to gain shore or reenter a craft. The trip is normally done with two nights of camping on the river, but at flows above 5000 cfs, this run can be a day trip!

The weather begins to warm up in June, but snow and rain are good possibilities in late May and early June. December, January, and February are very cold. The river can freeze during these months, but they are good times for observing winter populations of bald eagles and big game animals. In summer, shorebirds such as sandpipers and killdeer nest in the same areas that people use for camping. Please be on the lookout for nests to avoid destroying them. Bear Creek seems to have the highest incidence of rattlesnake sightings, and occasionaly a scorpion has been seen. Treat or boil drinking water, because streams originating beyond the canyon rim may be contaminated. These lower river sections receive heavy use. The carry-out method for solid human waste is preferred.

The put-in at Minam is at the confluence of the Minam River with the Wallowa River. The first 10 miles of the run are on the Wallowa River, which merges with the Grande Ronde River at Rondowa. The first 6 miles below Minam contain nearly continuous rapids. A mile and a half below the put-in is the Minam Roller or Hatchery Hole. The roller develops at about 3,000 cfs, and becomes a great surfing and ender hole at about 5,000 cfs. Beyond this volume the roller becomes a boat-eater and thrasher because of the pronounced backwash. This hole consumes swimmers, who may not surface until 30 feet downstream. This rapids is located on the first major right-hand bend in the river, and is recognized by several large basalt rocks on river left. Open boats should avoid the Minam Roller at flows exceeding 5,000 cfs by holding to the right bank.

Minam State Recreation Area is at mile 2. Because of its campground, this is a popular alternate put-in. A mile farther down is House Rock Drop. The chute is to the left of a house-size boulder that fell into the river during construction of the railroad. The preferred route is close to the left side of the rock to avoid the large hole farther left.

At mile 5, Blind Falls, also called Vincent Falls, class 2–3, may surprise many boaters. A rock garden leads into a ledge that is difficult to see. Look for it 0.5 mile below railroad marker 42 after catching a glimpse of a power line. The confluence of the Wallowa with the Grande Ronde is marked by two bridges at mile 10. Many nice campsites exist for many miles below here. Sheep Creek Rapids occur at mile 12. At mile 20 the long, heavy rapids among rocks is sometimes called Martin's Misery.

Many other rapids, some of which lead into headwalls, occur between here and Wildcat Creek. At Wildcat the unpaved road from Troy crosses the river on Powwatka bridge, and an unimproved picnic area is available on the right. This is an alternate take-out. A second alternate take-out is found 0.5 mile downstream on the left opposite Mud Creek. The 8 miles to Troy are somewhat slower than the above. The take-out is on the right at the bridge on the approach to Troy, or 1.5 miles downstream at a boat ramp on the right.

More detailed information can be found in *Wildwater Touring* by Scott and Margaret Arighi and in *Oregon River Tours* by John Garren (see Bibliography).

Hazards. The Minam Roller can swamp or flip boats at high water. Blind Falls (Vincent Falls) is difficult to see when approaching. It develops a keeper hole at low water. It and Sheep Creek Rapids should be approached with caution or scouted. Most of the rapids require more maneuvering at lower water. Sometimes rocks become decorated with twisted or broken canoes and ripped rafts.

Access. To reach the put-in from I-84 in La Grande, take Oregon 82 north to Minam. The put-in is near the store on the south (left) side of the river bridge at Minam. An alternate put-in is at Minam State Recreation Area about 2 miles downstream. This recreation area, with a campground, is at the end of a gravel road along the left bank of the river.

There are two routes to the take-out. Go east on Oregon 82 from Minam to Wallowa. Turn left on Troy Road (a poor road), and follow it to Wildcat and Troy.

A route longer in distance (80 miles), but not in time, is to continue even farther east on Oregon 82 to Enterprise, then take Oregon 3 northward 32 miles. Turn left at the Flora–Troy junction and follow the signs to Troy. Parts of these routes get rough in spring and summer, slick when wet, and snow-covered in winter. Shuttle service is available. Call the Minam Motel (541-437-4475) or Minam Store (541-437-1111).

Gauge. Located at Troy. Call the River Forecast Center in Portland. Accurate flow for the Wallowa between Minam and Rondowa can be estimated by subtracting the Elgin gauge reading from the reading at Rondowa. The latter gauge gives a more definitive flow reading for the Grande Ronde below Rondowa.

Gary Lane

194 Grande Ronde River
Troy to Boggan's Oasis

Class: 2; 2+(3)
Flow: 1,400–3,500 cfs; 5,000–12,000 cfs
Gradient: 17 fpm

Length: 19.5 miles
Character: canyon; roaded
Season: year-round

Below Troy the lines of trees spilling over the canyon rim begin to withdraw from the more arid side slopes, and the canyon becomes progressively steeper and drier. The brushy draws and grassy rimrock are frequented by mule deer instead of the elk that are dominant upriver. Rattlesnakes are more common on this stretch. There are a few ranches along the river, connected by a gravel road that parallels the run for the entire distance. A small park with outhouses, and a tiny store with a cafe and gas pumps, greet boaters at Boggan's Oasis, in the state of Washington.

Hazards. High flows create some interesting waves and strong headwall cross currents. Such places are accompanied by surging boils and large whirlpools that may require some heavy stroking to avoid.

Access. To reach the put-in, see run 193, Grande Ronde River: Minam to Troy, for directions to the Troy accesses and shuttle services available.

The take-out is at Boggan's Oasis store and cafe on Washington 129/Oregon 3 (it changes at the state line) between Enterprise, Oregon, and Lewiston, Idaho. This highway winds steeply down to the bridge that crosses the Grande Ronde at the store. The infamous Rattlesnake Grade claws its way tortuously out of the river canyon from here. A good all-weather route to Powwatka and the put-in at Troy strikes westward immediately off the north end of the river bridge. Shuttle service for the 75-mile drive is available.

Gauge. Located at Troy. Call the River Forecast Center in Portland.

Gary Lane

195 Grande Ronde River
Boggan's Oasis to Snake River

Class: 2(4); 3(4)
Flow: 1,400–3,500 cfs; 5,000–12,000 cfs
Gradient: 17 fpm

Length: 27 miles
Character: valley desert
Season: year-round

Below Boggan's Oasis the canyon becomes increasingly arid and devoid of coniferous forest. Semi-desert vegetation, characterized by hackberry trees and prickly pear cactus, becomes common. This river run is not known for its inviting campsites. Overnighters in the canyon rarely fail to encounter a rattlesnake, scorpion, or black widow spider.

In low water, a few class 2 rapids occur. In high water, there are several class 2 and 3 rapids, and some very large, powerful eddies. The Narrows, class 4, is toward the end of the run and is considerably more difficult than the other rapids. The Narrows is located 21.4 miles from the put-in or 5.5 miles below Slippery Creek, a major tributary that enters from the left. The approach is marked by a big natural "X"-like form on the left, one bend above the rapids. Some imagination must be used to see the "X." Look a little above eye level on an open hillside near the apex of the bend. The appearance of power lines as the river bends right warns of The Narrows below.

The rapids in The Narrows are created by irregular ledges and volcanic debris that contort the river as it flows through a cut in solid basalt. There are normally two sections to The Narrows. The upper part is a long set of irregular waves that give a roller-coaster ride. The second part is about 100–150 yards farther downstream, where most of the river funnels left to form a large, cresting, back-curling wave. The size of this curler varies widely with water level, but it has eaten many a craft. At flows above about 10,000 cfs, additional cresting waves develop immediately below the curler. These waves can become the nastiest part of The Narrows. The take-out is at Heller Bar on the Snake River, 0.3 mile below the confluence.

Hazards. The Narrows, class 4, is considerably more difficult than the other rapids. Be on the alert for rattlesnakes when scouting.

Access. The put-in is at Boggan's Oasis (see run 195, Grande Ronde River, Troy to Boggan's Oasis).

To reach the take-out at Heller Bar, drive north on Washington 129 to within 1 mile of Anatone. Turn right onto Montgomery Ridge Road and follow the sporadic signs to the Snake River. At the junction with the river, turn right (upriver) to the Heller Bar boat ramp.

Gauge. Located at Troy. Call the River Forecast Center in Portland.

Gary Lane

Solitude on the Snake River (photo by Jerry Arvin)

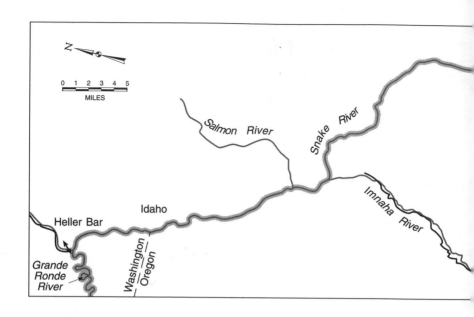

196 Snake River
Hells Canyon Dam to Heller Bar

Class: 3(5)   **Length: 78 miles**
Flow: 8,000–60,000 cfs   **Character: desert canyon; roadless**
Gradient: 9 fpm, PD   **Season: year-round**

Typically a pool-drop river, the Snake allows plenty of time to retrieve flipped boats and swimmers below the major rapids, if the water flows are in the 8,000–16,000 cfs level. It can usually be negotiated by the average boater. Above these levels, skilled river runners find tremendous challenge as the big drops become bigger, the water pushier, and the flow much faster. Biggest water is encountered at about 20,000 cfs; above this level the rapids begin to wash out slightly while strong eddy lines and currents begin to develop. Flows in the spring and early summer can easily reach 60,000 cfs at the put-in and may double after the Main Salmon enters at 61 miles from the put-in.

Late spring trips are a real treat; the canyon is still green, the weather is usually pleasant. Summer is paradise: hot days and 70-degree water. Into late September and early October the weather remains pleasant, the water cools a bit, and quick squalls can pop up. Year-round upstream winds can be encountered; it's best to boat in the morning to avoid them. Camping and hiking opportunities abound with large sandy beaches, more than 200 archaeological sites, and good trails. This area is protected by federal law, so do not disturb archaeological

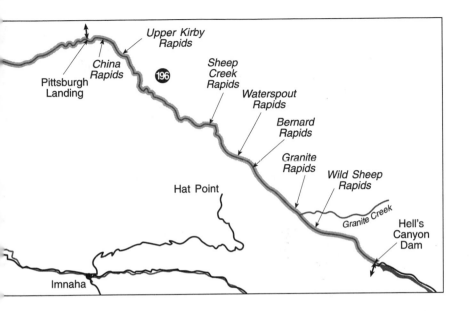

sites. More information can be found in *Idaho Whitewater* by Greg Moore and Don McClaran (see Bibliography).

The two major rapids on the Snake can be run by intermediate boaters with a little guidance from skilled boaters. The first rapids is Wild Sheep, located not quite 6 miles from the put-in. Look for a large lone pine tree on the left and take out. A trail located up the bank leads to a good scouting point. At low water, work either left or right of exposed rocks at the top before working to the center of the river for the final drop. The large diagonal waves from the left at the bottom can easily flip an 18-foot raft if not hit straight on.

Downstream about 2 miles is Granite Rapids. The best scouting is from river right where boaters can see the favored route: a tongue just right of center. Depending upon skill and size of boat, there are optional routes. After Granite Rapids, many lazy miles of river with a few class 2–3 rapids, towering canyon walls, and possible wildlife sightings lie ahead.

An alternative to running the lower section of the Snake, which some people find uninteresting, is to take out at Pittsburg Landing and shuttle to Whitebird, Idaho, for a Lower Main Salmon trip that ends at Heller Bar on the Snake. Best bet is to hire a car shuttle to Heller Bar and arrange a truck to shuttle boats from Pittsburg to Whitebird. Permits are required; contact Hells Canyon National Recreation Area, P.O. Box 699, Clarkston, WA 99403.

Hazards. Wild Sheep and Granite Rapids have big waves and holes that can flip a large raft. Scout these two. Watch out for jet boats on the river, especially during the fall hunting season.

Access. The put-in is located just below the Hells Canyon Dam where a BLM ranger checks permits. The BLM can supply permit holders with a list of people who run vehicle shuttles, or you can run your own. From I-84 in eastern Oregon, between Huntington and Ontario, take any of several exits to US 95 in western Idaho, and proceed north to Weiser. From Weiser, drive 31 miles north on US 95 to Cambridge, then turn left onto Idaho 71 and continue 29 miles to the dam.

To reach the take-out, return to US 95 and go north to Lewiston; cross the Snake River to Clarkston, Washington. Go south on Washington 129 to Anatone. At the light, bear left and proceed to Heller Bar. The take-out is a very convenient concrete ramp with food and telephone available.

Gauge. The Snake is runnable at all flows. Contact the River Forecast Center in Portland for the discharge from Hells Canyon Dam.

Ron Mattson

OWYHEE RIVER AND TRIBUTARIES

The Owyhee River arises from the mountains of northern Nevada and southern Idaho. Because the snowpack in the headwaters is normally not deep, the springtime runoff is rather short-lived despite the impoundment at Antelope and Wild Horse reservoirs far upstream.

This is arid country covered by sagebrush with some hackberry and juniper trees along the river. Wildflowers and grasses add their color to the surroundings. So does poison oak, so beware! The canyon also supports a large population of birds and rattlesnakes, which may inhabit the numerous campsites. Drinking water may be found in springs along the river, but springs become sparse as the season wears on and typically are not located near campsites. Boaters should carry enough water for a day's use and fill their containers whenever possible. Often the springs are mere trickles; a "U"-shaped tent stake placed in the trickle to form a spout can be indispensable. If river water is used for cooking or drinking, it must be purified, but the river water may contain farm chemicals unaffected by boiling.

The Owyhee is a very isolated river. There is no access for one stretch of 35 miles, and even where there is access it is still a long hike to summon help. Boaters forced overland unexpectedly in this inhospitable country could be in serious trouble.

Each of the three river runs described below should be considered as a major river expedition, with three to six overnights and almost no way of hiking out to civilization for help. More information on the first two runs can be found in *Idaho Whitewater* by Greg Moore and Don McClaran (see Bibliography). For permit information, contact the BLM, Boise District, 3948 Development Avenue, Boise, ID 83705.

197 East Fork Owyhee River
Garat Crossing to Three Forks

Class: 3(6) P   **Length: 65 miles**
Flow: 1,000–6,000 cfs   **Character: desert canyon**
Gradient: 12 fpm, PD   **Season: snowmelt**

The trip is fantastic, through remote desert canyons in the region where Oregon, Idaho, and Nevada meet. There are mile-long stretches where sheer walls drop to the river, and boaters would have to search hard to find a place to climb out. There are side canyons to explore, and in the less steep areas, it is possible to hike up to the canyon rim for spectacular vistas of the Owyhee Mountains. Eagles abound, but boaters are unlikely to see another human soul. Because of the challenges and the remoteness, the trip requires solid class 3 paddling skills and thorough preparation for wilderness expeditions. Given the portages, 6 days is a comfortable time to allocate. There is little or no competition for campsites.

Most of the rapids are easy class 1 and 2 whitewater, with a few class 3 rapids. However, there is a *mandatory portage* at Owyhee Falls, class 6, which is about 22 miles into the trip. Two miles farther is a probable portage at Thread the Needle, class 4. These are not easy portages, especially the one at Owyhee Falls. In addition, Cabin and Cable rapids, located about 11 miles below the confluence with the South Fork, are class 4 and 5, respectively, and need to be lined or portaged by most boaters.

The crowning glory is a warm spring located about 2 miles upstream of the take-out. It is truly a world-class spa. You can't miss it, and you will have earned it. There is more to know about this remarkable wilderness river than can be reported here. Before going, contact the BLM office in Boise, Idaho (208-384-3300) for maps and information about access, river conditions, and regulations on river use.

Hazards. The two mandatory portages and two probable portages present difficulties. At 6,000 cfs the approach to the portage of Owyhee Falls requires care because the water is fast. The canyon is in very remote desert country. Purify water and watch for rattlesnakes.

Access. The put-in is at Garat Crossing, near the southwest corner of Idaho. Take I-84 east into Idaho, exit at Mountain Home, and head south on Idaho 51. Beyond Riddle, near the East Fork Owyhee, turn right and proceed to Garat Crossing, Idaho, several miles west of the Duck Valley Indian Reservation. Garat Crossing, the put-in, is a gas pipeline crossing.

For the take-out, return north on Idaho 51. Turn left on Idaho 78, go to Murphy, turn left on Idaho 45, and continue to Jordan Valley, Oregon, just across the state line. From Jordan Valley, take US 95 west 2 miles, turn left on a secondary road, and proceed 37 miles to the take-out at Three Forks. (Three Forks is not a community.) The final 2-mile pitch down into the canyon is steep and rough. The take-out is possible

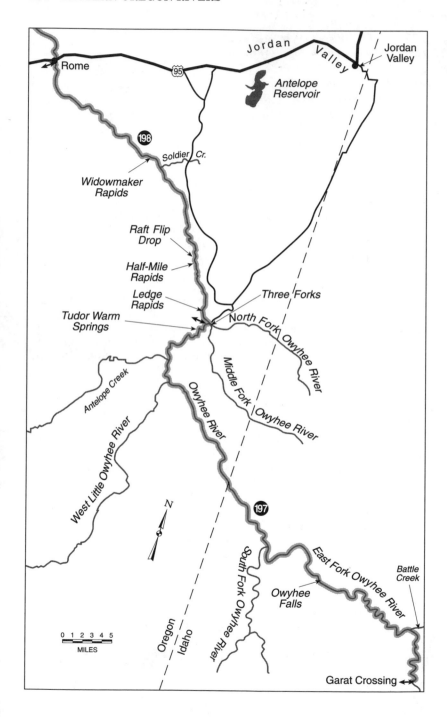

without four-wheel-drive, unless it rains; inquire with Jordan Valley shuttle drivers Eva Easterday (541-586-2352) and Kenneth Haylett (541-586-2406).

Jordan Valley can also be reached from central Oregon via US 20 or US 395 to Burns; from Burns, take Oregon 78 southeast to US 95, turn left onto US 95, and proceed northeast to 2 miles west of Jordan Valley.

Gauge. Located at Rome. Contact the River Forecast Center in Portland. About 1,000 cfs is the minimum, although folks in canoes and inner tubes have been known to bump down at much lower flows.

Paul Norman and Alex McNeily

198 Owyhee River
Three Forks to Rome

Class: 4(5)	**Length:** 37 miles
Flow: 1,200–8,000 cfs	**Character:** inaccessible gorge; desert
Gradient: 22 fpm, PD	**Season:** snowmelt

The Owyhee River has cut a canyon as deep as 3,000 feet down through volcanic rock. In many places the cliffs rise 1,000 feet straight up from the river. The countryside is arid with little vegetation and no inhabitants. There are no access roads or trails between the put-in and take-out, although there are a few places where a person could climb out of the canyon in an emergency. The steepness of the cliffs and narrowness of the canyon provide a fascinating experience. The normal trip is two or three overnights.

In contrast to the pastoral scene at the put-in, numerous rapids lie downstream. Ample time should be allotted for the necessary scouting of rapids, and for savoring the experience of isolation. Boaters may find hot springs, petroglyphs, and a large cave that makes an unusual camp shelter.

The weather in the bottom of the canyon can be oppressively hot in April and May, when this stretch is normally high enough to run. However, one should also be prepared for cool weather, cold water, and even snow flurries. The canyon has one of the densest rattlesnake populations in Oregon, so people may feel more at ease sleeping in tents. Camping areas are not nearly as plentiful here as on the next run or on most other eastern Oregon rivers. This river is becoming more and more popular.

At flows much over 3,000 cfs, the river becomes very fast, but some of the rapids wash out. (For comparison, the Middle Fork of the Salmon, at the same flow, is considered easier than the Owyhee. Further information can be found in *Wildwater Touring* by Scott and Margaret Arighi; see Bibliography.)

Three Forks, the put-in, is a slow-flowing pool. In 1.5 miles is Ledge Rapids, class 4. As the canyon narrows and water picks up to class 2, The Ledge is approached. The Ledge consists of several narrow chutes between boulders. Rafts have been wiped out at Ledge Rapids. Land near the base of large rocks on left and scout from the left. About 400 yards of class 4 boulder garden follow. In another mile, where there is a sheepherders' abandoned cabin on the right, there's a warm spring just downstream and a hot spring on the left 100 yards down. There are several class 2 rapids in another 2.5 miles.

At mile 8.5, after several class 2–3 rapids, look for a bend to the right. Stop before the bend and scout Halfmile Rapids, class 4+. Some rafts have never reached beyond this nearly 0.5-mile-long rapids. The rapids have an upper section and a lower section, with a short class 2 pool in between. Scout from the right. At low water, the lower section becomes extremely rocky; at any level, there is a tendency for rafts to get swept too far right and lodged against boulders. It is only 100 yards to the next major rapids, Raft Flip Drop.

Raft Flip Drop (mile 9), class 3–4, can be sneaked by kayaks on the left through the small left channel at high water levels, but rafts find a deceptively powerful roller at the bottom of the main chute that can flip a raft. In another 2 miles, several class 3- rapids run for 2 miles. A mile later, Subtle Hole (mile 14), class 3+, is longer than Raft Flip Drop. It leads into Bombshelter Drop, class 3, at mile 14+. A large cave on the left, just above river level, is a possible campsite. In a couple more miles are some fast class 3 rapids. A mile later is Finger Rock Rapids (mile 17), class 3. A small and a larger rock stick up at the head of the rapids. This is followed 1 mile later by several class 2 rapids. Soldier Creek (mile 19) enters from the right, with an extensive gravel bar.

The next mile brings springs on the right and several class 3 rapids among boulders in a steep canyon located 100 yards above Widowmaker, with class 3 water leading to Widowmaker (mile 20.5), class 5. The approach to Widowmaker is identified by a 200-yard stretch of straight, narrow canyon. The river seems to disappear among large boulders ahead. On the right a talus slope extends down to the river. As the flow of this run approaches 3,000 cfs, Widowmaker appears ominous. At flows below 2,000 cfs, competent boaters may run the class 3 rapids before stopping to scout Widowmaker, but all others should land on the right above the class 3 rapids. Although it looks very tempting to kayakers below 1,800 cfs, a portage is highly recommended. The portage is difficult on either side, but is usually done on the right. It is possible for medium-size rafts to thread the chutes on the right. Skilled rafters run the right series of two chutes of the big drop. The drop from the class 3 rapids to the bottom of Widowmaker is about 20 feet, with Widowmaker itself about a 10-foot drop.

There are numerous class 2 and some class 3 rapids for the next 8 miles. Small beaches occasionally dot the river banks. At mile 29, there are class 2+ rapids; below here, the canyon begins to open up. Several camping beaches and flat water can be found for the next 2 miles. The last rapids (mile 31), class 2, is followed by flat water to Rome, as the canyon rim fades away.

Halfmile Rapids on the Owyhee River (photo by Phil DeRiemer)

Hazards. This pool-drop river is much more difficult than the gradient of 22 fpm implies. A number of class 4 rapids of varying length and one class 5 rapids await the boater. Because of the remoteness of the canyon and extreme difficulty of hiking out, river conquerors must be conservative on this run. The road to the put-in becomes impassable after a rain. When scouting along the riverbank, be alert for rattlesnakes.

Access. To reach the put-in, see run 197, Owyhee River: Garat Crossing to Three Forks. Or, from Rome, drive 16 miles east on Oregon 78 to a dirt road marked "THREE FORKS ROAD." Head south 35 miles, then descend to the river. The dirt road, especially the last mile, can be muddy and impassable.

The take-out is located about 0.2 mile upstream from the Rome bridge on US 95 on the east bank. A large parking area, boat ramp, and toilets are here. Shuttle service can be obtained in Jordan Valley (see run 199, Owyhee River: Rome to Leslie Gulch).

Gauge. Located at Rome. Call the River Forecast Center in Portland. Although 1,200 cfs is the normal minimum runnable flow, it reportedly has been run, with steep, rock-scraping drops, at 400 cfs.

Rob Blickensderfer

199 Owyhee River
Rome to Leslie Gulch

Class: 3(4)   **Length: 66.5 miles**
Flow: 1,000–4,000 cfs   **Character: roadless; desert**
Gradient: 15 fpm, PD   **Season: snowmelt**

This run on the Owyhee has an interestingly diverse landscape. The canyon in general is broad and shallow, although there are several stretches with narrow, steep-walled inner canyons. The predominant basalts found in the upper canyon are interbedded with rhyolitic ash and sediments, which add various shades of white, red, green, and black to the canyon walls. Lambert Rocks are colorful badlands eroded from these sediments.

Because the Owyhee is unregulated above Rome and depends on snowmelt, the boating season is short and variable. It is usually runnable during April and May. Some years the season may extend into early June, while other years it may end by mid-May. The weather also is undependable, with temperatures ranging from freezing to 100 degrees Fahrenheit and above. Be prepared for rain or drought. The normal trip is four or five overnights. The rapids on this run are mostly class 2, making it a nice river for intermediate kayakers and rafters. However, the few class 3 and 4 rapids and the remoteness of the river demand that experienced boaters accompany less skilled boaters. Further information can be found in *Wildwater Touring* by Scott and Margaret Arighi (see Bibliography).

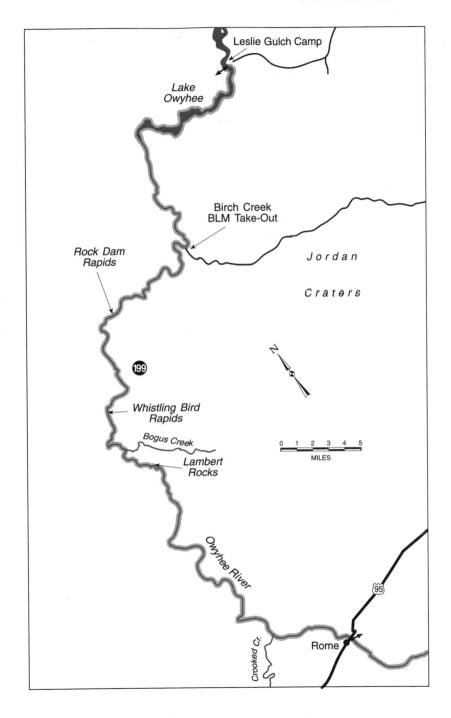

Leslie Gulch Camp

Lake
Owyhee

Birch Creek
BLM Take-Out

Rock Dam
Rapids

Jordan

Craters

199

Whistling Bird
Rapids

Bogus Creek

Lambert
Rocks

0 1 2 3 4 5
MILES

Owyhee River

95

Crooked Cr.

Rome

Six and one-half miles from the Rome put-in, Crooked Creek comes in on the left, marking the start of the canyon. The canyon opens for several miles; about 6 miles below Crooked Creek is Upset Rapids, class 3, followed by Bulls Eye, class 2–3. Artillery Rapids (mile 21.5), is a straightforward class 3. After the beautiful Lambert Rocks, Bogus Creek Falls is seen on the right at mile 27.5. Another 1.5 miles farther is class 3 Dogleg; after 2 more miles comes Whistling Bird Rapids.

Whistling Bird is preceded by a large rock wall on the left 0.5 mile upstream. A dry wash on the left, the rock face and slab on the right, and the noise of the rapids mark its location. Whistling Bird Rapids (mile 31), class 4-, should be scouted on the left by those unfamiliar with it. The current washes into a large slab that has fallen from the canyon wall. This should be avoided by pulling to the left.

In 2.5 miles, Montgomery Rapids (mile 33.5), class 3, is located in a steep-walled canyon after a left turn followed by a pool. It may be tricky for unsuspecting rafters at low water levels. The river drops and turns right, pushing boats toward a rock on the left. At high water there is plenty of room to maneuver.

In 5.5 miles, a small gully enters the river on the left just above Rock Dam Rapids, and part of an old concrete diversion dam is visible on the right. The noise of the rapids at the broken dam alerts boaters to its presence. Rock Dam (mile 39), class 3–4, should be scouted on the right. Possible routes at high water are on the left or in the center. At low water rafters may choose to line this rapids on the right.

After about 15 miles, boaters encounter slack water. At mile 53.5 is a water wheel on the right. Owyhee Lake, an 8- to 12-mile flat stretch, is the toughest part of this run. In light rafts without a headwind, expect a minimum of 4 hours. Lazier folks (some might say smarter) may wish to arrange beforehand for a tow (see Access, below). Leslie Gulch (mile 66.5) comes in on the right where the lake bends left. Take out here.

Hazards. Scout Whistling Bird Rapids to avoid the large slab-rock; scout Rock Dam. Be prepared for changeable weather, as well as rattlesnakes.

Access. Shuttle service may be obtained from two sources in Jordan Valley: Eva Easterday (503-586-2352) and Kenneth Haylett (503-586-2406). Haylett can also arrange for a tow along Owyhee Lake to the Leslie Gulch take-out.

Those wishing to run their own shuttle should take US 95 east to Jordan Valley and then north to the Succor Creek–Leslie Gulch turnoff about 18 miles north of Jordan Valley. To keep trip expenses down, obey the speed limit in Jordan Valley. From the turnoff, follow the signs to Leslie Gulch (approximately 26 miles).

Gauge. Located at Rome. Contact the River Forecast Center in Portland. A flow of 1,000 cfs is considered minimum.

Dan Valens and Lance Stein

COASTAL SURF KAYAKING

Riding ocean waves in kayak, surf shoe, or surf ski is a thrilling form of whitewater boating that requires knowledge of ocean conditions, strong swimming skills, and suitable equipment. Rugged headlands, expansive beaches, and direct exposure to North Pacific ocean swells make the Oregon Coast one of the most spectacular surfing areas in North America. However, these same factors can produce hazardous ocean conditions that are subtle and unique to the Pacific Northwest. The following terms offer important safety tips for kayak surfing along the Oregon Coast. In addition to reading these sections, we strongly suggest that boaters unfamiliar with the ocean arrange initial trips with experienced wave riders.

Waves. Storm winds at sea produce irregular waves that are transformed into smooth ocean swells as they travel away from the storm center. Swells approaching shore typically begin to shoal (drag on the bottom) in water depths one and one-quarter times the swell height, as measured from crest to trough. Steep beaches produce steep, plunging breakers with wave crests that plunge from top to bottom. Flatter beaches produce spilling breakers with wave crests that gradually tumble down the wave face. Swell size, wind conditions, and tidal height also control wave shape. These conditions can change dramatically within a few hours.

Small spilling breakers in the 2- to 4-foot height range are ideal for beginning surf kayakers. Plunging breakers in the 6- to 8-foot height range can rip paddles from boaters' hands and pop spray skirts, forcing even the most skilled boater to swim for shore. Since larger waves break in deeper water, they also break farther from shore, leading surfers to greatly underestimate their size. For this reason, it is prudent to start surfing close to shore, and then move out gradually to the larger surf as true wave size is confirmed. Such an approach also ensures that surfers will observe the infrequent sets of very large waves called "clean-up sets" before committing themselves to a thorough cleaning!

Beaches, Reefs, and Points. In their search for waves, surfers usually concentrate on beaches with offshore sandbars and reefs, as well as on points such as headlands and harbor jetties. These features cause swells to refract, or bend toward shore, and produce waves that break right or left along the shore, giving long rides to surfers.

Currents. Coastal currents can be wide and with velocities of several knots, twice the speed of a swimmer. They present a great danger to boaters out of their boats. **Rip currents** are particularly dangerous because they move out to sea a distance of 0.5 mile or more. Particularly strong rip currents occur alongside headlands and jetties. **Nearshore currents** are generated by shoaling waves that push water inshore from the breaker zone. Escaping water flows parallel to the shore in **longshore currents**, and then heads back out to sea in rip currents, through gaps between offshore sandbars or reefs. Currents are intensified during conditions of large surf. The least hazardous "current" is the **undertow**, which is not really a current at all, but just the backwash of a wave on a steep beach. The backwash dissipates a few yards from the beach face, and is of little concern to experienced swimmers.

Rip currents heading out to sea can sometimes be identified by choppy surface water, turbid zones, or streaks of sea foam. Nearshore currents cover broad areas and can be difficult to recognize in the turbulent surf zone. Surfers and swimmers in the surf zone should keep an eye on fixed points on shore to see if they are drifting in a nearshore current. To get out of any current, swim or paddle perpendicular to the direction of current flow. In large surf, it might take 20 minutes or longer to swim out of a rip current and into shore. When an open-water rescue by other boaters is not possible, a tired or chilled swimmer should leave the boat and head for shore. Waves and wind will eventually put the boat ashore.

Sticks and Skins. Eskimos spent thousands of years developing the ultimate all-purpose sea kayak. Modern kayaks have evolved from Eskimo kayaks. Flotation bags, support walls, and grab loops are necessary on today's boats. Boaters should use helmets and wear belted life jackets that can't be pulled up over the shoulders by turbulent waves. Most important, a full wetsuit or drysuit is essential for safe boating in cold coastal waters where large surf can force boaters to take long swims. For winter kayak surfing, a hood and booties are worthwhile additions to the full wetsuit or drysuit.

Paddling Out and Dropping In. Conflicts or collisions sometimes occur between kayak surfers and board surfers. These conflicts can be avoided if kayakers follow the rules of wave etiquette. Surfers should paddle out to the breaker zone off to the side of other surfers who are catching and riding waves. The surfer who is closest to the breaking part of the wave has the right-of-way over others riding the wave face. Other surfers trying to catch the wave should back off to avoid dropping on the surfer who is already in position. Unlike at the favorite play wave on the local river, there isn't a well-ordered lineup of boaters waiting to catch waves out in the surf zone. So all boaters must make a conscious effort to share waves and to avoid catching waves that might propel them into other surfers. Finally, remember that most board surfers are not used to surfing with kayakers. Give them plenty of room.

Good waves, mates!

Curt Peterson, Rick Starr, and Dale Mosby

NORTH COAST

200 Columbia River South Jetty

The area just south of the Columbia River South Jetty marks the northernmost surfing location on the Oregon Coast and provides some of the longest rides to be found on Oregon waves. Like most other south jetty breaks, the Columbia River South Jetty produces slow, mushy wave peaks during high tide, with 2- to 4-foot swells approaching from the west–northwest. An increase in swell height (to 4–6 feet) and a drop in tide level can result in the spilling breaker zone moving farther seaward with longer walls lining up to the south and shorter wave shoulders dying into the rip current channel against the South Jetty. Larger swells (6–8 feet) force the breaker zone more than 1 mile offshore, driving hazardous longshore currents and rip currents against the jetty.

Hazards. Moderate to large swells from the west–southwest drive strong longshore currents northward, which turn and flow seaward along the South Jetty.

Access. Beach access is easily found northwest of Fort Stevens, north off US 101 west of Astoria. Follow the road signs to Columbia River South Jetty. Surf conditions can be scouted from the observation stand adjacent to the South Jetty parking lot.

201 Seaside Cove

The cove and point breaks just south of Seaside lie on the northern flank of Tillamook Head and thus are protected from direct exposure to large winter swells that approach shore from the southwest. As the big swells wrap around the point and break over the rocky bottom, surfers test their skills on some of the largest waves (12+ feet) ridden in Oregon.

However, smaller winter swells (6–8 feet) and westerly summer swells (4–6 feet) travel farther shoreward before shoaling in Seaside Cove. At medium to low tide these spilling breakers form long walls, breaking from south to north. Understandably, the cove is a popular spot for board riders, leading to a congested surf zone and competition for waves.

Hazards. The cove waves are noted for substantial punch, and cleanup sets are frequent. In addition, a rocky bottom and potential long swims can make Seaside Cove a poor choice for inexperienced surfers.

Access. Take one of several coastal access roads immediately south of Seaside, on US 101, to reach the beach. Turning south at the beach, drive 1–2 miles on the frontage road while looking for parking and trails to the beach. Surf conditions can be scouted from along the road and the cobble beach berm.

202 Cannon Beach and Arch Cape

Several beach breaks can be found between Cannon Beach and Arch Cape, two small coastal communities separated by about 5 miles. A series

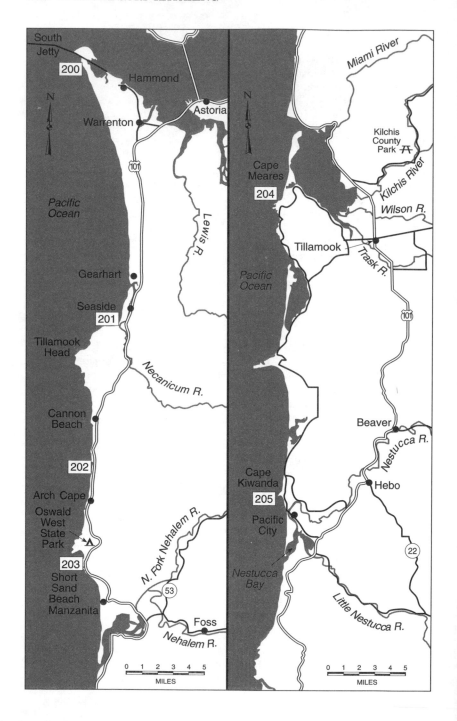

of small headlands and offshore sea stacks protect offshore sandbars from direct exposure to ocean swells, while offshore bar irregularities produce spilling breakers with short wall sections. Well-formed beach breaks can be found at Cannon Beach and Arch Cape areas during most tide levels and during westerly swell conditions of 2–6 feet. Strong onshore winds in summer months can blow out surf at either area, so early-morning conditions are preferable.

Hazards. Both Cannon Beach and Arch Cape beach breaks become unridable (close out) and form strong rip currents between offshore bars with swell conditions in excess of 6 feet.

Access. Beach breaks are easily located and scouted from beach access and frontage roads at Cannon Beach and Arch Cape, just off US 101.

203 Short Sand Beach

This delightful beach is less than 1 mile in length but has some of the best summer surf on the northern Oregon Coast. The small pocket beach is protected from summer onshore winds by headlands to the north and south. Crescentic offshore sandbars create well-formed wave peaks that break both north and south on medium tide with ocean swells of 2–6 feet. The waves commonly turn into plunging breakers at low tide and form spilling breakers during high tide, thus offering a variety of wave shapes throughout the day. The short length of this beach does not permit the development of strong nearshore currents, and the wide separation of wave peaks makes it easy to paddle out in small to moderate-size surf. Short Sand Beach has proven to be a popular surfing beach for beginning and experienced surfers alike.

Hazards. You won't want to leave this tiny sandy beach and its forested headlands.

Access. Short Sand Beach is located in Oswald West State Park, between Arch Cape and Manzanita on US 101. From the Oswald West parking lot next to US 101, walk down a paved path about 0.5 mile to the beach. In the past, the park service has provided carts to transport gear down to camping sites by the beach.

204 Cape Meares

A broad surf zone occurs immediately north of Cape Meares. Under the right conditions, spilling breakers form long lines that alternately shoal and re-form in several successions before finally collapsing on the cobbly beach face below the cape. These breakers are often at their best during low tide, with moderate ocean swells of 4+ feet. Strong onshore winds in summer months can blow out these delicate waves, so save this spot for those late spring and early fall outings. Due to the long paddle out and the gradually shoaling breakers, this spot is rarely surfed by board surfers, leaving the long, gentle breakers to more mobile kayakers. Brief excursions around the cape can spice up the afternoon when the surf is low.

Hazards. The long paddle out can lead to long swims for boaters with marginal rolls.

Access. To reach Cape Meares, take the Three Capes Scenic Route west of Tillamook, on US 101, and follow road signs to Cape Meares. In Cape Meares, follow the beach-front road south until it ends in a small parking area. Surf conditions can be scouted from either the parking area or the beach cobble berm.

205 Cape Kiwanda

Several beach breaks can be found just south of a tiny headland, Cape Kiwanda, during medium to low tide and during westerly to northwesterly ocean swells of 2–6 feet. Small spilling breakers form in the lee of the tiny headland, and a small sea stack forms near the end of the headland. Larger plunging breakers form farther south of Cape Kiwanda but, as a result of greater exposure to ocean swells and on-shore winds, these breakers are more sensitive to swell and wind conditions. Summer weekends can be busy at Cape Kiwanda, as hang gliders are attracted to the windswept bluffs on the north side of the headland, and fishermen launch their double-ended dories in the south lee of the cape.

Hazards. Beach breaks south of Cape Kiwanda become unridable (close out) and generate strong nearshore currents during large winter surf.

Access. Cape Kiwanda forms the northern beach-front boundary of Pacific City, a coastal resort town several miles west of US 101 and about 15 miles north of Lincoln City. Surf conditions can be scouted from a parking lot just south of the cape or from beach access roads to the south in Pacific City.

CENTRAL COAST

206 Gleneden Beach

Some of the fastest-breaking waves on the central coast can be found at Gleneden Beach during medium to low tide, with westerly swells of 4+ feet and offshore winds. Irregularities in offshore sandbars produce plunging breakers that peel to the north or south, often forming hollow wave faces. "Going for the tube" in a kayak is something like dropping sideways into a nasty river hole: guaranteed excitement and a probable thrashing in the end! Strong wave surges on steep beach faces, such as those at Gleneden Beach, make getting in and out of the surf zone difficult for a kayaker; bring a friend who doesn't mind getting wet feet to lend a hand.

Hazards. Beach breaks at Gleneden Beach become unridable (close out) with ocean swells greater than 6 feet. Longshore currents and rip currents between offshore bars are well developed even in moderate surf conditions, but are greatly intensified by large winter surf.

Access. Gleneden Beach County Park is found by following road signs in Gleneden, a coastal community off US 101 about 7 miles south of Lincoln City. Surf conditions can be scouted from the parking lot at the state park.

207 Otter Rock

A beach break forms off sandbars to the south of Otter Rock, a small headland known for an unusual rock formation called the Devil's Punch Bowl. The beach break is sheltered from winds and large surf by the headland and offshore reefs, resulting in ridable surf when other beach breaks are closing out. However, the headland is relatively short, permitting small summer swells to wrap around the point and shoal in the small cove just south of the headland. The spilling breakers formed in the cove are typically small but increase in size to the south, where offshore sandbars are more directly exposed to ocean swells. Ridable waves are formed over a wide range of conditions at Otter Rock, but rarely break with consistently good form.

Hazards. Large winter surf generates a moderately strong rip current that flows seaward along the headland.

Access. Take the Otter Rock exit off US 101 about 9 miles north of Newport and follow road signs to the Devil's Punch Bowl. Wooden steps lead down to the beach from the parking lot, from which there is a good view of surf conditions in the small cove.

208 Yaquina Head Cove

Yaquina Head produces some of the most consistently ridable surf on the central coast. Westerly to northwesterly ocean swells of 2–8 feet wrap around the long headland and form spilling to plunging breakers in the cove south of the headland. As the ocean swells increase in size, or as the tide level drops, the breaker line moves farther offshore, and long walls line up to the south.

In moderate-size surf, wave shoulders die into the rip channel along the south side of the headland. The rip channel offers an easy paddle out to the breaker zone. However, during conditions of larger ocean swells (6–8 feet), waves break across the rip channel and against the headland, making paddling out between sets very interesting. During conditions of small summer swells (2–4 feet), small breakers offer short rides close to shore, with the gentle wave crests protected from onshore summer winds by the large headland.

Hazards. Large winter surf generates strong longshore currents that flow north and turn seaward at the headland, producing a strong rip current that flows several hundred yards seaward along the headland. Submerged rocks underlie the surf zone in the cove during high tide, but are avoidable by staying several hundred yards south of the headland.

Access. To find and scout Yaquina Head Cove, park in a paved lot just south of Yaquina Head off US 101, about 4 miles north of Newport. Follow a wide path a couple of hundred yards southwest to the beach.

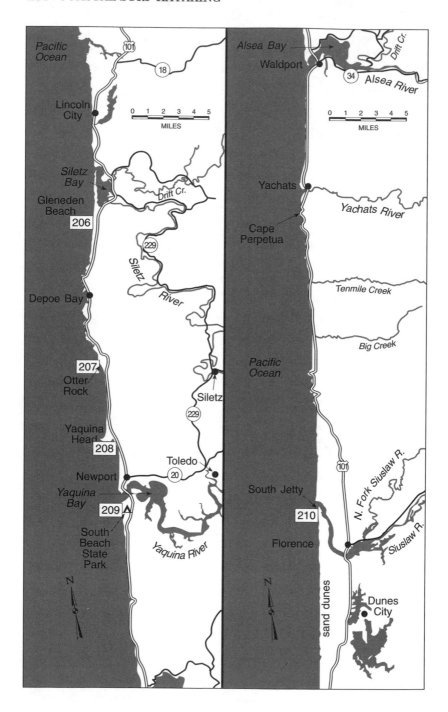

209 Yaquina Bay South Jetty to South Beach

A series of beach breaks form between Yaquina Bay South Jetty and South Beach State Park, about 1 mile south of the bay entrance. These beach breaks are formed over offshore sandbars separated by rip channels and are protected from direct exposure to northwest summer swells by the long jetty system that extends about 0.5 mile seaward off the beach. Spilling breakers shoal over a shallow sandbar immediately south of the south jetty during low tide, with westerly swells of 4–6 feet. The breaks farther south of the jetty are more exposed to ocean swells. Plunging breakers form at most tide levels with ocean swells of 2–6 feet, approaching from either the west or northwest. These breakers become unridable (close out) when ocean swells exceed 6 feet. In addition, the unsheltered beach breaks are often blown out by summer onshore winds. Either arrive early in the morning or wait for windless fall conditions.

Hazards. Many surfers have frightening stories of getting caught in the south jetty rip current during large winter surf. Large southwest swells drive longshore currents northward against the south jetty, forming a wide rip current that extends beyond the end of the jetty.

Access. Scout surf conditions from either the south jetty or the beach dunes at South Beach State Park. The south jetty is found by exiting off US 101 immediately south of Yaquina Bay bridge at Newport and following road signs to the south jetty. To find the South Beach State Park access road, which leads to the beach parking lot, continue south on US 101 another mile beyond Yaquina Bay bridge.

210 Siuslaw River South Jetty

A short beach break occurs just south of the Siuslaw River South Jetty at medium tide with westerly ocean swells of 2–4 feet. The south jetty break forms spilling breakers with short wall sections that are very susceptible to summer onshore winds. Sometimes when the surf is large in the winter, ridable waves break between the jetties.

Hazards. Like other Oregon jetty systems, a strong rip current flows seaward along the south jetty during conditions of large winter surf.

Access. A south jetty access road turns off US 101 immediately south of the Siuslaw Bay bridge just south of Florence. Take the road to the end of the spit and scout surf conditions from the south jetty.

SOUTH COAST

211 Winchester Bay South Jetty

Perhaps the finest jetty beach break to be found on the Oregon Coast occurs south of the Winchester Bay South Jetty. Westerly to northwesterly ocean swells of 2–6 feet reflect off the south jetty wall and form wave peaks that turn into long wall sections that break north and south. Lower tides and larger ocean swells produce top-to-bottom–plunging breakers while higher tides and smaller surf result in spilling breakers with well-formed shoulders. The high jetty wall deflects much of the onshore wind energy in summer months, but windless morning conditions are preferable. The height of the south jetty wall and the distance offshore to the breaker zone have led many experienced surfers to underestimate wave size. Scout the surf conditions carefully before paddling out to the breaker zone.

Hazards. Large fall and winter surf conditions generate strong nearshore currents well south of the jetty and a wide rip current that flows seaward along the south jetty.

Access. Turn off US 101 at Winchester Bay about 5 miles south of Reedsport and follow road signs to the harbor and then to the south jetty. Surf conditions can be scouted from the beach at the south jetty parking lot.

212 Bastendorff Beach

Bastendorff Beach is situated between the Coos Bay South Jetty and a small headland 1 mile south of the bay mouth. The jetty and headland alternately protect either end of Bastendorff Beach from direct exposure to prevailing wind and ocean swells. This results in spilling breakers south of the south jetty in summer months and larger plunging breakers north of the headland in stormy winter months. The beach breaks here are ridable over a wide variety of ocean swell and tide conditions, but paddling out is difficult in large winter surf when clean-up sets close out rip current lanes.

Hazards. Large ocean swells close out much of the central part of Bastendorff Beach with freight-train walls that often break in only a few feet of water.

Access. Leave US 101 at North Bend or Coos Bay and head west for Charleston, where road signs point the way to Sunset Bay and ocean beaches. One mile south of Charleston pass the Coos Head Naval Facility turnoff and take the next right to Bastendorff Beach, following road signs to the beach front.

213 Lighthouse Beach

This popular surfing area is also a nice residential area. The waves at this beach are midway in intensity between Bastendorff and Sunset. It is probably the most popular beach in the Coos Bay area. Depending on conditions and distance from shore, the surf here challenges everyone.

Hazards. There are none in particular.

Access. See run 212, Bastendorff Beach, for directions to Charleston. Proceed west from Charleston beyond the Bastendorff Beach turnoff. About 100 yards past milepost 11, just before Sunset Beach, turn right onto Dead End Road. Proceed about 100 yards and then park off the pavement. The dirt/mud trail on the right winds down to the beach.

214 Sunset Bay

Sunset Bay is a tiny cove that offers small waves when other breaks are closed out by large storm surf. The cove is only 0.25 mile across and

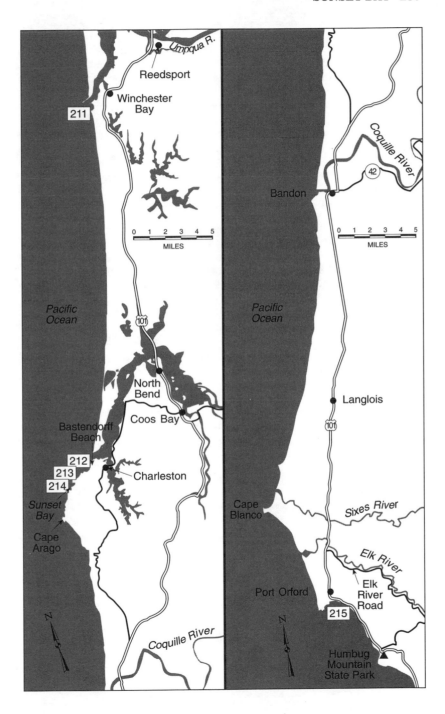

is connected to the open ocean by a narrow strait only 300 yards wide. The narrow entrance and shallow reefs offshore greatly reduce the size of ocean swells that can enter the cove, resulting in ideal beginner conditions with small spilling breakers during high tides. A small, sandy beach fronts the landward side of this delightful cove. Interesting rock formations and nearby tide pools are additional attractions.

Hazards. The interior of the cove is entirely protected from strong nearshore currents. However, shallow reef areas at the cove entrance are directly exposed to powerful waves and strong nearshore currents during periods of large storm surf.

Access. Leave US 101 at North Bend or Coos Bay and head for Charleston. Follow road signs pointing the way to Sunset Bay State Park, about 3 miles south of Charleston. Surf conditions can be scouted from the beach parking lot.

215 Port Orford

Long glassy walls characterize early morning waves that form offshore of steep beaches between Battle Rock and Humbug Mountain south of the tiny port of Port Orford. These classic summer beach breaks are protected from direct exposure to northwest ocean swells and onshore winds by Oregon's most westward land mass, Cape Blanco. Medium to low tides and moderate-size ocean swells (4+ feet) produce spilling breakers that peel to the north and south. Wave size and steepness generally increase with increasing distance south of Battle Rock. After a morning of wave sliding, barter with returning fishermen for fresh fish at the Port Orford pier.

Hazards. Some of the beach breaks form over a shallow rocky bottom and become unridable (close out) when ocean swells exceed 6 feet.

Access. The Port Orford beach breaks can be scouted from the Port Orford waterfront or from US 101 to the south.

Curt Peterson

OTHER CLASS 1 RIVERS

There are many class 1 runs that are not described elsewhere in the book. Some of these less well-known or less popular runs are described briefly here. Keep in mind that class 1 includes some whitewater with small waves, holes, and eddies, and is slightly more difficult than class C, which is swift flat water.

Five Rivers: 10 Miles to Mouth (Region 1)

Flow: 600 cfs　　　　**Length: 10 miles**
Gradient: 12 fpm, PD　**Season: rainy**

Several small ledges, a 2-foot shelf 1 mile below the put-in, and some meanders are the features of this run.

Access. Take out at the confluence with Alsea River, 20 miles west of the town of Alsea on Oregon 34. Put in 10 miles upstream on the road along Five Rivers.

Luckiamute River: Helmick Park to Willamette River (Region 5)

Flow: 500 cfs　　　　**Length: 14 miles**
Gradient: 1 fpm, C　　**Season: rainy**

Brushy banks, two class 1+ ledges, and narrow places are found on this run.

Access. Put in at Helmick State Park, on US 99 between Corvallis and Monmouth. Take out on the Willamette River at Buena Vista.

Siletz River: Sam Creek to Old Mill Park (Region 1)

Flow: 400–2,000 cfs　　**Length: 10 miles**
Gradient: 10 fpm, C　　**Season: rainy**

Small rapids and riffles occur in the upper section; the lower part is flatter.

Access. Put in at the boat ramp at Sam Creek Road 3 miles upstream from the town of Siletz. An alternate put-in at Siletz County Park in Siletz gives a 6-mile boat ride for only a 0.5-mile shuttle. Take out at Old Mill Park on the north side of town.

Santiam River: Jefferson to Buena Vista (Region 5)

Flow: 1,500–4,000 cfs   Length: 11 miles
Gradient: 6 fpm, C   Season: year-round

This run has slower water than upstream, plus some gravel bars and riffles. Be alert for snags.

Access. Put in at the public boat ramp in Jefferson, on river right, 100 yards downstream of the US 99E bridge. Take out at Buena Vista on the Willamette River. Alternate take-out after only a 5-mile run is the I-5 rest area on river right.

Yamhill River, South Fork: Sheridan to Amity–Bellevue Road (Region 5)

Flow: 700–3,000 cfs   Length: 11 miles
Gradient: 4 fpm, C   Season: rainy

There's fast water in willows 1 mile below the put-in; the last 8 miles meander.

Access. Put in one block upstream of the Oregon 18 bridge in Sheridan. Take out at the bridge between Amity and Bellevue.

YES, IT HAS BEEN RUN

Boaters often wonder whether a certain section of a river or creek has ever been run. The list below includes runs that we know have been done. These include extremely difficult hair runs, and runs with very poor access or very difficult portages, as well as runs that are not popular for other reasons. We do not know for certain that the people listed were the first to make the descent. If you can substantiate first descents that were made earlier than those given below, or if you know of additional runs, please send the information to the authors for inclusion in the next edition of *Soggy Sneakers*.

Alsea, North Fork: Upper Section to Fish Hatchery (Region 1)

Class: 4(5)   **Gradient: unknown**   **Length: unknown**

This run has a waterfall and lots of logs. Run in 1987 by Lance Stein and others.

Blowout Creek: Cliff Creek to Detroit Lake (Region 5)

Class: 4   **Gradient: 93 fpm**   **Length: 3.5 miles**

This twisting creek with high banks is fun but dangerous at high flows; there are logjams at low flows. Take out at trailhead parking area. Run in 1990 by Eric Brown.

Blue River: Mann Creek to Quentin Creek (Region 4)

Class: 4(5)   **Gradient: 240 fpm**   **Length: 4 miles**

This is a small log-choked stream starting 4 miles above the normal put-in. There are ledges. A rock slide leads to a class 5 triple drop. Run in April 1989 by Jens Mullen and Jim Reed.

Boulder Creek: Little Boulder Creek to North Fork Siletz (Region 1)

Class: 5   **Gradient: 300 fpm**   **Length: 3.6 miles**

Hike 0.8 mile to the put-in. The creek has steep drops and waterfalls in very narrow gorges. Logs and potential pin spots require much scouting. Run in March 1989 by Eric Brown and Phil Banon.

Canal Creek: Upstream to Mouth (Region 5)

Class: 4–5   **Gradient: 152 fpm**   **Length: 1.2 miles**

This is a small stream that feeds into Quartzville Creek. It's class 3 in the upper part, with a class 4 rapids near the end. It's class 5 at high flows. This is a good alternate put-in for the lower Quartzville Creek run. Run about 1986 by Eric Brown.

Canyon Creek: Elbow Creek to Owl Creek (Region 5)

Class: 4(5) P   **Gradient: 250 fpm**   **Length: 3 miles**

This run is almost impassable because of logjams and slides resulting from clear-cutting. Run in 1991 by Eric Brown.

Cedar Creek: Forest Road 2207 Bridge to Shady Cove Campground (Region 5)

Class: 4+(5)   **Gradient: 133 fpm**   **Length: 5 miles**

This is a pool-drop tributary of the Little North Santiam. All drops were run, but several are not recommended. This is a creek boater's dream, others' nightmare. Run in January 1991 by April Hoffman and Eric Brown.

Chetco River: Slide Creek to South Fork (Region 2)

Class: 4   **Gradient: 46 fpm**   **Length: 26 miles**

This run starts as a small stream, then goes through a difficult gorge with a gradient of 120 fpm. There's a long class 3 middle section, with class 3 and 4 rapids near the end. A 2-mile carry to the put-in is required. Run about 1985 by Phil DeRiemer et al.

Christy Creek

Class: 5+   **Gradient: 300 fpm**   **Length: 7 miles**
Run in December 1991 by David Gilmore.

Clatskanie River: Upper Section to Swedetown (Region 8)

Class: 2(3)   **Gradient: 70 fpm, C**   **Length: 6 miles**

The river drains into the lower Columbia River. It's a twisty, log-strewn run through deep dreamy forest with little whitewater. Swedetown is 7 miles upstream from Clatskanie. The put-in is along Apiary Road. Run in 1990 by Paul Norman.

Coquille, North Fork: Uppermost Bridge to Bridge Above Moon Creek (Region 2)

Class: 3   **Gradient: 40 fpm**   **Length: 13 miles**

This run has sandstone ledge-drops, sweepers, and private logging. The put-in is 25 miles east of Coquille. Run in 1987 by Craig Thurber, Sally Boyer, Dave Cutlip, Dave Mustonen, and Richard Dierks.

Coquille, East Fork: Three Miles East of Dora to Bridge on Gold Brick Road (Region 2)

Class: 3(4)   **Gradient: 30 fpm**   **Length: 3.3 miles**

Midway, beneath a footbridge, is a 5-foot ledge-drop into an 8-foot chute. There's a flat 1.7-mile paddle out. Run in 1979 by Bernie Eskeson, Ward Crane, and Craig Thurber.

Coquille, Middle Fork: Bear Creek Campground to Bridge West of Camas Valley (Region 2)

Class: 3(4)   **Gradient: 45 fpm**   **Length: 5 miles**

The put-in is just below a high-gradient, boulder-choked section. The run culminates with 1 mile at 73 fpm. Below are many accesses for low-gradient runs. Run in 1989 by Craig Thurber, Dave Taylor, and Richard Dierks; lower sections run in 1970s by Forest Millinex.

Coquille, South Fork: Coquille Falls to 16-Mile Bridge (Above Powers) (Region 2)

Class: 5–6   **Gradient: 235 fpm**   **Length: 0.8 mile**

Reach spectacular falls by a 0.5-mile trail from Forest Road 3384 past Squaw Creek. There are continuous big drops among large boulders. Low flow permits necessary scouting. Run in 1987 by Richard Dierks, Dave Mustonen, Craig Thurber, Don Wells, and others.

D River: Source to Pacific Ocean (Region 1)

Class: 1   **Gradient: 50 fpm**   **Length: 0.05 mile**

Known as the world's shortest river until one a few feet shorter was claimed in the Midwest, this river is very shallow, with gravel bars. At low tide the length of the run is nearly double that at high tide. Run in 1967 by John and Rob Blickensderfer.

Fall Creek: Portland Creek to Bedrock Campground (Region 4)

Class: 4   **Gradient: 150 fpm**   **Length: 1 mile**

This is a tight gorge in a logjam hell. Run in spring 1991 by David Gilmore.

Floras Creek: Bridge at Confluence of South Fork to Bridge 1.5 Miles from US 101 (Region 2)

Class: 3(5) P   **Gradient: 44 fpm**   **Length: 7.8 miles**

This run is 13 miles south of Bandon. There is activity among boulders for the first 5 miles, then comes class 5 Half-Mile Gorge with a gradient of 180 fpm. Run on March 8, 1992, by Richard Dierks, Dave Cutlip, Sally Boyer, and Doug Woodman.

Hood River, East Fork: Six Miles Above Parkdale to Bridge at Parkdale (Region 7)

Class: 4   **Gradient: unknown**   **Length: 6 miles**

A flood and road construction have destroyed this run. It is completely log-choked and not runnable. Run on June 14, 1976, by Michael Kay and Harvey Shapiro.

Hood, East Fork: Bridge at Parkdale to Dee (Region 7)

Class: 3(4) P   **Gradient: 120 fpm**   **Length: 7–8 miles**

This run is very fast over continuous gravel bars and many trees. Portage the old dam at the Dee lumber mill. Run on April 16, 1982, by S. Heindic and Harvey Shapiro.

Hood, East Fork: Bridge on Oregon 35 10 miles South of Town of Mount Hood to Bridge 5 Miles South of Mount Hood (Region 7)

Class: 4+   **Gradient: unknown**   **Length: 5 miles**

After an easy 0.5 mile, there are 4 miles of continuous class 3 and 4+ water. Run in winter 1992 by Rex Simenson and Steve Scheel.

Lake Creek: Triangle Lake to Fish Creek (Region 1)

Class: 5   **Gradient: 162 fpm**   **Length: 1.7 miles**

The waterfall section has gradient of 640 fpm. There are shallow pools below vertical drops. Logs and fishladders present problems. Run in January 1991 by April Hoffman and Eric Brown.

Little Luckiamute River: Sams Creek to Falls City (Region 5)

Class: 4   **Gradient: 92 fpm**   **Length: 3 miles**

This is a highly technical run with many logs, especially the parts not visible from the road. Take out above the waterfall at Falls City. Run in 1989 by Eric Brown.

Lobster Creek (Rogue River)

Run in 1986 by Don Wells and Brent Parks.

Lobster Creek (Rogue River): Takilma Gorge

Run in 1987 by Don Wells, Brent Parks, and Don Sors.

Millicoma River, East Fork: Bridge 19 Miles Above Allegany to Bridge at Little Creek (Region 2)

Class: 5   **Gradient: 150 fpm**   **Length: 6.3 miles**

This run has narrow technical drops and is sweeper-imperiled. It is private, not accessible to the public. Run in 1987 by Richard Dierks, Craig Thurber, Dave Taylor, Sally Boyer, and Dave Cutlip.

Millicoma River, West Fork: Trout Creek Road to Henry's Falls (Region 2)

Class: 2+ **Gradient: 53 fpm** **Length: 4.5 miles**

This run is scenic. Portage Stall Falls. There's a long shuttle on Deans Mountain Road. Run in 1980 by Richard Dierks, Dave Taylor, Craig Thurber, et al.

Moose Creek: Cub Creek to South Santiam River (Region 5)

Class: 3 **Gradient: 105 fpm** **Length: 4 miles**

This run is very technical in the sections along the road. It enters the South Santiam just above Tomco Falls, class 4. Run in 1988 by Eric Brown.

Mosby Creek: Gate on Mosby Creek Road to Waldon (Region 4)

Class: 1+(2+) **Gradient: unknown** **Length: 4.5 miles**

Watch for logs. A class 2+ ledge is at about mile 3. Run in 1991 by John Rose.

Nehalem River: Upper Section (Region 1)

Class: 2 **Gradient: unknown** **Length: unknown**

Explored on April 1, 1972 by Margie and Scott Arighi and others.

Nehalem River, North Fork: Fish Hatchery on Oregon 53 to Boat Ramp (Region 1)

Class: 2–3 **Gradient: 32 fpm** **Length: 5 miles**

There are five definite drops, and only one can be seen from the road. Good when the Wilson is over 7 feet. There are good surfing waves, and one long meandering stretch. Run about 1990 by Linda Starr and others.

Packer Creek: Entire (Region 4)

Class: 4+ **Gradient: unknown** **Length: 3 miles**

It flows into the west side of Hills Creek. The run is technical, with logs. Run in spring 1990 by David Gilmore.

Packer's Gulch: Packer's Gulch Road Bridge to Quartzville Creek (Region 5)

Class: 4+ **Gradient: 140 fpm** **Length: 1 mile**

This is a small tributary that makes an alternate put-in for Quartzville Creek. It's continuous class 4 with logs involved. Run in 1988 by Eric Brown.

Pistol River

Run in 1986 by Don Wells and Brent Parks.

Quartz Creek: Fourth Bridge Over Quartz Creek on Forest Road 2618 to Pond Road Bridge (Region 3)

Class: 3(4-)   Gradient: unknown   Length: 7 miles

Scout the first drop below the put-in bridge. The remainder is continuous class 3 with logs. Run in 1990 by David Ryan.

Quartzville Creek: Freezeout Creek to Greg Creek (Region 5)

Class: 4+(5)   Gradient: unknown   Length: 3.3 miles

This run has a concentration of steep drops. Gorges make portaging and scouting intimidating. Low water is recommended (Quartzville gauge at 2,500 cfs). Run in April 1991 by Eric Brown.

Rock Creek: 5 Miles to Siletz River (Region 1)

Class: 2-   Gradient: unknown   Length: 5 miles

This is a small meandering stream with several 1- to 3-foot ledges. Run in April 1990 by April Hoffman and Eric Brown.

Salmonberry River: Beaver Slide Road to Nehalem River (Region 1)

Class: 3(4)   Gradient: 70 fpm   Length: 10 miles

This run is remote, but with a railroad along it. The shuttle is difficult. Heavy rain of 2 inches (Nehalem and Wilson rivers over 6 feet) is needed. This is an excellent run (a more detailed description is needed). Put in near Belding Creek; turn off US 26 1 mile east of the Sunset rest area. First-run information unknown.

Sharps Creek: Staples Creek to Row River (Region 4)

Class: 2(3)   Gradient: 37 fpm   Length: 7 miles

This run has one class 3 and several class 2 fun rapids, most in the first and last miles. Run in 1988 by Arthur Koepsell.

Siletz River, South Fork: Valsetz Dam Site to North Fork Siletz (Region 1)

Class: 3   Gradient: 86 fpm   Length: 4 miles

The most difficult rapids, class 3, is at the put-in. There are small ledges and good surfing. Run in April 1989 by April Hoffman and Eric Brown.

Silver Creek: Silver Falls State Park to Silverton (Region 6)

Class: 4(6) P   Gradient: 60–85 fpm   Length: 10 miles

This run has ledges, falls, and slides ranging from 4–15 feet. It requires a 1-mile hike to the put-in; if the easier put-in is chosen, take a parachute to run the falls. Run in February 1983 by Craig Colby, Hank Hays and Murray Johnson.

Sixes River: Bridge at Locked Gate to Sixes River Recreation Site (Region 2)

Class: 3(4) **Gradient: 37 fpm** **Length: 5 miles**

The class 4 gorge at mile 3 requires scouting or portaging. Run in 1978 by Bernie Eskeson, Ward Crane and Craig Thurber.

Soda River: Taylor Creek to South Santiam River (Region 5)

Class: 4- P **Gradient: 133 fpm** **Length: 1.2 miles**

Watch for ledges and probable logs. The shallow drop at the confluence needs portaging. Run in 1988 by Arthur Koepsell and Eric Brown.

South Santiam River: House Rock Campground to Soda River (Region 5)

Class: 3+(5) **Gradient: 120 fpm** **Length: 2 miles**

There are logjams in the first mile, then a sloping 35-foot falls followed by a class 4 boulder garden. Run in 1990 by April Hoffman.

White River: Oregon 35 Bridge to Barlow Crossing (Region 8)

Class: 5–6 **Gradient: high** **Length: unknown**

Explored by Hank Hays and Scott Russell, date unknown.

White River: White River Falls to Mouth (Region 8)

Class: 3 **Gradient: unknown** **Length: 2 miles**

This run necessitated carrying, lining, wading, swimming, and paddling upstream from the Deschutes. The scenery is great. Run by Oregon Kayak and Canoe Club members, date unknown.

Wiley Creek: Middle Bridge to South Santiam River (Region 5)

Class: 2(4) **Gradient: about 30 fpm** **Length: 5 miles**

Must portage or run a blind drop at the bridge 0.8 mile above US 20. Run in 1984 by Gary Adams and Rob Blickensderfer.

Willimina Creek: Blackwell Park to Yamhill River (Region 5)

Class: 1(3) **Gradient: about 20 fpm** **Length: 5 miles**

Mostly Class 1 and flatwater, but Class 3 at put-in and at 4-foot ledge 2.5 miles downstream of put-in. Run in 1982 by Rob Blickensderfer and Rich Brainerd.

Wind River: 5 Miles Above Stabler (Region 7)

Class: unknown **Gradient: unknown** **Length: 5 miles**

Run by Bruce Warner and others, date unknown.

BIBLIOGRAPHY

Arighi, Scott, and Margaret Arighi. *Wildwater Touring—Techniques and Tours*. New York: MacMillan Publishing Company, 1974.

Bechdel, Les, and Slim Ray. *River Rescue*. Boston: Appalachian Mountain Club, 1989.

Campbell, Arthur. *John Day River—Drift and Historical Guide*. Portland, Oregon: Frank Amato Publications, Inc., 1980.

Carrey, Johnny, Cort Conley, and Ace Barton. *Snake River of Hells Canyon*. Cambridge, Idaho: Backeddy Books, 1979.

DeLorme Mapping Company. *Oregon Atlas and Gazetteer*. Freeport, Maine: DeLorme Mapping Company, 1991.

Garren, John. *Oregon River Tours*. Beaverton, Oregon: The Touchstone Press, 1979.

Jones, Philip N. *Canoe Routes of Northwest Oregon*. Seattle: The Mountaineers, 1982.

Moore, Greg, and Don McClaran. *Idaho Whitewater: The Complete River Guide*. McCall, Idaho: Class VI, 1989.

Quinn, James M., and James W. Quinn. *Handbook to the Klamath River Canyon*. Medford, Oregon: Educational Adventures, Inc., 1983.

Quinn, James M., James W. Quinn, and James G. King. *Handbook to the Deschutes River Canyon*. Medford, Oregon: Educational Adventures, Inc., 1979.

———. *Handbook to the Illinois River Canyon*. Medford, Oregon: Educational Adventures, Inc., 1979.

———. *Handbook to the Rogue River Canyon*. Medford, Oregon: Educational Adventures, Inc., 1978.

Schwind, Dick. *West Coast River Touring: The Rogue River and South Including California*. Beaverton, Oregon: The Touchstone Press, 1974.

State of Oregon, Oregon State Parks and Recreation Branch. *Willamette River Recreation Guide*. Salem, Oregon: Oregon Parks Department (525 Trade Street Southeast, Salem, OR 97310), 1976.

RIVER REGULATION AGENCIES

Cougar Dam
(541) 822-3344
U.S. Army Corps of Engineers
Blue River, Oregon

Detroit Dam
(503) 897-2385
U.S. Army Corps of Engineers
Detroit, Oregon

Foster Dam
(541) 367-5132
U.S. Army Corps of Engineers
Sweet Home, Oregon

Lookout Point Dam
(541) 937-3852
U.S. Army Corps of Engineers
Lowell, Oregon

Northwest Water Resources Data
    Center
(503) 231-2024
U.S. Department of Interior
Portland, Oregon

Reservoir Control Center
(503) 221-3741
U.S. Army Corps of Engineers
Portland, Oregon

River Forecast Center
(503) 261-9246
U.S. Department of Commerce
National Oceanic and Atmo-
    spheric Administration
Portland, Oregon

River Forecast Center
(206) 526-8530
U.S. Department of Commerce
National Oceanographic and
    Atmospheric Administration
Seattle, Washington

River Information Center
(916) 653-9647
California Department of Water
    Resources
Sacramento, California

Watermaster
(541) 388-6669
Oregon Department of Water
    Resources
Bend, Oregon

Internet river flow data for many of the rivers in this book is available from the U.S. Geological Survey, Army Corp of Engineers, and the Idaho and California water offices. It is summarized daily into a table that lists the run, its flow and status relative to flow levels recommended in this book. The data is available at:

http://www.physics.orst.edu/~tpw/kayaking/levels.html.

APPENDIX B

WHITEWATER BOATING ORGANIZATIONS

Grande Ronde Whitewater
   Boaters Club
1610 Cedar
La Grande, OR 97850

Lower Columbia Canoe Club
1714 SE 52nd Avenue
Portland, OR 97215
   http://www.teleport.com/
   nonprofit/LCCC

McKenzie River Paddlers
38305 Jasper–Lowell Road
Fall Creek, OR 97438

Northwest Rafters Association
P.O. Box 19008
Portland, OR 97219

Oregon Kayak and Canoe Club
P.O. Box 692
Portland, OR 97207

Oregon Ocean Paddlers Society
P.O. Box 69641
Portland, OR 97201

Santiam Whitewater Association
32560 SW Arbor Lake Drive
Wilsonville, OR 97070

Southern Oregon Association of
   Kayakers
P.O. Box 462
Jacksonville, OR 97530

Willamette Kayak and Canoe
   Club, Inc.
P.O. Box 1062
Corvallis, OR 97339
   http://www.peak.org/
   community/whitewater

Corrections, updates, and new runs for the next edition of Soggy Sneakers should be sent to the Willamette Kayak and Canoe Club at the address shown above. Updates and new runs, current river levels, and general boating information can be found at the Club web site.

INDEX

THE MOUNTAINEERS, founded in 1906, is a nonprofit outdoor activity and conservation club, whose mission is "to explore, study, preserve, and enjoy the natural beauty of the outdoors. . . ." Based in Seattle, Washington, the club is now the third-largest such organization in the United States, with 15,000 members and four branches throughout Washington State.

The Mountaineers sponsors both classes and year-round outdoor activities in the Pacific Northwest, which include hiking, mountain climbing, ski-touring, snowshoeing, bicycling, camping, kayaking and canoeing, nature study, sailing, and adventure travel. The club's conservation division supports environmental causes through educational activities, sponsoring legislation, and presenting informational programs. All club activities are led by skilled, experienced volunteers, who are dedicated to promoting safe and responsible enjoyment and preservation of the outdoors.

The Mountaineers Books, an active, nonprofit publishing program of the club, produces guidebooks, instructional texts, historical works, natural history guides, and works on environmental conservation. All books produced by The Mountaineers are aimed at fulfilling the club's mission.

If you would like to participate in these organized outdoor activities or the club's programs, consider a membership in The Mountaineers. For information and an application, write or call The Mountaineers, Club Headquarters, 300 Third Avenue West, Seattle, Washington 98119; (206) 284-6310.

Send or call for our catalog of more than 300 outdoor titles:

 The Mountaineers Books
1001 SW Klickitat Way, Suite 201
Seattle, WA 98134
1-800-553-4453